HOW to Study

THE BIBLE

ℋOW to Study
THE BIBLE

A Practical Guide to Biblical Hermeneutics

KEVIN W. RHODES

P.O. Box 3687
Cleburne, TX 76033
HopkinsPublishing.com

Copyright © 2016 Kevin Rhodes
Paperback: 978-1-62080-069-0
Hard Cover: 978-1-62080-070-6
eBook: 978-1-62080-071-3
Library of Congress Control Number: 2016936838
Version 1.0

**Discover Other Titles
By Hopkins Publishing
HopkinsPublishing.com**

Table of Contents

❖

For Tracy,

A godly woman,
truly a helpmeet for me;
a wonderful mother;
and the love of my life.

Acknowledgements

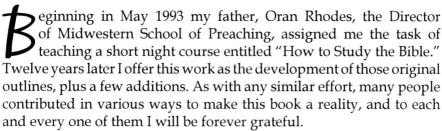

eginning in May 1993 my father, Oran Rhodes, the Director of Midwestern School of Preaching, assigned me the task of teaching a short night course entitled "How to Study the Bible." Twelve years later I offer this work as the development of those original outlines, plus a few additions. As with any similar effort, many people contributed in various ways to make this book a reality, and to each and every one of them I will be forever grateful.

Although mentioning all who have helped this work come to fruition would be impossible, I must recognize those who made special contributions in their own different ways. Sue Ann Arnett probably never realized the challenge she made when she requested my class material in a printed form, but her suggestion lies behind this book's existence. Thank you, Sue Ann. All those who encouraged my writing over the last several years will never know just how you lifted my spirits and spurred me on. Especially am I thankful for two gospel preachers whom I respect highly, Wayne Jackson and Johnny Ramsey, for their encouragement and their confidence in what I have to offer. I must also thank Dave Dugan and my good friend, Don Toth, for their persistent optimism in the value of this material.

I will always be thankful for those congregations with which I have had the privilege of working throughout the various stages of this manuscript. From the Bible Class in Harrisonville, Missouri, to the pages of the bulletin at Bowie Street in Wellington, Texas, to both classes and bulletin formats in Morris, Alabama, and Granbury Street in Cleburne, Texas, the brethren, and especially the elders, always supported me and gave me reason to believe this undertaking was worthwhile.

I have the advantage of a family that supports me in ways far beyond what I deserve. I thank my father and mother, Oran and

Sandra Rhodes, for their patience, their examples in both Christianity and marriage, for their unwavering support, and for the spiritual training I received through their effort. To my wife's parents, Chuck and Florence Ramseyer, I extend a special thanks, for welcoming me into your family from the beginning and not only loving me but also honoring me with your respect. To the world's best siblings, Renee', Tracey Lee, and Mark: I am so thankful that we remain close despite the miles between us. I am a better person today because I grew up with all of you.

Most of all, I am thankful to and for my beautiful wife, Tracy, whose graceful touch is present on almost every page through her careful proofreading over the years and gentle suggestions on helping improve my communication of some of the more technical problems. Your willingness to give so much of yourself to me, Makaria, and Hannah is a testimony of the strength of your character. You truly have always been my very best Bible student; therefore, it is only appropriate to dedicate this book to you.

January 14, 2005   Kevin W. Rhodes
Cleburne, Texas

Preface

A book attempting to explain the process of how to study the Bible is not a novel idea. Therefore, the need for greater understanding in this area must have been around for a while. Indeed, anyone working with a congregation of the Lord's people will comprehend in short order that ignorance of God's Word among God's people is bordering an epidemic. However, many preachers seem to believe that they themselves are the remedy to this disease, but, sadly, some of them are actually part of the problem. People do not learn best by being told. People learn best by teaching themselves. While preachers remain integral to congregational education, their role should be supplementary rather than elementary. Far too many people rely on the preacher to tell them the obvious and get upset should he choose instead to challenge them to greater heights of spirituality.

Previous efforts to help people learn how to study the Bible have concentrated on information and method. While these are certainly necessary, as an approach I believe they are wanting. While offering valuable material, they tend to assume far too much. Most tend to be brief outline guides for studying the Bible, when most people need to have it "fleshed out" for them as well, at least in the early stages of their learning. As a result, they remind me of my old algebra textbook in high school. For their examples they choose some of the easiest problems possible and then leave you to figure out the hard ones. Perhaps this makes these books less controversial and more marketable, but it does not make them effective.

Most people who wish to understand the Bible are not confused as a result of not knowing where Perea is or because they are not aware of the basic rules of hermeneutics. They are confused because it is much easier to cite rules than to explain and apply them. Studying the Bible is not just a matter of having the right information and understanding a method; it is an acquired skill. It is not enough to talk about the importance of context; we must investigate and comprehend the concept and application of context.

There are, of course, those who think an effort to teach people how to study the Bible is worthless. To them, the Bible "means what it says." But as many have discovered, knowing the Bible says "law" does not tell you which law. Seeing the word "Spirit" does not guarantee that it is actually a reference to the Holy Spirit or, even when it is, how His role is to be interpreted. The Bible's references to "grace" and "faith" might also be included in this category. Understanding the Bible, then, is not always an easy proposition.

What this should tell us is that there are factors that influence our understanding of the Bible prior to our ever opening the cover. Without taking into account the fact that each student brings something to his study from the very beginning — right or wrong — and addressing these issues, we will be "spinning our wheels." While a correct attitude does not guarantee a correct understanding, a correct understanding of scripture is unlikely without a correct attitude.

The operative word throughout this study is "skills." Reading this book alone does not create a better understanding of how to study the Bible. This book is itself only a tool through which I hope to help you develop for yourself the skills necessary to improve your exegetical prowess. Therefore, your willingness to evaluate yourself constantly, to absorb lessons and readjust your worldview, and to practice and apply the methods taught is central to your becoming a better Bible student. But, I emphasize once again, the key is not in learning how to "fill in the blanks" of some method. The key is to learn the investigative skills necessary to unlock the treasure trove of God's Book and begin putting the puzzle together until you can enjoy the beauty of the picture God has painted.

Despite my criticisms of others' works, I also realize that my own contribution is not the panacea for Bible study. It very likely contains errors (though I certainly hope not doctrinally) and important omissions. I take full responsibility for them. However, I hope that you find my efforts useful and that this work will fill in a gap so that you as a reader might also become a better student of the Bible.

January 14, 2005   Kevin W. Rhodes
Cleburne, Texas

Preface to the
10th Anniversary Edition

❖

The original reception of the first edition of How to Study the Bible surpassed my own hopes and expectations. From a project born out of a simple class and bulletin series sprang a volume designed to pass on the various lessons I have learned in studying the Bible daily both personally and in my work as a preacher and teacher. I appreciate all who have used this earlier work and found it helpful, for it truly proved a joy to write. So, whether you were introduced to its pages through your personal study, through a college class, or through the study of hermeneutics in preaching school, I am truly grateful.

In recent years people have found it increasingly difficult to secure a copy of How to Study the Bible at a reasonable cost and without some problem. I am thankful that Hopkins Publishing, my partner now for many endeavors, has been willing to publish this new edition so as to keep it available for years to come.

After ten years, it seems appropriate to address a couple of issues related to the original publication of the work. The most marked difference readers of the previous volume will recognize is the decision to use the New King James Version rather than the King James Version. While I used the King James Version in my youth and in my writing for much of my adult life, I have preached using the New King James Version for twenty years now. This, with the additional recognition that fewer readers today are as familiar with the language of the King James Version, beautiful as it is, caused me to reevaluate and, as in my other efforts, adopt the New King James Version as the Bible used in my writing. This created some interesting problems when addressing certain passages where the NKJV is admittedly flawed, but as a growing number of people use different versions in their study, this change will make the book more easily accessible to the most readers.

Changing the translation used as the foundational text required a number of additional changes to maintain consistency and continuity. I hope I have addressed these successfully. Additionally, I took the opportunity to make other minor changes in wording, though probably with much less consistency than I would prefer. In reverting to my original transcript, I also have returned to capitalizing pronouns when used to refer to God, Jesus, or the Holy Spirit. While this is somewhat out of favor today and though my personal tendency is to miss a capitalization in one place and insert one where it does not belong, with the reader's indulgence, I hope this also will be received well. I have also made a couple of organizational changes in this edition, moving the chapter on Logic (previously chapter seven) to become Chapter 4, just after the discussions about attitude and before addressing Biblical Authority since this seems like a more natural progression of thought. I am also relocating the chapter on Biblical Tools (previously chapter eight) to become Chapter 13, just after the discussion of Biblical Principles but before the other more practical chapters discussing study methods. I also took the advice of an early reviewer and renamed Chapter 20 "Epilogue" in keeping with its actual function.

After ten years I remained as convinced as ever of the need for this study. We are far too willing to settle for shallow surveys of the Bible that only reinforce familiarity without even challenging us to grow spiritually, whether personally or congregationally. However, much of this, I believe, is due to insufficient skill and the lack of confidence this produces. I pray that How to Study the Bible might become a catalyst for greater and deeper Bible study for years to come, offering the path to greater proficiency as a Bible student and thus a means to greater knowledge of God's Word and greater service in the kingdom.

September 4, 2015   Kevin W. Rhodes
Cleburne, TX

CHAPTER 1

Why Study the Bible?

—————— ❖ ——————

INTRODUCTION

Why do people gather together in groups both small and large across the country, each one carrying a book that was originally published almost two thousand years ago? Why have so many been willing to give their lives just to own a copy of this book? And why have some men tried so desperately to destroy this same volume? The Bible certainly deserves attention in the history books. It has caused controversy throughout its entire existence. It remains the best-selling book of all time. People definitely express interest in the Bible. However, we should not assume that this means people are interested in studying the Bible. There is a tremendous difference between showing interest in the Bible, reading the Bible, and truly studying the Bible.

The person interested in the Bible considers it a curiosity, perhaps even an important relic of history — an archaeological artifact to be examined and investigated. Television programs such as *Ancient Prophecies* and *Mysteries of the Bible* appeal to those who show interest in the Bible as a document and an artifact. However, those who produce these programs do not demonstrate any real interest in the content of the book — apart from what they believe they can either sensationalize or trivialize. In fact, they often spend their time disagreeing with what it teaches and disputing its origin. Among elitist "scholars" belief in the Bible as anything but an historical document of questionable origin provides conclusive proof that a person lacks scholarship completely and should be ignored and ridiculed with a touch of condescension. Obviously, these people see little value in studying the content of the Bible, because they have chosen to reject its relevance with a wave of the hand and have washed their hands of the matter.

Others retain a casual interest in the Bible not quite so callous as the first category. These individuals pick up the Bible from time to time as a source of comfort, enjoy the Bible stories, and generally believe that the world would improve greatly if people would live as the Bible teaches. They do not hold any particular animosity toward the Bible but rather an apathetic indifference. They shrug off the claims of Bible skeptics, believing, for the most part, that the Bible is true. They are generally classified as good people, though their interest in religion tends to be more social and passing than spiritual and zealous.

Some people, on the other hand, love the Bible so much that they dedicate themselves to reading it often. In years past, congregations would often count the number of daily Bible readers each week as an encouragement to members to take their Bibles in hand each day for a few moments to enjoy its precious words. How sad it is that (due to numbers falling so low that admitting them would be an embarrassment) we now rarely hear of such a practice! Reading the Bible keeps it close to our heart, reminds us of the stories we have heard for so long, and comforts us when facing adversity in life. However, reading the Bible never teaches us something that we did not know, falling far short of actual study.

Who may be the smallest in number but most definitely the most precious in value are those people who understand the marvelous treasures hiding in the pages of God's Book, who understand the importance of its role in their lives, and who earnestly and diligently spend their time trying to learn more of God's will each and every day. The only thing that will hold these people back is their skill in the art of studying. But even in this they will apply diligence so that the difficulties they discover along the way will soon melt away in an ever-growing knowledge and understanding of God's will. They persevere because they love God, love Jesus, and love the Bible with all their heart and soul.

There are many reasons why people pick up the Bible. They may wish to critique it, they may wish to soothe their consciences, or they may wish to comfort themselves. But those who will truly benefit from the Bible are those who take it in hand, open its pages, and peruse its contents in order to learn. Preachers present sermons from the Bible in order to help people learn. Teachers instruct students regarding the Bible's lessons so that they might learn. Christians talk to the lost about the Bible, hoping that they will learn. But none of these would ever be possible unless an individual, not unlike yourself, decided that he had to make the time and have the dedication to study the Bible personally in order to learn.

STUDY BECAUSE IT IS THE WORD OF GOD

Students pour over textbooks daily trying to learn pieces of knowledge that man has accumulated over time. Youthful scientists sit with mouths agape as they read the genius of Albert Einstein. Scholars tingle with excitement at the discovery of additional writings of such men. How much more should we tremble in both awe and delight every time we open the Bible? "For the word of God is living and powerful, and sharper than any two-edged sword, piercing even to the division of soul and spirit, and of joints and marrow, and is a discerner of the thoughts and intents of the heart" (Heb. 4:12).

The Bible is the written record of what your Creator has spoken to you (2 Pet. 1:21). It amazes me that people will listen to the words of the President of the United States because of how his policy may affect the world, that people will listen to advice from a broker because of how it may affect them financially ("When E.F. Hutton talks, people listen."), that people will listen to celebrities and sports figures when determining their next purchase, but that few people truly listen to God when He speaks through the pages of Holy Writ! When Jesus said, "It is written" (Matt. 4:1-11), the power in these words came not from the fact that they had been recorded but because God had spoken them.

The Bible is God's own breath. Paul said in 2 Timothy 3:16, "All scripture *is* given by inspiration of God." This phrase could be translated literally, "All scripture is God-breathed." This is a very personal way of describing God's communication with man. The Bible is not a series of stories and provisions originating with God that have undergone constant revision so long that its origin is of little consequence. When we read the very words of the Bible (1 Cor. 2:10-13), it is as if God is in our very presence uttering these words so that we can feel His breath as He speaks to us. This is a message coming straight from the heart of God to the ears of all mankind.

The Bible is God describing and revealing Himself. In many ways, the Bible is God's autobiography, because throughout its pages it either says or implies, "This is Who I am." When the Bible says, "In the beginning God created..." it has described an eternal, omnipotent, omniscient, and omnipresent spiritual Being. As we read the New Testament, the life of Jesus Christ and related teachings, our God exposes us in a more complete way to His moral character. Jesus Christ Himself is an "explanation" of God (John 1:18), so everything about Him leads us to a better understanding of God (1 Pet. 1:16; John 4:24; 1 John 1:5; 4:8). As God thus describes Himself to us in the pages of the Bible, He also includes His actions on behalf of mankind. "But God demonstrates His own love toward us, in that while we were still sinners, Christ died for us" (Rom. 5:8).

God had something to say to mankind. God had something that He wanted us to know. For this reason, He inspired the Bible, His personal message for mankind. That God has spoken to you should be more than adequate reason for you to study the Bible. "All Scripture *is* given by inspiration of God, and *is* profitable for doctrine, for reproof, for correction, for instruction in righteousness, that the man of God may be complete, thoroughly equipped for every good work" (2 Tim. 3:16–17).

STUDY BECAUSE IT IS THE ONLY WAY TO SALVATION

One need only humbly observe the universe to conclude that man exists as but a lowly creature subject to the design of an omnipotent, omniscient, and omnipresent Being. We should realize our dependency in the daily needs of life—food, oxygen, and water. We might think that we had done something by going to get them or by taking them in, but the fact remains that they pre-existed us and anticipated our needs. Therefore, recognizing that we are but creatures and therefore subject to our Creator, who is greater than we are in every way, we should then wonder what our responsibilities are to Him. Though the natural revelation of creation demonstrates the existence of God and our need for God, and though we can have a sense of morality as a result of God having introduced that concept originally to free moral agents, only through God's special revelation, the Bible, can we understand that our primary obligation is complete obedience and that, having sinned, our primary need is now forgiveness from that sin (Rom. 3:10-11).

You only learn about sin by studying the Bible. You may feel the twinge of the conscience when you fail to meet the expectations of social mores, but you can only understand right and wrong by reading God's Word. It alone reveals God's will and law for mankind (Jas. 1:25). Having now been revealed, it shows us what sin is, for "sin is lawlessness" (1 John 3:4). The Bible also provides the only means by which you can learn what you need to know about Jesus Christ. Although the ancient historians Josephus and Tacitus refer to Him, only the Bible explains fully His identity and reason for coming to the earth (John 3:16; 1 John 3:8). Without full and correct knowledge of Jesus Christ, salvation from sin remains impossible because Jesus is the only way (John 14:6) and the only authority (Acts 4:12) by which God will forgive (Acts 2:38). Only the Bible describes the Person of Jesus and His mission, making it the only source of true faith in Him (Rom. 10:17; John 8:24). Therefore, you can only learn how to be saved from sin by going to this book (2 Tim. 3:15). Many act as if the Bible is irrelevant to salvation. They want to rely on their subjective feelings and imagined contact with the Holy Spirit, when the Holy Spirit uses the message of the gospel as His instrument to convict and convert (John 16:8; Acts 2:14-42) through the preaching of that message by Christ's disciples (Mark 16:15-16).

James wrote, "Therefore lay aside all filthiness and overflow of wickedness, and receive with meekness the implanted word, which is able to save your souls" (Jas. 1:21). Stuck in quicksand with time running out, God has thrown us a rope strengthened with the same mighty power that created this world. The gospel is able to save, but we must take hold of it, use it, and then go in the direction of the "rope" (Jas. 4:8). "For I am not ashamed of the gospel of Christ, for it is the power of God to salvation for everyone who believes, for the Jew first and also for the Greek. For in it the righteousness of God is revealed from faith to faith; as it is written, 'The just shall live by faith'" (Rom. 1:16–17).

STUDY IN ORDER TO PROVE
ALL THINGS

It has been said on more than one occasion, "You can prove anything from the Bible." What this generally means is that, if you want to twist the context of passages and omit a few things here and there, you can create any number of doctrines, as the denominational world bears witness. Some people obviously study the Bible for this purpose. However, Paul's brief imperative to the Thessalonians carries a meaning quite different from the application cited above. He said, "Test all things; hold fast what is good. Abstain from every form of evil" (1 Th. 5:21-22).

Instead of approving any "interpretation" made from God's Word, by inspiration Paul cites the necessity of discerning the difference between right and wrong and then clinging to what is right — not only in doctrine but also in practice. The word translated "prove," "examine," and "test" in our English versions means literally to put to a test in order to verify genuineness. It is the word Peter uses to describe being "tested" by fire in reference to the smelting process whereby precious metals could be distinguished from those with similar appearance (1 Pet. 1:7). Thus, it implies we should put all doctrines and activities to a strenuous test in order to determine what is indeed good. John mentioned the same process when he told us to "test the spirits" (1 John 4:1). In other words, we must not listen and accept whatever someone says about the Bible. We must verify not only that the verses cited are correct but also that the teaching fits the overall context. Luke said of the Bereans that, "These were more fair-minded than those in Thessalonica, in that they received the word with all readiness, and searched the Scriptures daily to find out whether these things were so" (Acts 17:11). The test that any doctrine and practice must pass is the test of truth (John 17:17). If it is not true, it has no value to man. Therefore, we should apply ourselves earnestly to the study of the Bible, for only through diligent effort will we learn what has God's approval so that we can hold tightly to it. Since God has revealed "all things that pertain to life and godliness" (2 Pet. 1:3) and given us the responsibility of using this information properly (John 12:48;

1 Cor. 10:13), it behooves us to give our utmost to knowing and doing God's will there revealed.

Therefore, instead of making assertions such as, "The Bible doesn't say it's wrong," and arguing with Bible class teachers and preachers to accept our opinion as valid, we all have the responsibility of going to the standard of right and wrong, God's Word, in order to verify that what we are taught is truth and to test our own beliefs against what God actually says. It is easy to believe a lie if it appeals to us (2 Th. 2:10-11). After all, appeal is what temptation is all about (1 John 2:15-17). So we must study the Bible vigorously to know beyond any doubt (Rom. 14:23; Rom. 10:17) that what we believe and what we practice does indeed have Christ's stamp of approval (Col. 3:17) and is righteous (Rom. 1:17).

STUDY IN ORDER TO BE APPROVED OF GOD

We are all seeking approval in one way or another. Young children look for the approval of parents and grandparents. Teenagers often look for approval among their peers. In marriage we all seek someone who will validate our self-worth and "approve" of us despite our (sometimes-obvious) flaws. Some have had a desire for approval that became a stumblingblock: "for they loved the praise of men more than the praise of God" (John 12:43). Having approval is an important component of our psychological and social makeup. Seeking approval is a vital aspect of life because of how it positively motivates us to improve ourselves without our needing any immediate reward. But these examples demonstrate how important it is *whose* approval we value most, because this will determine our ultimate direction in life. Luke writes that Jesus "increased...in favor with God and man" (Luke 2:52).

When Paul wrote Timothy, he told him, "Be diligent to present yourself approved to God, a worker who does not need to be ashamed, rightly dividing the word of truth" (2 Tim. 2:15). Above all others, we should desire and long for God's approval. It should matter to us what *He* thinks of us, and it should matter most to us what it takes to *have* His approval. When we love God with our whole being (Matt. 22:37-38), we will give our all to doing what makes Him happy, to the point of ignoring what others might want and even denying our own "intuition" as well (Luke 9:23). But to have God's approval requires us to give all diligence to learning what *has* God's approval and then to dedicating ourselves to do it. As Paul states, we can only learn these things by "rightly dividing the word of truth." Many people vainly attempt to claim they have God's approval — for their lives, their activities and their doctrines — instead of delving into the revealed truth of God's word (John 17:17) and then making the necessary adjustments — to their lives, to their activities and to their doctrines. But claiming God's approval and having God's approval are two separate and distinct entities. The Jews claimed to have God's approval; Jesus studied and lived so as to possess it. On Pentecost Peter told the Jews, "Men of Israel, hear these words: Jesus of Nazareth, a Man attested by God to you by miracles, wonders, and signs which God did through Him in your midst, as you yourselves also know —" (Acts 2:22). His point is not that Christ's miracles created God's approval but that God demonstrated His approval for Christ's life and message through them.

People often make appeals to God in prayer seeking His approval. They sometimes live according to conscience, as if this alone assures God's approval (Acts 23:1). Many assume they have God's approval because they are "religious" or "attend church services regularly." But the only way to have God's approval is to devote yourself to learning His will as it is revealed in the Bible and then doing it. Then, and only then, can we have the assurance of hearing, "Well done, good and faithful servant" (Matt. 25:21).

STUDY IN ORDER TO GROW SPIRITUALLY

Far too often we direct our Bible study toward confirming what we know instead of learning so we can grow spiritually. We sit passively in Bible Study, silently disagreeing with the teacher yet unwilling to allow our own beliefs to be tested. We believe that if we understand the words given that we also understand the background, context, deeper implications, and application that go with those words. We confuse Bible reading with Bible study and often judge accuracy according to what we have always believed instead of by what the Bible actually says. Therefore, **in our Bible study we have conditioned ourselves NOT to learn and NOT to grow.** Spiritual growth requires being challenged and then meeting that challenge. It takes more than just attendance, more than quoting a few scriptures, more than reading a commentary or two. Neither is spirituality the sum of emotional highs maintained by constant hugging. In order to grow spiritually, we must devote ourselves to acquiring spiritual knowledge that we may apply. Peter described it in this manner: "as newborn babes, desire the pure milk of the word, that you may grow thereby" (1 Pet. 2:2).

Though spiritual knowledge alone does not assure spiritual growth, spiritual growth is impossible without first acquiring spiritual knowledge. One must know what it means to be spiritual and act spiritually before it can become a basic component in life. As Peter later wrote, "but grow in the grace, and knowledge of our Lord and Savior Jesus Christ" (2 Peter 3:18a). Spiritual growth requires deeper thinking into the character and nature of God (2 Pet. 1:4). It includes learning to think in spiritual terms and with spiritual concerns (Rom. 8:5; Phil. 4:8). It means reorganizing our lives to have spiritual priorities (Matt. 6:33). Thus, we must study the Bible in order to know these things and more. God has revealed Himself to us through His Son (John 1:18) who is likewise revealed to us through the gospel (1 Cor. 15:1-4). To know God and to know Jesus, one must know the Bible. If we desire intimate knowledge of the Almighty, we must understand intimately the divine revelation (2 Tim. 3:16-17).

Yet we should never equate purely intellectual understanding with spiritual growth, because true spiritual growth does not occur until what we learn intellectually from God's Word begins living within us. There is no spiritual growth without spiritual application (Jas. 1:22). There is no spiritual growth without spiritual commitment (Rom. 12:1). There is no spiritual life until we actively apply Christ's way of life to our own (Gal. 2:20). We must study the Bible intensely so that we may thoroughly digest the things of God's Word, so that they live inside of us and grow instead of allowing them only to pass through our system for a short while. "Let the word of Christ **dwell** in you **richly...**" (Col. 3:16a). Many people desire the comforts, joys, and peace that come with spiritual growth but simultaneously neglect God's Word. The truth is:

it is both the quantity and the quality of time we spend in God's Word that make these spiritual blessings a personal reality.

STUDY IN ORDER TO DETECT ERROR

God inspired the Scriptures for the benefit of mankind (2 Tim. 3:16-17), using the written word to instruct men in "all things that pertain to life and godliness" (2 Pet. 1:3). However, some men have contrary designs. For various evil purposes, men have distorted the pure and simple gospel message (Gal. 1:6-9; 2 Pet. 3:16). Sometimes these false teachers will simply leave out a portion of the message God intended. At other times they might add to it or modify it. Regardless of their motives, it is essential for Christians to know God's Word well enough to detect these departures from truth in order to refuse it themselves, warn others about it, and rebuke those espousing it. The apostle John wrote, "Beloved, do not believe every spirit, but test the spirits, whether they are of God; because many false prophets have gone out into the world" (1 John 4:1).

Contrary to popular belief, it is not important or even necessary to enter a study of the various denominational doctrines and world religions in order to confront them and expose them. While such studies may be beneficial in helping a Christian anticipate where someone is coming from or where he might be heading with an argument, there is a simpler and far more beneficial way to detect error: Know truth. If we will learn the truth, then we will automatically be able to know error when we hear it. "I have not written to you because you do not know the truth, but because you know it, and that no lie is of the truth" (1 John 2:21). However, we must not automatically equate "what we currently believe" with truth. Rather, we should be as the Bereans who "were more fair-minded than those in Thessalonica, in that they received the word with all readiness, and searched the Scriptures daily to find out whether these things were so" (Acts 17:11). The question is not whether a teaching differs from what we previously thought but whether or not that teaching is in harmony with God's Word. A strong dedication to truth (Prov. 23:23) will expose error quickly if properly applied. If someone should argue that Jesus was created, based upon Colossians 1:15-16, belief in His deity alone is not a substantive refutation. Only sufficient knowledge of the scriptures (to make manifest the contradictions created by the false teaching, Heb. 1:1-3; John 1:1-18; John 8:58) and developed interpretive skills (to demonstrate the extent and limitations of the context) will suffice. But these are not developed through refuting false teaching but only through diligent attention to truth (John 17:17).

False teachers utilize every known gimmick and persuasive technique in their power to cause people to accept their interpretations (2 Pet. 2:1-3). Primarily, they try to create a stronger emotional tie with their followers than the follower has with the Bible and truth. They may claim direct guidance by the Holy Spirit. They may attack or try to "redefine" inspiration. They may promise you the world. But you must see such tactics for the sophistry they are. You must not allow yourself to be led by men — any man. And the only answer for all such men is the same: love, hold fast to, and be devoted to truth. Only by relying on the revelation that is from above can one overcome the turmoil created by those below. "Sanctify them by Your truth. Your word is truth" (John 17:17).

STUDY IN ORDER TO GAIN KNOWLEDGE

Long ago the prophet Hosea cried out, "My people are destroyed for lack of knowledge. Because you have rejected knowledge, I also will reject you from being priest for Me; Because you have forgotten the law of your God, I also will forget your children" (Hos. 4:6). The overall level of knowledge among members of the Lord's church today can only be described as abysmal. It is becoming harder and harder to teach in some ways because it is necessary to provide so much background information on Old Testament history, the life of Christ, or the acts of the apostles just so that the lesson will make sense. Our attention to basic facts — such as knowing the books of the Bible, being able to quote scripture, and having a basic grasp of the scheme of redemption and the message of each book of the Bible — has given way to a general feeling of disinterest in what the Bible says because people are often content with what they *feel* about the Bible. Worse yet, the truth is that we do not know all that we think we know, and a lot of what we know may be wrong!

We console ourselves in our ignorance by claiming that we cannot remember "all of that." What amazes me is how much we can remember about other aspects of life while claiming a poor memory as an excuse for not knowing the Bible. While our children are learning computer skills and keyboarding at an increasingly early age, our expectations about their ability to learn Bible facts is dropping. While our teenagers are taking chemistry, physics, and calculus, we sit by idly while they act like they are incapable of studying and comprehending God's Word. The truth is that most people know a lot of things; they simply do not know a lot of things that are truly worth knowing! When we claim our children are not capable of learning the books of the Bible, yet they can quote a Disney movie verbatim, there is a problem—and it is not with their minds. When teens can memorize a playbook but not the names of the apostles and judges, the problem is not their lack of intellect. We adults know many facts necessary to doing our daily work but claim that we cannot remember five verses about the plan of salvation.

Think about it. We spend years trying to acquire knowledge of various sorts, but how much of that time is spent in learning how to make a living and how to recreate versus learning how to live properly before God? How can we say that we know how to implement God's Word into our lives when we do not even know how to give an overview about what God's Word says? Learning to know God begins by learning about God. Learning how to trust more in God cannot be taught until we first teach the fact that we need to trust in Him. Appreciating Jesus Christ begins by knowing what happened in the life of Jesus Christ. After all, what Jesus taught was generally centered on what Jesus did. While basic factual knowledge is not the end all/be all of Bible study, facts are the building blocks. We must take the time to get to know God by studying His Word. If we do not, we will miss out on the most precious knowledge we can gain in this life—not just something true, but "the truth" (John 8:32).

STUDY IN ORDER TO TEACH OTHERS

One of the fundamental laws of teaching is, "You cannot teach what you do not know." Unfortunately, many believe the only criterion for being a teacher is the willingness to teach! This inevitably leads to the blind leading the blind (Matt. 15:14), so that ignorance begets ignorance, which begets ignorance. Teaching others carries a great responsibility (Jas. 3:1), and this responsibility includes knowing God's Word well enough to communicate it to others. Thus, diligent study must go hand in hand with those who would teach. The writer of Hebrews said, "For though by this time you ought to be teachers, you need someone to teach you again the first principles of the oracles of God; and you have come to need milk and not solid food" (Heb. 5:12). How can we avoid having such a denunciation apply to us? Only through studying the Bible.

Every Christian has the responsibility of taking the gospel to the lost (Mark 16:15; Matt. 28:18-20). Though some may not have the greatest ability and while some may be so young in the faith that they do not know much, neither of these works as an excuse. The responsibility to teach implies the responsibility to study in order to teach. Paul told Timothy, "And the things that you have heard from me among many witnesses, commit these to faithful men who will be able to teach others also" (2 Tim. 2:2). The gospel is perpetuated by teaching people the gospel **and** by teaching people to teach the gospel. At the very least, every Christian should know how to teach the plan of salvation, the unique character of the church, the nature of true worship, the church's work and organization, as well as a basic summary of Christian morality, also presenting scripture for authority on each subject. Does this seem odd? Does it seem like this is asking too much? These are the basics that are necessary to carrying out the great commission! If we cannot explain to others why we live, worship, and act the way we do, we are failing one of the most elementary tests of our Christianity (1 Pet. 3:15).

Those who would teach Bible classes are responsible for knowing and discerning truth in regard to the material they are teaching (Jas. 3:17; John 17:17). Preachers must know the word so that they can preach the word, instructing those who should have good knowledge to start with (2 Tim. 4:2). Elders must know enough to teach mature Christians (1 Tim. 3:2), enough to correct those in error (Tit. 1:9ff), and enough to lead a congregation humbly but forthrightly in the practice of truth. It is not enough to know more than the ignorant. We must study so as to **be** among the knowledgeable.

Bible knowledge is the key to good Bible teaching. Too often, we have come to rely on manuals and commentaries so much that we never really absorb the actual Word. Therefore, we must learn to use each as a help but never as a crutch. Of course, few people would recognize when these helps have become crutches, and that is part of the problem. We rarely are willing to admit how quickly we run to the bookshelf when a problem presents itself or how often we have asked someone else and just accepted his answer. It will require effort and time, but if we are to teach God's message, His message must be the one we really know (Psa. 119:11, 97, 105).

STUDY BECAUSE THERE IS A GREAT NEED

We have grown lazy in our Bible study in the last few years. We have come to expect things — life — to be easy. Since World War II, we have experienced a technological revolution. We now have so many items of convenience that we expect everything to be convenient. Dishwashers save us time washing the dishes. Electric washers and dryers save us time cleaning our clothes. Microwaves save us time cooking. Fast food saves us time spent in a restaurant. And computers save us time by making corrections easier than ever thought possible. But have you noticed how we now think about these items of convenience? Most of us wouldn't know how to live without them! And computers are now becoming faster and faster. People who have older computers are no longer satisfied. Why? There are now faster processors on the market. We want things to come quickly and easily for us. But despite those who might argue to the contrary, there is not a short cut to learning the Bible. You can't buy Cliff's Notes. There certainly are marvelous tools available to help the serious Bible student. But without a determined, diligent, honest, hard-working student, they are just trophies collecting dust on a shelf.

In order to study the Bible, we must renew our commitment to thinking and exercise our minds accordingly. We spend far too much time watching television programs promoting immorality, and even when the content is good we often allow the television to "think" for us. Students in school prefer to be given the answers rather than work to arrive at the proper conclusion. Cheating is on the rise not only in our public schools but also in our universities. Beyond this, students today are learning to study in order to pass a test instead of studying to learn.

But life—and thinking—is not like this at all. It requires hard work and effort. Schoolwork is designed to work the mind. Much of higher mathematics, besides having practical applications, encourages logical thought. College courses should require you to use your mind. Today, many attending colleges seem to think that they are just supposed to soak in information. If this were the case, where would we get the discoveries of tomorrow? It will not happen without someone choosing to think. There is peer pressure today in many fields, attempting to produce uniformity through conformity. But peer pressure is just an excuse not to think and act for yourself. Thinking requires us to accept the facts even when they disagree with common thought. Disagreement itself does not make one courageous or thoughtful. It is the disagreement on the principle of truth that separates the thinker from the pack. Unfortunately, thinkers are becoming a dying breed. We seem content just to limp along and accept mediocrity—in our schools, in our work, and in our Bible study. But you can help reverse the trend! You can be an active, thinking Bible student. Now is the time to apply yourself. Don't wait around until you are not so busy, because that time will surely not come! The Lord needs knowledgeable elders, preachers, teachers, and members. The church needs members who know the Book and can recognize error. You can become just what is needed. So, start studying now; learning will never be any easier.

CONCLUSION

On the surface it may seem that motivations for studying the Bible are so obvious that one might reasonably assume its importance without the need for entering an extended discussion. However, no matter how much lip service we may pay to Bible study, the fact remains that, on the whole, basic Bible knowledge among Christians continues to plummet and those with a more intimate knowledge of

God's will are few and far between. In days gone by the church knew Christians who were prepared to answer the queries of their religious neighbors with a "Thus saith the Lord" and "book, chapter, and verse." Today, the prepared response seems to be "I'll have to ask the preacher." We must ask the question, "Why study the Bible?" because observation demands the conclusion that fewer and fewer people deem Bible study a worthwhile practice in any meaningful way.

However, our determination to learn God's will should extend far beyond direct Bible answers to the false practices of those around us. It must take us beyond the rudimentary memorization of names, verses, and events. We must learn that there are questions that require more than one word answers—of which the top three are "God," "Jesus" and the "Bible." Though all of these are essential and important fundamentally, to be truly beneficial Bible study must become more comprehensive. Factual questions need to be augmented with conceptual questions. If a student understands *what* a passage says but does not comprehend *why* it matters or *how* to apply it, Bible study is reduced to an intellectual exercise (if it can even be called that) and loses true significance. Christians often approach the Bible in a casual, non-studious way because they tend to believe that they already have a grasp of its meaning. Thus, we have conditioned ourselves to accept our current level of knowledge as acceptable without considering the appropriate standard for what is acceptable.

The apostle Peter wrote, "as newborn babes, desire the pure milk of the word, that you may grow thereby" (1 Pet. 2:2), yet he does not tell us directly what it is that should cause us to desire it beyond growth. He implies that there are sufficient reasons but does not specify all of them. He assumed that spiritual growth would be sufficient motivation for his readers. Yet studying this passage should include consideration of the particulars that would motivate us to grow spiritually. The seriousness with which we approach Bible study, both congregationally and personally, depends upon the strength of our faith in the power of God's word (Rom. 1:16) to accomplish in us what God says is possible and desirable, and our willingness to draw nigh to God (Jas. 4:8) in order to have the best relationship possible with Him. Your attitude toward God's Word will largely determine your love for Bible study. The deeper your love, the deeper you will take your study. "Oh, how I love your law! It is my meditation all the day" (Psa. 119:97).

Surely just **one** of the reasons cited above would be enough to motivate us to study the Bible, yet we have discovered many. Without a doubt, then, there is ample reason to study the Bible! You have so much to gain by applying yourself to this magnificent treasure—and so much to lose should you fail to do so. Studying the Bible is a noble pursuit, with the most promise and the greatest rewards. It is the means by which we come to know our Creator. It is the only way for us to reach our full potential as human beings. Why should you study the Bible? Because your eternal destiny depends upon it!

We should study the Bible because:

- **It is the Word of God**
- **It is the only way to salvation**
- **It is the only way to prove all things**
- **It is the only way to be approved of God**
- **It is the only way to grow spiritually**
- **It is the only way to detect error**
- **It is the only way to gain spiritual knowledge**
- **It is the only way to know what to teach others**
- **There is a great need**
- **Your eternal destiny depends upon it.**

Recommended Reading

Geisler, Norman L. and Nix, William E. *A General Introduction to the Bible.* Chicago, IL: Moody Press, 1986.

Harris, R. Laird. *Inspiration and Canonicity of the Scriptures: An Historical and Exegetical Study.* Greenville, South Carolina: A Press, 1995.

Warfield, Benjamin B. *The Inspiration and Authority of the Bible.* Philipsburg, New Jersey: The Presbyterian and Reformed Publishing Company, 1948.

Questions for Discussion

1. What reason cited motivates you to study the Bible the most? Why?
2. What problems exist today that are directly related to a lack of Bible study?
3. How do we develop our desire to study? How do we develop a desire to study in others?
4. How reliant are you right now on the opinions of others? How can you tell?
5. Who is the best and most dedicated Bible student you know? Why do you think so?

CHAPTER 2

Improper Attitudes

——————— ❖ ———————

INTRODUCTION

After Paul arrived in Athens, he was taken to Mars Hill. Taking the opportunity given to him, he preached a powerful sermon about "the unknown God." As he brought his lesson to a close, he emphasized the resurrection of Christ and the certainty of judgment to come. "And when they heard of the resurrection of the dead, some mocked, while others said, 'We will hear you again on this matter.' So Paul departed from among them. However, some men joined him and believed, among them Dionysius the Areopagite, a woman named Damaris, and others with them" (Acts 17:32–34). What made the difference in these three groups of people? They all heard the same sermon. They heard the same speaker. Yet some laughed at the sermon, others declined to commit one way or the other, while some truly believed. What was the difference between the three? Attitude.

Even today different people can pick up the Bible and arrive at different conclusions. While in some cases the differences may stem from inadequate preparation or poor skills, more often than not our attitudes sway us. Why? Our attitudes influence how we use or do not use the skills we possess. Our attitudes determine whether or not we will listen to a given point of view. Our attitudes guide us through the corridors of facts presented and tell us which way to take—even if it should disagree with the map. Our attitude is the lens through which we study the Bible. If our lens itself is out of focus, it blurs the truth revealed in the Bible and distorts what we see, causing us not to see the truth—not because it is not there, but because our lens is out of focus.

When was the last time you did some serious introspection regarding your attitudes toward the Bible? Take, as an example, the last time you became upset by something someone said in regard to your religious beliefs, whether in a Bible class, a sermon, or a personal encounter. Were you truly open to the point of view being presented to you? Were you upset afterwards? Why? Were you angry? Did you feel threatened? Now, how much time did you take to examine what the Bible said about it afterwards? Many times we expose the dirt on our lens in Bible study when we fail to evaluate what the Bible says. We then complain about how dirty people look when we actually need to apply the cleaning cloth to our attitude (Matt. 7:1-5).

Attitude is important. It affects our approach to life, and, more important still, it affects our approach to the truth of God's Word. When we think we already know what God says, our attitude keeps us from learning. When we refuse to accept what God says, our attitude makes us dogmatic about our own opinions. We must make sure that we do not have any improper attitudes affecting our Bible study or we have condemned ourselves to willful ignorance, because improper attitudes will keep the truth away from our eyes, leaving us to live and operate in a self-created illusion that has no substance.

TRYING TO PROVE SOMEBODY OR SOMETHING WRONG

One of the surest ways to get people into their Bibles is to challenge their firmly held beliefs and force them to prove that their beliefs are accurate. Unfortunately, however well this may work at getting people to open the text, it has many drawbacks that undermine good, honest Bible study. The most glaring difficulty with taking such an approach should be obvious: it starts with the belief held and then goes to the Bible for confirmation. Bible study should begin with the Bible and build belief (Rom. 10:17) — not the other way around. Some have desired to oppose error so much that they accepted something that was itself erroneous just because it "solved" the problem of one particular error. So while the truth prevails upon us at times to demonstrate that someone else holds an erroneous position, this should never become a fundamental approach to our study of God's Word.

When we approach the Bible with our belief "already in hand," we will often end up using a text out of context in order to prove something we believe but that the text does not say. Many people, and many preachers, when trying either to comfort a small congregation or justify a person's absence from the assembling of the saints (Heb. 10:25), will say, "For where two or three are gathered together in My name, I am there in the midst of them" (Matt. 18:20). However, this text has nothing whatsoever to do with an assembly of the Lord's people! It refers to the Lord's approval and authority for an action toward a brother who has sinned based upon following His will. The situation is found in verses fifteen and seventeen. The "two or three" refer to the "witnesses" of verse sixteen. Authority is the context of verses eighteen and nineteen.

Another problem created by trying to prove something or somebody wrong is majoring in minors. Jesus said, "Woe to you, scribes and Pharisees, hypocrites! For you pay tithe of mint and anise and cummin, and have neglected the weightier matters of the law: justice and mercy and faith. These you ought to have done, without leaving the others undone" (Matt. 23:23). The Pharisees of Jesus' day spent most of their time trying to show how wrong other sects and people were. In this passage Jesus charged them with majoring in minors. They had become so concerned with proving other people wrong that they had completely overlooked some of the most important principles of what God said. Why? Because of their attitude.

The apostle Matthew wrote, "Then the Pharisees went and plotted how they might entangle Him in His talk" (Matt. 22:15). The Pharisees were so concerned with proving Jesus wrong that they had no room left in their hearts to accept that He was right. While we must stand firmly against error, studying in order to try to prove something or somebody wrong demonstrates the wrong attitude toward the Bible.

HOLDING ON TO PRECONCEIVED IDEAS

An old saying I have heard attributed to both Mark Twain and Will Rogers goes something like this: "It isn't all the things we know that hurt us. It's all those things we know that ain't so." How true this is in regard to Bible study! Most people think that they understand the

Bible, at least to some degree, before they ever seriously begin studying it. However, the sincere Bible student must guard against holding on to preconceived ideas, because they are roadblocks to truth.

When Naaman, the commander of the Syrian army, heard that a prophet of God could heal him of his leprosy, he headed toward Israel. However, "Elisha sent a messenger to him, saying, 'Go and wash in the Jordan seven times, and your flesh shall be restored to you, and you shall be clean.' But Naaman became furious, and went away and said, 'Indeed, I said to myself, "He will surely come out to me, and stand and call on the name of the Lord his God, and wave his hand over the place, and heal the leprosy"'" (2 Kings 5:10–11). Naaman's anger, which originally caused him to ignore the prophet's instructions, was rooted in his preconceived idea of what the prophet **should** do. It was only when he was willing to accept the truth regarding what he was told that, following his compliance, he was healed (2 Kings 5:14).

In the Sermon on the Mount, our Lord said, "Do not think that I came to destroy the Law or the Prophets. I did not come to destroy but to fulfill" (Matt. 5:17). Jesus knew that His disciples were likely to make suppositions as to His purpose, so He warned against drawing conclusions before considering all the facts (all His teaching) (John 12:48). Still, many of the Jews held to false assumptions about the Messiah in the first century, such as assuming He would be a political leader and deliverer. Jesus did not meet up with their expectations *because they expected the wrong thing!* They were so busy looking for a Messiah that met their own preconceived ideas that they neglected and mistreated the Messiah when He was right there among them (John 1:10-11; Mark 12:10-11). Some people today think they know what is right, then they go to the scriptures to support their ideas. Such an attitude will inevitably produce failure because, just like the Jews before them, these will spend so much energy looking for the wrong teaching that they will overlook, neglect, and mistreat the truth. A good Bible student must be willing to toss aside all creeds — whether written or implied — and reject all assumption, then accept the Bible as God's revealed truth (John 17:17).

All of us have preconceived ideas. We all carry baggage toward our Bible study. We have all been taught **something** about the Bible prior to our independent study. But we must not hold on to these preconceived ideas as if they themselves are truth. We must be willing to evaluate our previous ideas using God's Word as our standard and discard false notions — no matter their origin — else we will attach ourselves to the unwieldy burden of our own presumption, making true Bible study futile and thereby drowning in unbelief.

THINKING THAT WE CANNOT UNDERSTAND THE BIBLE

The apostle Paul wrote, "All Scripture is given by inspiration of God, and is profitable for doctrine, for reproof, for correction, for instruction in righteousness, that the man of God may be complete, thoroughly equipped for every good work" (2 Tim. 3:16–17). Yet the attitude some have toward Bible study would indicate that Paul's words in this passage were meaningless. While some would say that understanding the Bible is a noble objective, they would also argue that it is essentially impossible. Yet Paul tells us that the Bible was penned **specifically** for us to understand and apply! A few have even argued that because man is so low it is impossible for him to understand the things of God. However, this does not exhibit humility; it denies the power of God. Do we really believe that God created a being with which He wished to communicate but was not able to do so? Also, God Himself reveals the fact that some things will remain unknown to us because He does not reveal them (Deut. 29:29), but does this not imply that what He reveals we can know and understand? "God is not the author of confusion" (1 Cor. 14:33).

Another segment of people would alter this objection only slightly, claiming that while it is possible to understand the Bible, it is not possible for us to understand the Bible alike. This view really teaches that it is possible for us to *misunderstand* the Bible but not to understand it. God, by His very nature, could only have one meaning in mind when He inspired the Scriptures. Any interpretation of His words besides the one He intended is erroneous (Matt. 22:29-32). Only one view is acceptable because truth, by its nature, is not relative, biblically or otherwise. Jesus said, "And you shall know the truth, and the truth shall make you free" (John 8:32). Spiritual freedom comes through understanding and applying the religious truth revealed in the word of God (John 17:17). If you cannot understand it, you cannot be free.

Unfortunately, many people would rather claim that the Bible cannot be understood than make the diligent effort necessary to understand it (2 Tim. 2:15). In actuality, they are spiritually lazy, not willing to make any effort to understand something if they do not comprehend it fully at the first hearing (Matt. 13:9). Others use this excuse when the truth revealed would require them to change their way of life (Matt. 13:10-17). When the Jewish leaders asked Jesus, "By what authority are you doing these things" (Matt. 21:23), He replied by presenting a logical dilemma to them. God, in the flesh, revealed the truth to them. But they replied, "We do not know" (Matt. 21:27). However, the previous verses revealed that they knew the logical conclusion all too well; they just did not like it. Like these Jews, many people deny that it is possible to understand what God has said, but the problem lies in their hearts — not in God's Word. **You** *can* understand the Bible, and we can *all* understand the Bible alike. But we must prepare our hearts to accept truth and diligently work toward that end (Ezra 7:10).

PRIDE

Pride is one of those "attitude" sins that touches every area of life, and Bible study is no exception. The wise man said long ago, "Pride goes before destruction, And a haughty spirit before a fall" (Prov. 16:18). Whenever a Bible student begins his study thinking that he already knows the answers, his motive is wrong. Bible study is about learning what God has to say — not seeing whether or not He agrees with you. It is pride that causes us to suppose that we **must** be right and that creates the desire within us to try to control right and wrong — at least in our own minds.

When Paul preached in Thessalonica, "the Jews who were not persuaded, becoming envious, took some of the evil men from the marketplace, and gathering a mob, set all the city in an uproar and attacked the house of Jason, and sought to bring them out to the people" (Acts 17:5). The Jews' envy existed because of their arrogant presumption of spiritual superiority, which Paul had exposed by his preaching, and their jealousy at Paul's success. Their pride not only caused them to reject the gospel themselves but to assault those who accepted it. Pride caused them to seek solace in their physical control over the house of Jason and others when they could not control the message. Sometimes, even today, people first become defensive, due to their pride, when their assumptions are challenged and then strike back offensively with verbal assaults and illogical arguments, once again from pride.

Earlier in Acts, when the apostles were preaching, the Jewish leaders in Jerusalem had shown the same disposition, "being greatly disturbed that they taught the people and preached in Jesus the resurrection from the dead" (Acts 4:2). Later, among themselves, they acknowledged that a miracle had been performed, but due to pride, they refused to admit their mistake publicly and even tried to suppress any knowledge of the event. Some people may privately admit that their ideas, beliefs, and teaching do not match the biblical record, but at the same time, their pride keeps them from admitting this publicly or making the changes required. However, this problem generally stems from other problems. More common in personal Bible study is the belief that questioning previously held positions is a lack of faith or a sign of weakness. However, nothing is as strengthening and faith-building as the reassurance brought by an independent examination of the evidence. The only thing to lose by such an examination is an erroneous belief. However, in order to expose these, you must first be willing to lose your pride.

Pride convinces us that nothing is as important as our own position and blinds us to the value of truth. Pride makes us believe that we could not possibly be wrong. Pride keeps us from ever considering that we might have accepted an erroneous teaching. Therefore, as we approach Bible study, let us remember the apostle Paul's words, "Therefore let him who thinks he stands take heed lest he fall" (1 Cor. 10:12).

SELF-JUSTIFICATION

One of the greatest difficulties we face in studying the Bible is that we have already developed a certain lifestyle and way of thinking prior to our study. Therefore, at some point in our study (and often in many) God's Word will confront us—our ideas and our way of life—and challenge us to change. This challenge creates an internal conflict, a battle between our will and God's. We must either accept God's will or attempt to justify ourselves. Otherwise, the internal conflict will overwhelm us with guilt. It is indeed unfortunate that many prefer to justify themselves rather than repent and accept God's will (Acts 17:30). The rich young ruler went to Jesus seeking the way to enter the kingdom but went away sorrowful when Jesus confronted His covetousness (Matt. 19:16-22). Paul wrote, "For I know of nothing against myself, yet I am not justified by this; but He who judges me is the Lord" (1 Cor. 4:4). Self-justification effectively places the individual in charge of judging himself instead of accepting that the Lord will judge according to His Word (John 12:48). When we attempt to justify ourselves, we are essentially trying to avoid applying what God says to our lives. When the Pharisees asked Jesus about marriage and divorce, He did not let it stay a doctrinal dispute about the Law of Moses but made a universal application of righteousness that applies in a very personal way (Matt. 19:1-6). The Pharisees sought self-justification in the Law, but Jesus pointed them toward the higher way of righteousness (Matt. 19:7-9), a strict conclusion that caused even His disciples great dismay (Matt. 19:10) because Jesus' application struck at the very heart of the self-justifying excuses of that day, the types of excuses that still prevail in our own society.

When a man knowledgeable in the Law approached Jesus and asked Him, "Teacher, what shall I do to inherit eternal life?" (Luke 10:25), Jesus called him back to the Word (Luke 10:26). The man correctly quoted the obligations of loving God (Deut. 6:5) and loving one's neighbor (Lev. 19:18), but his life obviously fell short of God's will. So it says, "But he, wanting to justify himself, said to Jesus, 'And who is my neighbor?'" (Luke 10:29). He did not want Jesus to actually answer the question (though the Savior did indeed do so with the story of the good Samaritan in subsequent verses). Rather, he desired an answer that would exonerate him and confirm the good opinion he had of his own righteousness. However, this is not the role of God's Word. When we assume our own righteousness from the start, we miss the primary role of the Word to save (Rom. 1:16-17).

Self-justification causes us to proclaim our innocence despite the overwhelming preponderance of facts against us. It creates a false image of right and wrong that is based in personal practice rather than divine direction. It leads us to reject truth and accept lies (2 Th. 2:10-12), turning life itself into a lie (1 John 1:6-10). Self-justification puts the sinner in the position of God as the standard, as the judge, and as the redeemer.

APPEALING TO THE WRONG STANDARD

Any time we encounter disagreement in the spiritual realm we generally rise to defend our beliefs. The most appropriate defense is an appeal to a standard. In fact, Jesus did this each time the devil confronted Him in the wilderness when He replied, "it is written" (Matt. 4:1-11). However, it matters very much what our standard is to defend our beliefs, because our defense can only be as strong as the standard we use. All too often we forget the necessity of biblical authority for our behavior and beliefs and begin employing phrases in our personal defense that betray adherence to the wrong standard. Jesus said, "He who rejects Me, and does not receive My words, has that which judges him—the word that I have spoken will judge him in the last day" (John 12:48). Therefore, since Jesus established the word as the standard of judgment, it must be the standard to which we appeal.

When some scribes and Pharisees found fault with Jesus' disciples for not washing their hands "the correct way," it was because they judged "according to the tradition of the elders" (Mark 7:3-5). To this, Jesus replied in part, "All too well you reject the commandment of God, that you may keep your tradition" (Mark 7:9). The Pharisees' problem was not in accepting something passed down (tradition), but that they accepted something that did not come from God (2 Th. 2:13-15). Creeds may have begun as an attempt to summarize what someone or some group believed the Bible to say, but when an individual cannot demonstrate that belief from the Bible itself, the creed has become the standard. Such is often the case today. Many people will defend their beliefs vehemently despite the fact that they have never entertained a serious examination of them. For these, what they were taught growing up or what they have always believed has replaced the Bible as the standard. Likewise, children can grow up in a wonderful Christian home, learning the proper way to worship, serve, and live, yet actually have no real faith because their basis for acting is on their parents' faith rather than on Jesus Christ and His Word. How many times in Bible class has someone quoted some commentary as if that settled the matter? It is the wrong standard. Some people will believe what a favorite preacher says—no matter what! That is the wrong standard. If we are not firmly relying upon the Word of God and reasoning from it ourselves, we have fallen prey to appealing to the wrong standard.

The directives to rightly divide the word of truth (2 Tim. 2:15) and search the scriptures (Acts 17:11) imply that God's Word is the only correct standard to which we should appeal, and that we each have the individual responsibility to verify that what we believe and practice agrees with what God has said (1 Th. 5:21). What other people have accepted, what other people have taught, and what other people have practiced is totally irrelevant. The only standard that matters now is the standard that will be used on Judgment Day, and that is the all-sufficient, inspired Word of God (2 Tim. 3:16-17).

CLOSED-MINDEDNESS

The concept of being "closed-minded" has received great abuse in recent years, mostly because it has been twisted and defined incorrectly. Rejecting certain ideas does not alone make someone closed-minded. Rather, being closed-minded refers to someone's refusal to consider pertinent facts and evidence. After Jesus healed a lame man, certain Jews ignored this miracle's attestation to the truth of Jesus' words because they had eliminated any possibility of accepting what He had to say. Jesus challenged them to search the scriptures for further evidence of the truth in His words (John 5:38-40), but these Jews, despite their claims, had no real interest in what the Bible said (John 5:45-47). They had closed their minds even to the possibility that Jesus could be God in the flesh, causing them to reject Him—not due to the evidence, but because they did not want to know the evidence. When Jesus taught in his hometown of Nazareth, the people did not deny His wisdom or the miracles He did (Matt. 13:54), but they closed their minds to His teaching because they would only accept what they had always assumed — that He was Joseph the carpenter's son (Matt. 13:55).

While it would be nice to think that people today are not this closed-minded, the evidence suggests otherwise. It seems so easy for people today whose beliefs are challenged by the Bible to respond, "That's just your interpretation!" (These people generally cite 2 Peter 1:20, "knowing this first, that no prophecy of Scripture is of any private interpretation," not realizing that this passage is speaking of the origin of Scripture through inspiration.) What would be truly remarkable if it were not so sad is that people will say this even when all a person has done is read the scriptures without providing any commentary. They reject the evidence God has provided because they have closed their minds to truth. It is so easy to ignore evidence. The Pharisees went to Jesus saying that they wanted to see a miracle. Jesus refused to perform one — not because of their unbelief but because they had witnessed a miracle already. They had evidence at their disposal but had closed their minds to what that evidence indicated (Matt. 12:38-42). Some will even say, "I don't care what the Bible says." This implies that they recognize the disparity between their beliefs and what God says and closed their minds to God's Word (2 Tim. 4:2-4).

A closed mind shuts out possibilities not already accepted, including God's revealed truth. Thus, a closed mind limits itself to what evidence it considers helpful and rejects all evidence that might disprove previously held conclusions or require a change. A closed mind is a mind that fears facts, fears evidence, and fears truth. A closed mind rejects what is the Bible student's greatest help — the evidence of the Scriptures — unless it supports a conclusion already assumed. A good Bible student will be open to all the possibilities and allow the evidence found in God's Word to guide his thoughts in his search for truth instead of ignoring evidence just because it might not support his position.

WISHING SOMETHING WERE TRUE

Saul of Tarsus had a great education, trained by Gamaliel in Jerusalem (Acts 22:3a), and obviously was a man of great intelligence. He had a great zeal for God (Acts 22:3b) that caused him to make havoc of the church (Acts 8:3), involving himself in threats, imprisonments, and even murder (Acts 9:1-2), which later caused him to assert that he was the worst of sinners (1 Tim. 1:15). Yet Paul still maintained that this was done in good conscience (Acts 23:1), saying, "I did it ignorantly in unbelief" (1 Tim. 1:13). Why would a man of such superior intellect act so recklessly? What caused him to deny Christ and the truth so long? He simply wanted to believe that he was right and that Christianity must therefore be wrong.

Many Bible students mistakenly go to the scriptures looking for what they want to be true. This can be a very innocent mistake. When we have been told what to assume about a passage or a doctrine (meaning that it has been interpreted for us in a given way over a long period of time so that it is part of how we think), then we will want to believe it is true, even when the evidence does not necessarily agree. Many a person has cited Romans 5:1 in support of the doctrine of faith only: "Therefore, having been justified by faith, we have peace with God through our Lord Jesus Christ." However, the word "only" does not appear in this verse. It certainly teaches justification by faith; it in no way teaches justification by faith only. But those who have listened over and over again to a "faith only" interpretation generally read "only" into the text, though it does not exist there in fact. Why? They want to believe that it is true. Likewise, many people err in their Bible study in their efforts to avoid painful conclusions. Many people actually reject the gospel because they do not want to have to face the painful conclusion that their parents or other loved ones are lost. Herod imprisoned John the Immerser because he, and especially his wife, Herodias, found John's message personally painful (Matt. 14:3-4). Many people find the conclusions of Jesus' teaching about marriage and divorce painful (Matt. 19:1-9) just as his disciples did (Matt. 19:10), so they adjust what they believe in order to avoid the pain that those conclusions bring. Some people want so badly to find fault with others that they overlook applications that apply to them personally. The Pharisees wanted to believe that Jesus was wrong and that He was not the Messiah so badly that they spent their time trying to catch Him in an error while failing to apply the law to their own lives (Matt. 9:10-13; 11:16-19; 12:1-8).

We must be prepared to accept what God says without reading our own prejudices into a passage. We must accept the conclusions that follow from what God says, regardless of how painful that may be. We must stop trying to find reasons to condemn others and instead make sure that we are applying God's Word to our own lives. When we go to the Bible wanting to believe something is true, we have things in the wrong order. We study the Bible in order to discover truth so that we know what to believe (John 8:32).

A WILLINGNESS TO IMPUGN GOD'S WORD

It should go without saying that one's attitude toward the Word of God itself will affect interpretation greatly. However, time and time again in my studies with individuals I have seen people willing to impugn God's Word rather than accept the truth. They would rather imply that the Bible is inconsistent or wrong than admit being inconsistent or wrong themselves. The Pharisees were so intent on proving Jesus was wrong that they were willing to assign Jesus' healing power to Beelzubub (Matt. 12:22-24). To this Jesus replied, "Therefore I say to you, every sin and blasphemy will be forgiven men, but the blasphemy against the Spirit will not be forgiven men" (Matt 12:31). Jesus told them that in their efforts to circumvent Jesus' teaching they had in fact brought indictment against the Holy Spirit who had provided the means of the miracle. Likewise, when we take a position that implies that the Bible is in error, we have effectively committed blasphemy against the Holy Spirit, impugning the Source, because we are implying that what God says is not really from God (2 Tim. 3:16-17).

Many people commit this moral felony when they refuse to examine the entire context of a passage. How many people have quoted Jesus saying, "Judge not, that you be not judged" (Matt. 7:1), and then interpreted that to mean that all judging is wrong? Jesus also said, "Do not judge according to appearance, but judge righteous judgment" (John 7:24). Therefore, Jesus could not have meant in Matthew 7 that all judging is wrong. Yet some people would rather act as if Jesus was right in Matthew 7 but wrong in John 7 in order to try to justify their own position. This essentially pits scripture against scripture. I have taken people to various passages in the Bible in an attempt to teach them only to have them try to jump here and there in the Bible looking for some scripture *that would contradict* the scripture I pointed out to them. This attitude itself is wrong! How are we better off by treating God's Word as if it is full of contradictions? Again, this is an attack against God Himself. When you have two verses contradicting one another, you can be sure that your interpretation of at least one of them is wrong. "For God is not the author of confusion, but of peace, as in all the churches of the saints" (1 Cor. 14:33).

Satan tried to pit scripture against scripture when he tempted Jesus. Rather than agreeing that there was some contradiction or inconsistency, Jesus pointed out that Satan's interpretation was incorrect and therefore the problem (Matt. 4:6-7). Some try to mask their own inconsistency in doctrine by calling it "tension." Others try to play down the fact that they are undermining verbal plenary inspiration. Any time we study the Bible, we must examine the entire context, not only of the passage and book, but also of the entire Bible, in order to make sure that our interpretation does not create inconsistency in our beliefs (Acts 20:27). The Bible is always right; we are often wrong. Let us not confuse these two.

APPLYING THINGS TO EVERYONE BUT YOURSELF

Most preachers will tell you that everything would improve immensely in the church if people would only apply what they believe. However, I am convinced that the vast majority of people are more than willing to apply lessons they learn from the Scriptures— just not to themselves. Invariably, after a hard-hitting lesson someone will come up and say, "I sure hope Brother 'Fill-in-the-Blank' was listening." And while Brother "Fill-in-the-Blank" probably did indeed need that lesson, the purpose of sermons *and* of Bible study is not to see if we can find fault in others but to see how well we can see fault *in ourselves* and then make the appropriate correction (Jas. 1:23-25). Yet few seem willing to approach Bible study in this way.

It seems rather simple to point out the principle of treating our bodies with respect and taking care of them (1 Cor. 6:19-20) to someone who smokes or drinks alcohol, but for some reason we do not want to apply this ourselves when illness demands a change in our behavior or diet. The principle is no different. We simply do not see the application because it is too close to home. Many have no trouble recognizing and applying the command to give each first day of the week (1 Cor. 16:1-2) but cannot see the parallel application in regard to partaking of the Lord's Supper each first day of the week (Acts 20:7). There are parents who rightfully point out the immodesty of mini-skirts and low-cut blouses while allowing their own children to wear skin tight clothing that leaves little to the imagination (1 Tim. 2:9-10). Why does it seem so easy to notice where others need God's guidance but so hard to see where we need it ourselves? First, the detachment we feel from others helps make the hard applications easier to admit, whereas our close proximity to personal sins tends to blur our spiritual vision and our "application acuity." Overcoming this propensity is therefore essential if we are to benefit from Bible study. Second, most of our Bible study is centered, incorrectly in my view, on teaching others God's Word first. Therefore, we are *looking* for examples to illustrate *our* points. We then draw our examples from our own observation, which is clearly dominated by what others do. Therefore, the problem is not that we have trouble understanding how to apply what the Bible says to real life situations but that we tend to judge only those situations that apply to others.

Bible study must begin with a willingness to take a long, hard look into the mirror of the soul without blaming the reflection on someone else. For our Bible study to help us we must be willing to see and accept its lessons *for us*. James said, "But be doers of the word, and not hearers only, deceiving yourselves" (Jas. 1:22). We must apply God's Word to our own lives *first*, before we have any business looking elsewhere. Jesus surely had this in mind when He said, "Hypocrite! First remove the plank from your own eye, and then you will see clearly to remove the speck from your brother's eye" (Matt. 7:5).

CONCLUSION

All people of genuine sincerity undoubtedly desire to avoid having improper attitudes regarding the Bible. Unfortunately, the desire alone does not accomplish the task. We cannot simply wish away an improper attitude, nor should we behave as if we are above such failings. The inspired apostle Paul wrote, "Therefore let him who thinks he stands take heed lest he fall" (1 Cor. 10:12). Therefore, as we have been commanded to apply diligence in our study of God's Word (2 Tim. 2:15), this diligence must begin with reining in any improper attitudes — and keeping them reined in. This must be an ongoing process, for it is a never-ending battle that Satan wages against us (1 Pet. 5:8). If he perverts our attitudes, he can easily persuade us to accept a perverted doctrine (Gal. 1:6-9). Therefore, we must give the most earnest effort imaginable to keeping our attitudes pure (Matt. 5:8). This alone does not guarantee that we will reach the truth in our study, but it is certain that the truth will elude us if our attitudes fail us.

The first step toward avoiding improper attitudes is to become aware of them. A foe that lurks in the darkness can more easily inflict harm than one within our sight. If we realize the nature of these attitudes and their accompanying dangers, then we are in a better position to expose them for what they are. Many people become frustrated in trying to explain their beliefs because their beliefs are neither logical nor true. They have become the victims of their own attitudes. Once we are aware of these damaging attitudes we must determine to examine ourselves and our attitudes at every turn (2 Cor. 13:5). Every Bible study session should begin and end with a close examination for any attitudes that might have caused us to accept a conclusion from improper motivation. In fact, Bible students need to constantly incorporate this self-examination into Bible study. But in order to do this, we must remain conscious of our own beliefs and be honest about our possible motivations. Perhaps the hardest step in avoiding improper attitudes is learning to separate yourself from what you believe. If you identify yourself with any belief save that of accepting truth, then accepting truth will become an unbearable task, because it will require you to deny not only a false belief but, for all practical purposes, your own identity. Thus, we should all reflect on Jesus words, "If anyone desires to come after Me, **let him deny himself**, and take up his cross, and follow Me" (Matt. 16:24).

One last word of warning. Just because you may have proved that your belief is correct does *not* guarantee that your attitudes are right. Even if your "position" is right, any of the attitudes already cited are harmful and wrong, because they will inevitably lead you away from the truth at some point and on some matter. We must therefore give diligence to avoiding these harmful, improper attitudes and devote ourselves toward developing the proper attitudes that will ward off future difficulties (Prov. 23:23).

We should avoid the improper attitudes of:

*   **Trying to prove something or somebody wrong**
*   **Holding on to preconceived ideas**
*   **Believing that we cannot understand the Bible**
*   **Pride**
*   **Self-Justification**
*   **Appealing to the wrong standard**
*   **Closed-mindedness**
*   **Wanting to believe something is true**
*   **Willing to impugn the word of God instead of admitting error**
*   **Applying things to everyone but yourself**

Recommended Reading

Apple, Jody L. *Hermeneutical Agnosticism: A Critique of Subjectivisim in Biblical Interpretation*. Media, PA: New Testament Christian Press, 1985.

Dunn, Frank J. "Attitudes That Help or Hinder Proper Interpretation." Chapter in *Rightly Dividing the Word: Volume I – General Hermeneutics*, ed. Terry Hightower, 7-23. Pensacola, FL: Firm Foundation Publishing House, 1990.

Questions for Discussion

1. What improper attitudes are the most difficult for you personally? Why?
2. To what do you attribute the origin of your improper attitudes?
3. Rank these improper attitudes in the order of the damage they can cause, then discuss.
4. Give examples of where you perceive these attitudes in people with whom you disagree on spiritual matters. What might those same people say about you?
5. How do you correct improper attitudes when it requires an attitude in the first place?

Assignment

On separate sheets of paper, write down three disagreements you have had recently. Include one with a religious neighbor, one with your preacher, and one with a fellow Christian. Then evaluate the attitude and posture you took toward each of them at the time.

CHAPTER 3

Proper Attitudes

❖

INTRODUCTION

While eliminating improper attitudes is essential to Bible study, doing so does not guarantee that a person will develop the proper attitudes. Rather, a person might simply enter an attitudinal vacuum or react so violently against formerly held attitudes that he adopts new attitudes that, while different, are just as dangerous as those originally held. Perhaps "attitude" itself is a little misleading. It would be wrong to place these characteristics in the same category with optimism or pessimism or to equate them with a general outlook. The traits mentioned below are intended to portray various aspects required in order to maintain objectivity.

In the same way that improper attitudes will lead us to bring foreign ideas to Bible study that intrude on the accuracy of our conclusions, proper attitudes ensure that we wait to allow the study to determine the conclusion, helping us to remain open to all possible interpretations until they can be eliminated with reason. Having the proper attitude also requires focus. It helps us to remember why we are studying in the first place. Therefore, the proper attitudes help the Bible student focus on God's truth and how it applies to his life.

Attitudes, interestingly enough, can be shaped by the intellect as well as shape the intellect. It is possible to mold one's attitudes through attention and intellectual self-examination in order to determine why we think or feel a certain way. Once we reform our attitudes, it is possible for our correct attitudes to help us develop the intellect. That is not to say that attitudes increase our intelligence but that proper attitudes lead to greater clarity of thought. As a result, the intellect is less cluttered with disinformation and more open to truth.

Our attitudes are what lead to our first impressions, and, without great effort, our first impressions often become lasting impressions. Nowhere is this quite as obvious—and dangerous—as in Bible study. Therefore, the Bible student must begin developing the proper attitudes lest all his efforts ultimately be made in vain.

OPEN-MINDEDNESS

Almost every person alive would consider himself open-minded. Thus we must consider it an admirable trait. However, this does not necessarily mean that such personal evaluations are accurate. Indeed, the differences that continue to exist, especially in the religious realm, should be enough to demonstrate that at the very least people maintain very different ideas regarding what being open-minded entails. When we speak of being open-minded, it implies that we are open to accept something, but we must define what it is we are open to accept. Do we mean that we are likely to accept almost anything? Do we mean that, while we will not necessarily adopt what others believe, we are open enough to allow people to believe something we think is wrong without voicing strong disagreement? Do we mean that we are open to listen to others' ideas just long enough to develop an argument against it? These concepts mistake gullibility, tolerance, and debate for open-mindedness. In the first instance, there is no discernment; in the second, there is no acceptance; and in the third, there is no real consideration of other points of view. Neither of these provide for the acceptance of an idea or belief based upon the merits of that belief.

What then does it mean to be open-minded? It means that we are always open to and willing to accept and adopt truth. An open mind is willing to consider anything but always compares it with the standard. It was this openness to truth that Jesus implied when He said, "If anyone has ears to ear, let him hear" (Mark 4:23). Therefore, in Bible study the standard to which we must compare all beliefs is the word of God itself. "Sanctify them by Your truth. Your word is truth" (John 17:17). While this may seem basic to many readers, maintaining such an attitude is often more difficult than it might seem. Open-mindedness requires a person to always consider the possibility that he might be wrong. This does not mean that we are constantly in doubt or that we lack confidence in our understanding. It means that we confidently hold to our beliefs until the truth requires that we discard them. Our biggest problem with this lies in how much we associate our beliefs with our identity. If we identify ourselves by what we already believe, then it is unlikely that we will be open to accept the truth should it disagree. However, if we will integrate a love and desire for holding to truth in all matters, then we will not only be willing but eager to reject our false notions in favor of newly discovered truth (either due to personal study or someone else's comments).

The Scriptures commend the Bereans for having an open mind: "These were more fair-minded than those in Thessalonica, in that they received the word with all readiness, and searched the Scriptures daily to find out whether these things were so" (Acts 17:11). The Bereans' claim to nobility, you will notice, centered on their willingness to consider Paul's message and their determination to accept it only if it agreed with the Scriptures. Such open-mindedness must characterize us as Bible students or we will never discover the beautiful truth of God's Word and thus remain forever burdened with the baggage of erroneous belief — a failure in faith that will, more than likely, translate into a failure in pleasing God (Rom. 12:1-2).

SPIRITUAL MINDEDNESS

What does it mean to be spiritually minded? The question itself seems ridiculous, because the answer should be obvious. However, many people have exchanged spirituality for pseudo-spirituality. They want the appearance of being spiritual without the responsibility that goes with it. Some equate zeal with spirituality, yet Paul indicated that zeal alone does not ensure the proper spiritual mindset (Rom. 10:1-2). Others get caught up in emotional hype, relying on the excitement, often of externals, to give them the strength by which to live. But neither of these is true spirituality. They fail to provide any strength and comfort after the initial "high" and create a dependency on the fervor and emotion of the moment rather than a trust in the God of eternity. Somehow people have equated these emotions with being "Spirit-filled" and spirituality. God, on the other hand, always connects spirituality with our reception of and our living by the message revealed by the Spirit (Rom. 8:1-4). "If we live in the Spirit, let us also walk in the Spirit" (Gal. 5:25).

Spiritual-mindedness is not a feeling but a determination—a determination to direct our thoughts and our lives according to God's revealed will. Jesus taught in parables, especially early on in His earthy work, in order to stimulate spiritual thinking (Mark 4:10-12). "And He said to them, 'Do you not understand this parable? How then will you understand all the parables?'" (Mark 4:13). In asking these two questions, Jesus showed that their problem in understanding the parable was a failure to think spiritually. Many times people err in their Bible study because their thinking remains centered on the physical. Some can only think of a kingdom as a political and geographical entity, failing to understand that Jesus was speaking of the spiritual kingdom of the church over which He now reigns (John 18:36; Matt. 16:18-19). Others can only see life after death in physical terms (indeed, many think of heaven in this way). Our ability to see the glory of the spiritual is often obscured by our own concentration on the material (Mark 7:14-23). Thus, being spiritually minded means thinking on spiritual things. "For those who live according to the flesh set their minds on the things of the flesh, but those who live according to the Spirit, the things of the Spirit" (Rom. 8:5). When we are spiritually minded we will meditate upon what God has said in His Word and let His words guide our view of everything else, and we will be looking for how our lives should change to match God's Word.

The essence of a spiritual mind is a concern for matters of the spirit, a diligent search for answers in God's Word, which is the product of the Holy Spirit's inspiration (1 Cor. 2:12-16), and a constant reflection on the personal need to make the inspired words of the Spirit take life in our own lives. Spiritual-mindedness and spirituality are not the effect of an emotionally charged atmosphere but are the turning of the mind to the things of God, understanding that He alone has the answers to life's questions and needs. A spiritual mind turns from man's doctrines and creeds to God's Word. A spiritual mind turns from worldliness and sin to the eternal and truth. A spiritual mind rejects intuition and opinion and accepts God's answers. A spiritual mind does these things because it first turns toward God's Word.

PASSION FOR TRUTH

A Bible student **must** have at his very core an unyielding passion for truth. And while this is easy to say, achieving it in practice requires the fervor of a zealot. Though our society still utters the words "the truth, the whole truth, and nothing but the truth," it seems obvious that such a phrase has little or no meaning to a large segment of the population. Nowadays our dedication to truth often disappears should the truth actually cost us something, hurt our feelings, or require something of us (like paying the taxes we owe, admitting fault, or accepting a painful conclusion). When the truth is convenient or suits our purposes, we love truth. But when the truth works against us, we will find a way to subvert it. This subjects truth to our whims of fancy and personal aggrandizement, while a genuine passion for truth causes us to subject ourselves to that truth.

Jesus prayed to the Father, "Sanctify them by Your truth. Your word is truth" (John 17:17). The word of God therefore reveals religious, spiritual reality. (This also shows that realism and idealism are not mutually exclusive. God's will is the ideal in which, through Jesus Christ, He has provided for the reality of man's sin.) What God says may be denied by men, but it cannot be changed. When we deny God's Word, we deny reality. However, this is exactly what many men do. They deny portions, if not all, of God's Word because they do not like what that truth costs them (Luke 14:28). A well-developed passion for truth, however, desires to know truth in order to abide by that truth. The apostle Peter recorded, "as newborn babes, desire the pure milk of the word, that you may grow thereby" (1 Pet. 2:2). When we have a passion for truth, we will not only accept the truth of God's Word when it is presented to us, we will also seek it out! To a true lover of truth, it is not enough to make correction when another discovers and points out his error, rather he applies himself to knowing truth so that he might discover his own errors and make appropriate correction— not to avoid the embarrassment of being wrong but rather to fulfill his passion for possessing truth. The person who longs for the right relationship with God of righteousness will seek out not only God's Man of salvation but also God's Plan of salvation (Matt. 5:6)! Both of these are revealed in the truth of God's Word (Acts 4:12; 2:38).

Respect for truth has diminished greatly throughout the last few years. An oath to tell the truth has become almost a meaningless formality. Individuals will vouch for the good character of a friend or family member despite knowing all too well the vast extent of his flaws. People will complain about the politicians who lie and then reward the ones who lie the most. The greater sin by far, however, lies in the vast array of people who do not love the truth of God's Word enough to seek and search it out in order to come to know God's will. They will hear the truth maimed in proclamation yet never stand up to defend it. They may disagree with what they have been told, but they do not care enough to see what is right. Where is our passion? Where is our fire? Studying the Bible, whether by ourselves or with others, will truly benefit us only when we will accept nothing but the truth. "Buy the truth, and do not sell it, Also wisdom and instruction and understanding" (Prov. 23:23).

PERSISTENCE

Two common approaches to Bible study seem diametrically opposed to one another at first glance while actually stemming from the same problem. Some people look at the Bible and read it fairly casually, afterwards asserting, "That is so simple anybody ought to be able to understand it." Others look at the Bible and are overwhelmed by both the mass of material contained in its pages and the difficulties presented by some passages. Many things in the Bible are simple to comprehend, while others bewilder the best of scholars. The basic message is so straightforward that it sometimes becomes a stumblingblock (1 Cor. 1:18-21). Yet there is no denying that some places require much depth of study, as Peter also affirmed (2 Pet. 3:15-16). What both the casual reader and the overwhelmed student lack is persistence.

Paul told Timothy, "Be diligent to present yourself approved to God, a worker who does not need to be ashamed, rightly dividing the word of truth" (2 Tim. 2:15). The word translated "study" in the King James Version and "be diligent" in the New King James Version, as well as others, means "to give one's best, regardless of the labor required." Therefore, Paul recognized that the effort necessary to understand holy writ surpasses the casual, implying that it takes great effort to understand it correctly. Many students approach the Bible with too much confidence in their own intelligence, by which I mean that they mistakenly believe that if they cannot understand what the Bible says, fully and completely, their first time through it, then it must not be worth knowing. When this happens, the Bible student may very well cease his studies when he has come up with an easy explanation, not continuing his thought process long enough to discover that he is, in fact, very, VERY wrong. One Calvin and Hobbes cartoon demonstrates this attitude well. Calvin asks his father what makes the wind blow, to which his father responds, "Trees sneezing." Calvin replies, "Really?" After which his father admits, "No, but the truth is more difficult." The next frame shows Calvin out in the wind saying to Hobbes, "The trees sure are sneezing today!" Sometimes we accept the easy answers because we lack the necessary persistence to discover the truth.

Persistence in Bible study means that we must prepare ourselves for an expedition to dig for truth. Paul wrote, "Till I come, give attendance to reading, to exhortation, to doctrine" (1 Tim. 4:13). Notice that he began with "reading." The word means in its origin "to know again," carrying with it the idea of review. Persistence also includes taking the time to reflect upon what God says. In the same passage Paul says, "Meditate on these things; give yourself entirely to them, that your progress may be evident to all" (1 Tim. 4:15). Persistence in Bible study causes us to seek the truth (John 17:17), the whole truth (Acts 20:26-27), and nothing but the truth (Gal. 1:6-9). It does not allow us to settle for basic knowledge or simply facts but to make the struggle necessary to get to the background of the passage to find the meat beyond the milk (Heb. 5:12). Persistence does not mean that we never draw conclusions, but it does mean that we work feverishly to make sure our conclusions are correct "from top to bottom." Persistence causes us to realize there is always more available to learn, while also giving us the heart to seek it out (Psa. 119:97).

ACCEPTANCE OF TRUTH

Studying the Bible requires a person to lower those defense mechanisms built up over time that inevitably lead to internal fights between previously accepted beliefs and new, sometimes conflicting, information. This does not mean that you should throw caution to the wind, but many a person has despised truth simply because it was new to him. Therefore, our attitude in studying the Bible must include an awareness of this natural struggle that occurs within us so that we do not fight truth, once discovered, simply on the basis that it does not meet our prior expectations. This is, essentially, an attitude of "hearing." Do we study the Bible or listen to someone presenting it with an ear for truth or with an ear for having our own beliefs substantiated? Jesus said, as He concluded the parable of the sower, "Therefore take heed how you hear. For whoever has, to him more will be given; and whoever does not have, even what he seems to have will be taken from him" (Luke 8:18). The difference between the two categories presented lies in their willingness to hear truth and accept it as truth.

Some people spend the majority of their study time trying to explain away what the Bible teaches instead of accepting it. They come across moral imperatives and attempt to disregard them as "cultural prerogatives." They see verses that obviously contradict their teachings and then twist evidence to reinvent the meaning of the words in that passage. Some will even go so far as to admit the truth on a scholastic level yet never adapt to it on the doctrinal level. Many religious groups are building their reputation by calling themselves "Bible-believers" while ignoring much of what the Bible says (2 Tim. 4:2-4; Acts 20:26-27). Truth, by its very definition, does not allow for variation, notwithstanding the moral relativists of our present day. Therefore, our acceptance of truth often depends on our determination to see that "all the facts line up." A person who can content himself with inconsistency and/or hypocrisy does not have the character necessary to discover and accept truth. When two beliefs are not consistent with one another, one must be rejected. However, we must make sure that the inconsistency lies within the beliefs themselves rather than in our own desires. Faith and works are consistent with one another (Jas. 2:14-26) as are grace (Eph. 2:8-10) and law (Rom. 8:2). Yet some who emphasize one or the other of these will reject another very biblical doctrine—not because it is inconsistent with the Bible but because it is inconsistent with their own teachings.

Accepting the truth means that we are willing to accept it at "face value," without the trappings of dogma. Sometimes we decide that "It can't mean that!" based upon an objection that is more personal than biblical. Therefore, we must learn to develop a heart that accepts truth as the compass of the soul, so that our concern is no longer trying to impress others with our knowledge but to have confidence that we are going the right direction. "How sweet are Your words to my taste, Sweeter than honey to my mouth!" (Psa. 119:103).

MORAL COURAGE

Any mention of courage tends to provoke images of a hero scurrying through machine gun fire in order to lift an injured friend and then carrying him back to safety. While we would never want to demean or diminish such bravery, there is a greater courage yet, and it is required of the Bible student. Every individual who delves into the pages of God's Word must possess moral courage, the internal fortitude to accept truth and its consequences bravely while withstanding the flurry of fiery darts from the wicked one—from frontline forces, snipers, and friendly fire. Moral courage requires more endurance because we must have it not only for a few moments of heroism but also for the struggle that often ensues shortly afterwards with our friends, family, and even ourselves. "But Jesus said to him, 'No one, having put his hand to the plow, and looking back, is fit for the kingdom of God'" (Luke 9:62).

It takes moral courage to accept the responsibilities that come with the freedom truth brings (John 8:32). "If anyone comes to Me and does not hate his father and mother, wife and children, brothers and sisters, yes, and his own life also, he cannot be My disciple. And whoever does not bear his cross and come after Me cannot be My disciple" (Luke 14:26-27). When we sit down to study and suddenly realize the depth of commitment required of us and the immense task it is to devote oneself to the discovery of religious truth, it can be overwhelming. And moral courage is a necessity when the consequences of truth require more of us than we expected—as they usually do. Some people have made significant strides in correcting their lives only to be faced with the truth of God's Word that indicates they are not even Christians in God's eyes. It takes courage to accept such a conclusion and to adjust your frame of mind accordingly, but this demonstrates the necessity of moral courage. "For which of you, intending to build a tower, does not sit down first and count the cost, whether he has enough to finish it" (Luke 14:28). The conversion of Saul of Tarsus presented a problem for many Christians. After all, this same Saul had instigated many of the hardships that the church in Judea faced (Acts 8:1-3). Therefore, who could blame them for fearing him (Acts 9:26)? Barnabas, however, had the moral courage to do what was right (Acts 9:27).

As Jesus roamed the Galilean countryside, many people followed him in order to see what miracle he would do next — especially if they could enjoy the fruits of his labor by having another meal! But when Jesus taught them the necessity of accepting Him and His will, totally and absolutely, they reneged, saying, "This is a hard saying; who can listen to it?" (John 6:60 ESV). Peter was willing to physically defend Jesus with his sword but later denied him (Luke 22:49-60; John 18:10). What we must realize is that Bible study requires a new type of bravery and a new paradigm of heroism. Bible study requires moral courage, because it is by moral courage that we submit to God's will, it is by moral courage that we can forsake our prior understanding of scripture, and it is by moral courage that truth understood becomes truth undertaken. Bible study will become just an intellectual exercise unless the Christian combines it with moral courage.

LOGICAL

For one reason or another, a perceptible divide can arisen between religion and logic. Perhaps this stems from an emotionalist reaction to the secular rationalism developed during the "Age of Reason." Perhaps some do not see how emotion and reason can coexist. However, the Bible clearly teaches that, while we are to be a caring and loving people whose hearts are deeply moved by God's love (1 John 4:7-11), we also must be a logical people. God expects us to reason! Paul told the Thessalonians, "Test all things; hold fast what is good" (1 Th. 5:21). The word "test" means "verify," to compare objectively to a standard. That God intended a study of His Word to be based in reason is clear from the words of Peter, "as newborn babes, desire the pure milk of the word, that you may grow thereby" (1 Pet. 2:2). The phrase "of the word" translates the Greek word *logikos*, from which we have derived our word logical. The context indicates that Peter was emphasizing that the gospel does not seek to appeal to people through trickery or emotional hype but through reason. Therefore, since God communicated using reason and appeals to us using reason, He must also (as Paul already stated) expect us to use reason in order to understand His message properly.

We must begin by understanding the nature and purpose of logic. Logic is the means by which we force objectivity on ourselves. It is through logic that we can put our beliefs to the test against God's standard. When we act as if God's Word can be understood subjectively (you have your interpretation; I have mine), then we are rejecting logic and reason in favor of personal opinion. God, by His very nature, can have only ONE opinion and accept only ONE interpretation—one that is consistent with His own (Gal. 1:6-9)! It is through logic that we check to make sure that our interpretation agrees with God's. Logic, then, is no more incompatible with emotion than God's nature of light (1 John 1:5) is incompatible with His nature of love (1 John 4:8). These are not separate "natures" but rather, along with spirit (John 4:24), comprise His one nature. It is only through logic that you can learn the when and how of making the proper emotional response. Without logic you could respond emotionally with joy without reason for doing so. You can feel saved without being saved. Emotion can give you the feeling but cannot provide the substance. Logic leads you to the substance whereby you can also enjoy the feeling—with confidence.

Unfortunately, many today fear logic. They are afraid of having their beliefs tested. Remember: truth has nothing to fear. Jesus encouraged and expected others to apply logic to God's Word and rebuked them for failing to do so (Matt. 22:23-33, 41-46). He never asked people to follow blindly but always appealed to evidence and reason (John 10:31-39). In our Bible study it is imperative that we employ logic. You must be willing to think for yourself and strive for complete objectivity or the truth will elude you. Logic points out our inconsistencies and reveals where our beliefs contradict themselves. Thus, through this never-ending process, logic leads us to reject those beliefs that cannot be reconciled with the totality of God's Word (Acts 20:27). Any belief that cannot be logically substantiated is not worth believing.

TRUST

One cannot read through Psalm 119 without the writer impressing you with his great respect for and trust in God's Word. He regards it as the cure for sin: "Your word I have hidden in my heart, That I might not sin against You" (Psa. 119:11). He treated it as the guide for life: "Thy word is a lamp unto my feet, and a light unto my path" (Psa. 119:105). And he adored it as the one thing that deserved his constant attention: "Oh, how I love Your law! It is my meditation all the day" (Psa. 119:97). Throughout the entire chapter there is an abiding trust in God's Word. He does not question what God has said; he accepts it. He does not argue with God; He submits to Him. Behind all of these is trust. Unfortunately, today many people lack a basic trust in God's Word. They feel free to cast it aside, or portions thereof, at a moment's notice should it not suit them. At the heart of such arrogance and presumption lies a failure to trust what God says, whether it pertains to science, history, archaeology, or doctrine.

Trusting God's Word requires more than simply accepting the truthfulness of the biblical account. We must trust the Bible and respect it as inspired revelation (2 Tim. 3:16-17). As the product of the mind of God, the Bible must be perfect (save for the intervention of man, such as with scribal errors or translation difficulties) in all matters, else on what basis should we trust it on any matter? If God errs in historical facts or in scientific facts, then what is to say that He has not also erred in presenting the plan of salvation? Behind this attitude of distrust is the design to make variation within the Word of God somehow acceptable by attempting to emphasize man's role, both in the communication of His message and in man's difficulties in interpreting it. But the end design in both is to allow man more leeway in trusting himself and his ideas rather than accepting God and God's ideas. It is possible for men with their various personalities to have participated in the process of inspiration and for God still to have ensured the accuracy of each and every word. This is, after all, what the writers themselves claimed (1 Cor. 2:10-16)!

When we trust the Word of God (which includes trusting by reasoned faith that the Bible is from God), we will also accept it as wholly authoritative and obey it. Jesus accepted the inspiration and authority of the Old Covenant as completely binding insofar as it was intended (John 10:35; Matt. 5:17). Christ presented His message as totally authoritative because it originated with God the Father and because it would stand as the standard of judgment for men (John 14:28). Therefore, trusting in the gospel, we make our appeal to the authority of our Lord and to the message He left (Col. 3:17). The Scriptures were written with purpose (Jas. 4:5), for the instruction of man toward the salvation of His soul (Jas. 1:21). Yet many times Bible students will start making excuses for God's "mistakes" instead of searching for the answers that are needed to complete their own understanding. Why do such cases exist? People do not trust God's Word enough. When we trust it completely, then we will accept its authority and reconstitute our beliefs and our lives in accordance with what God, in His inerrant and infallible Word, teaches.

CURIOSITY

As a young child I used to pepper my mom and dad with all sorts of questions. I wanted to know what everything was, how everything worked, who made it work, and why it worked that way. After every answer I received, I usually managed to come up with at least two more questions to ask. Perhaps you remember similar experiences. In any case, curiosity such as young children generally exhibit is often missing from our Bible study. Whether due to inhibition, fear of correction, or lack of interest, few people today have the will to ask and ask and ask questions about the Bible. Rather than assuming that their motives are somehow impure, I believe that the problem lies in a basic satisfaction with their current understanding of the Scriptures. Many lack the motivation to study harder because they are satisfied that they know all they need to know, so they will learn nothing.

After Jesus healed a lame man on the Sabbath day, a certain element of the people became very distressed at what they considered a great infraction of the Law. They never stopped to consider that they might not understand the Law correctly and failed to appreciate the difficulties that their misunderstanding created for them. When Jesus addressed them, though, he not only pointed out their dilemma but also addressed the root of the problem—their lack of curiosity in what the Law DID say. "But you do not have His word abiding in you, because whom He sent, Him you do not believe. You search the Scriptures, for in them you think you have eternal life; and these are they which testify of Me. But you are not willing to come to Me that you may have life" (John 5:38–40). These Jews were satisfied with their understanding and therefore had ceased to investigate the scriptures. This did not mean that they never picked up their Old Testaments, but rather Jesus implied that they were not motivated by curiosity and a desire to learn. Therefore, their lack of curiosity kept them from searching long enough to discover the truth about Him.

A problem that seems even more pervasive in our current era, however, is that many people are not even curious enough to study God's Word when someone has challenged their beliefs. How sad it is when people are so intellectually lazy that they would just as soon remain wrong as to go to the trouble of learning the truth. "You believe your way, and I believe mine" and "That's just your interpretation" are cop-outs, exhibiting a lack of curiosity that offends Jesus Himself. We must have enough curiosity about what the Bible teaches to cause us to study diligently a matter when a view different from our own has challenged us. Curiosity bids us to examine the evidence fully and completely lest our disinterestedness lead to our own destruction. Luke praises the Bereans, for "These were more fair-minded than those in Thessalonica, in that they received the word with all readiness, and searched the Scriptures daily to find out whether these things were so" (Acts 17:11). A Bible student is under no obligation to accept all ideas presented to him, but he is obligated to consider them. Curiosity guards us from the twin evils of religious traditionalism and religious liberalism, pushing us to learn the truth for the satisfaction of our own conscience.

HUMILITY

Humility remains an enigma in many ways. It seems that while most everyone agrees that humility is a desirable attribute, not everyone agrees on what humility is. The basic meaning of humility is that of lowliness, taking a lower position instead of a higher one. Yet it is certainly possible for men to have only the pretense of humility (Col. 2:18, 23). Some associate humility with lowliness in such a way that would contradict confidence and leadership. Paul's example should be enough to dispute this view (Acts 20:19-21). Others believe that humility is best expressed when we express doubt. But doubt is contrary to faith (Matt. 21:21)! Our faith and trust in God create humility in the sincere heart. Humility causes us to measure ourselves according to the divine standard rather than against some self-contrived one and to see ourselves as God sees us — sinful, weak, and needy — instead of in the self-congratulatory way we often see ourselves.

Peter wrote, "Likewise you younger people, submit yourselves to your elders. Yes, all of you be submissive to one another, and be clothed with humility, for 'God resists the proud, But gives grace to the humble.' Therefore humble yourselves under the mighty hand of God, that He may exalt you in due time" (1 Pet. 5:5-6). Humility causes us to be more mindful of the needs of others and of our own needy condition. It is quite fashionable today to proclaim ourselves independent and self-made. However, every person who has ever lived needs God. We all need God's care to sustain our existence and to provide for all the things we take for granted on a daily basis. Self-made indeed! But greater than our acknowledgement of these physical needs is the necessity of realizing and acknowledging the need we have for God spiritually. "Therefore whoever humbles himself as this little child is the greatest in the kingdom of heaven" (Matt. 18:4). Herein lies the importance of humility in our Bible study. Our humility must extend far enough to recognize that in a discussion of spiritual necessities and doctrinal questions, we must look to God for the answers. Many people start off well but somewhere misplace their loyalties in Bible study. They realize that "their way" and "God's way" do not match, but they refuse to adapt. Do they think that they do not need God for that particular piece of information? As we study, sometimes we need to ask, "Would we argue with the author to His face?"

Several years ago I proposed the following proverb: "Be confident enough to think that the other man is wrong, but be humble enough to think that you might be the other man." Humility forces us to accept the fact that we could be wrong. Without this attitude, Bible study will be forever fruitless. We must be willing to admit our own limitations while not pushing our limitations off onto God. Humility is what will bring us to admit our error, when it has been adequately demonstrated, and adapt to the truth. Humility causes us to view reality as God sees it, both regarding ourselves and His Word, recognize the need to accept God's will, and recall perpetually all that God has done on our behalf (John 3:16). Therefore, "Humble yourselves in the sight of the Lord, and He will lift you up" (Jas. 4:10).

SINCERITY

During the first century the common view among Jews was that a person's wealth indicated righteousness while poverty implied God's disfavor. They assumed that since material riches were given by God they could serve as a gauge for measuring how pleasing one's life was to God. However, Jesus Himself was not rich in worldly possessions — far from it. Yet He was richer than all spiritually because of His righteous life (Col. 2:3; 1 John 2:1; Heb. 4:15). Therefore, when a certain rich young ruler approached Jesus one day asking, "Good Teacher, what good thing shall I do that I may have eternal life?" (Matt. 19:16), he most likely viewed himself as one already having God's favor. Moreover, when Jesus told him to keep the commandments, the man asked, "Which ones?" (Matt. 19:18), as if there were some you had to keep and others where obedience was not necessary. When Jesus quoted several commandments to him, the man asserted that he had done all of these things. Then he pressed the matter further, "What do I still lack?" (Matt. 19:20). It was a good question. It was an important question. However, Jesus' reply and the man's subsequent actions proved that he really did not mean what he asked. Jesus told him to sell all that he had and give it to the poor. "But when the young man heard that saying, he went away sorrowful, for he had great possessions" (Matt. 19:22).

The rich young ruler had done so much that was right, and he asked the right question. The problem was that he did not do it sincerely, and this illustrates an essential point for Bible study. Every time we open God's Word we have the opportunity to ask Jesus the question, "What do I still lack?" However, the question, and our Bible study, will only help us if we are sincere about it. The rich young ruler expected a different answer to his question than the one he received, and so it often is in Bible study. When we go to the Bible expecting God simply to rubber stamp our lifestyle, our beliefs, and our practices, or at the most to ask us only for slight modifications, then we lack the necessary sincerity for God's Word to benefit us.

Sincerity is the opening up of the heart and the mind to accept God's answers and recommendations for our lives. It is the willing heart that says, "What shall I do, Lord" (Acts 22:10). It is the open mind that studies to learn and apply instead of treating Bible study as a purely intellectual exercise in theoretical religion (Jas. 1:22). Without sincerity a Bible student will end up much like the rich young ruler, adhering to all those practices with which he already agrees but failing to change when Jesus' words require more than what he expected. Without sincerity a Bible student is stuck spiritually. He will remain forever fixed in the quagmire of his own low expectations. A Bible student must approach God's Word sincerely, for only when he is totally open to any and all that God says (Acts 20:26-27) will he be able to reach the heights for which God made Him (Eph. 4:17-24). The rich young ruler went away sorrowful—not because Jesus did not answer his question, but because he was not prepared for and did not appreciate the answer he received. All of this could have changed if the young man had one special quality—sincerity.

PRAYERFUL

Perhaps it ought to go without saying that anyone who opens the pages of God's Word should also spend much time communicating with the Author. Paul said that we are to "pray without ceasing" (1 Th. 5:17), and surely we would want to pray before entering any study of the Bible. However, we must also understand clearly for what it is we should be praying. Some people will utter prayers before they study asking God to guide them. Others ask for God to give them knowledge. Many religious groups pray for the Holy Spirit to descend upon them so that they will have the right understanding of Scripture. As sincere as these people may be, they are praying for the wrong thing. God should indeed be our guide, but He guides us through His revealed truth (Psa. 119:105). God does indeed provide us knowledge, but He does so through His Word (John 8:32). The Holy Spirit certainly plays an important role in our coming to understand God's Will, but His role is limited to providing the inspiration for the penman who wrote the books we now find in God's complete revelation, the Bible (John 14:26; 2 Tim. 3:16-17; 2 Pet. 1:19-21). Therefore, God has provided His guidance, the knowledge we need, and the means to understand it; He did so by inspiring His Word in such a way that all men could know what He wanted, if they will devote themselves to studying it.

However, while prayer will not provide some mysterious power by which we can understand the Bible better (else everyone would automatically understand it alike), prayer still plays an important role in Bible study for the student. Prayer helps us to understand our need and to appreciate our God more in providing for our needs, especially in regard to our salvation and His Word that reveals His plan to us (Jas. 1:21). Prayer helps us to focus on the task at hand and concentrate on the importance of God's will (Matt. 6:10) and the importance of understanding it. When we pray, we should pray for wisdom (Jas. 1:5). But it is important to understand what wisdom is, as opposed to knowledge and understanding, so that we know for what we are asking. When James told Christians to pray for wisdom, he was discussing the benefits of overcoming temptation. Wisdom refers to the application of knowledge, putting those things we learn from our study into practice in our daily lives so that we can overcome temptation. Through exposure to God's will and experience in handling temptation, we can come to a better understanding of what to do when temptation lures us. Thus James wrote, "But be doers of the word, and not hearers only, deceiving yourselves" (Jas. 1:22). Thus we should pray for wisdom, appreciating our opportunities to apply our newfound knowledge in overcoming temptation and therefore pleasing God.

Prayer is often treated as the answer for everything. It is not. We must appreciate prayer for what it is and what it can do without attributing to it something God has not. Prayer is an opportunity for us to communicate with the Author of the Bible. Bible study is how He communicates to us. The person who thinks He can grow closer to God solely by prayer has learned nothing. The person who thinks that He understands God but does not pray to Him is fooling himself. Prayer is a blessing, and prayer can do much (Jas. 5:16). Prayer must be a constant companion of Bible study, but it is not a replacement for it.

INTEGRITY

If all of the qualities discussed earlier could be summed up in one, that one quality would have to be integrity. However, the word "integrity" has been used so often for so many things that its basic meaning has been lost. Integrity is far more than just honesty. You can be honest about doing something that is completely heinous. Individuals who were honest about their intent have carried out many of the publicized shootings in recent years, but this does not mean that they had integrity. Integrity requires at least three components: 1) the earnest search for what is right (2 Tim. 2:15), 2) the willingness to act in accord with what is right once it is discovered (Jas. 1:22-25), and 3) the forthrightness to tell others what you have discovered is right (Amos 3:3; Rom. 1:16-17). Without integrity, a Bible student will stumble and his efforts will all be for naught. Without integrity, he may not work hard enough to find truth. Without integrity, he may not be willing to adapt to truth when he finds it. And without integrity, he may be ashamed of what he knows is right. After the Jews returned to Jerusalem from their captivity, Ezra demonstrated integrity, pointing God's people back to the law. "For Ezra had prepared his heart to seek the Law of the Lord, and to do it, and to teach statutes and ordinances in Israel" (Ezra 7:10). The Bible student must have the same kind of integrity: to seek truth, to practice truth, and to proclaim truth.

A person of integrity never ceases his search for right. He never assumes he understands everything perfectly. He does not feel content with his current knowledge. He must learn more. He does not understand or respect those who are content with less (though he still loves them), because this search for truth drives his very being. A person of integrity finds hypocrisy and inconsistency distasteful. He has no use for it in his own life or in the lives of others. To know something is right and not do it is as unfamiliar to him as anything could be. Therefore, he accepts the fact that he must make changes in his life as he learns new things; in fact, he welcomes such changes, because he knows that they are the right thing to do. A person of integrity cannot silently sit, ignoring others who either do not know what is right or do not do what is right. He must speak out. He must help them. He must teach them. Because nothing is more important than being right, living a life that is in accord with truth, a life of righteousness — right with God, right with God's law, right in relationships with men.

Apollos was an eloquent and knowledgeable man (Acts 18:24), but his eloquence and his knowledge were not enough because he had not yet learned of Christ. He taught accurately the things he knew, but he did not know enough. But when Aquilla and Priscilla took him aside to teach him more perfectly, Apollos did not take offense; he took advantage of the opportunity. He eagerly learned something he had not known. He accepted it and adapted to it, and then he boldly proclaimed it (Acts 18:25-28). Apollos' integrity was what made his eloquence worthwhile! We must commit ourselves to maintaining integrity in our Bible study. It is not always an easy thing to search for the hard answers, to change when something new is learned, or to tell others what they need to know, but a person of integrity will do all of these, and more, *because he must.*

CONCLUSION

Hopefully, no one will now deny how essential the proper attitudes are for studying the Bible. Our attitudes often shape how or whether we examine the facts. While proper attitudes alone do not save and do not provide knowledge, they are essential for salvation and for learning truth (John 8:32). While the wrong attitudes can become stumblingblocks, the right attitudes can become spiritual building blocks. Paul said that he had "lived in all good conscience before God" (Acts 23:1) yet also confessed to being the chief of all sinners (1 Tim. 1:15). His actions prior to His obedience to God's Word were wholly against God, even to the point of persecuting the church (Acts 7:58-8:3). While his knowledge had been inaccurate, his attitude was one of deeply held reverence. Once confronted by Jesus, His attitudes led him to accept the truth and obey the gospel (Acts 9:1-22; 22:16). Saul of Tarsus had conviction and zeal prior to his conversion, but he had to be confronted with truth in order to make the necessary changes so that his conviction and zeal were directed properly.

Whenever we study through the books of Matthew, Mark, Luke, John, and Acts, we should take time to note how important the attitude of those mentioned in the narrative affected their reception of the message of Jesus Christ. Time and time again we see spiritual leaders who failed to accept Christ, not because they did not have access to the truth or have the ability to discern the truth but because their heart was set against the truth. People throughout the world today have access to God's Word, and most, if not all, of these have the ability to discern what God has said. Yet more religious division exists today than at any point in history. Why? Attitude. Religious error stems either from the existence of improper attitudes or indifference towards proper attitudes. It is not enough to say we respect God's Word; we must demonstrate it. It is not enough to claim unity; we must pursue it. It is not enough to accept "most" of what God says; we must receive it all.

Some perhaps believe that attitudes toward God and His Word are inborn, and therefore that it is up to God to change them. However, inasmuch as God has provided the gospel to all peoples (Acts 2:39) so also has He provided the power to change (2 Th. 2:14; Rom. 1:16). The question of our reception of the Word is not a matter of God's intervention but of our own mindset—the proper attitude—toward God's Word. "These were more fair-minded than those in Thessalonica, in that they received the word with all readiness, and searched the Scriptures daily to find out whether these things were so" (Acts 17:11). Attitude is not everything. But it is essential. May your attitude toward God's word be such that Paul's commendation may be true of you, "For this reason we also thank God without ceasing, because when you received the word of God which you heard from us, you welcomed it not as the word of men, but as it is in truth, the word of God, which also effectively works in you who believe" (1 Th. 2:13). Therefore, by first securing a godly attitude, we open ourselves up to receiving godly instruction, and receiving godly instruction makes possible our living a godly life (Tit. 2:11-13).

We should develop the proper attitudes of:

- Open-mindedness
- Spiritual Mindedness
- Passion for Truth
- Persistence
- Acceptance of Truth
- Moral Courage
- A Logical Outlook
- Trust
- Curiosity
- Humility
- Sincerity
- Prayerfulness
- Integrity

Recommended Reading

Carter, Stephen L. *Integrity*. New York: HarperCollins Publishers, 1996.

Questions for Discussion

1. What attitude do you need to work on the most? Why?
2. What attitude do you find missing from others the most? Why do you suppose that is?
3. How does attitude influence action?
4. How does integrity sum up the other attitudes?
5. How do you develop the proper attitude?

Assignment

After examining your chosen subject of study, consider how each of these attitudes would contribute to a better and proper understanding of the subject or text and write down your conclusions.

CHAPTER 4

Logic

———— ❖ ————

INTRODUCTION

*M*arilyn Vos Savant, who writes a column in the pop-culture entertainment magazine *Parade* and has the highest I.Q. on record, replied to a reader's question regarding the compatibility of faith and science. Ms. Vos Savant responded in part by saying, "It's not hard to hold conflicting beliefs *if* one of them comes from the heart—like religion—and the other one comes from the head—like science." She continued, "That's because I think science arises from the intellect, and religion arises from emotion."[1]

This misconception seems to dominate the religious world and society in general, as well as the culture of elitists such as Marilyn Vos Savant. Scientists have convinced many people that science alone is the realm of reason, while religion is the realm of belief that is contrary to reason. Scientists themselves have much at stake in convincing people that they alone are reasonable. Their purpose is to attempt to persuade people that only natural explanations are reasonable and that anything that requires reference to something beyond what occurs in nature cannot be classified as reasonable. Thus, they are trying to win an intellectual war by first winning the battle for definition and classification. Sadly, many have fallen prey to such twisted logic as that suggested by Ms. Vos Savant. They neatly fold away their religious beliefs into a tight little corner into which they do not allow reason to tread because they have been convinced that religion is not the place for reason. I beg to differ.

When the Lord spoke through His prophet Isaiah, He said, "'Come now, and let us reason together,' Says the Lord, 'Though your sins are like scarlet, They shall be as white as snow; Though

---

1 Marilyn Vos Savant, "Ask Marilyn," *Parade*. February 2001.

they are red like crimson, They shall be as wool'" (Isa. 1:18). God not only *allowed* reason in religion, He *required* it! Peter describes the gospel as the *logikos* milk, the logical milk (1 Pet. 2:2). Furthermore, references such as 1 Thessalonians 5:21, "Test all things," discussed earlier, clearly require the Bible student to employ logic. When Peter told his readers to "be ready to give a defense" (1 Pet. 3:15), he used a word that implies "a **reasoned** defense." When a person eliminates logic from the equation in his search for truth, he has defeated himself before ever beginning.

Countless thousands in the religious world have bowed their knee to the secular humanists who have bullied their way into the mainstream of America by ridiculing faith and promoting naturalism. But people abandoned reason long before that, and in the process the religious world has accepted both doctrine and division that are contrary to the word of God (Rom. 16:17). Why? They accepted the fact that their doctrinal conclusions would not make sense, they delighted in contradiction and hypocrisy, and they reveled in the diversity and confusion thus created. God is not so (1 Cor. 14:33), nor is He pleased by such (1 Cor. 1:10). Our Creator is a God of wisdom and reason, not a god of emotional pandering. Reason and faith are not contradictory unless we make them so!

THE NATURE AND PURPOSE OF LOGIC

The very use of the word "logic" in conjunction with a religious topic can be enough to make one suspect — at least to some. To them, logic refers to human wisdom and human understanding, human abilities and human weaknesses, and so they believe logic stands in opposition to the gospel. The New Testament does indeed show the folly of human wisdom (1 Cor. 1:18ff; Col. 2:8); however, each time the inspired writers condemn human wisdom it is within the context of an attempt to ignore the gospel, replace the gospel, or impugn the gospel — not to interpret the gospel. Human wisdom was condemned by God as an attempt to cast off divine authority — not to discover it and submit to it. Additionally, God Himself *requires, condones,* and *commends* human thought and discernment (1 Th. 5:21; 1 John 4:1; Acts 17:11) rather than discouraging it.

Therefore, the human thought process is an essential part of the equation in Bible study.

The difference between this and "human wisdom" is the subject and standard by which a person discerns. "Human wisdom" contemplates human possibilities, human accomplishments, and human philosophy. "Human wisdom" thus has for its standard either *a* human or humanity as a whole, both of which God condemns (Jer. 10:23; Prov. 14:12). "Human wisdom" attempts to determine the way of salvation apart from God's Revelation (Rom. 1:16-17). God provided the gospel as the subject and truth as the standard (John 17:17). Therefore, the gospel should be the focus of our studies and truth the standard against which we compare all doctrines and beliefs. This is essentially where and why logic plays a role in Bible study. **Logic is the process by which we can make a comparison of our beliefs with God's objective standard.** Logic itself does not offer itself as an alternative to God's will; it simply provides the basis for the determination of the exact content of God's will. Without logic all biblical interpretation would fall into the realm of subjectivity, and sadly, this is why many reject logic. Ironically, those who oppose logic by calling it "human wisdom" embrace human subjectivity created by the absence of logic, which is exactly what God condemned.

However, it is logic that gives an argument and belief credibility, because it is logic that can establish that a belief is consistent with truth. Logic begins with what is undeniably true and then proceeds to demonstrate what is and is not consistent with that known truth. Without logic there cannot be any comparison with a standard or any credibility. The rejection of logic forces religion into the field of speculation and insecurity, where the Bible becomes something to be molded by men instead of that by which men themselves are molded. The philosopher David Hume once said, "No man turns against logic until logic turns against him," and the recent retreat from objectivity made by many "religionists" has only amplified Hume's point. Logic is the means by which the truth of God's Word is discerned. It is provided by God but derided by men. Skeptics counter that humans sometimes err in their thinking. This I fully admit. However, when humans err in their thinking it is not because they used logic but because they *failed* to do so.

THE LAWS OF THOUGHT

Whenever we hear the word "law" we tend to think of the rules government uses to maintain order or perhaps our minds go to those who enforce this order, but other disciplines besides government routinely refer to their "laws." Various fields of science have laws — the law of biogenesis, the law of gravity, the laws of thermodynamics among them. These laws are simply an expression of universal fact, a rule recognized as binding because of the absence of exceptions. The laws of thought are rules that should govern our thinking, and more specifically, the conclusions we draw. These rules are not random impositions of the Age of Reason but are the result of careful investigation into what will guarantee the correct conclusion. Logic might be called the literary sister of math. Many of the laws of thought are applications of mathematical principles to the realities of life.

While "the laws of thought" may sound quite imposing, most people employ them in at least a popular sense all the time. Though I have never heard someone say, "You ought to consider the law of rationality before you determine what that means," I have often heard people say, "Don't jump to conclusions!" Many a parent has instructed a child, "Don't touch the stove; it's hot," only to have a different child burn himself by touching it. The parent, after appropriate consolation, might ask the second child, "Didn't you hear me tell your sister that the stove was hot?" without ever realizing that he was relying on the law of identity. We also understand how silly it would be to talk about a woman being "kind of pregnant." She either is pregnant or she is not pregnant. There is no in between. There is no "partially pregnant." There is no "kind of pregnant." This seems self-evident, yet many people routinely ignore the law of excluded middle in religious discussions. A common saying even today is "You can't have it both ways," an acknowledgement of the law of contradiction. Detectives, lawyers, teachers, and parents all draw conclusions without being eyewitnesses to a particular act. How is this possible? Well, they can "put two and two together," and so they confirm the law of implication and inference.

Certainly the laws as presented here are in a simple form, yet they *are* present; they are pertinent; they are accepted. Logic simply codifies these laws and provides structure for them so as to encourage people to evaluate the validity of their thought process, which obviously has an impact on their belief system. The laws of thought do not stand in opposition to any belief itself; they serve as a guardian against an incomplete or inaccurate thought process, which in turn may very likely produce an inaccurate conclusion. In the same way that failing to regard all of the instructions or ingredients in a recipe will most likely alter the likelihood of a delicious culinary experience, failing to regard all of the laws of thought, more often than not, will lead to a conclusion that does not reflect reality. The laws of thought therefore are the guardians of discourse, providing the structure by which to evaluate conclusions and making it possible for us, if we are willing, to distinguish between fiction and reality.

THE LAW OF RATIONALITY

According to Dr. Thomas B. Warren, the "law of rationality says that men should draw only such conclusions as are warranted by the evidence."[2] The emphasis of this law falls upon the necessity of evidence and the importance of limiting the scope of consideration to what that evidence allows, realizing that no conclusion should go beyond this. Thus the law of rationality rules out presumption and speculation as having any legitimate role in determining truth. Should a person choose to deny this law he would essentially be denying evidence, objectivity, and truth. It is important for us to discover the location of evidence and to consider *all* of the evidence if we are to be successful in our quest for an accurate conclusion. When approaching a study of the Bible, this same "law of rationality" does not change.

Since the law of rationality establishes the essentiality of evidence in order to make a truthful determination regarding any question of fact, then it follows that one must gather all of the evidence available pertaining to that question if a conclusion is to have any legitimacy. In Bible study, the Bible itself is the main body of evidence to consider. Bible study also requires consideration of history, archaeology, and other fields of study, but if one seeks religious truth,

2 Thomas B. Warren. *Logic and the Bible*. Jonseboro, AR: National Christian Press, 1982 , p . 14.

he must examine the evidence presented by the Bible. Many people dismiss the Bible and argue against its legitimacy as a source without considering the evidence. They *assume* there is a disparity between the Bible and rationality, so they exclude the Bible from the evidence. But while eliminating evidence may help you feel comfortable with the conclusion you have accepted, it will never help you find or establish truth. Truth can withstand any test; it welcomes examination. So anyone who prefers to withhold evidence is not really interested in truth.

Despite the various proofs of inspiration showing that the Bible is the authoritative body of evidence regarding religious truth, many will break the law of rationality when it comes to questions of religious truth. On more than one occasion the author has read from the Bible only to hear people say in one form or another, "I don't care what the Bible says!" When confronted with biblical evidence that contradicts their beliefs, people often will violate the law of rationality and not accept the evidence rather than changing what they believe. Others will accept some of the evidence but not all. They will point to all of the passages that talk about faith's role in salvation (Rom. 5:1; John 3:16) but will avoid verses about salvation that mention requirements other than faith (Rom. 10:9-17; Acts 2:38). In both instances it is important to note that the unwillingness to consider all the evidence does not change the conclusion warranted by the evidence. Truth is objective. It exists outside of individuals. Many people act as if truth depends upon their acceptance of the evidence. To the contrary, the endurance of God's truth does not depend upon any person's will (1 Pet. 1:22-25), but the salvation of every person's soul depends upon his willingness to seek, examine, and accept the evidence for and requirements of God's truth (John 17:17; John 8:32)

THE LAW OF IDENTITY

The laws of thought discussed here may seem obvious to the average reader. They may seem so simplistic that calling them laws gives them an undeserved weight. However, the fact that these laws are so obvious is what makes them laws. They always apply. They always are true. And all reasonable people accept them as a basic part of life. So it is with the law of identity. "The law of identity states that if something is true, then it is true."[3] It is hard to be more obvious than that! However, while most people realize and accept the obvious in principle, they will sometimes reject it in application. So while logic demands that a fact is a fact—no matter who may object—there will be some who do not like the fact itself and will therefore reject it. A particular fact may not fit with someone's doctrine, but rather than making a change in his doctrinal position that person often chooses to reject the fact. It is in just such a case that the law of identity stands strongest. Truth is truth—no matter who rejects it and no matter what someone says about it. Denying truth does not eliminate truth or the force of the facts. "This law says, in effect, that if a proposition is true for one person, then it is true for another person."[4] Therefore, in the religious realm what God says in His Word is truth (John 17:17). We can accept it or reject it, but we cannot change it (Rev. 22:18-19). People may choose to "agree to disagree," but in doing so at **least** one person is wrong because the truth is the same for every person.

The law of identity rejects the idea that truth can be subjective. Therefore, within the framework and context of the Bible, when God binds an action on one person, it applies to all people to whom that covenant is given. When God binds a principle upon one group of people, that principle applies to all people to whom that covenant is intended regardless of the passage of time. These qualifications are necessary because not every person has lived under the new covenant and because it is important to understand whether God binds an action or principle in order to know the extent of its application. (For example, it is important to know whether Jesus intended to bind the act of washing feet in John 13 or the principles of humility and service.) But neither of these two distinctions changes truth. Since all people living today are amenable to (answerable to) the new covenant (Heb. 8:8-13; John 12:48), then everything the new covenant says is true and applies to all people living today. It is therefore impossible for people to live under the same covenant and be saved from sin in two different ways. If the Bible teaches that women are not to lead in public worship (1 Cor. 14:34-35; 1 Tim. 2:9-15), then it is true for all women for all time.

---

3   Ibid, 20.
4   Ibid.

If the Bible teaches that one person should pray to the Father through Jesus Christ, then it is true for all people (Eph. 5:20). Truth is truth.

Some people seem to always claim, "That's just your interpretation," as if there can be several equally good interpretations of biblical truth. If an interpretation is not true, then a Bible student should be able to demonstrate such. Interpretation does not mean that a person can pick and choose his beliefs arbitrarily. Proper interpretation depends upon the laws of thought and objectivity. Truth expresses reality, and though people might be out of touch with reality from time to time, their unwillingness to accept it does not change truth nor the consequences of their unbelief (2 Th. 1:7-9). Therefore, the law of identity is essential for the Bible student to understand. It implies that for all of us to get to heaven, we must all take *the same* path to get there (Matt. 7:13-14).

THE LAW OF EXCLUDED MIDDLE

One cannot discuss morality for long with most people before the always available "gray area" emerges as the argument of choice. In the movie version of Tom Clancy's *Clear and Present Danger* (I only recommend an edited version), the hero—Jack Ryan, working as Deputy Director of the CIA—is determined to expose an illegal governmental operation. As he confronts one man, this guilty party responds with a very typical argument that not everything is black and white, complaining that Ryan looks at life in such a "simplistic" way. Ryan's reply, delivered by Harrison Ford, is classic: "Not black and white. Right and wrong!" Unfortunately, more and more people are relying on the villain's argument as a moral philosophy rather than on the hero's.

The law of excluded middle applies both to "things" and to "propositions." According to Warren, "The law of excluded middle for things is: any thing either has a certain property or it does not have that property."[5] A cat either has a tail or it does not have a tail. A man is either bald or he is not bald. There is no in between. Now it may be necessary for us to define what constitutes a tail or what qualifies for baldness, but the existence of a standard eliminates gray areas. Therefore, the New Testament, as our God-given moral standard (John 12:48; 2 Cor. 5:10), has the information within it in order to conclude

---

5   Ibid, 20.

whether behaviors are moral or immoral (John 17:17). If it cannot, then it is imperfect and insufficient. It is neither (2 Tim. 3:16-17). A person has either sinned or he has not sinned. A dress is either modest or it is not modest. But people insist on maintaining their "gray areas" when they are unable to demonstrate that a behavior pleases God and wish to soften the impact—and sometimes the consequences—of their actions. As the law of excluded middle for things tends to apply to morality, the law of excluded middle for propositions tends to apply to doctrine. Warren states, "The law of excluded middle for propositions is: every precisely stated proposition is either true or false (not-true)."[6] A proposition essentially is a statement that says, "This is how things are." Some, influenced by religious pluralism, have argued that the Bible does not set forth propositions because they do not want to face the law of excluded middle. Does the Bible set forth the proposition that baptism is for remission of sins? Read Acts 2:38. Does Jesus teach that how we worship matters? Read John 4:24. Does the Bible say that obedience is necessary? Read Hebrews 5:8-9.

The law of excluded middle exists to help people overcome the problem of "Yes, but...." In such a situation, "Yes," is generally the response to the proposition and "but..." is a proposed reason why the "Yes" does not mean "Yes." It is certainly possible that some statements are not precisely stated. For instance, the Bible *does* say to keep the Sabbath holy (Ex. 20:8). But this was given to the Jews and only to the Jews, and the law in which that statement is made was nailed to the cross (Col. 2:14). Therefore, it is important to be specific and precise, recognizing when the Bible qualifies itself. However, if we include every clarifier necessary, we must be willing to abide by the truth of a proven proposition. Between black and white there is middle ground (blue, red, green), but as Warren adds, "there is no middle ground between black and not-black!"[7]

THE LAW OF CONTRADICTION

"You can't have it both ways!" That is the essence of the law of contradiction. And while most may believe that they understand this

6   Ibid, 21.
7   Ibid, 20-21.

principle and appreciate its implications, chances are that they have accepted contradictory conclusions from time to time. Contradictions occur when a person holds two (or more) views concurrently which cannot both be true. In a very sad way, people in abusive relationships have accepted a contradiction. They live daily with a person who claims to love them yet treats them in a manner totally inconsistent with love. Warren describes the law of contradiction for things by saying that "nothing can both have and not have a given characteristic (or property) in precisely the same respect."[8] Jesus noted this principle in the Sermon on the Mount. "No one can serve two masters; for either he will hate the one and love the other, or else he will be loyal to the one and despise the other. You cannot serve God and mammon" (Matt. 6:24). Serving two masters is contradictory because the two will inevitably give conflicting orders, making a choice necessary and voiding the proposition that both are masters.

The same concept applies to propositions, because as Warren points out, "no proposition can be both true and false, in the same respects."[9] As the law of excluded middle eliminated the possibility of accepting some "in between" area, the law of contradiction eliminates the possibility of accepting both sides of an argument. In a football game it is simply impossible for both sides to win. "In the same respects," just as "precisely stated," is an important element, however, because it is possible that two ideas, while different, are not mutually exclusive. The proposition that salvation is by faith (Rom. 5:1) does not contradict the proposition that salvation is by works (Jas. 2:24). However, should one add the word "only" to either of these, they would by definition contradict. "In the same respects" comes into play in this instance as well, denoting that the New Testament uses "works" in different ways to refer to different actions. The works mentioned in James 2 are a necessary expression of faith — obedient works (Heb. 5:8-9) — while the works mentioned in Titus 3:5 refer to self-determined actions rather than a faithful response to God's Word (Rom. 10:17). If a person insists that "works are works" (meaning that he accepts the idea that faith and works *are* mutually exclusive) he necessarily involves himself in a contradiction, or more specifically, forces one

---

8   Ibid, 23.
9   Ibid.

upon God, which would be inconsistent with God's character (1 Cor. 14:33). He is also left with a quandary to explain Jesus' assertion that faith itself is a work (John 6:29). Part of this is solved when we recognize that the word "work" simply means "activity." Activity can be righteous or unrighteous, obedient or disobedient, self-determined or God-determined. Appreciating these distinctions is essential in order to understand various Bible passages in such a way so as not to introduce a contradiction.

Despite how tempting it might be at times, one must avoid contradiction. Above all, we must not accept a proposition that contradicts God's Word in any way. When we accept a contradiction, we accept inconsistency. When we accept inconsistency, we accept error. When we accept error, we accept hypocrisy. How then do we reconcile God's plea and design for spiritual unity (John 17:21-23; Eph. 4:4-6) with denominationalism? We cannot. They contradict one another. Bible students must commit themselves to a constant examination of doctrinal positions. Without such, contradictions will soon become part of that individual's worldview and spiritual outlook, regardless of the inconsistencies, regardless of the error, and regardless...of the consequences (John 12:48).

THE LAW OF IMPLICATION AND INFERENCE

In some ways, implication is at the heart of logic, for it provides the connection that exists between stated truth and unstated truth. Implication is not that which is taught or said explicitly (in so many words) but the teaching which must result from these explicit teachings. Implication refers to the consequences of stated truth based upon other laws. Once one has compiled all of the evidence, this immediately eliminates some possibilities. Knowing a stated fact often provides more knowledge than simply what is stated, and two related facts work in such a way as to narrow the possibilities that are consistent with reality.

If a person knows (by the law of identity) that "Only immersion accurately describes the mode of baptism taught in the New Testament," then he knows that sprinkling and pouring are not taught in the New Testament as modes of baptism even though the statement did not explicitly say so. To deny this reality would require violating the law of contradiction. The law of excluded middle should keep someone from describing baptism (as Hollywood is so fond of portraying it) as someone standing waist deep in water while having water poured over his head. The law of implication and inference requires that a person consider all of these laws and draw only those conclusions that are consistent with these laws.

Implication itself depends upon the concept of a common frame of reference. So when compared to the same point of reference, two objects or propositions can then be related to one another. When the point of reference has been shown to be genuine, the conclusions drawn by comparison with this point of reference will also be true if a person follows all the laws of thought correctly. Syllogisms essentially illustrate implication. They take a general truth and apply it more specifically within a category. The classic example goes something like this: All men are mortal. Kevin Rhodes is a man. Kevin Rhodes is mortal. If a person accepts the first two sentences as true, then he must accept the last. If an individual refuses to accept it, it is because he has not truly accepted one of the first two statements.

Inference is the action by which the mind discerns what has been implied. When God told Abraham to offer Isaac as a sacrifice, though God had promised to make a great nation through him, Abraham set out to do so, concluding that God would raise Isaac from the dead (Gen. 22; Heb. 11:17-19). Abraham knew that God's two statements to him must reconcile. He accepted their truth but also inferred God's implication that Isaac would return home with Abraham (Gen. 22:5). Since faith is the product of the word (Rom. 10:17) and since Abraham's inference regarding Isaac was commended as faith, then it must follow that faith accepts not only the explicit statements of the Bible but also their implications.

Bible students have the responsibility, as Abraham did, to accept what God implies as well as what He explicitly says. Failure to do so is a rejection of Christ (John 12:48). (Not only are His "words" binding but also the whole "word," including its implications.) Failing to infer (accept) what the Bible teaches does not in any way limit the implications of the Bible, nor does it loosen personal accountability. Warren's words on the subject still succinctly capture the point: "Let it be noted by all that doctrine which is *implicitly* taught by the Bible is bound on men, not because men have inferred it, but because God has *implied* it."[10]

GATHERING THE EVIDENCE

Most people associate logic with the syllogisms and proofs offered by polemicists in debate — at least as a formal study. However, one cannot **demonstrate** truth until one has taken all of the necessary steps in order to **discover** truth. *Induction must precede deduction.* Therefore, the gathering of evidence is an essential step in the process by which one comes to understand the Bible. As a corollary, one must diligently pursue anything pertinent to the study or the lack of complete data will skew the results. In the media's parlance regarding law enforcement they call this "a rush to judgment." Likewise, almost every fictional detective, from Sherlock Holmes to Hercule Poirot, finds success by uncovering clues that others missed, and those people missed them either because they decided the matter before they considered all the facts or because they did not search diligently enough for evidence.

How often does this prove true in Bible study! Some people have built entire doctrines based upon one verse, which, after having misinterpreted it, caused them to misinterpret every other passage that pertained to it. They came to a conclusion before considering all of the facts. If one only looks at 1 Corinthians 15:29 one might conclude that Christians in the first century practiced baptism for the dead. But once one gathers additional evidence, this option becomes untenable. Jesus taught that upon death a person's destiny is sealed (Luke 16:26), and the writer of Hebrews taught this as well (Heb. 9:27). Therefore, since one cannot hold to a belief in a "fixed gulf" and in "baptism for the dead" without accepting contradiction, then one must not be true. Additional research shows that the Lord will judge people based upon their actions while living (2 Cor. 5:10) and that God designed baptism to be the response of an individual because of his own need spiritually (Acts 2:37-38). Therefore, one must reject baptism for the dead as Christian doctrine. (Some have argued that Paul is referring to

10   Ibid, 32.

the spiritually dead, but this would make no sense in the context of the physical resurrection.) Looking next to immediate context one notices that after Paul made a logical argument to the Corinthians regarding the reality of the resurrection, he then used illustrations for emphasis showing how others accepted it as fact. This does not imply that they all taught and believed truth. In fact, Paul's reference to them as a third group of people (note the pronouns) indicates that they were not Christians. Thus, the remote context demands that the Bible student reject baptism of the dead as a false doctrine (1 John 4:1) and provides evidence regarding what Paul meant in the immediate context. Bible students should use clear passages in order to interpret the difficult ones — not the other way around.

A Bible student **must** withhold judgment until all of the evidence is in; otherwise, he will never reconsider positions or beliefs. This is why the Bible student's attitude is so important. He must be willing to reevaluate his conclusions when new evidence is uncovered or presented by another. However, since the Bible is the source of all pertinent evidence (2 Pet. 1:3), his studies should encompass the entire Bible as the standard for doctrine as well as those areas that provide information regarding the situation and setting in which the author wrote. He must look at that evidence from every angle possible in order to consider every solution imaginable, eliminating false conclusions by applying the laws of thought. When a person desires to understand a subject, he should consult every passage that refers in any way to that subject. Gathering evidence is essential if one is to understand every aspect of the context and to have access to all relevant information. Bible students must therefore avoid opinions — which offer nothing new factually — while diligently collecting evidence.

REASON

The apostle Peter tells us in his first epistle, "But sanctify the Lord God in your hearts, and always be ready to give a defense to everyone who asks you a reason for the hope that is in you, with meekness and fear" (1 Pet. 3:15). In the context of suffering, Peter emphasizes the necessity of mental preparedness to defend and explain the willingness to suffer for the cause of Christ. The word translated "defense"is *apologia*, from which we receive the word "apology." But this word does not mean saying, "I'm sorry." This compound Greek word contains two ideas. *Apo* indicates separation—that the object in question does not remain with its host. *Logia* indicates reason, generally vocalized. Thus, an *apologia* is a reasoned response. God fully intends His people to think through their situation, their faith, and their hope. He also implies that a *reasonable* answer exists to explain why a person would suffer rather than forsake Christ. So a person can defend New Testament Christianity effectively by means of reason. While the appeal of the gospel certainly has emotional currents (2 Cor. 5:14), it also has a firm basis in fact. If the gospel is only an emotional story, it will affect the feelings momentarily. But it is the historical (and spiritual) truth of the gospel that gives it its power to affect lives eternally (1 Cor. 15:1-4; Rom. 1:1-17; John 8:32).

Therefore, a belief that does not pass the test of reason does not pass the test of truth, and that which does not pass the test of truth is error and not part of the gospel (1 John 4:1-6). Since gathering all the evidence available to the Bible student requires great diligence, so also the dedication required in order to reason through all the evidence to ensure that nothing that violates the laws of thought enters the domain of our belief system requires the utmost of our character. Reason is essentially the process of eliminating possibilities by comparison with known facts in accordance with the laws of thought in order to reduce the options to one, which must be the truth. So, having gathered all of the evidence, the facts, and the propositions of the Bible, one must then consider what is and is not consistent with the evidence according to the laws of thought. It is not enough to find one passage that fits a belief (or rather that a person thinks fits his belief); one must ensure that all passages in the Bible are completely consistent with that belief. We are commanded to "Test all things" (1 Th. 5:21).

God's call for reason is a call for objectivity. Therefore, every individual must look beyond himself for an adequate explanation of his beliefs (Jer. 10:23). Many religious groups claim to gather evidence only from the Bible. Since God is not the author of confusion (1 Cor. 14:33), some men have failed to think carefully enough about the evidence they hold in their hands. However, the responsibility for reasoning correctly falls upon men's shoulders. God has made us with the capability of doing so, and He expects us to employ that ability. If God does not expect men to reason, then there is no purpose for the evidence. God inspired His Word (2 Tim. 3:16-17) to be more than a storybook; He wants every person to read what He has said and think about it (Psa. 1:2; 119:97).

DRAWING CONCLUSIONS

In an amazing display of mental gymnastics, a growing number of religious people simultaneously attempt to argue that they have a deep and abiding respect for the Scriptures and even for the necessity of thinking about them but that, despite these two, they find it improper to draw conclusions from the combination of the two — at least in such a way that would accept the universal binding of those conclusions. "This is what it means to me" has become their mantra, preaching postmodern relativism and not the gospel of Christ. Subjectivity has replaced objectivity, and they love to have it so. "Conclusions" to them are personal statements of belief but not statements of fact. They are thus essentially agnostic, believing that objective religious truth remains outside the grasp of mere men. Yet in a fit of inescapable hypocrisy they will become quite dogmatic about their approach. Therefore, they allow room for every conclusion but one that would condemn them. The current non-denominational movement (which is ecumenism with an evangelical twist) is the most obvious expression of this way of thinking. To them a person may draw conclusions but may not bind conclusions — at least not very many.

The laws of thought, however, link evidence and proper reasoning to a conclusion that necessarily applies universally. To draw varying conclusions one must first avoid or mishandle evidence or use faulty reasoning. If this is the case, then the person does not truly believe in the evidence (the Bible) or in reasoning (logic). What that person believes in is his own opinion, and so we reach the crux of the matter. Those who speak out against (or harbor doubts about) the existence of objective conclusions do so because they have reached their own conclusions without full consideration of the extant evidence and the laws of thought. Thus, they desire freedom to infer without being bound by what God has implied (Matt. 16:18-19). But these two — implication and inference — must work together or they do not work at all. Implication is the process by which God supplies the evidence of religious truth. Inference is the process by which man discerns from the evidence what that objective religious truth is. Once a person discovers through his study a truth new to him (that which God implied and he inferred), then this new information, as a conclusion founded upon full evidence and proper reasoning, is as legitimate as the evidence upon which it is based. It then becomes the basis for additional investigation.

This spiraling series creates the situation whereby a person can build an understanding of God's will. Without the ability to draw objective moral conclusions, a person could arguably pick up the Bible, read the same passage day after day, and reach different conclusions because of the changes in his experiences. This necessitates contradiction, which in turn denies (or defies) logic itself. Any conclusion demands evidence and thinking. The correct conclusion demands full and complete evidence and logical reasoning. Most people actually want to have the freedom to draw conclusions; they just do not want the "burden" of having to accept only those that are true (John 17:17).

WHY DO PEOPLE ESCHEW LOGIC?

Despite the obvious benefits of logic, among some there remains a heated antagonism toward the very idea and principles of logic. In the postmodern era society has become so increasingly sensitive to the opinions and thoughts of others that certain people insist on the equality of ideas and opinions — no matter how ludicrous they might be. However, this drift toward the equality of ideas and away from the discernment of truth and logic has not occurred through a frontal assault against logic but rather through what might be called guerrilla warfare, where opponents of reason attack each tenet of objectivity and logic independently in order to create doubt in others. Their approach is subtle, but the consequences are devastating because the unwritten agenda underlying these things is to develop an atmosphere where their own opinions and ideas can find greater acceptance without the "burden" of having to pass any test of truth and reason (1 John 4:1; 1 Th. 5:21). Thus, false teachers and their followers value originality, speculation, and all kinds of biblical skepticism. After all, these will give them credibility on a wider scale. (This also explains why those in academia, and those who esteem them highly, often have this problem.)

The attacks themselves come in various disguises, but their objective remains consistent: undermine the concept of truth. Therefore, since evidence, reason, and conclusion essentially capture the essence of logic, these three constantly find themselves under assault. The Bible, God's spiritual evidence, has repeatedly undergone attack in regard to its inspiration and inerrancy. The basic purpose of German rationalism and higher criticism was to influence people to treat the Bible more like the work of men than as the work of God (1 Th. 2:13). Lower views of inspiration and the acceptance of alleged contradictions and inaccuracies both work to undermine the Bible as credible evidence, whether some of those who accept these premises comprehend it or not. Concurrent with this battle, some have gone to emphasizing the fallibility of human reasoning. While all would agree that men are fallible and that men often err in their thinking, this is not their point. Rather than arguing that men are sometimes wrong, they maintain that man can never be sure he is right. (Interestingly enough, those who espouse these ideas are sure that their own ideas are superior!) They say that God is so far above man that man cannot possibly understand God's will. This is false humility gone mad! Is God unable to create a being with whom He can communicate? Or is God incapable of communicating to His creation in a way that the creation can comprehend? It thus leads to total agnosticism, which itself is full of self-contradiction. (If man's abilities are so inept, how could he possibly comprehend his own inadequacies?) Finally, the call for a new system of hermeneutics (which is actually old error with a new name) sought to throw out the validity of implication and thereby of conclusions. They argue that the current system has produced disunity rather than unity and should be discarded. However, they mistakenly blame the system for what is the fault of men. Their "solution" is to ignore the possibility of their own shortcomings and instead place the blame on logic. It is thus a self-serving means of absolving themselves of ethical responsibility (Acts 17:11).

Logic does not necessarily occur just because someone has drawn a conclusion or thought a little or even gathered some evidence. Rather, logic requires *correct* and *complete* evidence and *correct handling* of that evidence in order to ensure a *correct* conclusion (2 Tim. 2:15). Logic's antagonists seek to undermine truth because they themselves refuse to adapt to it. In the process, they are destroying their only hope for salvation (John 8:32; John 17:17). Logic is the means of discovery. The only other alternative is ignorance, and ignorance is not an alternative that God accepts (2 Th. 1:7-9).

CONCLUSION

The current atmosphere in the religious world seems turned toward subjective and emotional interpretation of the Bible, making how a person *feels* about what the Bible says more important than what God has written. Many people find this attractive because it requires little thought, it allows them to believe whatever suits them, and it attempts to avoid controversy by saying that varying and contradicting interpretations does not mean that one of them is wrong. For some people the use of logic is synonymous with the human wisdom condemned in the Bible (1 Cor. 1:18ff; Col. 2:1-8), but what God condemned was the attempt of man to reason without considering God's Word.

The rationalistic movement of the eighteenth century did move toward pushing God's Word out of the picture, and therefore many deists emerged from that era. German rationalism of the nineteenth century tried to apply human wisdom to God's Word as if what man said about the Bible held more importance than what God said in the Bible. But neither of these movements invented logic; they both digressed from it whenever it fit their fancy. Some have claimed that the Restoration Movement actually sprang from rationalism because they mistakenly believe that logic either came into existence after the Bible or that rules of interpretation change to accommodate society (Rom. 12:2). Logic is not an arbitrary discipline. Therefore, opponents of logic cannot discard it as if it were a passing fad anymore than they can the law of gravity. It exists and has meaning for them whether they recognize it or not. In the same way that the law of gravity applied before Isaac Newton came on the scene, logic also applied before someone began studying it and designated it as a particular discipline.

Logic is not an attempt to "out-think" God. Even the mention of such a thing is preposterous (Isa. 55:8-9). It is instead the method of identifying truth. Science has identified various laws to describe how the universe works. The fact that scientists have discovered the reality of these laws does not mean that they invented them, nor does it mean that the scientists have any claim to equality with the One who put those laws into motion (Gen. 1). That many of these same scientists continue to insist on the theory of evolution despite the evidence against it surely settles that; however, their failure to apply the scientific method to evolution does not mean that all of their conclusions have been false. As science works to identify truth revealed in nature, logic works to identify truth revealed in words (John 17:17).

A Bible student who does not appreciate logic is neglecting the very avenue through which one can effectively enhance his understanding of God's truth. Logic is not the end of Bible study; it is the means. It is not an arbitrary system of rules developed by men but the recognized system of thought created by God. So using logic does not in any way exalt man. To the contrary, it enables man to come to a greater understanding of God's will and marvel at His wisdom. The person who rejects logic has locked himself out of true spiritual growth (1 Pet. 2:2; 2 Pet. 3:18), settling instead for emotionalism and the passing fancy of the doctrine of "felt needs." Spiritual growth will occur only when a person has thought through his life in relation to God's Word, but **that** requires logic (Psa. 1:2; 1 Tim. 4:15).

In order to hold a rational view of Scripture we must remember that:

- **Reason and faith are not contradictory unless we make them so.**
- **No man turns against logic until logic turns against him.**
- **Men should draw only such conclusions as are warranted by the evidence**

- Anyone who prefers to withhold evidence is not really interested in truth
- Truth is truth — no matter who rejects it and no matter what someone says about it
- A behavior is either right or wrong; there is no gray area in morality
- We must never accept a proposition that contradicts God's Word in any way
- Implication provides the connection that exists between stated truth and unstated truth
- Inference is the action by which the mind discerns what has been implied
- Bible students should use clear passages in order to interpret the difficult ones — not the other way around
- If God does not expect men to reason, then there is no purpose for the evidence
- To draw varying conclusions, one must first avoid or mishandle evidence or use faulty reasoning
- False teachers and their followers value originality, speculation, and all kinds of biblical skepticism
- Logic requires correct and complete evidence and correct handling of that evidence in order to ensure a correct conclusion.
- To neglect logic in our studies of the Bible is to ensure that we will avoid proper conclusions.

Recommended Reading

Hedges, Levi. *Hedges' Rules of Logic.* Faith and Facts Press.

Rhodes, Kevin. "Prove All Things." In *The Faith Once for All Delivered,* edited by Tommy J. Hicks, 130-145. Lubbock, TX: Hicks Publications, 1998.

Warrren, Thomas B. *Logic and the Bible.* Jonseboro, AR: National Christian Press, 1982 .

Questions for Discussion

1. Can you name three different issues where people treat faith and reason as contradictory?
2. What is the biggest failing of most people in the process of gathering evidence?
3. Provide one additional biblical application for each law of thought.
4. If an interpretation of a verse is itself controversial should it be used as the sole foundation of an argument?
5. What is so offensive about logic to some people?

Assignment

Put the title of your study at the top of a sheet of paper, then make a list of all facts available on that subject. On a separate sheet of paper, make a list of implications that follow from these facts, citing the laws of thought that apply whenever possible.

Religious Authority

INTRODUCTION

Religious discussions between individuals often bog down into meaningless controversies or heat up into ongoing arguments because of the differences in how people view religious authority. These differences generally account for the differences in various religious practices as people distinguish themselves religiously into their respective groups. These differences generally fall into the following categories: 1) what is required 2) what is prohibited 3) and what is optional — all of which extend from whatever is used as the basis for religious authority. In the name of creating unity the current ecumenical trend has placed more and more into the "optional" category. By treating so much as optional there has been an explosion of even more differences and corresponding different religious sects. Thus the answer for achieving unity does not lie in eliminating the first two categories (for we would first have to establish that we have the right to do so), nor does it lie in eliminating the third. Rather, the answer to religious differences is to discover, through diligent effort, the view of religious authority that is consistent with God's own view.

Within society we can distinguish at least five views regarding moral authority: 1) all is allowed 2) all that the conscience allows is allowed 3) all that the church allows is allowed 4) all that is not prohibited is allowed and 5) all that of which God approves is allowed. First, to the secular humanist all is allowed, though not preferred, because he does not recognize any moral absolutes. Right and wrong are simply matters of taste. Thus, no one can condemn another person's actions. The media's current love affair with "tolerance" betrays their worldly philosophy. Second, many may not allow everything, yet they want to become the standard themselves. They will condemn Hitler, but cannot find any basis for doing so outside of their own conscience. Situation ethics (which many religions have unwittingly accepted) puts the individual in total control of right and wrong, and so follows the ethics of the days of the judges (Jdg. 21:25), a standard inherently flawed (1 Cor. 4:4; Acts 23:1). Third, many people appeal to what their church teaches as the standard of right and wrong. This actually extends the previous position into a corporate body. It still places men in charge of right and wrong and makes God subject to following the decisions of men, misinterpreting Matthew 16:18-19. Fourth, many people will look to the Bible and accept God's prohibitions as identifying wrong behavior. They recognize God's right to declare certain things sinful, but they only recognize as sinful those things that God specifically prohibits (Ex. 20:1-17). Many religions fall into this category. Finally, there are those who believe that we must have God's approval of a given behavior before acting, recognizing His authority over mankind to be all encompassing of our moral decisions (1 Thess. 5:21-22; Col. 3:17).

What many people find difficult is leaving their current view of authority behind in order to discover the view of which God demonstrates approval. The easy road accepts what one has always thought and been taught. The road to truth is more difficult. It requires Bible searching as well as soul searching. The Bible student does not have the right just to look at the choices cited above and choose the one he finds most appealing. Rather, a person who has the right desire and the right attitude must pursue the course that proves consistent with God's Word at every turn instead of blindly accepting the first or second view to which he becomes acquainted. In order to act morally a person must first obtain moral authority. This is the essence of any religious question or argument. This is the bottom line in religion and the cornerstone of life. Until we can establish firmly God's view of His authority and how He expressed it, we remain destined to wander aimlessly amid life's moral choices, and sure to fail in our quest for a heavenly home.

WHY DO WE NEED AUTHORITY?

That we need authority in order to act we derive from the fact that God is, that God is greater than man, and that God has expressed

His will for man. The existence of God—that eternal, omnipotent, omniscient, omnipresent Spirit who willed the existence of man and the universe in which man now resides—follows logically from the very fact that the universe and man are neither eternal nor self-caused, implying the necessity of a Creator, as well as from other equally logical proofs. Thus, since by right of definition God is the Creator and thus greater than His creation, man must be subject to Him. However, one can only express such a relationship in relation to and as far as the Creator has expressed His will. Therefore, throughout human history, mankind has been subject to the will of God inasmuch as He expressed it and directed it to man at that time. Since God now has expressed His will fully and completely to mankind (John 8:32; 2 Tim. 3:16-17; 2 Pet. 1:3; Jude 3), it follows that all mankind is subject to God and that any actions in which we choose to participate must coincide with God's will thus expressed (Col. 3:17).

This concept, while basic to every action in life, remains elusive to many. But even Jesus' enemies understood the need for moral authority. "Now when He came into the temple, the chief priests and the elders of the people confronted Him as He was teaching, and said, 'By what authority are You doing these things? And who gave You this authority?' But Jesus answered and said to them, 'I also will ask you one thing, which if you tell Me, I likewise will tell you by what authority I do these things: The baptism of John—where was it from? From heaven or from men?' And they reasoned among themselves, saying, 'If we say, "From heaven," He will say to us, "Why then did you not believe him?" But if we say, "From men," we fear the multitude, for all count John as a prophet.' So they answered Jesus and said, 'We do not know.' And He said to them, 'Neither will I tell you by what authority I do these things'" (Matt. 21:23–27). The foregoing account demonstrates: (1) that we need authority in order to act and (2) that when we act we do so either based upon man's authority or upon God's. Jesus' miracles demonstrated that He acted based upon God's authority, as He elsewhere argued (John 10:31-39). In fact, everything He did constituted submission to the Father's will (Phil. 2:5-8; Matt. 5:17; John 8:29; Matt. 26:39). So if Jesus Himself, God in the flesh (John 1:14), recognized and submitted to the authority of the Father, then we who are sinful and weak by all means must submit to God's authority.

We need authority to act because, despite the proud claims of evolutionists, mankind is not the pinnacle of existence. We need authority because we are the needy, the weak, and the sinful. We need authority because we do not know what is best for us (Jer. 10:23) and we are incapable of improving our own situation apart from God (Eph. 2:8-9; Jas. 1:17). We need authority because we live in a world that is not our own (Psa. 24:1). We need authority because we owe our present existence to God and the quality of our future existence to God (Col. 1:16-17; 1 John 2:25). We need authority for all that we do because nothing that we do steps out of the realm God created for us. We are His subjects. We need His authority.

WHERE DO WE FIND GOD'S AUTHORITY?

Throughout every corner of the world, societies have, in some way or another, recognized the hand of the Almighty in the affairs of men. While their understanding of Jehovah God may have left much to be desired, most primitive cultures recognized the need to seek the Creator (Heb. 11:6). Thus, men have long attempted to communicate to God and express their devotion in various ways. But their sincerity did not necessarily make those attempts pleasing to God. Today's New Age movement reverts to these practices of trying to achieve "spirituality" through individual preferences. Many established religious groups indicate that submission to God's authority comes through internal urges, once again placing God's authority into the realm of subjectivity. Religious people commonly will say, "God put it on my heart" to do thus and so, not realizing that they have arbitrarily assigned an action to God that He has not Himself "signed on to."

How can we possibly maintain that it is God's will for us to do something when God has not Himself said as much? We can be subject to God's will only so far as He has expressed His will, and our authority to act can extend only so far as God has made His will known. Since He has expressed His will fully and completely in the Bible (2 Pet. 1:3; Jude 3) thereby revealing all truth (John 8:32), then we have no authority to act beyond what the Bible says. This concept is absolutely essential in order to understand God's authority and our relationship to His authority. Since God has totally revealed His will in the pages of the Bible, then only to the extent that the Bible provides authority to act can we do so with God's approval (2 Tim. 3:16-17). When Satan tempted Jesus in the wilderness, our Savior responded each time with some form of "It is written" (Matt. 4:1-11). Why? Jesus recognized the Scriptures as God's expression of His authority (John 10:35). How dare people today try to excuse their actions as God's will without being able to show so in God's Word!

Think for a moment about some of your actions—in life, in worship, in service. Where has God given His permission for you to do them? Any answer besides, "The New Testament," is a wrong answer (John 12:48; Col. 3:17). Do you act, then try to justify? Or do you find assurance of God's approval in His revealed will and then act? These questions go to the heart of authority. They address our motives and our priorities. Anyone can carry the Bible and cite Scripture. Christians are known ultimately through their reverence for God, their reliance on what God has revealed, and their respect for the authority found therein. There is no authority in papal decrees, in church councils, in denominational creeds, or in individual feelings. These can only appeal to the authority of men (Matt. 15:8-9), and their power to save rests with men. Therefore, let us say with Paul, "I am not ashamed of the gospel of Christ, for it is the power of God to salvation for everyone who believes, for the Jew first and also for the Greek. For in it the righteousness of God is revealed from faith to faith; as it is written, 'The just shall live by faith'" (Rom 1:16-17). My friends, there is no divine approval if there is no biblical authority.

IS THE CHURCH SUBJECT TO THE BIBLE OR THE BIBLE SUBJECT TO THE CHURCH?

During the Reformation Movement of the sixteenth century, people had to confront a fundamental question about biblical authority: Was the Bible the product of the Church and therefore subject to the Church's tradition and interpretation or was the Church the product of the Bible—or, more specifically, divine revelation—and therefore subject to its specifications? While originally the former view was solely the position of the Roman Catholic Church, in the years since the Reformation many of the denominations created as a result of this movement have adopted an attitude similar to what their forefathers opposed, making their "church's interpretation" (which is really equivalent with tradition) the real standard to which the Bible is subject.

Since the church was established on the Day of Pentecost following the resurrection of Christ (Acts 2:1-47) somewhere between 29 and 33 A.D. and since the New Testament was not completely penned until 90-96 A.D., then certainly the question is relevant. However, dating *these* events does not actually answer the question. The fact that the gospel did not exist in *written form* before the establishment of the church does not imply that it was not there. In fact, as we review the New Testament record, it becomes obvious that **the message of the gospel preceded the church**. John the Immerser and then Jesus Himself preached the message concerning the coming of the kingdom of heaven (Matt. 3:1-2; 4:17). This was not a political kingdom (John 18:36) but a spiritual kingdom, the church (Matt. 16:18-19), and it was established, as promised, in the generation of the apostles (Mark 9:1; Col. 1:13-14). Thus the message was partially revealed during the ministry of Christ. However, the complete message of the gospel would have to wait until Christ's work was done—after He had died, been resurrected, and ascended to His Father—because this was central to the victorious message of the gospel of hope (1 Cor. 15:1-4; 55-57). Those early disciples had submitted themselves to the message about the coming kingdom. When Peter presented the gospel message on the Day of Pentecost (Acts 2), the people submitted themselves to that message in order to become Christians and thereby members of the church. Not even the apostles were allowed to modify God's message (Gal. 1:6-9). To the contrary, they also had to submit to it (Gal. 2:11).

In any century God's will can be known only by what God has revealed and is not subject to man in any way. If doctrine is simply a matter left to the interpretation of the church, then each individual can simply choose the church that interprets the Bible in a way that pleases him. Thus, on every level, this subjects God's revealed will to man's religious whims. God revealed His will by inspiration, first orally and later in writing. It is this inspired message that carries God's authority, and this is what all men must obey (Heb. 5:8-9) in order for God to save them and add them to *His* church (Acts 2:38-47). The character of God demands that man conform to Him rather than God adapt to man (1 Pet. 1:16). The church is the product of the gospel, the product of individuals submitting to God's will and thus achieving oneness — not by the vote of majority or by a superimposed power structure, but by each individual choosing to submit to God (Jas. 4:7).

IN THE NAME OF THE LORD

The phrase "in the name of the Lord" carries different connotations for different people, depending upon their backgrounds and the modes of expression that surround them. These six words, and others like them, often are used to try to create the impression of spirituality and dedication by affirming that a particular action is done "in the name of the Lord," by which most people essentially mean that they will do whatever they feel compelled to do but in the process give credit to God for making it possible and giving them the talent. However, the Bible does not use the phrase so arbitrarily.

"The name of the Lord" signifies the Lord's power and authority, His design and approval. When Jewish leaders called Peter and John into question regarding their healing of the lame man at the gate Beautiful, "when they had set them in the midst, they asked, 'By what power or by what name have you done this?'" (Acts 4:7). In the idiom of their day they were asking, "Who gave you permission to do this?" or "Who made this possible?" Their reply is significant: "let it be known to you all, and to all the people of Israel, that by the name of Jesus Christ of Nazareth, whom you crucified, whom God raised from the dead, by Him this man stands here before you whole" (Acts 4:10). The apostles not only gave credit to Jesus for the healing of the lame man but also established the sovereignty of Christ and His approval of their action and teaching based upon the miracle they performed. They then took His authority one step further by saying, "Nor is there salvation in any other, for there is no other name under heaven given among men by which we must be saved" (Acts 4:12). There is no other means of obtaining salvation from sin outside of Jesus Christ. No one else has the power to make forgiveness possible. But, as such, no one but Jesus has the right to determine how this is to be accomplished. Since He is the one who makes salvation possible, then He and He alone has the right to say what saves and whether an action is right or not. There are many things that people do in the name of religion and Christianity for which they do not have the Lord's approval. To whom will they appeal for salvation?

The apostles could say that the man was healed by the name of the Lord because it was fully in keeping with His will, as the miracle gave evidence. However, it is impossible for something to be done "in the name of the Lord" if the Lord has not expressed His permission and approval for it. The Lord's approval of the action *preceded* the apostles' taking action. This must always be our model. For us to do something in the name of the Lord we must first find His approval for it in His will. In the military, when something is requisitioned, someone in authority must "sign" to demonstrate approval and authorization. So it is with Christ. In the gospel He has revealed His will; it bears His signature. But anything beyond what is revealed cannot be said to have Christ's approval and therefore cannot be done "in the name of the Lord." Paul wrote, "And whatever you do in word or deed, do all in the name of the Lord Jesus, giving thanks to God the Father through Him" (Col 3:17). Therefore, whatever we say or do must be limited to those things for which the Lord has given His approval.

JESUS' VIEW OF BIBLICAL AUTHORITY

Recent trends among modernists have downplayed the role of authority in biblical interpretation, preferring to relegate all interpretation to the place of subjective opinion. Many have tried to compromise with this pluralistic approach by limiting authority to the "core gospel" or to the specific words of Jesus. They realize the central role of Jesus (1 Cor. 15:3-4) yet, in order to hold these positions, they also refuse to accept His view of biblical authority. Though Jesus lived under the Old Law and we live under the New, Jesus Himself should be the standard and model for how we conduct ourselves (1 Cor. 11:1), and this must begin with how we view biblical authority.

Jesus' boyhood obviously included much time with the Law. When He was twelve, His familiarity and understanding of it amazed the scholars of His day (Luke 2:46-47). When Satan tempted Jesus in the wilderness, our Savior responded with scripture each time, implying that what God had revealed settled the matter of right and wrong (Luke 4:1-13). On His return to Nazareth, Jesus read from the Law in the synagogue and declared that His being there fulfilled the prophecy included in the reading (Luke 4:16-21). Such a strong statement indicates His total respect for the Old Covenant (which included the prophets!) and that He accepted God's will as absolute truth. The fact that God said it meant that it would happen. Thus, when God says something, it also must, of necessity, be obeyed. He appealed to the Scriptures as a final authority regarding His identity and fulfillment of prophecy (John 5:39). Furthermore, He appealed to the Old Covenant as a foundation and standard for judging right and wrong, for "the scripture cannot be broken" (John 10:34-36). In the Sermon on the Mount, Jesus said, "Do not think that I came to destroy the Law or the Prophets. I did not come to destroy but to fulfill" (Matt. 5:17). Jesus Christ Himself—God in the flesh—did not consider it His right to set aside the Law and disregard it. To the contrary, He recognized His need to obey it completely (Phil. 2:5-8). For Jesus, everything in the Law and about the Law needed to be completed in His life—not only the prophecies but also the directives. What higher degree of respect could there be?

Jesus regarded the Old Covenant as authoritative during His lifetime. It was the standard of right and wrong for Jews *because* it revealed God's will for them. As such, no man could alter it without doing it damage, and no man could disregard it without being held responsible. In the same way today, men have no right to alter the Lord's message through interpretation or otherwise (Gal. 1:6-9), and no man can disregard it without suffering divine retribution for doing so (John 12:48). The New Covenant is a better covenant (Heb. 8:6-13), a higher covenant with greater responsibilities as well as greater promises. While we marvel at the grace of God bestowed upon mankind in the person of Christ (Eph. 2:10; John 1:16), we must never assume that we are under any less an obligation to respect divine authority. In fact, in that we have access to all truth (John 8:32; 17:17), God must also hold us to this higher standard of accountability (Heb. 2:1-4).

THE AUTHORITY OF DIRECT STATEMENTS

Any intelligible document contains direct statements — statements designed to indicate facts and conditions, requests and commands. These statements may take the form of declaratives (simple statements of fact), imperatives (commands), interrogatives (questions), hortatories (Let us...), or exclamations (Behold!). While there are variations on these basic units of expression, these five are easily identified and understood. The purpose of any statement is communication. Everyone makes statements in attempts to communicate. This alone does not make a statement authoritative. The authority of any statement does not depend upon that it is said or upon what is said but upon who said it.

Direct statements have authority when they indicate communication from one with authority. Anyone can provide a statement regarding the meaning of the First Amendment to the U.S. Constitution; however, only the statements made by the Supreme Court carry any authority because those justices alone are in positions that make their statements authoritative. In the same way, many people can make statements about religion and spiritual matters, but this does not mean they have the authority to do so — including the Supreme Court. A direct statement becomes authoritative when it is communication from God that requires something of the recipients of the message. So while recorded in the Bible, some statements carry no authority because of who said it. Statements of the Pharisees do not carry any spiritual weight because they did not have God's approval. But when God communicated to man in the days of direct revelation, whether that message came orally through a prophet or in writing, that message was authoritative.

Jesus respected the authority of God's direct statements. Each time Satan tempted Him, Jesus responded by citing Scripture. When He said, "it is written," this carried the strength of "God says." In the first instance, "when the tempter came to Him, he said, 'If You are the Son of God, command that these stones become bread.' But he answered and said, 'It is written, Man shall not live by bread alone, but by every word that proceeds from the mouth of God'" (Matt. 4:3-4). The authoritative answer to Satan's challenge was the citation of scripture.

In a sense Jesus answered Satan by saying, "It would be wrong for me to do that because what God said through Moses in Deuteronomy 8:3 is authoritative." While Moses' statement in Deuteronomy was directed specifically to the Israelites of his day, the message from God was authoritative for all people under that law. God had thus made a declarative statement regarding the relative importance of food to listening to God. Jesus then acted in such a way that was consistent with what God said was true, demonstrating respect for God's statements. Similarly, when we open the New Testament, we find many of God's statements revealed through inspired men, as well as quotations of Jesus. Since this is God's communication, then all of those statements that communicate God's will are authoritative statements of truth (John 17:17). In order to submit to this authority, we must make sure that what we do in life is consistent with the statements God has made in regard to our conduct.

Since direct statements in God's Word provide information pertinent to our salvation, then it is necessary for us to ensure that our lives and actions are consistent with the information provided. Therefore, since the Bible says that "faith comes by hearing, and hearing by the word of God" (Rom 10:17), then any belief and subsequent practice that does not originate with and conform to God's revealed will does not have God's authority (or approval) behind it. Before His ascension Jesus declared, "He who believes and is baptized will be saved; but he who does not believe will be condemned" (Mark 16:16). This simple declaration establishes certain facts regarding salvation, and **it is up to each individual to model his life in a way that is consistent with these facts.**

The apostles understood correctly that the question asked by the inspired prophet David in Psalm 2, "Why did the nations rage, And the people plot a vain thing?" (Psa. 2:1; Acts 4:25), revealed important information (Acts 4:27). Likewise, when Jesus asked, "The baptism of John—where was it from? From heaven or from men?" (Matt. 21:25), He established the two categories of religious authority. So questions are also direct statements that have authority. Paul often combined information from a rhetorical question with an exclamation in order to provide the model for our lives. In Romans 6:1-2 he wrote, "What shall we say then? Shall we continue in sin that grace may abound? Certainly not! How shall we who died to sin live any longer in it?" His first question notes that a conclusion follows from his earlier statements. The second question poses one possible conclusion. The exclamation demands that his readers accept another conclusion. The third question provides explanation as to why the first conclusion, posited within the framework of the second question, would be unacceptable. Therefore, questions and exclamations also provide much information regarding the direction our lives should take or not take.

Sometimes people confuse "direct statements" with "commands." As noted above, many direct statements are not commands but still carry authoritative information. But commands are indeed direct statements and can carry authority, depending upon whether or not the command originated with God. In Acts 2 the baptism of the Holy Spirit, which provided the apostles both with the gospel message and the ability to speak in other languages, demonstrated that the apostles' words originated with God. Therefore, when Peter told the people on the day of Pentecost, "Repent, and let every one of you be baptized in the name of Jesus Christ for the remission of sins" (Acts 2:38), this imperative (actually two distinct imperatives) carried God's authority. Since the reason for the action (need for forgiveness) still exists today and the means (change of thinking and immersion in water) are still possible today, then, being the divine mandate, they are still authoritative today. God's direct statements, regardless of their type, provide information as to how we are to conduct life. **Only by acting in ways that are *completely* consistent with *all* of these revealed statements can we *know* that we are pleasing God.**

THE AUTHORITY OF ACCOUNTS OF ACTION

The Pharisees, always hoping to catch Jesus in a mistake, must have grinned from ear to ear when they saw His disciples plucking grain on the Sabbath (Matt. 12:1). After all, according to their interpretation of the Law plucking grain constituted work, and God had forbidden work on the Sabbath. So the Pharisees said to Jesus, "Look, Your disciples are doing what is not lawful to do on the Sabbath!" (Matt. 12:2). While Jesus was not Himself plucking grain, He was allowing

His disciples to do so; therefore, as their Teacher, He was responsible. Jesus took the charge laid at His feet and turned it into a question of authority, that is, whether or not plucking grain, as the disciples were doing, was in fact wrong. He responded, "Have you not read what David did when he was hungry, he and those who were with him: how he entered the house of God and ate the showbread which was not lawful for him to eat, nor for those who were with him, but only for the priests? Or have you not read in the law that on the Sabbath the priests in the temple profane the Sabbath, and are blameless? Yet I say to you that in this place there is One greater than the temple. But if you had known what this means, 'I desire mercy and not sacrifice,' you would not have condemned the guiltless. For the Son of Man is Lord even of the Sabbath" (Matt. 12:3–8). Jesus referred to an approved account of action from the Old Covenant—priests working on the Sabbath—in order to demonstrate a principle, which He also cited.

Jesus' reference to the work of the priests on the Sabbath is significant. He deliberately chose an action that the Pharisees recognized as authorized and demonstrated that it necessarily implies that the Pharisees' own position in regard to what constitutes prohibited work was incorrect by showing that according to their interpretation of prohibited work the priests would be profaning the Sabbath. Such a position is untenable, and they knew it. The Pharisees could not argue that the priests were wrong in what they did because the LORD told the priests to do it; therefore, the only conclusion left is that the Pharisees' interpretation of what constituted prohibited work was incorrect. Jesus proved all this by appealing to an approved account of action.

Jesus used the priests' behavior as an example of God's approval of such actions, into which category the disciples' efforts would also fall. (Some of the sacrifices offered by the priests also provided food for their meals.) Jesus then argued that this demonstrated *how* people should understand the pertinent commands. The priests did work on the Sabbath and were blameless. The disciples were not plucking grain for personal profit but for survival, and the work they were doing was for God; therefore, their actions were not wrong. Jesus then employed an *a fortiori* argument, from the lesser to the greater. Since the priests' caring for the temple was not wrong, how could the disciples' efforts on His behalf be wrong? Thus, this established authoritative precedent. Jesus then cited the principle by which He applied these events: "I desire mercy and not sacrifice" (cf. Hos. 6:6). While the Pharisees had designed rules for the Sabbath, they failed to understand priorities correctly. Service to God qualified the meaning behind the Sabbath day work restrictions. Jesus used an account of action to demonstrate authority for His disciples' actions as having the right priority.

How one understands Jesus' reason for referring to David's eating the showbread depends upon the interpretation of the Old Law. The Law mandated certain limitations (Lev. 22:10, 15; Lev. 24:5-9; Num. 18:11); however, David's reasoning emphasizes that the bread was no longer holy since it had been removed from the table, and Ahimelech seems to have agreed (1 Sam. 21:1-6). Therefore, it seems likely that the limitations applied to the bread when it was on display but not afterwards. There was certainly nothing special about the bread; what was special was the function it served. If after serving that function it did indeed become common once more, then the priests could allow others to eat it.

Demonstrating Christ's recognition of the authoritative nature of certain accounts of action, while very important, does not explain when an action is authoritative versus when an action is not authoritative. Sinful actions obviously have no authority, nor do recorded actions for which there is no approval cited. Joshua's recounting of Rahab's lie does not give it credence (though some have sought to justify it), nor does the factual account of Judas Iscariot's suicide demonstrate God's approval for taking your own life, and this should be self-evident. However, we must also distinguish between actions that are optional, incidental, or essential. An action may have God's approval, but the question remains as to whether it is essential for all to participate in the specifics as given or whether that action is one of many authorized options or whether certain elements are simply incidental without any intention of implying obligation.

When Jesus finished the account of the Good Samaritan, he said, "Go and do likewise" (Luke 10:37). However, the Bible student must determine what events in the narrative are optional, incidental, or essential. For instance, while taking care of people who have been beaten and left for dead is certainly included, did Jesus limit His lesson this narrowly? Does the fact that the events took place near Jericho require us to travel that road until we find someone dying along the way? Certainly not! But *why* not? What makes the place incidental? What makes these specifics optional? And what makes specifics in other places obligatory? As Jesus' question and its answer indicate, the purpose of the entire story was to present a picture of someone who demonstrated mercy toward others. Therefore, within the framework of the narrative itself, Jesus indicated that the specifics given were put forth in order to illustrate a principle. It was this principle of showing mercy to all people that He declared as universally authoritative. While the place was incidental, and the specifics optional, the underlying principle is essential. The major reason that we know this lies in the fact that "showing mercy" is identified elsewhere with actions *other* than those cited in the story of the Good Samaritan.

The disciples partook of the Lord's Supper on the first day of the week (Acts 20:7). Unleavened bread and grape juice are the only elements cited as part of the Lord's Supper observance (1 Cor. 11:23-29). Elders are only found in a plurality (Phil. 1:1). These accounts of action by the early church carry authority because they all carry the approval of God as demonstrated through the apostles, who either participated in them or wrote in favor of them. Moreover, since God provides no coordinate account of action with these cited above, then that example becomes obligatory. So while the apostles sailed in order to go preach the gospel, the fact that they also walked shows that "sailing" is not a binding action. Jesus used the washing of feet (John 13) simply as an illustration of humility, an attitude that can be expressed in many ways, as the New Testament itself shows. Thus, an account of action is obligatory when God, in His Word, demonstrates His approval for that action, and presents no other option within that particular category.

THE AUTHORITY OF IMPLICATION

After Jesus had silenced the Pharisees yet again, representatives from the sect of the Sadducees came to him with a religious question. They proposed a scenario in which a woman married a man who subsequently died, leaving no children. She then married one of his brothers only to have the same thing happen. This continued until she had married seven times, and then she died. And so they asked Jesus, "'Therefore, in the resurrection, whose wife of the seven will she be? For they all had her.' Jesus answered and said to them, 'You are mistaken, not knowing the Scriptures nor the power of God. For in the resurrection they neither marry nor are given in marriage, but are like angels of God in heaven. But concerning the resurrection of the dead, have you not read what was spoken to you by God, saying, "I am the God of Abraham, the God of Isaac, and the God of Jacob" ? God is not the God of the dead, but of the living'" (Matt 22:28–32). This passage must truly confuse some people today, because Jesus relied on the authority of implication in order to make a conclusive argument regarding scripture.

The Sadducees' question presupposed many things erroneously; primarily, they did not believe in a resurrection from the dead. Therefore, while Jesus answered their question by teaching that marriage relationships will not exist following the resurrection (perhaps emphasizing that He did not subscribe to some of the beliefs about the resurrection then popular), He also answered the underlying assumption by appealing to the authority of scripture, quoting from Exodus 3:6. However, there is no *explicit* reference to the resurrection *at all* in that passage. The word is not mentioned. Yet Jesus *insisted* that this passage answered the question as to whether or not there was a resurrection. While He did not think it necessary to include all of His reasoning, His intention is clear. The Lord said, "I am the God of Abraham, the God of Isaac, and the God of Jacob." Thus, God had identified Himself by means of His relationship with previous patriarchs, but more specifically, His wording—"I am"—indicated that these relationships continued beyond death. Therefore, one must believe that there is life after death in order to remain consistent with what the Lord said in Exodus 3:6.

This is what implication is all about. Implication occurs when facts may not be explicitly stated but must logically follow from the information provided. Even the verb itself in the Hebrew is only implied in this instance. Yet Jesus accepted this passage as authoritative and used it as such. After quoting the verse, He stated the logical conclusion *implied* by the verse: God is not the God of the dead but of the living. And Jesus had earlier stated that the Sadducees were wrong for not accepting this fact, that their failure to accept this implication constituted ignorance of the scriptures, and that their teaching denied God's power (v. 29). Their failure to accept implication *had implications!* Some people today want to hide their unbelief behind the ruse of hermeneutical agnosticism. They simply do not want to accept the teaching that God has implied, and so they act like it is impossible to accurately understand such. Yet Jesus demonstrated that not only is it possible to understand the implications of scripture, it is absolutely necessary to do so if we are to know God's will.

People sometimes misunderstand what implication is. Some believe that implication means the same thing as inference, assumption, and speculation. But this simply is not the case. Assumption and speculation refer to drawing conclusions without adequate evidence. Inference refers to what an individual believes the evidence indicates. Implication, however, refers to those conclusions that naturally and necessarily follow the demands of the evidence, though that information is not explicitly stated.

People often wonder about the origin of Cain's wife. We know that God ceased creating after the sixth day (Gen. 2:2). We also know that His creation of humans consisted of Adam and Eve (Gen. 1:26-27; 2:18-24), and that Eve is the mother of all living (Gen. 3:20). So when we see that Cain married his wife (Gen. 4:17), we can know her origin, though it is never explicitly stated. Since creation is limited to God, and God ceased creating after Adam and Eve, then God did not create any more women. Therefore, we must consider what other means existed whereby a woman could exist for Cain to marry. Since the supernatural explanation of creation can be eliminated due to God's statement in Genesis 2:2, we can conclude that Cain's wife came to be through natural processes. Furthermore, in Genesis 5:4 it says, "And the days of Adam after he had begotten Seth were eight hundred years: and he begat sons and daughters." Therefore, we know that Adam and Eve had daughters, though none of them are named. We can also know, according to this statement, that Adam and Eve had sons other than Cain, Abel, and Seth. With the information provided, we can conclude that Cain's wife was most likely his sister, or possibly his niece. (Cain was most likely the firstborn based upon Eve's statement at his birth (Gen. 4:1). However, since Adam and Eve had both sons and daughters besides the three sons listed, it is possible that a son and daughter married earlier and had a daughter who then became Cain's wife, though Genesis 5:4 would seem to indicate that these sons came later.) So while we know by implication that Cain married a close relative, we still may only speculate as to the specifics. Some have objected to this idea because of God's later condemnation of such close intermarriage. However, the fact that He made it unlawful *later* is very important. Such a prohibition did not apply to Cain, nor could it if the world was to be populated.

We accept the principle of implication all the time. We understand that if Bob is taller than Fred and Fred is taller than John then it would be true to say that John was shorter than Bob, though it was never explicitly stated. Why? Because the information provided allows for only one conclusion. This is implication. Some people today act as if implication cannot be binding because it requires fallible individuals to think, sometimes inferring incorrect answers. First, people must think in order to understand explicit statements. Second, any failure to understand the implications of a text does not mean that understanding it is impossible. Third, a rejection of implication ultimately, and perhaps intentionally, leads to "interpretation by consensus" rather than by logical processes, putting what people *want* to believe God said above the text itself in order of importance.

While the New Testament treats implication as authoritative, many have difficulties accepting its authority when applied to more specific matters in life and therefore reject implication in principle, despite what Jesus did. However, as in all matters biblical, discarding biblical principles solves nothing. To the contrary, it creates multitudinous other problems. A man may claim to be without sin, yet this is known to be untrue because Paul said that all men have sinned (Rom. 3:10-11, 23). However, it is still only by implication that this is known because no particular individual is specified by the text. Implication makes it unnecessary. In the same way, the existence of sin in men's lives already affirmed implies that law exists to which men currently are amenable because John wrote that sin is the transgression of the law (1 John 3:4).

God's use of principles makes implication all the more necessary. Principles allow for application within a stated framework without requiring each and every detail. When Paul cited "revelries" as a work of the flesh in Galatians 5:19-21, this automatically condemned all the activities inherent in revelries. By including "lewdness," which includes all behaviors that provoke sexual desire, he was including by implication the modern dance, "making out," and immodesty. Furthermore, Paul's adding of "such like" to the list not only *allows for* implication, it *requires* implication. There is simply no way to understand and apply Paul's condemnation of "such like" without employing implication. Everything that falls into a given category by definition partakes of the character of that category, including when that character is condemned.

When Jesus instituted the Lord's Supper, He used the symbols present at the time. Since He did this during the Jewish Passover (Mark 14:12-26), since the Jewish Passover required eliminating all fermenting and leavening agents from the home (Ex. 12:14-20), and since Jesus kept the law perfectly (Heb. 4:15), then it is a *fact* that Jesus used unleavened bread and unfermented grape juice. The text does not explicitly say so, but it does imply it. Likewise, many people try to justify social drinking by appealing to John 2 where it records Jesus' turning water into wine. However, these people would have Jesus condoning, contributing to, and participating in an action that God had condemned (Prov. 20:1). This would make Jesus Himself out to be a sinner (Eph. 5:11), besides ignoring the meaning of the underlying Greek word *oinos* (which simply refers to the product of the grape generically). Jesus made fresh grape juice, not alcoholic wine. This much is implied and an ascertainable conclusion.

For some reason, there are people who believe that two plus two equal four in every realm but religion. They do not want to accept the implications of Bible statements, largely because they do not want to submit to the implications of Bible statements. But regardless of how implication is accepted, it is authoritative and binding. To deny facts known by implication is essentially to attempt removal of part of God's Word (Rev. 22:18-19). A Bible student must consider the implications of revelation and accept the consequences of the facts presented. Jesus held the Sadducees responsible for both the explicit statements and the implications of God's Word (Matt. 22:29-32), and the same is true for people today.

GENERIC AND SPECIFIC AUTHORITY

To hear some people's perspectives on how God chose to write the Bible would border on the comical if such opinions were not so serious. Some believe that the Bible is too long, boring, and repetitive. They argue that many of the specifics listed are superfluous, unnecessarily taking up space. Others think that the Bible is not specific enough and wish that God had provided more "Ten Commandment style precepts" and left less to be covered by principle. These interpretive leanings manifest themselves when one group ignores the specifics that illustrate *how* God intended a principle to be applied and when the other ignores the generics that explain the motivation and principle behind the stated specifics. Thus, balancing generic and specific authority is essential in order to understand the Bible correctly. Accordingly, direct statements, accounts of action, and implication all present both generics and specifics, and it is important that they be accepted equally and completely.

If one were to insist on specific authority alone to demonstrate how to travel in order to reach the lost, he would be limited to walking and sailing. Such reasoning would eliminate riding in automobiles and on airplanes or using radio and television. The terms "go" (Mark 16:15) and "went" (Acts 8:4) are very general and include all forms of transportation and other ways of getting the message out. That the scriptures express more than one example under the general heading of "going" indicates that they were not intended to limit "going" but to illustrate it. The Greek word *euangelizo*, generally translated "preach" or "preach the gospel," basically means "spreading the good news," and thus we have authority for employing the means available to us to do just that. However, we must make sure that the message gets out untainted and without violating God's word. "Dramatic presentations" would include many assumptions and great speculation. Additionally, employed in worship, any female leadership would violate 1 Corinthians 14:34-35. So while there is generic authority for spreading the gospel, this does not mean that it carries unlimited authority or that there are no scriptural boundaries.

The scriptures also provide us with generic authority for rest, relaxation, and recreation both by Jesus' example and by words that express or imply these. However, the specific activities authorized are limited by other statements, examples, and implications in God's word. Generic authority to recreate does not "trump" God's principle of taking care of the human body (1 Cor. 6:19-20). Generic authority to worship is limited by the requirement to do so "in spirit and in truth" (John 4:24). Therefore, for something to be worship that pleases God it must both fit the definition of worship (*proskuneo*) **and** match our requirement of having the proper attitude and actions. Generic authority is limited by the context in which it is found and by further prohibitions expressed through inspiration. *Notice that in all of these cases we are referring to the authority expressed in the scriptures, not the silence of the scriptures, which we will address later.* Understanding generic and specific authority requires much attention, including an appreciation for the intent of the writer, the extent of the writing, and a broader comprehension of the Bible as a whole (Acts 20:27).

The most difficult aspect of generic and specific authority is to identify whether God is instituting a practice, recognizing circumstances that pleased Him, regulating a practice (holy kiss), or simply stating incidental matters. Matthew and Mark wrote about Jesus' taking unleavened bread and grape juice, which were used during the Passover meal, and giving them new significance, a significance apart from the Passover (Matt. 26:26-30; Mark 14:22-26). Luke recorded the direct statement, "do this in remembrance of me" (Luke 22:19-20), which instituted a new practice that was to continue past that one incident. Eating unleavened bread and drinking grape juice were not new practices, but doing them in remembrance of Christ was. Thus, while "do this" is a very generic statement, the context (more on this later) limits what "this" refers to—specifically to those actions taken by Christ and recorded by inspiration and to the purpose He designated. So Christ provided both a direct statement requiring His disciples to observe the Lord's Supper and an authoritative example of *what* to do and *why* to do it. However, He did not at this time address *where* or *when*.

Even though Jesus instituted the Lord's Supper on a Thursday night, he did not institute a particular time for observance that evening. And while Paul wrote to the Corinthians to regulate the Lord's Supper (1 Cor. 11:17-29) due to their abuses of it, specifically addressing their having strayed from its purpose, he indicated only certain conditions that disciples needed to meet (being assembled, for one) but did not refer to *when*. Luke, however, later wrote in recognition of the fact that the disciples observed the Lord's Supper on the first day of the week (Acts 20:7). This is the only reference to the *time* that the Lord's Supper is to be observed, which means it is the only time God authorized. It is not as though Matthew, Mark, Luke and Paul had given some authority to partake of the Lord's Supper *any* day of the week and that Luke's specification limited what was elsewhere generic. To the contrary, Luke was supplying information that was needed but not addressed in scripture anywhere else.

While these examples illustrate the relationship of generics and specifics, it is essential from the beginning for the Bible student to recognize whether the relationship between two pieces of information is coordinate or subordinate. Playing a piano is not in a subordinate category to singing. They are coordinate. They both are subordinate to the category of making music, a generic that is not found in the New Testament (at least not in an accurate translation). Also, the requirement of faith (Heb. 11:6) does not fulfill or nullify the requirement of baptism (Acts 2:38). They are coordinate: both equally necessary in order to obtain forgiveness (Jas. 2:24). The question ultimately comes down to determining the most generic authorization provided without any prohibition added. The biblical text designates "bread" as an item designated by Christ to be part of the Lord's Supper (1 Cor. 11:23-29). In addition to this, the context shows that since Jesus instituted the Lord's Supper during Passover that no leavening agents would have been present, indicating that it was without doubt unleavened bread. Now, flour is essential in order to make bread, but there were several grains available as there are today. The designation of "bread" demands the existence of flour, but it does not imply any particular grain. The Catholic Church requires the bread they serve to contain at least some unleavened wheat, which becomes a significant problem for those who are wheat-gluten intolerant.[1]

The hermeneutical interaction of generics and specifics may seem a little remote to some readers; however, they are at the heart of many differences among those concerned with biblical authority. Many disagreements, such as whether or not to have divided Bible classes, how many cups to employ in the Lord's Supper, contributing to orphan homes, and helping non-Christians financially, often come down to different perspectives regarding generic and specific authority. The main point to remember is that a specific does not limit a generic unless it involves prohibition. The fact that a specific way of doing something is mentioned in the bible does not limit a practice that is authorized generically. But if a specific prohibition exists, then it does limit the extent of generic authority because prohibition automatically indicates that a practice is unauthorized. Therefore, one must establish that a given action falls into a generic authorization and that no other biblical injunction prohibits it. Thus, generic authorization has direct ties to implication and relies on implication in order to establish authority. It is incorrect to allow a practice that has no generic authority and equally wrong to prohibit a practice that has generic authority where no God-given prohibition exists.

CONCLUSION

Religious authority can be both fairly complicated and very controversial. However, a Bible student who has the necessary desire, has purged himself of prejudicial attitudes, and has dedicated his heart to the discovery of God's will in its purity will also give all diligence to unraveling these complexities without allowing the controversy to deter him or a point of view to dissuade him from accepting the conclusions that God demands. Unfortunately, most people accept a view of religious authority prior to studying the Bible that does not itself come *from* the Bible. Thus, from the outset a perverted view of authority taints their study, distorts the truth, and leads down the pathway of ignorance and error.

1 John Curran, "Grain Line: Family Fights for wheat-free Communion wafer," **Fort Worth Star-Telegram**, 20 August 2004.

An appreciation of and respect for divine authority should begin with a careful handling of revealed truth. No matter how passionate, no matter how sincere, no matter how dedicated a person might be, without God's moral authority establishing the parameters of study and the perimeter of the Christian walk, that individual will wander hopelessly, confused in study, confused in ethics, confused in life.

But this need not be the case. God Himself has revealed the way to understand the message of His book. God Himself has provided the example of how to recognize His authority and apply it to interpretation. God Himself has shown us the way out of religious division and confusion. But we must be willing to follow. This is the opportunity set before the Bible student. It is a challenge, yes, but it offers rewards beyond comparison.

In order to comprehend religious authority a person must:

- **Evaluate his actions morally**
- **Recognize that he must submit to God's moral authority**
- **Seek out God's will as God has *revealed* His will**
- **Realize that the Bible—not tradition and not church leaders--expresses God's will**
- **Establish divine approval biblically before taking action or claiming divine approval**
- **Follow the example of Jesus in respecting scriptural authority**
- **Submit to direct statements communicating God's will**
- **Model his own actions after accounts of action to which God has given His approval**
- **Accept the Bible's implications as equally authoritative**
- **Avoid confusing implication with personal speculation, assumption, and incorrect inference**
- **Remember to investigate the finer points of generic and specific authority**

Recommended Reading

Beals, George. *How Implication Binds and Silence Forbids*. Ann Arbor, MI: PC Publications, 1998.

Dungan, D.R. *Hermeneutics*. Delight, AR: Gospel Light Publishing Company.

Hightower, Terry, ed. *Rightly Dividing the Word: Volume I – General Hermeneutics*. Pensacola, FL: Firm Foundation Publishing House, 1990.

Hightower, Terry, ed. *Rightly Dividing the Word: Volume II – Special Hermeneutics*. Pensacola, FL: Firm Foundation Publishing House, 1991.

Warren, Thomas. *When is an Example Binding?* Moore, OK: National Christian Press, 1989.

Questions for Discussion

1. Why do people assume that they have God's approval without even studying the Bible?
2. How do you overcome an attachment to a preacher, religious belief or body, or tradition when it might lead to a conflict with God's Word?
3. Why do people so often suggest or participate in an activity prior to establishing God's approval?
4. Without implication is there a biblical definition of marriage and family?
5. What types of problems are you likely to have if you misunderstand generic and specific authority?

Assignment

On a separate piece of paper, write down what you know God approves of regarding the Lord's Supper, citing the scriptural reference on which the authority is based and the type of authority that provides the authorization, then compare this with **every** aspect of your current practice.

CHAPTER 5

Biblical Silence

INTRODUCTION

We the People of the United States, in Order to form a
more perfect Union, establish Justice, insure domestic
Tranquility, provide for the common defence, promote
the general Welfare, and secure the Blessings of Liberty
to ourselves and our Posterity, do ordain and establish
this Constitution for the United States of America.

This document and these words have provoked many
discussions in this country up to the present day about the nature of
the Constitution and how it should be interpreted. Some politicians
describe the Constitution as "a living document" that should be
adapted according to the times in a sort of "fluid interpretation" model.
Others argue that the purpose of creating a written Constitution was
expressly to overcome the difficulties our Founders encountered
with the unwritten, and therefore "fluid," British Constitution,
where legislative or judicial whim could change the whole direction
of government. In other words, the text and its context itself should
govern interpretation.

The Federalist Papers were a series of essays published
anonymously in newspapers in selected states designed to encourage
ratification of the Constitution and are still the best commentary on
constitutional context (sometimes called intent). *The Anti-Federalist
Papers* were written by those who worried that the federal government
would usurp its authority (as they believed Britain's had done) and
desired a weaker national government as a result. In effect, these
groups were arguing over the extent of federal authority intended by
the Constitution and the possible ramifications of how its silence would

be interpreted. Amazingly enough, this same difference in approach is what divides the religious world. How should we understand the silence of the Bible as it pertains to religious authority? Does its silence permit all that is not expressly or implicitly prohibited? Or does its silence prohibit all that is not expressly or implicitly authorized? Any document that is intended to be authoritative, if it is of any value, includes an explanation of how its silence should be understood. This is one reason why the Federalist and Anti-Federalist factions added the Bill of Rights to the Constitution. Though some Anti-Federalists objected to these amendments on the basis that the Constitution's silence, by not mentioning these rights, automatically guaranteed that Congress could not infringe upon them, assuming that all would accept a limiting view of silence, other Anti-Federalists worried that some citizens (and legislators) might not always share this view of interpretation; therefore, they proposed these amendments. While we are more familiar with some of the earlier amendments, the Bill of Rights closed with the Tenth Amendment: "The powers not delegated to the United States by the Constitution, nor prohibited by it to the States, are reserved to the States respectively, or to the people." According to this amendment, the silence of the Constitution should be interpreted as prohibiting action by the federal government not authorized by the document itself.

In the same way, the Bible, and the New Testament in particular, explains how Bible students should interpret its silence. In various passages God has provided instruction regarding the meaning of His silence. Therefore, we must respect the principle of silence He Himself affirms and apply it consistently in our interpretation of scripture. "If anyone speaks, let him speak as the oracles of God" (1 Pet. 4:11a). It is thus inappropriate to affirm or deny something based upon "what God did not say" until we first can demonstrate what God intended by His silence.

COLOSSIANS 3:17 AND BIBLICAL SILENCE

Paul's epistle to the Colossians contains a very specific discussion defending the deity of Christ against the teaching of some early Gnostics, emphasizing the authority implied by the identity of

Jesus Christ and addressing the practical effect this should have on the lives of individuals. This book has two pivotal passages, Colossians 2:6-7 and Colossians 3:16-17. Colossians 2:6-7 creates the transition from Paul's discussion about the deity of Christ to his discourse on the implications this has for people and their conduct, using Christ's death, burial, and resurrection as the model. Colossians 3:16-17 then makes the transition from the discussion regarding the perspective and attitudes required of a Christian to how these pertain to various relationships in life. Therefore, the context preceding Colossians 3:17 indicates Paul's focus: Jesus Christ's identity implies His authority; His word communicates His authority; and it is our responsibility to live in accordance with His stated authority. Such is the foundation laid when Paul penned, "And whatever you do in word or deed, do all in the name of the Lord Jesus, giving thanks to God the Father through Him" (Col. 3:17).

The first phrase in this verse, "And whatever you do in word or deed," demonstrates that Paul addressed everything in life. The original language emphasizes this: "And everything, any*thing that may come up*, what ever *its nature, whether* in word or in action." "Everything" covers life generically. "Any*thing*" covers specific things in life. "Ever" covers any contingency. "In word or in action" simply emphasizes more directly that he is addressing all of life. God has given us all things that pertain to life and godliness (2 Pet. 1:3). The question is whether or not we will accept and abide by what He has given.

The second phrase in this verse, "do all in the name of the Lord Jesus," has become the major point of disagreement among commentators. Many interpret this to mean, "Whatever you choose to do, praise Christ when you do it." However, this does not fit the character of the book's context or the meaning of the phrase "in the name of" already discussed. All that Paul had said to this point in the book focused on the limits of behavior, whether this referred to Christ's teaching as the basis for these limits instead of the Old Covenant (Col. 2:6-23) or to the limits Christ's teaching placed on individual behavior (Col. 3:1-15). "In the name of Christ" means simply that an action has Christ's signature on it, indicating His approval. He has provided His signature of approval through His word. Therefore, anything we do MUST have Christ's prior approval. So according to Colossians 3:17, unless Jesus has given His stated approval in His Word, an activity is prohibited.

The third phrase, "giving thanks to God the Father through Him," is significant not only in speaking of prayer and of Christ's mediation in prayer but also in stating the appropriate attitude we should have toward God for all that He has provided, including His will, so that we might know how to please Him. Therefore, instead of looking for license in the silence of the Bible, we should see the limitations God has placed upon us. To go beyond what has Christ's stated approval is to act on our own authority, creating a self-determined religion (Col. 2:23) that competes with Christ and Christianity.

SECOND TIMOTHY 3:16-17 AND BIBLICAL SILENCE

When Paul wrote to the young evangelist Timothy shortly before his death, he placed his concern squarely on the promulgation of the gospel message in its power (2 Tim. 1:8) and purity (2 Tim. 1:13) throughout future generations (2 Tim. 2:2). Therefore, he urged Timothy to treat that wondrous message with diligence and care (2 Tim. 2:15), exhorting him to continue his studies to gain wisdom in how to act in life (2 Tim. 3:14-15). This message, he affirms, is found in the Scriptures: "All Scripture is given by inspiration of God, and is profitable for doctrine, for reproof, for correction, for instruction in righteousness, that the man of God may be complete, thoroughly equipped for every good work" (2 Tim. 3:16-17).

That Paul referred to more than simply the Old Testament in verse sixteen, which was Timothy's guide in youth (v. 15), is manifest by Paul's own treatment of the New Testament as scripture in his earlier epistle to Timothy (1 Tim. 5:18) — remote context — and by Paul's characterization of what those scriptures accomplish, providing the way to salvation and producing faith in Christ Jesus (again v. 15) — immediate context. Since these fall within the confines of the gospel message (John 14:6; Rom. 10:14-17), Paul certainly did not intend to limit his meaning to the Old Testament in what followed. Furthermore, if Paul's reference to scripture in verse sixteen referred only to the Old Covenant, then he would be saying that it was fully capable of providing man what he needed, without any need for the new, which would contradict the teaching of other scriptures (Heb. 8:6-13). Rather, his designation of "the Holy Scriptures" makes plain that what God has said should be the authority by which we live. Timothy had accepted this while growing up under the Old Covenant and had followed the same principle upon becoming a Christian. Paul's designation of "all" in verse sixteen adds weight to the acceptance of the inspiration of the New Covenant on the same basis as the Old (2 Pet. 1:20-21). As such, the whole body of God-breathed literature serves as the basis for religious authority for all matters of life (though the covenants contained within that literature place divinely set limits on themselves).

With this in mind, we should also notice the extent to which the Scriptures pertain to life. They provide the information we need, they convict us of sin, they correct us when we stray, and they instruct us in what is righteous. The stated purpose for this training is our own spiritual preparation. God's Word gives us all the information we need in order to know both what we are to do and how to carry out properly the tasks assigned to us by God, and these tasks are described as "every good work." Now, if the Bible informs us through direct statement, account of action, or implication regarding every good work that God would have us do, we can conclude that any activity not found in the New Testament (as the covenant under which we live, Col. 2:14) *cannot* be a good work. God revealed every good work, and He did so in the Scriptures. Therefore, it is quite impossible for someone to justify an action that cannot be sustained by New Testament teaching. When anyone attempts to declare an action "good," he must do so with God's authority, yet God's authority is found in the scriptures. So in a great passage that declares the certainty of God's inspiration, Paul also teaches about the limitations placed upon us by God's silence.

FIRST THESSALONIANS 5:21-22 AND BIBLICAL SILENCE

Paul often ended his epistles with a series of short exhortations to the people. One of the most obvious examples of this practice is at the close of his first letter to the Thessalonians. These young Christians needed much instruction still, so Paul chose to include some basic guiding points for them, including the need to follow the guidance of the leaders, to be pure in motive, to appreciate the importance of prayer, and to rejoice in their new faith. As Paul then turned his attention to their relationship to the gospel message, he said, "Test all things; hold fast what is good. Abstain from every form of evil" (1 Th. 5:21–22).

The word "test" translates the Greek word *dokimazo*, a word that originally referred to the test that was made on metals to determine their authenticity. Therefore, it does not mean that we are to believe something and then try to prove it; rather, it means that we must verify the truth and goodness of *all things* before we accept and practice them. The next two phrases show that the test Paul has in mind is the differentiation between good and evil. Holding fast to what is good implies that the test performed confirmed conclusively that a given behavior has God's approval. To such things we are to commit ourselves wholly and completely, not only accepting them but also doing them. Thus, the test must come prior to the practice. It is only by putting an action or belief to the test that we can know whether or not it has God's approval, and this approval can come only through the revelation found in His Word. We should then abstain from anything that fails to provide proof of its goodness—no matter what the situation and no matter how tempting it may be to justify it.

What should strike the reader is that Paul presents only two categories—the category in which we can find behavior that is tried, tested, and true and the category in which all other beliefs and behaviors fall. There is no middle ground between right and wrong. It either has God's stated or implied approval or it does not. It either passes the test with adequate proof or it does not. It is either proven to be good or it is evil. God's silence *cannot* be construed so as to indicate His approval either stated or implied. Therefore, where God has not spoken to provide approval, one can assume that he has not given it. So it is necessary for the Bible student to scrutinize a belief or action first and verify—put to the test—that an action or belief has God's approval before he can say that it is good. **Furthermore, since the only way to know what has God's approval is to consult His Word, then** only those things found in God's Word can have God's approval, and only those things found in God's Word can be verified, regarding right and wrong. Some seem to believe that it is up to God to step in and say, "No, you can't do that!" But the Bible clearly indicates that the burden of proof is on us. Before we do anything, we must "test all things." You can *never* show that God approves of something by His silence. God's silence does not create some third category wherein we have liberty to do as we so choose. To the contrary, we only have permission to do as we can verify by means of the scriptures.

ROMANS 1:16-17 AND BIBLICAL SILENCE

Without question the book of Romans describes the beauty of the gospel message as well as its power. Paul's proclamation of the good news of Jesus Christ is a thorough exposition of man's universal need for the gospel (ch. 1-3), faith as the acceptance of the gospel (ch. 4-5), the necessity of obedience to the gospel (first in baptism and then throughout life) (ch. 6), the superiority of the gospel to the Old Law (ch. 7-8), the universality of the gospel call (ch. 9-11), the gospel applied (ch. 12-13), the love for one another created by the gospel (ch. 14-15), and faithfulness to the gospel (ch. 16). All of these things are captured in essence by Paul's opening thesis: "For I am not ashamed of the gospel of Christ, for it is the power of God to salvation for everyone who believes, for the Jew first and also for the Greek. For in it the righteousness of God is revealed from faith to faith; as it is written, 'The just shall live by faith'" (Rom. 1:16–17).

While verse sixteen is often quoted, the following verse sometimes does not receive the attention it deserves, most likely because it is difficult (made worse by idiomatic translation) and misunderstood. "For" indicates that the verse is a further explanation or clarification of what was said previously. "In it" refers to the gospel. So it says that "the righteousness of God" is "revealed" in the gospel. But we must then consider the meaning of righteousness in this passage. Righteousness essentially refers to all those things that it takes to have the right relationship with God, including God's character that extends opportunity, Jesus Christ who manifested that opportunity, the communication of God's will that defines the opportunity, and man's obedience by which he takes advantage of that opportunity. The context of verses sixteen and seventeen indicates the communication of God's will regarding what man is to do. Verse eighteen contrasts this action with disobedient man's unrighteousness. Therefore, "the righteousness of God" refers to the actions God has revealed in His will that God requires of man in order for any man to have the right relationship with His Creator. So "the righteousness of God" is equivalent to "God's plan for man's salvation."

The Bible allows for only two categories: righteousness and unrighteousness. And, according to 1 John 5:17, all unrighteousness is sin. Therefore, anything that does not fit the category of righteousness is wrong for us to do. Yet Romans 1:17 tells us that "righteousness" has been revealed in the gospel. So all those actions that contribute to having the right relationship with God are contained within the gospel message. If an action is not included therein, then it must fall into the category of unrighteousness and be sinful. Thus, when the Bible speaks in favor of an action, it reveals righteousness. When the Bible is silent about an action, it implies that the action under consideration is unrighteous. "Little children, let no one deceive you. He who practices righteousness is righteous, just as He is righteous" (1 John 3:7).

UNDERSTANDING THE PRINCIPLE OF BIBLICAL SILENCE

Most people are first confronted with the principle of biblical silence by the question of whether or not God allows the use of mechanical instruments of music in worshiping Him, though the principle applies beyond this one issue. For many people this issue has emotional power that often overrides an objective consideration of the important hermeneutical principles involved. This further explains why developing the correct attitude is so essential for good Bible study. Without doing so, present beliefs and practices never come under close scrutiny, and so the search for and acceptance of truth becomes derailed from the outset. Having previously established the validity of the silence principle from the scriptures themselves, it remains for the Bible student to accept the need to implement this principle into his framework of reference when examining any scripture or subject and then to apply it in every aspect of life. For greater clarity the student should consider sub-principles related to biblical silence.

Some have stated on occasion that the specificity of the New Testament's designation of singing in worship limits; this is not precisely true. It is the New Testament's silence regarding every *other* form of music in worship that forbids all but singing. Paul specified fornication as the reason to withdraw from the brother in Corinth (1 Cor. 5), but in writing to the Thessalonians he referred to laziness as another example that fell into the general classification of disorderliness, which implied the necessity of withdrawal. Paul's specificity in 1 Corinthians does not limit the basis of withdrawal to fornication because *in the same covenant* he provided authority on a broader basis. It is the non-existence of positive divine legislation (i.e. silence) that forbids our involvement, not specificity in one instance (Heb. 7:14). The point is that it is wrong to participate in *anything* or act in any way for which we do not *know* that God has stated His approval. We are to walk by faith (2 Cor. 5:7), and that faith can only come from what God has said (Rom. 10:17) — not from His silence. If you cannot say for certain that God approves of something, you can assume that He disapproves of it (Rom. 14:23). Since God has expressed what is *right*, then sin is not limited to just what God has expressly forbidden (1 John 5:17). God does not have to say specifically regarding every sinful thing, "Don't do that!" He took care of that when He said "Do this!"

God approves of actions in principle, and He disapproves in principle. By implication He approves of whole categories of actions without naming them individually. By His silence He forbids all actions for which He has offered no approval. Therefore, it is incumbent upon the student of the Bible to demonstrate God's written approval rather than to use God's silence as a cloak to cover personal desires. God has spoken in regard to music in worship. He approves of singing (Eph. 5:19; Col. 3:16; etc.) but is silent concerning any other form of music to be used in Christian worship. This may be the most obvious application of the silence principle because of the stark contrast this presents, but be assured, it is not the only application.

APPLYING THE PRINCIPLE OF BIBLICAL SILENCE

God, having sufficiently demonstrated the principle of silence in the pages of the Bible, has provided for all men in the New Testament complete instruction as to how to please Him (2 Pet. 1:3). Furthermore, the most obvious application of this principle—the limiting of music in worship to singing—is also one of the most frequently violated. Violators protest such a characterization in various ways, such as: (1) based upon what they like, (2) based upon a covenant not in force, (3) based upon a prejudiced understanding of a Greek word, and (4) based upon what God *does not say.* The first involves incorrect attitude; the second fails to accept the limited role of the Old Covenant (to be discussed later); the third results from making a decision and then trying to prove it using Greek (also to be discussed later); the final mistake stems from a misunderstanding or non-acceptance of biblical silence. However, rather than dwell on this one issue, it is essential that the Bible student apply the principle of silence consistently, which means that he must be willing to accept the limitations that go with biblical silence in all areas of doctrine—not just this one!

The principle of silence applies to the music God desires in worship whether a person is in the assembly or out. Those verses that discuss the assembly specifically (1 Cor. 14:15; Eph. 5:19; Col. 3:16) mention only singing, but when the New Testament refers to worshiping God in music privately (Acts 16:25; Jas. 5:13), it is just as limiting. Therefore, since God has spoken on the use of spiritual songs, they should never be used for entertainment purposes because such an action goes beyond the scope of what God established (John 4:24). Likewise, the Lord's designation of unleavened bread and grape juice (through historical understanding of the Passover) and the New Testament's silence eliminate other emblems from being used at the Lord's Supper (1 Cor. 11:23-29), just as the example of partaking the Lord's Supper on the first day of the week (Acts 20:7) provides authority for it *only on that day.* The Bible's silence regarding any other day of the week eliminates the other six days from consideration. A practice gaining popularity today is the use of "dramatic productions" and "skits" in worship (and elsewhere). Besides raising important questions regarding the role of women in these skits (1 Cor. 14:34-35), such productions necessarily imply things that the Bible does not, thereby implying untruth. Additionally, the New Testament does not tell us to "dramatize" the gospel but to "teach" and "preach" it (Matt. 28:19; Mark 16:15). Paul intentionally contrasts his preaching with the more dramatic oratory that was common in Corinth (1 Cor. 1:18-2:2) because the power of conversion is to come through the content of the message—not the presentation.

The so-called "progressiveness" of the times has contributed to the degrading of worship from an obligation and honor to render obeisance to our Lord "in spirit and in truth" into a cheap entertainment appealing to the senses and personal desires. More and more, man has made himself the center of attention in worship. Man's desires, man's ideas, and man's innovations have replaced reverence and obedience—yet men still have the audacity to call it "praising the Lord." However, God is not mocked.

Since the Bible's silence limits, it must limit in every case. Otherwise hypocrisy prevails and provides opportunity for those who prefer license to limits. That being said, the Bible student has the responsibility to reflect on all matters in order to determine where implication ends and silence begins—in regard to each and every doctrine and practice in which he may choose to participate. Is it no wonder, then, that many people prefer to abandon the rigors of diligent Bible study in favor of an open-ended (and man-originated) approach to pleasing God?

While the wording of Acts 20:7 and silence elsewhere limits the partaking of the Lord's Supper to the first day of the week, the wording of 1 Corinthians 11:23-29 and silence limits the conditions and situation in which Christians should partake of the Lord's Supper. This passage indicates that the Lord's Supper is to be taken where and when a congregation is assembled together and that all members of the congregation should partake in that assembly (though a specific time of day is not mentioned). To partake of the Lord's Supper in a situation different from this is simply going beyond what the New Testament says.

It is claimed by many throughout the religious world during the month of December that "Jesus is the reason for the season."

By this they mean to say that Christmas should be celebrated as a religious holiday in honor of Christ's birth. But can this belief and practice actually pass the test for genuineness required by the Scriptures? That shepherds were out at the time of His birth indicates a time other than the end of December. So if people are celebrating the birth of Christ they are doing so at the wrong time of year. But beyond this fact, one must first scrutinize the scriptures for evidence that God approves of specifically celebrating the birth of Christ in any way at any time! Since the account of His birth is in the Bible, it deserves our attention and study, but not at one time of year more than another. Also, the New Testament only gives authority for one day to be special as opposed to all others, and that is *every first day of the week when we remember Christ's death!* Now the Bible certainly provides authority for giving gifts and decorating your home. However, it nowhere indicates approval for observing any holiday in a religious manner. If we attempt to do so (by singing religious songs regarding the birth of Christ, decorating with "angels," manger scenes, etc.), then we do so on our own authority and without God's approval.

Additionally, the only way that the New Testament provides for the Lord's church to garner financial support is through the free will offering that is taken on the first day of the week (1 Cor. 16:1-2; 2 Cor. 9:6-7). Since it nowhere provides for fundraisers, garage sales, bake sales, and car washes, then the Bible's silence prohibits such activities. The same principle also applies to how the Lord's money, once collected, should be spent. The principle of biblical silence has far greater implications than many people have considered — even if they have accepted the principle in regard to one issue. Consistency demands that a Christian apply a principle that is biblical in every situation.

As in all matters of biblical authority, it seems that the closer to home the principle gets, the more likely people are to reject the principle. We end up allowing our own participation to be the standard of right and wrong rather than accepting the standard as God has revealed it. This explains why people are willing to accept the idea until it is applied to a part of worship, church-work, or life that implies the necessity of change.

One of the longest running arguments, between parents and children and preachers and parents, is the manner in which one determines the standard for modest dress. In the New Testament Paul discusses the principle (1 Tim. 2:9-10) as does Peter (1 Pet. 3:1-6), but the problem hearkens back to Adam and Eve who used fig leaves as a partial covering only to be informed by God Himself that their clothing choice was inadequate (Gen. 3:7, 21). Generally someone poses the question, "How short is too short?" But based upon the principle of silence, the actual question should be, "How long is long enough?" That is, it is not up to the preacher to prove a skirt or pair of shorts is too short or that a blouse is cut too low or that a pair of jeans is too tight. To the contrary, the individual Christian is responsible for establishing that God, without question, approves of his apparel.

By this time most people are trying to come up with some exception to the principle. What about recreation? God has stated His approval for both exercise (1 Tim. 4:8) and refreshing activities (2 Tim. 1:16); however this does not mean that such activities are not regulated. Though recreation is approved in general, it still must comply with being in the light (1 John 1:5-7) and not violate any other God-given principles (1 John 3:4). Therefore, even among those activities that God has generically authorized He also sometimes sets limits by principles stated elsewhere. Based on these principles, then, we can see that various school activities, for just one example, could fall under God's generic authorization of exercise and recreation, but the uniform may be immodest thereby violating another principle. A diligent Bible student must therefore first establish that a given behavior has God's approval and then confirm that He has set no limitations on any aspect of that activity.

The principle of biblical silence makes one matter very clear: Until you can demonstrate *from God's Word* that a given activity or behavior has God's approval, it is sinful for you. If it is not "of faith," it is sin (Rom. 14:23), and it cannot truly be of faith unless it comes from God's Word (Rom. 10:17). This also answers all of those "gray area" questions. If God has approved of it, then there is no problem. If there is no approval, then it is wrong. The "gray area" usually covers those behaviors that God does not authorize but people want to do anyway. So it is really not gray at all. In Christianity the burden of proof is not on the preacher or the elders to show you why something is wrong but upon you as a Christian to show that God approves of it (1 Th. 5:21). We have gone to treating living by faith (2 Cor. 5:7) as an option and a matter of opinion instead of as the acceptance and implementation of what God Himself has revealed. It is high time for us to change that attitude.

OLD TESTAMENT EXAMPLES OF THE PRINCIPLE OF SILENCE

Some may believe that the principle of biblical silence cited here is either some new thing, because they have not heard of it previously, or a concept with great limitations. However, it is important to note that under both Patriachal Law and Mosaical Law God operated in accordance with the principle of silence. God has employed the silence principle consistently throughout time and in every system that He has given. While the specific precepts differ between the Patriachal, Mosaical, and Christian systems, the principles establishing authority for approved action always remained the same.

After the world had degenerated morally following creation, God determined to destroy the world by flood, but Noah found grace in the eyes of the Lord as a person of righteous character. For Noah the requirements for pleasing God meant the building of what amounted to a gigantic crate (Gen. 6). God told Noah what to build. He told Him how to build it. He told him how big to make it. He told him what to use for building materials. There were many practical reasons why He did this. The ark had to hold all the animals, the feed, and Noah's family for over a year. The dimensions given were perfect to keep it from turning over. The wood had to be seaworthy. And there are probably several other reasons not quite as obvious. However, it is unlikely that Noah would have understood all of these reasons when God told him, nor was it important for him to do so. What mattered was that God told him what to do. His faith took over at that point, and he obeyed (Gen. 6:22). Noah could have used gopher wood for most of the ark but decided that oak would be nice for the door. He could have decided to add a crow's nest for a better view. But in doing so he would have violated the principle of silence; he would have gone beyond God's instructions. The ark floated and saved Noah and his family because Noah accepted God's way—not what God said plus a little bit of Noah's ideas.

Shortly after Moses had given instructions to the newly consecrated priests, Aaron and his sons, regarding what to offer as sacrifices and how to do so, two of these priests, Nadab and Abihu, chose to go beyond God's Word. "Then Nadab and Abihu, the sons of Aaron, each took his censer and put fire in it, put incense on it, and offered profane fire before the Lord, which He had not commanded them. So fire went out from the Lord and devoured them, and they died before the Lord" (Lev. 10:1–2). The fire was "profane" before the LORD because He had not commanded it. Nadab and Abihu were offering up something that the LORD had not requested. It does not say that they were not sincere. It does not say that they were offering it to idols. It does not say that God told them not to do it. What it says is that they offered something "which he commanded them not." They did not respect God's silence, and He judged them for their sin.

The New Testament instructs us regarding the nature of the church and how it is to work and worship. It teaches us how we are to conduct ourselves in life. The fact that God does not specifically condemn every nuance of sin does not mean He allows them. In Christianity, as before, God has told us what He wants. To add to it and go beyond it is sin.

CONCLUSION

After more than 200 years since the adoption of the United States Constitution in 1787, citizens of this country have forgotten, failed to study, or never considered the original purpose of this beautiful document, written in order to provide the framework for a new government in an infant country trying to correct the abuses observed under English domination. Instead of diligently considering the text of the Constitution in its context, people began reinterpreting the Constitution according to the moods and mores of contemporary society, essentially making the rule of law subject to the whim of the people. It did not happen overnight. To the contrary, it crept in by stealth, one issue at a time, gathering strength by popular opinion instead of by authoritative appeal. In order to justify such an approach, all people had to do was ignore the Tenth Amendment to the Constitution which provided the guidelines for interpreting the document's silence or alter it by further amendment (as in the Fourteenth). So we now have arguments from Supreme Court Justices that center on whether or not they are "in step" with certain societal norms instead of by their proven knowledge of and respect for the Constitution as the final arbiter of governmental action.

Unfortunately the same thing has happened to the New Testament. People as a whole have failed to study the nature of New Testament authority. Almost immediately upon its completion men came along and began restructuring doctrine and practice to fit their own designs. All they had to do was to ignore the scriptures God provided where He explained how He wanted man to interpret His silence. Now such changes have been accepted into the interpretive psyche of many as if God had altered by way of amendment what He said by way of the gospel. As changes to the Constitution did not occur overnight, neither has the violence done to the Bible happened overnight. The failure to appreciate the New Testament early in the second century led directly to the great apostasy that emphasized tradition and human authority with all its accompanying errors. In the Reformation, division was inevitable—not because of the nature of religion, but due to the failure of the reformers to respect the Bible's silence. The Restoration Movement began with a plea to go back to the Bible. Some ultimately decided the Bible was not enough for them. They left because they refused to acknowledge the principle of biblical silence. And such continues to occur.

When we undermine the silence principle (or allow it to be undermined and do nothing about it), then the floodgates are opened. Soon men's ideas, doctrines, and practices replace God's, and the original message of good news becomes perverted (Gal. 1:6-9) into the tradition of men (Matt. 15:9), losing its saving power in the process (Rom. 1:16). If we understand the importance of requiring a "Thus saith the Lord" from others to explain their religious actions (1 Pet. 4:11), then we all must make sure that we require it of ourselves before we participate in any practice, lest we be guilty of hypocrisy (Matt.

23:1-3). How we understand the Bible's silence is one of the core principles of hermeneutics—the science of interpretation. It colors our world and the glasses through which we see truth (John 17:17). A blindfolded man on a rooftop dares not take a step without instruction where and how to do so. All men are spiritually blind (John 9:39-41), and we dare not take a step without God's guidance lest we fall into the abyss (Col. 3:17; Jer. 10:23).

When applying the principle of biblical silence the Bible student must consider that:

- Any document that is intended to be authoritative, if it is of any value, includes an explanation of how its silence should be understood
- To go beyond what has Christ's stated approval is to act on our own authority
- An activity not found in the New Testament cannot be a good work
- We must verify the truth and goodness of all things before we accept and practice them
- Anything that does not fall into the category of righteousness is wrong for us to do, and the New Testament reveals all righteousness
- It is essential that the Bible student apply the principle of silence consistently
- The principle of biblical silence has far greater implications than many people have considered
- The closer to home the principle gets, the more likely people are to reject the principle
- The "gray area" usually covers those behaviors that God does not authorize but people want to do anyway—or vice versa
- The principles establishing authority for approved action always remained the same
- Nadab and Abihu did not respect God's silence, and He judged them for their sin
- How we understand the Bible's silence is a core principle of hermeneutics

Recommended Reading

Beals George. *How Implication Binds and Silence Forbids.* (Ann Arbor, MI: PC Publications, 1998).

Questions for Discussion

1. What makes the issue of biblical silence so difficult?
2. Given the various passages cited in support of biblical silence as prohibiting action, from what biblical passage would people seek to justify biblical silence as allowing behavior not specifically condemned?
3. Can you think of areas other than those cited where the principle of silence is often ignored?
4. How did Jesus treat the silence of the scriptures?
5. If biblical silence is not treated as limiting action, what effect would this have on respect for God's Word?

Assignment

Consider popular belief in regard to a topic or text of interest and then compare this with what the Bible says, applying the principle of silence.

CHAPTER 6

Biblical Expediency

INTRODUCTION

It is fashionable in some circles to treat expediency as some sort of "catch-all" category that justifies almost any activity. To many people expediency apparently means doing whatever is convenient for their own purposes. However, this is exactly why it is essential to understand biblical authority prior to any discussion of expediency. Expediency does indeed involve a determination of the most practical way to fulfill a certain purpose. But this is quite different from doing something solely for the sake of convenience. There are many things that might be convenient to a particular individual and yet not be right because they fall outside the realm of God's authority. Expediency then is a matter of choosing the best way to fulfill what God has commanded *within the limits and context of His authority.* Therefore, one must first determine whether or not an action is authorized before he can decide whether or not that action is expedient. If God does not authorize something, then it simply cannot be expedient. However, in some cases God has authorized an action generically so that there are several ways that the action can be carried out. Expediency is how one determines which way to fulfill that obligation to God.

Jesus gave the great commission to His apostles (and to all Christians by implication) shortly before ascending to heaven. "And He said to them, 'Go into all the world and preach the gospel to every creature'" (Mark 16:15). This statement provides authority for teaching the gospel to the lost, but the very nature of the word indicates that there are several ways to "go." A preacher could go personally, send either CDs or DVDs, use correspondence, engage people on social media, or work in other ways over the Internet. An individual could go on foot, by boat, on a plane, or in a car. All of these are permitted by Jesus' statement to go and preach, but the situation dictates which one is the best choice, inasmuch as it is obvious that going around the corner and going to China have different requirements. The point is to get there in the best way possible, following other biblical principles such as stewardship and redeeming the time.

Expediency is a matter of exercising judgment within the parameters of what God has authorized. God calls upon us to partake of the Lord's Supper on the first day of the week (Acts 20:7). The best *time* on the first day of the week, when the entire congregation can meet together, is a matter of expediency. God has given the elders in a local congregation the responsibility to see that the flock is fed (Acts 20:28). This might be accomplished partially through Bible Classes, gospel meetings, lectureships, the bulletin, home studies, or all of the above. The question is: What will work best to produce knowledgeable Christians? Expediency sometimes becomes confused with ease, and so produces difficulties. The easiest way to feed the flock is to rely on one sermon every week during the worship hour; however, this is not the best solution (if we are seeking true spiritual growth), and so is not expedient. Many times we have accepted traditional solutions to prior situations and have stuck with them despite the fact that they are not the best solutions. Expediency demands that we have God's authority for what we do, but it also requires us to follow the best option available to us (1 Cor. 10:23).

Unfortunately, many people who mean well judge what is "best" according to efficiency rather than by effectiveness. Efficiency measures the economy of the process; effectiveness measures the value of the result. It might be efficient to employ all monies in the area of evangelism toward mass media; however, it would not be very effective. Individual Christians talking to their friends and neighbors about their faith may not be the most efficient way to spread the good news, but it is very effective. Congregations should not judge their work according to what generates the most publicity or by what makes the work easiest. Congregations should judge their work—and the expediency of their decisions—according to how well they are fulfilling their mission. Therefore, a person who holds fifteen Bible studies per week but only converts one soul per year is not as effective as a person who holds three studies per week but converts three souls per year. The first person is certainly busier than the second, but assuming for the moment that all those involved have equal aptitude and attitude, the method the first person used would certainly not be expedient.

JESUS, MARK 2:18-22, AND EXPEDIENCY

The term "expediency" has been abused by certain people who wish to justify any and every action. I have no doubt that someone out there would argue that having the congregation gather at Cooter's Bar and Grill would be expedient if it meant that more people would attend—even if it **was** to watch the Super Bowl. On the other hand, there are also those who would deny that it is ever expedient to do anything that costs money.

For an option to be expedient it must first be authorized—given God's stated approval through direct statement, approved account of action, or implication. There can be no discussion of expediency until one first establishes proper authorization from God's Word (Col. 3:17). However, just because something is authorized does not make it expedient. It is authorized to buy expensive commercial time during the Super Bowl to advertise a gospel meeting; it is NOT expedient. Sadly, too often people rely on "instinct" and "common sense" in determining expediency rather than applying principles. Of course, a Christian must know what principles to apply. But, as in so many ways, Jesus provides the guidance needed. In Mark 2:18-22 the inspired writer records an incident that proves to be extremely helpful in establishing the principles of expediency.

An expedient action is an action that is authorized but not required. Mark writes, "The disciples of John and of the Pharisees were fasting. Then they came and said to Him, 'Why do the disciples of John and of the Pharisees fast, but Your disciples do not fast?'" (Mark 2:18). Jesus did not argue that fasting was wrong. In fact, His later comments demonstrate that He accepted the practice as authorized. However, at the same time, He argued *against* His disciples doing it. Fasting was an authorized activity, but it was not required activity. The disciples of John and the Pharisees were attempting to require something that God did not require. Some people who are seeking financial support can try to "guilt" people into supporting their work, acting as if the people are sinning if they do not. There are many different works congregations can choose to support, or they could choose to put all the money at work locally. To require some specifics beyond the God-given activities of evangelism, edification, and benevolence is to fail to understand expediency.

An expedient action is appropriate to the circumstances. Jesus' response to the question of fasting draws out yet another important principle. "And Jesus said to them, 'Can the friends of the bridegroom fast while the bridegroom is with them? As long as they have the bridegroom with them they cannot fast. But the days will come when the bridegroom will be taken away from them, and then they will fast in those days'" (Mark 2:19–20). Fasting implied sadness on some level. Therefore, Jesus illustrated by referring to a wedding that there are times when fasting is inappropriate because it does not fit the circumstances. Since Jesus was present upon the earth, it was a joyous time rather than a solemn occasion; therefore, fasting would be inappropriate. Before one can label an action or behavior as expedient, he must first demonstrate that the activity is appropriate to the circumstances. Since the command to "go" (Mark 16:15) generically authorizes various means of travel, one must determine what type is appropriate to the particular circumstances at hand. Flying on a jet is certainly authorized, but it is an inexpedient way of going to talk to your next-door neighbor about the gospel! Therefore, for something to be expedient it must be the most appropriate manner in which to address the situation.

To Be Expedient an Action Must Give the Right Impression to Others. We return to the question of fasting raised by the disciples of John and the Pharisees: "And Jesus said to them, 'Can the friends of the bridegroom fast while the bridegroom is with them? As long as they have the bridegroom with them they cannot fast. But the days will come when the bridegroom will be taken away from them, and then they will fast in those days'" (Mark 2:19–20). To the prior principle regarding the necessity of appropriateness, a Bible student must add the desire to give the right impression. It would be inappropriate for Jesus' disciples to fast while He was with them because it would give the wrong impression to people. Unfortunately, today many people seem more concerned about pushing the envelope and fitting in than they are about giving the correct impression to people. Could a song leader bring in a piano in order to serve as the means to determine the correct pitch for a song, as a sort of huge pitchpipe? If he used it only for that purpose, it would be authorized. But that does not make it expedient because it would leave the wrong impression with people — especially visitors — implying that *a capella* singing is a matter of preference rather than doctrine. A current trend in some places is to adopt the posture of raising the hands during worship. There is no question that the raising of hands in worship is authorized. This was a well-known posture for prayer during the first century that was accepted (1 Tim. 2:8). However, during the first century, the raising of hands during worship did not carry the same connotations as it does today. In the first century and before it was simply a posture of reverence; today it carries charismatic connotations. Therefore, raising the hands during worship is inexpedient behavior today because it implies a charismatic belief system built around emotionalism rather than God's Word (Rom. 10:1-2). Paul taught that if an action gave an impression that would cause others to stumble, even though the action itself was authorized, it should be avoided if other authorized possibilities exist (Rom. 14:13). Sadly, many who advocate such a prayer posture today know full well its connotations and implications and recommend it in order to blur the distinctions between charismatic evangelicalism and the Lord's church.

    To Be Expedient an Action Must Fulfill Its Intended Purpose. A few years ago some began misinterpreting Mark 2:22 trying to justify unscriptural adaptations to culture. They missed the fundamental point that Jesus was referring to questions of expediency rather than authority, using the matter of fasting as the vehicle. He said, "No one sews a piece of unshrunk cloth on an old garment; or else the new piece pulls away from the old, and the tear is made worse. And no one puts new wine into old wineskins; or else the new wine bursts the wineskins, the wine is spilled, and the wineskins are ruined. But new wine must be put into new wineskins" (Mark 2:21–22). In a further development on the theme of appropriateness, Jesus used two illustrations to show that fasting, which was a withdrawal from other activity in order to mourn or give attention to spiritual concerns, was inappropriate for His disciples since it would take them away from their learning from Him. The disciples of John and the Pharisees had allowed the external manifestation to dominate rather than its purpose. If the purpose of a particular program is to reach the lost but you have had no Bible studies in a two-year period, the program is likely inexpedient. Congregations often enjoy the illusion of activity while actually spending time on entrenched activities for which the members themselves cannot recall the original purpose. Also, some have argued that a freer translation makes the Bible easier to understand for them, but if it communicates the wrong message in an easy way, it does not promote a better understanding of the Bible at all! While some make these choices out of ignorance, others actively promote translations that make Bible reading easier while making Bible study harder. If the purpose is to understand God's message (as it should be), then it must begin with as accurate a translation of God's message as is possible that can also be read with a measure of understanding (otherwise we would have to force people to learn Hebrew, Aramaic, and Greek, which would make the translation question irrelevant).

Questions of expediency do not receive the attention they deserve. People have been taught that authority is the Bible's arena while expediency is the elders' arena, without realizing that elders have the responsibility to see that the Bible is taught accurately and followed exactly and that the Bible provides guidance in matters of expediency as well as in matters of authority. More elders need to ask themselves, "Why are we doing this?" and "Is there a better way?" instead of mindlessly continuing in the pattern of the past without any evaluation of the quality of that pattern. Liberal change agents should not be given a free pass to call everything they do "matters of expediency" without first proving that it is authorized (1 Th. 5:21) and then demonstrating that it is also expedient. However, in some places traditionalism has replaced submission for many who would be equally upset by a change in the time of worship as they would over the use of mechanical instruments of music. Without a correct understanding of expediency, Christians lose all perspective in regard to addressing matters according to principle. **People who cannot apply principles cannot practice true Christianity**.

A PERTINENT QUESTION

One of the current trends in this country and in the church is an attitude of permissiveness that seems to be the guiding light for most individuals. All one must do anymore is question something and the one involved will pipe back, "What's wrong with it?" Even if a person attempts to explain the various things wrong with such things as social drinking, smoking, dancing, immodesty, or any number of similar issues, the one to whom all of this is addressed will respond, "Well, I don't see anything wrong with it!" The same could be said regarding many of the religious practices of the various denominations — as well as the reasons given trying to justify their division. Herein lies the essence of the problem in understanding, appreciating, and abiding by God's authority. The problem is a difficult one, cutting deep into the fabric of even those who have a reputation for being "conservative." People have begun to think only in terms of not doing what is wrong instead of doing what is right. The only true standard of right and wrong is the word of God (John 17:17), but often individuals only look at it to find out what is wrong instead of asking themselves whether or not it is right. These have failed to appeal to God's authority, failed to observe God's silence, and bypassed these two in order to consider "expediency" without any regard for the necessity of respecting God's limits.

For one reason or another, some have limited their "need" for divine authority only to those realms where they do not mind submitting to it. But this is not submission at all (Jas. 4:8)! If Christians continue to attempt to limit God's role in their decisions — whether they pertain to the church, worship, or life in general — they have rejected Jesus Christ as Lord and placed themselves in that all-important role. Jesus said, "But why do you call Me 'Lord, Lord,' and not do the things which I say?" (Luke 6:46). Some, however, believe that as long as they technically *do* what Jesus says, the motivation or reason does not matter (baptism, for one example) and that this does not prevent a person from doing *more* than Jesus said (like Nadab and Abihu). But John stated a principle for divine authority when he wrote, "For I testify to everyone who hears the words of the prophecy of this book: If anyone adds to these things, God will add to him the plagues that are written in this book; and if anyone takes away from the words of the book of this prophecy, God shall take away his part from the Book of Life, from the holy city, and from the things which are written in this book" (Rev 22:18–19).

Many controversies, whether between teenager and parent, member and member, friend and friend, or Christian and God could be resolved quite easily if all involved would but follow the prescription given in the Bible. It is time that Christians considered their actions from God's viewpoint. It is not enough to stand against blatant sin if we are ambivalent toward righteousness. It is not enough for a preacher to denounce error boldly in principle from the pulpit if he says nothing against it when it is introduced in practice. Christians must diligently prepare themselves mentally according to God's direction or they will not be prepared spiritually when confronted with temptation. If people are not prepared spiritually, they will most definitely compromise morally, because compromise does not begin with deliberate action to defy God so often as it does by being ill prepared to live for Him daily (Rom. 12:2).

Many have suggested lists of questions similar to the one below, so I make no claim to originality in the approach. Some people carry such a list of questions around with them on a daily basis. However, this is far from a long-term solution. What each person must do is incorporate these questions and the underlying principles into his decision making process so that the underlying assumptions that people often use to justify their sins do not cloud his own judgment. Therefore, before taking an action, a person should ask himself:

§ **Is it wrong?** Sin is a transgression of the law in any form (1 John 3:4). Remember, an activity can be condemned generally in principle just as easily as specifically in name.

§ **Is it right?** Christ must authorize anything that we do in some way (Col. 3:17). Someone may have a great idea of how to raise money to send an evangelist to Outer Mongolia, but that does not mean that it is authorized.

§ **Does it set a good example?** Christians are to let their lights shine before men (Matt. 5:14-16). How is this possible when they involve themselves in even questionable activities?

§ **Would it lead others to Christ?** Paul believed in bringing others to Christ through his example (1 Cor. 11:1). Can Christians keep participating in every school organization and live as Paul did?

§ **Would it be a stumblingblock to other Christians?** If Christians are involved in an activity that is approved by God but that might cause others to fall, they should give it up for the sake of that person's soul (Rom. 14:13).

§ **Would it be seeking the kingdom first (Matt. 6:33)?** This is a question of priorities. Do Christians really put the kingdom first in planning their activities, while taking vacations, and while planning for the holidays? Do Christians schedule around God or do they expect Him to schedule around them?

§ **Would God be pleased if He saw you?** It is a shame that people do not realize that they have no secrets from God. Everything is known to Him and is "written down" (Rev. 20:12).

§ **Would it violate your conscience?** While the conscience is not a proper standard by itself, it is wrong to do something when you are not sure of it being right (Rom. 14:23). This would keep people from so many difficulties.

§ **How would the world see it (1 Th. 5:22)?** It is just as improper to give the wrong impression as it is to sin outright. Even though the world is confused about many things, Christians are to act in such a way that there is no doubt of their stand for God (2 Pet. 3:14).

§ **Would Christ have done it?** The popular phrase "What would Jesus do?" has good meaning but is often interpreted according to situation ethics rather than biblical truth. A person should consider "Did Jesus do it or approve of it?" (1 Pet. 2:21). It is wrong to justify an activity. Christians should be honest about what Christ would do by studying what Christ did.

These are ten simple questions that should help in making decisions. There are plenty who will want to continue dancing, drinking, using tobacco, smoking, gambling, wearing immodest clothing, worshiping their own way instead of God's way, involving the church in unauthorized activities, and more. But each time they act, they should be asked a very simple question, as all people should ask themselves before participating: *"What's right with it?"*

THE BEST COURSE OF ACTION

People have become so selfish in both attitude and action that they have drastically overhauled their standards—and not for the better. While religious people formerly (though erroneously) considered themselves above such, today's religious pluralism has led the charge. Defining deviancy down is no longer just a sociological term but now also a regular practice among even religious people. Instead of striving for the heights of Christian liberty (Phil. 3:13-14) people are quickly accepting more and more immorality. Declining doctrinal standards and declining moral standards have mutually assisted one another into society's descent. Those who have rejected God's morality for society's mores boast about their tolerance. But many who grieve over society's decadence fail to see their own contribution to it in their rejection of biblical authority. Yet those who still stand strong in proclaiming the virtues of following biblical authority often treat biblical expediency like a spiritual buffet. The lifestyles of these people may vary greatly, depending upon how far behind God's Word their own thinking has fallen, but there is a common bond between them all. In each case people have taken the easiest road available that suited their conscience (Jdg. 21:25).

Sadly, many people ignore the principles of expediency in order to test the limits of authority. Too many people are unwilling to recognize these signs of spiritual decline because they are accepting a "lowest common denominator" approach to Christianity. As a result, a growing number will oppose only what is "blatantly wrong" while others will oppose what is "inherently wrong." Hopefully there are still Christians who also oppose the failure to do what is right. But when are we going to start opposing the failure to do what is best? Some people "settle" in their choice of mate. Some people "settle" in their choice of occupation. But saddest of all are the people who "settle" for less than their best when it comes to Christianity. Expediency does not consist of taking the easiest authorized option but rather the *best* authorized option. This difference distinguishes expediency from convenience quite easily. The easiest way to confront a person in sin is through written correspondence. The best way is through a face-to-face meeting. Both are authorized, but the most personal method possible is the expedient option. However, as in so many things, even people who claim to honor biblical authority often seek convenience rather than excellence in its implementation.

PUSHING THE LIMITS OF EXPEDIENCY

Expediency has received very little attention throughout the years. After all, few Christians even know what expediency means. One might even argue that since expediency is the realm of judgment it would be ridiculous for anyone to concentrate on it. So is a study of expediency justified? The answer surely is a resounding "Yes." Dangerous attitudes and trends appear first in areas of expediency where the level of objection cannot center on "authorization." But biblical expediency is not about doing what you could try or get by with but rather it is about doing what is best for the Lord, His church, and His cause.

Expediency addresses many issues pertaining to the current climate of change in the brotherhood. Some seem intent on making every change possible while others resist change even when the change is both authorized and expedient. This reveals just how far away from the standard of Gods' Word we have drifted: one side does not care if the Bible says something is wrong, and the other side does not care if the Bible says it is right. The answer to both problems is to return the Bible to the center of every discussion.

Years ago "progressive" Christians attempted to hide their agenda under the cloak of expediency. Congregations conformed to the expectations or desires of the world because most of the suggestions made were indeed authorized generically. Larry Fluitt illustrated this behavior in his article, "We're Going to Build a Baptistry!," in which the dimensions described resembled those of a swimming pool. Does the Bible contain prescribed dimensions for a baptistry? Of course not. Could a multi-function building provide additional classroom space? Absolutely. Are they authorized? Yes. But why do people want them? Do they want a large baptistry because of their tremendous interest and success in evangelism or because they would enjoy swimming? Did the idea for a multi-function building stem from spiritual or recreational concerns?

If something is not required, then a Christian should provide *biblical* and *spiritual* reasoning as to why it should be considered. Hint: "The kids will love it" does not constitute biblical or spiritual reasoning. Yes, most of these people balk at "the very idea" of having to explain their motives and reasoning, usually because neither their motives nor their reasoning is very good. Could a congregation hold Bible Classes in various homes instead of at the building? Yes, but why would you want to? Is the instruction better when you are away from the building? Or is it more difficult for elders to oversee and easier to insert personal beliefs in a home atmosphere? Would it make evangelism easier by inviting people into the comfort of a home rather than to a strange building? Perhaps. Is it authorized? Yes. Is it expedient? No way. We can agree that meeting in smaller groups may be a good way to get to know people and even an excellent way to invite non-Christians into our home for a Bible study. But why could we not do these things *in addition to* meeting to worship and edify one another? A practice built on the assumption that we must subtract one type of meeting in order to have another cannot be called expedient because it appeals to convenience rather than spiritual conviction. Do we have authority to hold our hands above our heads in worship? Yes (1 Tim. 2:8). But why would people choose this option among all those available when doing so immediately identifies them with the charismatic and community church movements? Or might that be the motive? Could we anoint people with oil? For what purpose? Anointing with oil at one time had a cultural signification of choosing leadership but was not instituted for the church. Therefore, anointing your leaders only identifies you with an ancient culture and perhaps with some fake healers. Is it expedient? Hardly. Of course, if you have bronchitis and want the elders to come to your house, pray for you, and smear Mentholatum on your upper lip, then be my guest (Jas. 5:14). But somehow that part of anointing does not seem expedient to people.

If a songbook is authorized, so is using an overhead projector or a computer projection of a song. However, if the music is not included on the projection, then the songbook is more expedient. Also, one should consider which is easier to read by people with poor eyesight. Elders certainly have the authority, as a matter of expediency, to cancel the Sunday evening worship due to inclement weather and a concern for people's safety. However, calling off the Sunday evening worship in order to watch the Super Bowl can never be called expedient because doing so has no **spiritual** justification.

Some congregations, in order to combat a growing problem with "inadequate" singing, placed microphones throughout the auditorium in order to amplify the singing. These microphones soon found their way into the hands of the best singers in the congregation, some of which were women. These best singers are now being placed in front of the congregation on the stage. What was the original problem? People in the congregation were not singing out. So what has this "solution" done? Are more people singing out or is there now less a need for them to do so? The problem—congregational singing—was not really addressed at all. Instead, it is in the process of being gradually replaced. None of these stages contributed to better congregational singing; therefore, they did not fulfill a spiritual purpose and are inexpedient.

Singing is certainly authorized and required, as are particular types of songs (Eph. 5:19). However, the exact choice of songs is, to a degree, a matter of expediency. Any song that teaches error is not just inexpedient; it is unauthorized. But some songs are authorized, but may be inexpedient. Songs about the resurrection are authorized, but singing them on Easter is inexpedient because it would give people the impression that we celebrated Easter as a religious holiday. Singing songs about the birth of Christ around Christmas time is inexpedient for the same reason. Song leaders must also determine whether or not the congregation knows a song adequately. Worship on Sunday morning is an inexpedient time to teach a new song because it detracts from the spiritual purpose of the gathering. It would likewise be inexpedient to lead a song with an alto lead if the congregation's altos are out of town. Many songs we sing may not teach error explicitly but have strong shades of false teaching. If there is no question that all the people singing the song will understand it in a biblical context, the song may be expedient. But if anyone singing would understand the song improperly due to questionable lyrics, then singing the song is inexpedient. On a final note, songs sung in youth gatherings fall under the same rules of expediency as any others. Names other than "the church of Christ" are authorized; however, those in the church who are changing their name are not doing so for spiritual reasons but in order to distance themselves from certain defining doctrinal positions. Expedient? I don't think so!

Christians drifting along in the murky sea of inexpediency generally end up in the ocean of error. Why? Because their efforts from the beginning have centered on conforming to the world and appealing to the flesh. They learned to push the limits of expediency and then keep on pushing the bounds of authority. This makes them fairly predictable, which is why so many were able to proclaim with confidence years ago where all of this was heading. Many congregations did not listen then and are suffering the consequences now. Hopefully, people will start listening now and avoid suffering later.

CONCLUSION

Biblical authority and biblical expediency remain hotly contested issues despite the fact that the New Testament clearly outlines the principles God expects Bible students to follow. The most obvious reason for this is that people already have decided, through one means or another, what they like and then adopt principles of interpretation that will allow them to continue doing what they like. It is admittedly difficult to change one's whole approach to understanding the Bible (if this is what becomes necessary), but whether it might seem a burden to do so or not does not make such a change optional.

The New Testament is made up of many interrelated principles that serve as a skeleton of individual conduct. Certain principles, such as worshiping God (John 4:24), have specific actions already sketched out with great precision. For this reason, no one argues about whether or not God should be worshipped, but instead the disagreement lies in the specifics and whether or not those specifics are binding (and they are). Other principles, such as doing good (Gal. 6:10), are so broad that only a good understanding of the examples provided and other related principles makes it possible to define the limitations of this principle. Yet all actions, when correctly interpreted, will be consistent with God's character because God's character is the basis for His will (1 Pet. 1:16).

A growing element of religious people has rejected biblical authority as an entire concept, preferring instead to rely on emotional fervor as the gauge to measure divine approval. Yet this opposes very explicit statements in the Bible. It is possible to be sincere and yet be wrong (Acts 23:1); therefore, sincerity cannot be the standard. It is possible to be zealous and emotional yet be far from God (Rom. 10:2); therefore, zeal and emotion cannot be the standard for pleasing God. It is possible to have *an* understanding of the Scriptures and yet be *wrong* in that understanding of the Scriptures (Matt. 22:29). Somewhere along the way, we have grown so lax that "religiosity" or "spiritualism" has become an acceptable replacement for Christianity "by the book." Religious pluralism, the runaway child of denominationalism, has convinced society as a whole that truth is discovered subjectively and within instead of by studying the objective truth of God's Word (John 8:32; 12:48; 17:17). This provides evidence of secular humanism's success in our society. But it is important to note that as secular humanism has led to man-centered religion, so too it has compelled the adherents of such man-centered religion to rely on human authority for that religion. The question about the baptism of John is therefore also pertinent in principle for today's questions. Before we act, we must first ask whether the authority for taking the action is derived from heaven or from men.

An appreciation of biblical authority is essential for correct interpretation. Your understanding of authority colors how you view the context. Your comprehension of the context determines how you see doctrine. And your perception of doctrine affects the direction of your actions. Any actions, then, taken without Jesus' approval amount to a rejection of Jesus Himself (John 12:48). Acting out of "convenience" is not expedient; it is rebellion. Such is the nature of authority, and such is the consequence of not submitting to God's authority.

Biblical Expediency:

- Expediency is not a matter of doing what is convenient
- Expediency determines the most practical way to fulfill a spiritual obligation
- Expediency only considers possibilities within the range of authorized activities
- Expediency means choosing the best option available
- Expediency should be judged according to effectiveness — not efficiency
- An expedient action is authorized but not required
- An expedient action is appropriate to the circumstances
- An expedient action gives the right impression to others
- An expedient action fulfills its intended purpose
- Expediency does not ask "What's wrong with it?" but "What's right with it?" followed by "What is the best way to do what is right?"

Questions for Discussion

1. What guards the Bible student against confusing expediency with convenience?
2. Is it possible to emphasize practicality to the exclusion of spirituality?
3. Why would we ever choose a poor option rather than the best option?
4. Discuss the four principles of expediency Jesus applied to fasting and how they apply today.
5. What is the biggest difference between asking "What's wrong with it?" and "What's right with it?"

Assignment

Choosing an action related to a topic or text of interest, consider the various options possible scripturally, then apply the principles of expediency and supply argumentation regarding what the best course of action should be.

CHAPTER 8

General Context

INTRODUCTION

Context is one of those terms that everyone throws around but few actually understand or appreciate. Derived from Latin, this compound word means "with the text." It is never enough therefore to say, "It means what it says." This is only the text, the words. Every text has its own history and its own particular place in the larger scheme of the writing. To ignore these, as many are prone to do, is to turn a blind eye to essential information. The result is that people believe they understand a passage of scripture when all they really understand are the words. They often assume incorrectly that because the same word is used in two different places that it must refer to the same doctrine or concept.

Far too many try to interpret the Bible as if it had been written today directly to them. They then try to twist every piece of information in such a fashion as to make it apply directly instead of accepting the reality that the Bible was written years ago by individuals to particular people who had particular problems. The message, though thousands of years old now, most definitely still applies. But understanding *how* it applies depends upon our willingness to study more than just the words, though understanding them correctly is essential. We must study what goes *with* the words — the context.

Context is what bridges the gap of understanding between the original recipients and today's Bible student. The better the Bible student understands what the original recipients understood the more likely he is to understand the Bible correctly. But context requires more than just a consideration of historical consistency; it also demands an examination of literary and doctrinal consistency. The key word is "consistency." **Context is the major principle of interpretation whereby a person's understanding of a given passage is shown to be consistent with truth.**

The greatest problem for most students of the Bible is learning to discipline themselves in such a way that **all** contextual considerations override previous conclusions or doctrinal predispositions. Failing to consider just one aspect of context can be doctrinally fatal. It is an easy thing to look into the Bible and see what we wish to see. It is quite another to look into God's Word and see what God wants us to see. But this latter quest is what Bible study is all about. It takes little effort to come up with an explanation about a given passage. Just look at the many different religions today! Remember: the devil can interpret scripture too, but this does not make his interpretation valid (Matt. 4:5-7). The validity of our interpretation depends upon its being consistent with *all* of the evidence that context makes available. We must settle for nothing less than truth. "Sanctify them by Your truth. Your word is truth" (John 17:17).

BIBLICAL CONTEXT

When a person wishes to understand the context of a passage in a book, he must first understand the framework of the book itself. One could not provide a very good idea of the plot of *War and Peace* by simply opening it up randomly and reading a few lines. Yet this is the approach people sometimes take in interpreting the Bible. Martin Luther famously struggled with the inconsistencies of Catholicism then one day opened to Romans 1:17, "For in it the righteousness of God is revealed from faith to faith; as it is written, 'The just shall live by faith.'" He determined that this was the key to the interpretation of every other passage, which later caused him to call the book of James an "epistle of straw." Luther made the mistake of interpreting Romans 1:17 **before** considering the book of James. He forgot the importance of biblical context.

Mormons interpret the two sticks in the text of Ezekiel 37:15-20 as the Bible and the book of Mormon, maintaining that God wanted them joined together as one book. But even a general perusal of the Bible contradicts this claim. The faith was provided once for all (Jude 3), and any message different from the gospel Paul preached was to be disregarded even if supposedly given by an angel from heaven (Gal. 1:6-9). Furthermore, the Mormon interpretation does not fit the figures of the text when one considers how God employed those names in other texts. A student of the Bible must consider **all** of these factors **before** drawing any conclusions. The immediate context contradicts their claim as well (Eze. 37:21-22). However, consider for a moment what this interpretation would do to the framework of the Bible. It would make the entire book almost totally irrelevant! If one accepts the book of Mormon, he must reject the work of the apostles. Jesus promised that the Spirit would guide them into **all** truth (John 16:13). If there was another testament yet to come, either the Spirit failed in His work or Jesus was wrong. Both conclusions impugn the character of God. In the Mormons' efforts to support their *own* testament, they ignore biblical context.

Certainly these two particular examples are not the only ones available, nor is abuse of biblical context limited to these particular religious entities. They serve as examples and warnings to all people seeking truth. One cannot study one verse, one chapter, or one book of the Bible without considering the rest. Doing so produces doctrines contrary to the will of God because they do not stem from and are not consistent with the *whole* of the Word of God.

Biblical context also should consider the nature and purpose of the book in question. The Bible does not claim to be a science textbook. Its purpose is to inform man of his spiritual condition and of the solution available to him through Jesus Christ. But this does NOT mean that the Bible is scientifically inaccurate. To the contrary, the Bible demonstrates scientific foreknowledge through its references and by its avoidance of the erroneous science of the times during which it was penned. It is not necessary for God to name each *species* created. He described the various *kinds* and included scientifically accurate information—like begets like, a pretty basic genetic law. Scientists claim the Bible is inaccurate when it speaks of the sun rising and setting. But this is an attempt to evaluate the Bible as a science textbook instead of a spiritual book containing some scientific information. I dare say that evolutionists have no problem talking about watching a beautiful sunset! Their attacks against the Bible are an attempt to impose a different context upon it than the one it projects for itself.

Biblical context is simple and difficult at the same time. It does not require a correct understanding of the most difficult passages but only a familiarity with the basic structure, purpose, direction, and aim of the whole. However, without question a correct understanding of the whole depends upon a correct understanding of the parts. One may understand the purpose of the Bible as a presentation of the Scheme of Redemption, but this does not mean that one's understanding of the Scheme of Redemption is correct. Therefore, a Bible student should continually "move in and out and back and forth" between the whole and the component parts, constantly checking to make sure they are consistent with one another. Does the conclusion drawn from this passage of scripture fit into the overall plan of the Bible? How? Does one's current understanding of the overall picture mesh with what this passage of scripture is saying?

Today it is often considered old-fashioned when teaching or preaching from one passage of scripture to refer to another, what is commonly called a proof-text. It is certainly true that if the Bible says something once it is authoritative whether it is repeated or not. That is not the question. But providing a text outside of the immediate context helps to demonstrate to others (and ourselves) that our interpretation is consistent with overall biblical context (an important consideration for those references as well!) God is not the author of confusion (1 Cor. 14:33). The Bible, though penned by many, is authored by One. When we study it, we should treat it that way.

COVENANT CONTEXT

Most people recognize the division between the Old and New Testaments. Usually the publishers make it pretty clear. However, the distinction between covenants is not just a consideration for the printer. It is essential for a Bible student to understand that God has used more than one covenant with people over the ages and that it is improper to apply arbitrarily the words of one covenant to a people who did not or do not live under that covenant.

When God told Adam and Eve they could eat of the trees of the garden but not to eat of the tree of knowledge of good and evil (Gen. 2:16-17), He was making a covenant with them. In the beginning God spoke to the head of the family, the patriarch, in order to provide direction. He told Noah to build an ark (Gen. 6:14ff). He told Abram to leave his homeland (Gen. 12:1-3). He promised Abram a son (Gen. 15:5). The book of Genesis details various aspects of the Patriarchal Covenant, as does the book of Job. They were responsible to God according to what He revealed to them but not for what would come later.

When Moses led the Israelites out of Egypt, they were living under Patriarchal Law. It was only when the LORD gave the Law to Moses (Ex. 20:1ff) that the Israelites had a written covenant with Jehovah. The LORD gave this covenant to the Israelites—and only to the Israelites. Therefore, other peoples continued to live under Patriarchal Law. They would each be judged by what God had revealed to them (Rom. 2:12). The Gentiles were not held to the Mosaical Law because it had not been given to them. The Jews were not held to the Patriarchal standard because they had been given a better covenant with higher standards. The Gentiles did not have access to all of the same information that the Jews did, but whatever they had access to, God held them responsible for it. Sometimes people can be overly harsh in their criticism of those living under the Patriarchal system (Gen. 38), forgetting that they did not understand all that we do or should today.

Even the Israelites lived in a time when God was still revealing Himself gradually to mankind. They did not receive the Old Testament in one volume but in stages. And even when this entire covenant had been completely recorded it was imperfect. It was perfect for its purpose but not the full answer that man needed. Both Patriarchal and Mosaical systems required sacrifices for sins committed, but neither provided an answer for sin itself. Therefore, since neither covenant was given to us, it is inappropriate to appeal to them to justify an action today. And since they lack the complete answer for sin, why would we want to?

God's communications with mankind began as a one-on-one matter between God and the patriarch, who then had the responsibility of passing on this information to his family. Each family had a different patriarch; therefore, each received individual communication based upon the same principles but addressing their particular situation.

This communication was not constant, and the information imparted was incomplete—not because God did not know what He wanted but because man needed gradual revelation in order to understand God.

When the descendants of Jacob suffered affliction in Egypt, God chose to alter the manner of His communication. Instead of communicating to the head of each family, God chose one man to be His spokesman—Moses. Originally he gave them instructions from God that provided for their deliverance from bondage. Then, after escaping Pharaoh and crossing the Red Sea, they camped at the base of Mount Sinai where God called Moses up to receive the Law on behalf of the people. This Law was for all of Israel, instituted by God for an entire group of people. This was not a law of individual communication but a written code of conduct for all of Israel. God gave this Law to further reveal His character to mankind and to provide more exact knowledge in regard to sin and righteousness, a specific code known to be from God that was precise in its denouncement of sin and its call for moral behavior, including religious service and worship. God continued to use prophets from time to time to reveal Himself through His dealings with mankind (Heb. 1:1), but the Law of Moses always was the context for His interaction with the Jews—during the period of the Judges, the Kings, and the Captivity—and the Patriarchal Law remained the context for His interaction with the Gentile nations, as some of the prophets also record (Jonah, Nahum, etc.). However, each of these laws was incomplete. They provided some knowledge of God, some knowledge of sin, some knowledge of morality, some knowledge of worship, and some knowledge of God's plan, but neither provided all truth or the complete answer for the problem of sin (Rom. 1:18-3:23). The Patriarchal Law and the Mosaical Law forced man to admit that there was a problem, but the solution remained an enigma. Some people today want to live by the Old Covenant, but James warned about trying to do this (Jas. 2:10). "For the law was given through Moses, but grace and truth came through Jesus Christ" (John 1:17).

Jesus came to earth as a Jewish man (John 1:14), living under the Old Law (Gal. 4:1-6). By keeping it perfectly, including the prophecies about Him found therein, He fulfilled its purpose (Matt. 5:17), because through His sacrificial death on the cross He provided the answer for sin (Rom. 3:24-26) and ascending to heaven He could send the Holy

Spirit to provide the revelation of all truth (John 16:13), the good news for all mankind. For centuries man had struggled with only gradual access to God's plan. With the coming of Christ, God, in the person of Christ (John 1:18), revealed His character in its fullness (Heb. 1:1-4; Col. 2:9); however, this necessitated a change in covenant (Heb. 7).

As previously promised (Heb. 8:6-13), through the blood of Christ God established a new covenant—not with an individual family or with one ethnic group, but with all mankind. Therefore, the older, inferior covenants were nailed to the cross (Col. 2:14) because they treated men differently and had become a dividing wall (Eph. 2:14-16). The New Covenant is universal and unifying (Acts 10:34-35; Eph. 4:1-6). Unfortunately, many people today make the mistake of reading the Old Testament, whether it refers to Patriarchal or Mosaical Law, as if it is binding on us today. Some claim that we must keep the Sabbath. But this was only for those living under the Old Covenant given at Sinai. Others wish to justify some current practice by appealing to a Law-Covenant that is not in force and that provided only incomplete information. That is not to say that it has nothing to offer. The Old Testament's information was vital in leading mankind to the establishment of the New (Gal. 3:24-25). Its prophecies continue to provide a valuable resource by which the authenticity of Jesus as the Messiah can be demonstrated. Through these things our hope is strengthened (Rom. 15:4), and through the examples provided on its pages we can learn from the mistakes of those who have gone before us (1 Cor. 10:11). However, we should *not* turn back to these things for our spiritual authority.

Paul compared the need for the Jews to let go of the Old Law as religious authority to how a widow must let go of her dead spouse (Rom. 7:1-6). When we appeal to the Old Covenant for religious authority, we have forgotten that we are bound to the New Covenant. Granted, there are some similarities between the covenants. We should expect this since God gave them. However, if a principle is repeated in the New Covenant that was found in the Old, it is binding today only because it is taught in the New. Let us therefore use the Old Covenant in our studies but not abuse it (2 Tim. 2:15).

Most people do not have a problem understanding the distinction between the Patriarchal and Mosaical Covenants and the

New Covenant when presented in theory. However, when it comes to some particular teaching or practice, it seems that this understanding falters when confronting old assumptions. Context and consistency demand that we abide by the same principle regardless of how it might affect a particular belief or practice.

Some have taught that it is sinful for a couple to choose *not* to have children. After all, when God created man and woman he told them "Be fruitful, and multiply" (Gen. 1:28). Following the flood the LORD gave Noah a similar command, "Be fruitful, and multiply, and fill the earth" (Gen. 9:1), but then he added, "And as for you, be fruitful and multiply; Bring forth abundantly in the earth And multiply in it" (Gen. 9:7). In each of these instances the command was given under particular circumstances to particular people who lived under the Patriarchal Covenant. This becomes clearer when we look at one more similar reference. God gave Jacob the name of Israel and then said, "'I am God Almighty. Be fruitful and multiply; a nation and a company of nations shall proceed from you, and kings shall come from your body" (Gen. 35:11). God had a particular purpose in mind that required propagation in all of these cases. In the first two instances there were few human beings alive at the time. A command was important to ensure the growth of humankind. In the situation with Jacob God had a particular purpose in creating a nation from which the Messiah would come. Neither of these situations exists today. More important, all of these commands were given under Patriarchal Law and therefore do not apply to us anyway. Some then appeal to a New Testament reference: "Nevertheless she will be saved in childbearing if they continue in faith, love, and holiness, with self-control" (1 Tim. 2:15). While they have appealed to the correct covenant for a reference, these have missed the immediate context of this verse: Though women were not to take the lead spiritually (1 Tim. 2:11-14), God still gave women an important role they should value (1 Tim. 2:15).

If we are to accept one aspect of the Old Covenant, we must accept them all (Jas. 2:10). Yet few make arguments in favor of sacrificing bulls and rams or temple worship. What they have unwittingly done is treat the New Covenant as an amendment to the Old instead of a totally New Covenant that stands alone. While the Old Covenant provides a necessary context for *understanding* the New

Covenant, it does not carry any *authoritative* weight today. We must first find authority for an action in the New Covenant; then, and only then, should we look to the Old Covenant to possibly illustrate the principle.

Since Christians live under a new and different covenant than the Jews of old, we should not only accept but also expect that the worship God desires and ordains will also differ. Under the Old Covenant, participation in worship was more limited due to the priesthood. Under the Old Covenant God commanded some worship in a particular place—the temple. Under the Old Covenant the Jews kept certain feasts yearly. Under the Old Covenant priests who came from Aaron's lineage offered animal sacrifices. All of these things changed with the advent of the New Covenant. So although God still desires worship today, the manner and means by which He accepts it has changed (Heb. 13:15).

The Psalmist wrote: "Give unto the Lord the glory due to His name; Worship the Lord in the beauty of holiness" (Psa. 29:2). As the context of the two similar verses indicates (1 Chr. 16:29; Psa. 96:8-9), worshiping the LORD in the beauty of holiness was a statement of the character of worship (or more specifically the worshipper) but not a generic command authorizing anything offered, as other Old Testament passages remind us (Lev. 10:1-2, etc.). In regard to worship under the New Covenant, Jesus told the Samaritan woman that "the hour is coming, and now is, when the true worshipers will worship the Father in spirit and truth; for the Father is seeking such to worship Him. God is Spirit, and those who worship Him must worship in spirit and truth" (John 4:23-24). Similarly to how the Psalmist spoke regarding the character of worship under the Old Covenant, Jesus spoke here in regard to the New. Therefore, not every action offered to God as worship is acceptable. It must fit the specified character of being "in spirit and truth." Worship must include the right heart in combination with the right action. But remember: the right action is determined not by anything in the Old Covenant but only by what is in the New.

Acceptable worship, by the very nature of the word Jesus chose (*proskuneo*), limits itself to specific actions directed specifically to God with specific intent in accordance with His own request. The New

Covenant certainly includes singing as an acceptable act of worship (Eph. 5:19; Col. 3:16), but the question then arises as to whether or not one may use a mechanical instrument in conjunction with a song of worship. The New Testament never mentions such an instrument in conjunction with worship in the church (harps are mentioned only in heaven using symbolic language), though some have tried to create an instance in the use of *psallo*. However, most people choose to appeal to Psalm 150 and its inclusion of mechanical instruments of music in praise to God. Rather than spending time analyzing this Psalm, we must recall something of the utmost importance: it is irrelevant. What God accepted or even requested under the Old can never provide authority for that action today. He has not requested it; He will not accept it. It is not a part of God's revealed truth (John 17:17). The New Covenant does not permit mechanical instruments of music in worship — no matter what men may think or practice (Col. 3:17).

Several years ago a small movement began that claimed the various accounts of the life and teachings of Christ authored by Matthew, Mark, Luke, and John were not part of the New Covenant but rather part of the Old. They taught that since Jesus lived under the Old Covenant what He had to say only applied to the Old Covenant and those living under the Old Covenant. They thus maintain that the teachings of Jesus, as contained in those four short biographies, are not authoritative today.

Jesus certainly lived under the Old Covenant (Gal. 4:4); however, His enunciation of the principles of the coming covenant does not in any way violate His living under and keeping the Old. In fact, it fulfills the Old (Matt. 5:17). The Articles of Confederation provided the structure for the United States of America even while the Founders were discussing the new framework that would be provided in the Constitution of 1787. The Old Covenant is part of the historical background for the life of Jesus and therefore for the accounts of His life, but Jesus did not limit Himself to discussions about the Old Law. He came "preaching the gospel of the kingdom" (Matt. 4:23), which is the Church (Matt. 16:18-19; Mark 9:1; Acts 2:47; Col. 1:13-14). Jesus was preaching *in preparation*. Living under the Old Covenant, He taught people to keep the Old Covenant (Matt. 8:4) but not the traditions taught by men (Matt. 15:1-9). However, He also was teaching them about the time to come. Though not doctrinal, Jesus' prophecy of the destruction of Jerusalem (Matt. 24:3-35), an event that would take place after the Old Covenant had been replaced, demonstrates that He directed His instruction beyond the confines of the Old Law. Why could He not address both? Shortly before His arrest Jesus promised His apostles that He would send the Holy Spirit both to teach them all things and to remind them of *everything that Jesus had said* (John 14:25-26). The apostles were able to bear witness of all things pertaining to Jesus—including what He taught—because they had been with Him from the beginning of His ministry (John 15:27). This included the revelation of righteousness and truth which He began with His own teaching (John 16:10, 13; 1:16; Rom. 1:16-17). This, plus the additional instruction given by Christ after His resurrection, formed the basis for what the apostles were to teach (Acts 1:1-3). Jesus' words and word are the standard by which we will be judged (John 12:48; 2 Tim. 4:1-2). Finally, why would the Holy Spirit inspire Matthew, Mark, Luke, and John to write their books after the Old Covenant had been nailed to the cross if they were part of the Old Covenant? This would make God out to be a fool! However, it demonstrates quite clearly how far some people are willing to go in order to avoid the instruction and authority of Jesus Christ.

The very term "covenant" has caused some confusion over the years. "Testament," which we get through Latin, does capture one specific sense of the Greek word *diatheke*, but it does not address other uses of the word. "Covenant," on the other hand, can sometimes be too broad a translation if not understood properly. The New Testament use of this word stems from the Septuagint, the Greek translation of the Hebrew Scriptures, creating a link between the Hebrew word *beriyth* and *diatheke*. The original meaning of the Hebrew word implies a "cutting off" or "division" either in reference to a sacrifice offered to seal an agreement (and to demonstrate its serious and binding nature) or to the arrangements made as a result of the agreement. While the secular use of these words might imply ideas including "alliance," "agreement" and "contract," these words do not adequately portray the nature of God's intentions or the real force of the word.

The Greek word *diatheke* is a compound word derived from the preposition *dia* (through or because of) and the verb *tithemi* (to place). In John 18:11 the apostle uses the root *theke* to refer to the sheath (the proper place) of a sword. In Luke 12:24 the writer uses *apotheke* to refer to a barn (where you put things away). In 1 Timothy 6:20 Paul uses *paratheke* which is translated as "what was committed to your trust." Paul's use of *paratheke* emphasizes that something of value has been "placed" at Timothy's side (*para*) for safekeeping. In John 9:22 John records how the Jews "agreed" (*suntithemi*) about what to do should anyone confess Christ. They "put *their heads* together." The preposition *sun* emphasizes that the idea was mutually determined among equals. *Diatheke* combines the concepts of "the proper place" and "the involvement of two parties" to refer to how two parties can be placed together. *Suntithemi* refers to an agreement worked out between the two parties; *diatheke* refers to a document that is binding in the relationship between the two parties though only one created the terms due to his superior position in the relationship. It is a "disposition." Some seem to believe that the New Covenant of Christ is binding on an individual only when that person accepts the covenant. This is not the case. The Covenant became binding after Jesus died (1 Cor. 11:25) and the terms were first read (Acts 2). Therefore, all people everywhere are amenable to and subject to the New Covenant (John 12:48; Acts 17:30). Man does not get to set any of the terms of his reconciliation with, relationship with, and fellowship with God. If we are to be saved, it will be by our accepting God's terms. He made provision for this covenant through the death of His Son (Matt. 26:28) and announced the terms of the covenant when He provided the gospel (Rom. 1:16-17; Mark 16:15-16; 1 John 1:5-7). It is impossible to accept Jesus as our Savior if we do not accept the God-given terms of the covenant.

AUTHORIAL CONTEXT

Bible students often err by reading every passage of scripture alike without considering the background and style of the penman. While God is the ultimate Author of the Bible (2 Tim. 3:16-17) and the Holy Spirit the "Editor in Chief" (2 Pet. 1:19-21), God used the background and style of the penmen and allowed these to come through even while the Holy Spirit guarded every word (1 Cor. 2:10-13). Therefore, the style and background of the author become part of the context.

It is helpful to consider both an author's choice of words as well as any personal experiences that may have contributed to those choices. When Peter wrote, "Likewise you younger people, submit yourselves to your elders. Yes, all of you be submissive to one another, and be clothed with humility, for 'God resists the proud, But gives grace to the humble'" (1 Pet. 5:5), he used the word *enkomboomai* to refer to clothing oneself. This has specific connotations of a servant putting on an apron to do lowly work, which would have included washing feet—a perfect word considering the lesson Peter himself had to learn from the Savior shortly before His crucifixion (John 13:1-17). The experiences of Jeremiah and Hosea are central to their respective prophecies. Knowing who wrote some of the Psalms is extremely helpful in understanding those Psalms in greater depth. It is certainly true that knowing something about the author is not always necessary, such as with the book of Hebrews. However, while an understanding of the author may not be crucial, it certainly proves helpful. Paul's background in Judaism and career as a persecutor underlie much of his writing, making his arguments even more compelling. He demonstrates an intimate knowledge of the Pharisaical position and refutes it easily. John's emphasis on love and truth in each of his contributions stems not only from the situations of his day but from the very words of Christ he heard. Peter directly referred to events in his life within the context of his writing on more than one occasion (2 Pet. 1:14, 17).

We need to take more time in our Bible study to contemplate the background of the person writing. Moses' record of his own sins and weaknesses is significant coming from his own pen. The account of the conversion of Saul of Tarsus and his subsequent name change and work as an apostle takes on a special character when we consider the relationship that Luke had with Paul (Col. 4:14; 2 Tim. 4:11). The author's point of view, his relationship with God, and his relationship with the people to whom he wrote all create a panoramic backdrop for the content of the writing. They were inspired men, yes, but they were also real people.

BOOK CONTEXT

One of the oft-repeated mistakes of aspiring Bible students is to attempt exegesis of a passage of scripture without first reading the entire book, of which the passage is only one part. This often leads to an incomplete, and sometimes incorrect, conclusion. In Philippians 1:3-7 Paul refers to the "fellowship in the gospel" he shares with the Philippians, of their "good work," and to their being "partakers with me of grace." Without reading the entire book one would have great difficulty determining that these phrases referred to their financial support of the apostle (Phil. 4:14-18). A book's overall context can help significantly with its difficult passages and sometimes correct our understanding of a passage that we did not realize was difficult. Paul's use of "S/spirit" in the book of Galatians has proven to be difficult for readers who tend to plow forward based upon assumptions. But this could be alleviated by a consideration of Paul's use of "S/spirit" throughout Galatians where the meaning is clear, as well as close consideration of Paul's overall point to the Galatians of the necessity of following the New Covenant without mixing in anything else, including Judaism. From Paul's first use of the word in Galatians 3:2, he implies a close connection between "S/spirit" and revelation of the New Covenant. However, Galatians 3:5 clearly states that miracles provided by the Holy Spirit that reveal and confirm the message (Heb. 2:3-4) are the point, indicating a firm basis for understanding Paul's use of the term, and this understanding should guide the Bible student in interpreting "the promise of the Spirit" just a few verses below (Gal. 3:14) as well as the phrase "God has sent forth the Spirit of His Son into your hearts" (Gal. 4:6). These two examples are often interpreted without any consideration of the book's context, which emphasizes following the new revelation provided in the first century by the Holy Spirit and today found in the pages of the New Testament. Some also miss the emphasis in Galatians 4:29 of the Spirit as the standard, referring to His instruction, in opposition to following the misguided ways that men, and sometimes our own wisdom, might lead us—once again a theme of the book (Gal. 1:6-9).

In the first two chapters of Galatians Paul felt the necessity of establishing the basis of both his concern and his authority; therefore, he did not refer to the Spirit in either of these chapters. In chapters three and four, arguing in favor of the belief system of Christianity as revealed by the Holy Spirit, Paul contrasted the "Spirit" as the guide to our actions versus first the law and its activities (Gal. 3:2, 5), including circumcision, and then the flesh, representing man's wishes to make his own decisions apart from God's instruction (Gal. 4:29). Having thoroughly devastated the arguments of the Judaizing teachers and having made the distinction between following one's own path and following God's, Paul began to apply these lessons in chapters five and six, beginning with circumcision. Within this context he once again contrasted those whose actions stem from the law and those whose beliefs and actions stem from the Spirit's instructions (Gal. 5:4-5). Therefore, Paul has maintained his usage of "Spirit" into this next section.

Beginning with verse sixteen Paul began an entire section that could be entitled "Walking in the Spirit," and it is within these verses that people seem determined to abandon the book's context. In Galatians 5:16-17 Paul wrote, "I say then: Walk in the Spirit, and you shall not fulfill the lust of the flesh. For the flesh lusts against the Spirit, and the Spirit against the flesh; and these are contrary to one another, so that you do not do the things that you wish" (Gal. 5:16-17). Without context these two verses might seem to contradict one another. The first indicates that the individual is in control, while the second might lead some to believe that he has no control. But the point concerns which one a person listens to—himself or the Spirit. The book's context indicates that this does not refer to the Spirit's influence from within but externally through the message He delivered. This is essential for the next verse as well. "But if you are led by the Spirit, you are not under the law" (Gal. 5:18). Here, as in the previous verses, the apostle picks up the contrast he has presented all along. You are either going to follow what God has said through the Spirit, or you are going to disregard it and go your own way. You are either going to follow (be led by) the Spirit's instruction or you are going to accept the Judaizers' claim that you need to keep the Law of Moses. Some seem intent on replacing the book's context of the Spirit's guidance through the inspired message with some kind of direct means of influence. But Paul *never* says, indicates, or implies such. Throughout the book of

Galatians Paul emphasized that there is only one acceptable message from God, and that message is the gospel, the message delivered by the Holy Spirit in the first century through inspiration and now available in written form in the New Testament. Any addition, subtraction, or substitution to its influence on our decision-making is contrary to what Paul referred to in this epistle.

The apostle Paul is famous for his lists—a subject to which we will return at a later time. Galatians is known for two lists that appear together in Galatians chapter five: the works of the flesh and the fruit of the Spirit. However, many people fail to note that the contrast of these two lists is actually an extension of Paul's argument about the differences between following one's own will (or another man's, for that matter) and submitting to the will of the Father as revealed in Scripture through the inspiration of the Holy Spirit. Thus, these two lists serve to demonstrate the two very different directions life will take depending upon whose will dominates a person's heart.

Therefore, when Paul mentions the fruit of the Spirit in verse twenty-two, he is not referring to the Holy Spirit's personal presence within an individual as the factor that produces the qualities that follow but rather to the effect or product (fruit) of the Spirit's instruction through revelation. That these qualities result from the Spirit's influence is undeniable, but the nature of that influence is determined by Paul's usage throughout the book. Book context indicates the Spirit's influence to bring about this fruit is indirect rather than direct in any way. This interpretation is also supported by the contrast made with the works of the flesh. Left to go his own way without divine instruction, man will typically participate in the activities included in Paul's first list. Therefore, actions consistent with lust and doing things without regard for God are works of the flesh (Gal. 5:19-21), but actions consistent with the Spirit's instruction are the fruit of the Spirit (Gal. 5:22-23). A Christian may slip and choose to follow his own way from time to time and be guilty of the works of the flesh, and a non-Christian may follow some of what the Spirit has taught and develop some aspects of the good qualities His instruction offers. The level of development cannot be the same, however, because a non-Christian has not exhibited proper love for God (1 John 5:3; Heb. 5:8-9; Acts 2:38). Nevertheless, the origin of these good qualities is divine, and that is what Paul is emphasizing.

The issue Paul then addresses is whether or not the Christians in Galatia were willing to apply this knowledge to their own situation. Repentance, a requirement prior to becoming a Christian (Acts 17:30), demands the sacrifice of one's own will for God's (Gal. 5:24). It is the message that the Spirit inspired that provided spiritual life in the first place (Gal. 5:25a; John 3:5); therefore, the Spirit's instruction should continue to be our guide in developing Christian character (Gal. 5:25b). This would include any and all of the current problems that beset us, just as it did for the Galatians (Gal. 5:14-15, 26). Therefore, throughout this section dedicated to walking in the Spirit, Paul's use of "Spirit" never wavered. Paul remained true to the context of his book, and so should we.

The final chapter of Paul's epistle to the Galatians provides an excellent conclusion for the "flesh vs. Spirit" concept introduced in Galatians 4:29 and carried on throughout chapter five. Paul writes, "For he who sows to his flesh will of the flesh reap corruption, but he who sows to the Spirit will of the Spirit reap everlasting life" (Gal. 6:8). Which will are we going to give heed to, our own will or God's, revealed by the Holy Spirit in His Word? Whichever way we choose to proceed, we will bear the responsibility for the consequences.

If a Bible student's interpretation deviates from the author's consistent pattern, he must provide ample reason to explain why, beginning with the author's words. In one instance Paul clearly intended to indicate an attitude by his use of "spirit" because he described it as such—"in a spirit of gentleness" (Gal. 6:1). In the last verse of the book, he identifies the spirit as the human spirit by saying, "Brethren, the grace of our Lord Jesus Christ be with your spirit. Amen" (Gal. 6:18). However, most of the time, exegetes and commentators give no justification for veering away from the author's own definition and use of terms. Therefore, it is essential to remember that consistency is a requirement in order to call something "context," and that includes consistency throughout a writing. I personally found a renewed appreciation for book context when researching a lesson on only one verse—Judges 21:25—discovering that the author had built up a case for the stated situation of ethical, religious, moral, and political decay throughout the book before summarizing his conclusion in that final verse. As we have seen, however important the theme of a book may be, it is not the only consideration in determining book context. "The Church" is almost universally accepted as the theme of Paul's epistle to the Ephesians, but few seem to recognize the emphasis on unity through adherence to God's plan for the Church and for the individual Christian as part of that Body. We recognize Peter's theme of "Spiritual Growth" in his second epistle, but many ignore the prominent role that Peter gives to false teaching as an inhibitor of spiritual growth. James teaches about "Practical Christian Living," but specifically addresses how to handle temptation, which is what makes it so practical. Unfortunately, we often settle for clichés, slogans, and presumptions as our overall view of a book instead of first considering it as a whole before making pronouncements about one portion. The author wrote it as a whole, and therefore this is where the Bible student must begin.

A book's context is significant not only in creating a basic understanding of the theme of the book but also for helping the student interpret more difficult passages. This is true not only for how the author employs words and phrases but also for how he has introduced themes and subject matter. Most books of the Bible follow patterns established by the author within the framework of the type of literature employed. Therefore, authors will often introduce thoughts and subject matter and then build upon them later in the writing. This practice in writing helps in the identification of the context itself, but it also assists the Bible student in his efforts to understand the smaller portions of the text.

The book of Daniel gives us a good example of this principle. The first half of Daniel sets the historical context of the author, but it also provides useful information in preparing the reader to interpret the visions contained in the second half of the book. In the earlier portions of Daniel the prophet records both the dream or vision and its interpretation, thus demonstrating the symbolic nature of the visions and the context for an apocalyptic approach (a technique for which Daniel served as the prototype). Nebuchadnezzar's dream recorded in chapter two introduced the theme of the four earthly kingdoms and the coming of God's eternal kingdom. In truth, this is the theme of the entire book. Moreover, Daniel provided us with the interpretation so that we would later be able to identify these themes in later portions of the book. Chapter seven, which comes at the beginning of the second part of Daniel, is a recapitulation of chapter two in many ways because it recalls the theme of the four earthly kingdoms. Daniel had already identified Babylon as the first kingdom when he addressed Nebuchadnezzar (Dan. 2:36-38), so in chapter eight he progressed by identifying the second kingdom as the Persian kingdom, which consisted of both the Medes and the Persians (Dan. 8:20), and the third kingdom as Greece, even making an allusion to Alexander the Great and his successors (Dan. 8:21-22). Chapter nine emphasizes what most Jews did not recognize, that the Messiah's deliverance would be spiritual in nature and come during the time of yet another people (the fourth kingdom). The last vision elaborates further on the successors of Alexander, including an extensive discussion concerning the reign of Antiochus Epiphanes (11:20-39). However, some forget the book's context and try to force Daniel 11:40-45 into the Maccabean period, when Daniel himself had set the framework to include a kingdom beyond the successors of Alexander. This passage refers to the time of the fourth kingdom—Rome. The book's context requires it. The lesson then is straightforward: Let the author's context provide the first commentary on his work. Many create problems for themselves and others because they refuse to look at the book as one unit, intended to be viewed as a whole by the author. Many widely held doctrines depend upon viewing a verse or passage without reference to the whole book. Therefore, book context is invaluable in order to keep our mind's eye focused on truth.

THE THEMES OF OLD TESTAMENT BOOKS

In this brief overview the name of each book is given in **bold** type with a brief description of the book's contents or the reason behind its name or both. In *italics* is a suggested lesson to be learned from each of these books. While these short descriptions cannot replace personal study of the material, perhaps they will provoke interest and thought in regard to considering book context.

The Pentateuch (Theological Focus)

Genesis means "beginning" and is the book of beginnings. We find in it the beginning of the universe, the beginning of man, and the beginning of man's relationship with God. *God is our Creator.*

Exodus refers to the "going out" of the children of Israel from Egypt to Sinai. *God is our Deliverer.*

Leviticus is easily remembered by *Levi*, the tribe of priests. It is a book dedicated to the principles of worship to God and holiness. *God is Holy.*

Numbers refers to the census ordered by God of the people of Israel. It continues the record of the Israelites as they were continually cared for by God as they wandered in the wilderness. *God is our Provider.*

Deuteronomy refers to the second (*deutero*) giving of the law (*nomos*). This is Moses' last address to the people in which the law is repeated for the second generation of those who left Egypt. *God is our Lawgiver.*

The Books of History (Societal Focus)

Joshua is the record of the conquest of Canaan under the able leadership of Joshua. *Faith is the Victory.*

Judges refers to those leaders who delivered various areas of Israel from outside oppression. It also displays how quickly a people can turn away from God. *Sin Destroys Society.*

Ruth was a woman who lived in the time of the judges who, though not a Jew by birth, chose to follow Yahweh. *Enduring faithfulness.*

I and II Samuel describe the United Kingdom of Israel under Saul and David. *The Character of Godly Leadership.*

I and II Kings picks up the history of Israel recording the story of Solomon, the division in the kingdom, and the subsequent parallel histories. *Righteousness exalts a nation...*(Prov. 14:34).

I and II Chronicles is a condensed story of the times (*chronos*) of the kings to the carrying off of Israel by Assyria and the captivity of Judah by the Babylonians from the point of view of the captivity. *The Cost of Rebellion.*

Ezra helped rebuild the temple and reestablish respect for God's Law. *Principles of the Remnant.*

Nehemiah oversaw the rebuilding of Jerusalem. *Leadership of the Remnant.*

Esther was the Jewess who became queen and saved her people from annihilation. *Preservation of the Remnant.*

Books of Poetry (Perspective of a Godly People)

Job was a Gentile who showed great patience despite many trials and much suffering. *Patience Through Trials.*

Psalms is a book of individual songs. *God Deserves Our Praise and Earns Our Love.*

Proverbs is a collection of short sayings, most of which were probably written by Solomon. *The Practicality of God's Wisdom.*

Ecclesiastes is from the same root as *ecclesiastical* ("of the church") but simply refers to the sayings of the preacher. *Only Spiritual Priorities Give Meaning to Life.*

Song of Solomon is a beautiful book about the type of love a husband and wife should share for one another. *Marriage is Beautiful When You Follow God's Plan.*

The Major Prophets (The Consequences of Sin)

Isaiah is the prophet who saw Christ, the Suffering Servant. *A Sinful People must Look to God for Forgiveness.*

Jeremiah was the weeping prophet who endured much from an unbelieving people. *Even the Faithful will Suffer as a Result of Others' Sins.*

Lamentations refers to the *lamenting* or sorrowing of Jeremiah over the fall of Jerusalem. *Sin and its Consequences should Sadden Us.*

Ezekiel prophesied of the capture of both Israel and Judah but also foresaw the coming spiritual restoration. *Captivity Encourages Repentance.*

Daniel was a man of great moral courage who also prophesied of what would take place in the period between the testaments. *Salvation will come in the Coming Kingdom.*

The Minor Prophets (Man's Responsibilities)

Hosea married an ungodly woman to learn how greatly God has loved a sinful people. *God Loves Us, and We should Model our Love after His.*

Joel prophesied of Pentecost in the midst of telling of a coming plague of locusts (whether literal or figurative). *We must Look to God for Salvation.*

Amos was bold in what he said because he was convicted of what God had revealed to him. *We should be Bold and Sure of what We Believe, Say, and Practice.*

Obadiah reminds us that pride will be judged. *We must Learn to be Humble.*

Jonah prophesied reluctantly to the Gentiles living in Nineveh. *God Cares about the Souls of All Men, and So Should We.*

Micah showed righteous indignation at the sins around him. *Do Justly, Love Mercy, and Walk Humbly with your God* (Mic. 6:8).

Nahum proclaimed the coming destruction of Nineveh, describing very precisely how the Babylonians later destroyed the city. *We must Listen to God to Avoid Destruction.*

Habakkuk reminds us that sin of every kind will be judged. *We must Have Faith in God.*

Zephaniah promised that judgment was coming. *Repentance is the Only Answer for those who will be Judged.*

Haggai refused to let the people sit still as they enjoyed the comfort of a home while God's temple lay in ruin. *Get to Work for God!*

Zechariah announced in prophecy that *Christ would die for our salvation. We must Come to Him as He Requests.*

Malachi ended the time of revelation before Christ with a call for religious restoration. *Prepare for the Coming of the King.*

THE THEMES OF NEW TESTAMENT BOOKS

The Accounts of the Gospel

Matthew wrote to the Jews about the purpose of Christ, emphasizing the heavenly nature of the kingdom. *Jesus, the Promised Messiah.*

Mark wrote to the conquering Romans, showing them how that Jesus Christ conquered sin and death by His service and sacrifice. *Jesus, the Servant King.*

Luke wrote to Theophilus, a Greek, about the life of Jesus Christ. In this short biography Luke demonstrates to the Greek mind how Jesus lived and taught the perfect ethic, the goal of Greek philosophy. *Jesus, the Perfect Man.*

John wrote to Christians whose faith was being challenged by the Gnostics. In simplicity John proves the deity of Christ. *Jesus, God in the Flesh.*

A Book of History

Acts is the written record of various *acts* of the apostles. This was not written to be a complete history of the early days of the church but to show its beginning on the day of Pentecost and demonstrate the principles on which it is based. *The Cause of Christ.*

The Pauline Epistles

Romans is the most thorough treatise on the gospel of all the books of the Bible. *God's Plan for Man's Salvation.*

1 Corinthians was written to correct problems of division and fornication, to correct misunderstandings about Paul's apostleship and the resurrection, and to answer questions about marriage, eating meat offered to idols, spiritual gifts, and the collection for the saints. *Truth is the Only Solution for Problems.*

2 Corinthians is perhaps the most personal of all the letters bearing Paul's name. In it he relates some of the heartaches and hardships which often accompany the preaching of the gospel as he defends his work from outside attacks. *Spiritual Discernment.*

Galatians contains yet another defense of Paul's authority and also a powerful defense of Christian liberty, earning it the nickname, "The Magna Carta of Christian Liberty." *Spiritual Freedom is in Christ.*

Ephesians emphasizes how dependent the church is on Christ for salvation and how that should affect our daily behavior. *Unity in Christ.*

Philippians begins by emphasizing the importance of the gospel and then uses this as a base upon which to add unity, faithfulness, and a Christian mindset. *The Way to Christian Maturity.*

Colossians was written to answer Judaizing teachers and early Gnostics who taught that Christ was less than God but more than man. Paul answers these teachings and shows their consequences for believers. *The Preeminence of Christ.*

1 Thessalonians is addressed to a young congregation troubled over the recent deaths of fellow Christians. Paul writes to assure them that these will be present at Christ's second coming. *Transformation in Christ.*

2 Thessalonians was written to correct their misunderstanding of the first letter. These young Christians had believed Paul but had assumed that the second coming of Christ would be immediate. This epistle was sent to correct that perception. *Faithfulness.*

1 Timothy was sent to a young evangelist to encourage his faithfulness to the truth, his faithfulness in the work, and his faithfulness in life. *Advice for a Young Preacher.*

2 Timothy is Paul's final writing of which we have record. His message throughout the book is that the gospel must continue to be proclaimed after his death. *The Work Must Go On.*

Titus was told to appoint elders and to set in order the things that are wanting. Particularly this last admonition applies to preachers today who do not wish to "rock the boat." *Encouragement to a Faithful Preacher.*

Philemon is a personal letter in which Paul asks Philemon to be kind to Onesimus, his runaway slave who is returning as a new Christian. *The Principles of Christian Love Govern Moral Decisions.*

The General Epistles

Hebrews was written to stay a possible apostasy among Jewish Christians whose faith in Christ was wavering. Throughout this book, the unknown author demonstrates Christ's superior message, priesthood, covenant, and sacrifice. *The Supremacy of Our Savior.*

James is a sermon on practical Christianity. This book has often been called a commentary on the Sermon on the Mount. *Don't Just Talk Christianity; Live it.*

1 Peter was given to a people who were soon to experience physical persecution. But Peter teaches us that the physical trials of this life are only temporary and that through them we can grow. *Prepare for Persecution.*

2 Peter gives the ingredients for true spiritual development—spiritual knowledge, the right knowledge, and faith through knowledge. *Grow Spiritually through Knowledge.*

1 John In this letter, the apostle attempts to provide assurance for these Christians of the value of their faith by emphasizing the themes of fellowship and love. *The Nature of True Fellowship.*

2 John teaches us that truth is an absolute for religion and for life. *Truth is the Standard.*

3 John shows us the attitudes of four Christians—Gaius, Diotrophes, Demetrius, and John. *Examples of Christianity—Good and Bad.*

Jude reminds us that the common salvation will only stay common if we defend the gospel. *Contend for the Faith.*

Apocalyptic Literature

Revelation was written during the principate of Domitian (though some date it during the reign of Nero) to strengthen the resolve of Christians. *Never Give In to the World!*

CONCLUSION

Context helps the Bible student see the relationship a passage under immediate consideration shares with its author, the book of which it is a part, the covenant to which the historical characters and the recipients were amenable (which could be different—Matthew, Mark, Luke, and John), and the rest of the Bible. General context is the big picture of Bible study. It keeps the student mindful of why what he is studying has importance and deepens the student's appreciation for the unity of God's Word.

General context, however, is only the tip of the iceberg. It introduces many considerations for the benefit of the student but does not provide access to the entire picture. Therefore, it is important for the student to have a well-rounded view of context from the beginning. While general context provides the external skeleton to help identify the exact function of the text being studied, this alone does not give the study life. A student must continue his quest until he has explored all avenues that supply pertinent information rather than stopping at the first sign of success. Contextual perseverance, then, is a quality that cannot be underestimated in value.

General context includes:

- **A broad understanding of the scheme of redemption and message of scripture**
- **Consideration of the covenant under discussion**
- **Information regarding the penman**
- **The theme and structure of the particular book**

Recommended Reading

Laws, Jim, ed. *The Scheme of Redemption*. Pulaski, TN: Sain
    Publications, 1990.
Pledge, Charles. *Getting Acquainted with the Old Testament, Volume I*.
    Memphis, TN: Pledge Publications, 1970.
Pledge, Charles. *Getting Acquainted with the Old Testament, Volume II*.
    Memphis, TN: Pledge Publications, 1971.
Tenney, Merrill C. *New Testament Survey, Revised*. Grand Rapids, MI:
    Wm. B. Eerdmans Publishing Company, 1985, reprint 1989.
Wharton, Edward C. *Redemption Is: Planned, Needed, Provided*. West
    Monroe, LA: Howard Publishers, 1972.

Questions for Discussion

1. Summarize the theme of the entire Bible in one paragraph.
2. How would a doctrinal misunderstanding of the reason for man's sinfulness contribute to a misunderstanding of the entire Bible?
3. What causes people to confuse covenant context more than anything else?

4. What is the most important thing to know about an author of a book of the Bible?
5. What is the one word that best describes the determination of context?

Assignment

Take some time to read through the book of Ephesians and make short notes in regard to its general context, including how this affects various portions of the text.

CHAPTER 9

Literary Context

──────── ❖ ────────

INTRODUCTION

While the Bible is a special book—the inspired book—it is also still a book, which means that it is a piece of literature. Therefore, as a piece of literature—actually several related pieces—it is important to understand the nature of the literary approach the authors took in order to record the message of God. It is essential because the literary context defines the parameters and style by which the author chose, through inspiration, to convey the message. Since different literary approaches have different priorities and different literary philosophies, every form of writing has its own purpose and carries with it elements of style that demand consideration throughout the process of interpretation. Writing history is different even from writing a biography. Penning an epistle differs greatly from writing poetry. Apocalyptic writing maintains many distinctions from purely prophetic writing. Therefore, it is inappropriate to treat each piece of the Bible in the same way.

Each unit must be interpreted on its own terms as literature. Figurative language generally occurs to varying lengths depending upon the type of literature. One expects figurative language in poetry. One expects symbols in Apocalyptic. This remains true to a degree in prophecy. As the student studies the epistles he will notice that they employ a more straightforward tone of expression, though certainly maintaining a useful array of both similes and metaphors. History and biography take this even further because it is the nature of the literature. This does not mean they do not use figurative language. It simply means that the percentage of usage changes with the type of literature written.

A historical writing is event-oriented. A biography is typically character-oriented. Poetry is generally emotion-oriented. An epistle is person-oriented. Apocalyptic literature emphasizes a clash in cultures, while prophetic literature emphasizes the character of God and what it causes Him to do. These categories do exist; however, it would be wrong to understand them as anything but fluid. Some writings use a combination of these forms in order to communicate, depending upon their purposes.

Unfortunately, the advent of literary criticism has provoked a backlash. Whereas literary criticism scrutinizes the Bible as a work of man, looking for deficiencies (where there are none), many have responded by foregoing *any* conscious consideration of the nature of the literature in their interpretation. But if interpretation is to be accurate, it must accept what it interprets on its own terms, and that includes its rhetorical or literary context.

HISTORY

The Bible contains a wealth of historical information, though modern historians often scoff at this thought. They prefer to call Herodotus "The Father of Modern History," bypassing Moses in the process. To a modernist, any record that would imply God has a role in human events simply disqualifies it as "modern" history, no matter how accurate the record. This definition was somewhat necessary in order to distinguish Herodotus' work from the mythological literature of Homer. However, such a view also equates the history in the Bible with mythology, which is a gross injustice.

History is the record of significant events accompanied by an attempt to explain why the events occurred as they did along with their significance. The best history relies on sources closest to the events. Good narrative history provides background on the major actors interwoven with the story of which they are a part. Writing history often requires the author to develop one course of events to a particular point and then turn his attention to another coinciding set that pertains to the bigger picture in order to develop it. Otherwise, the reader cannot appreciate all that happened that led to a conclusion. History is not always chronological.

The historical portions of the Bible fit into this category very well. Much of the first part of the Old Testament records the history of Israel from its forefathers to its fight for independence from Egypt to its culture, especially religiously, to its expansion of territory, to its political intrigue within, to its wars without, to its subjugation to world powers, and to its return to its cultural roots. When understood in this light, how could anyone describe the Old Testament as boring? *This* is well-written history.

The books of Acts in the New Testament is excellent history as well. Luke weaves the story of the establishment and growth of the early church using two significant actors, Peter and Paul, and concentrating on the events that held the greatest significance in illustrating what the church is all about. Therefore, he explains the origin of the church on Pentecost, the reason for the animosity with Jewish leaders, the way in which persecution led to the spread of the gospel from Jerusalem throughout Palestine, how the Gentiles came to be included in the church, and how eventually the church spread throughout the Roman Empire. History is an explanation of events in order to provide perspective to its readers. The book of Acts does this, and more, admirably.

When we view these portions of the Bible as history—as explanations of how and why things are significant—perhaps we will cease viewing them as just stories and start seeing them as integral pieces of the puzzle that explain how we arrived where we are—culturally, historically, and spiritually. God deserves to be mentioned in history because He has been its most important participant. Furthermore, when we realize how perfectly accurate the Bible's history is in every fact that can be substantiated through human endeavor, perhaps we will begin to accept the Bible's accuracy—and significance—in every other way.

BIOGRAPHY

As Tacitus, Livy, and Josephus provide a background by which to understand the genre of history during the early days of the church, the writings of Suetonius and Plutarch help illuminate the characteristics of biographical writing during the same period.

Suetonius' descriptions of the early Roman emperors, while a bit tabloid-esque, explore the relationship between character and leadership. Plutarch's comparisons of various major characters of ancient history demonstrate exceptional skill in identifying pertinent, especially admirable, traits—lending support for the "Great Man" view of history. The biographies written during the early Roman Empire were generally short, centered on the most pertinent events in a person's life, and contained definite moral judgments. Considered from this perspective, the four short biographies of Jesus written by Matthew, Mark, Luke, and John not only measure up but also stand out as exceptional biographical pieces.

Modern biographical tomes, while longer, follow much of the same pattern. They attempt to capture the character of the individual through the main events in his life that the author believes best illustrate the individual's impact. This may differ depending upon the chosen emphasis and the intended audience. Biographies about Dwight D. Eisenhower might emphasize either his military career or his political career. The most recent biographies of the Roman Emperor Domitian are very different in presentation—one is more chronological while the other appears more topical. In any case, a biography attempts to capture the essence of the individual through events during his life—often the more dramatic events but always those that affected others the most. To write such a work the author would include basic information about the person based upon what the audience needed in way of introduction. He would then interweave events, quotations, and speeches (especially from that individual), and argumentation as to their meaning in order to produce a character study. Thus, biography is not the chronicling of a life; it is a well thought out attempt to explain a person's character and impact on society.

Jesus' inspired biographers performed this task splendidly. Each knew his audience, took the same facts, chose those events most likely to appeal to the reading audience, and developed a presentation best suited to highlighting Jesus' relationship to and impact on those reading, all while following a *general* chronology of the major events of His life. Together they present Jesus as Messiah and Rabbi, as a the ideal servant leader, as a philosopher and ideal man, and as deity. They are all true. However, while each author was a disciple of Jesus

Christ, as authors they rarely offer a purely moral judgment about Him. They rely on His life to demonstrate His character. This is not just good biographical writing. It is the best.

POETRY

When most people think of poetry (if indeed that occurs to most people!), they generally think of limericks, rhyming quatrains, or perhaps the haiku writing assignment they received in Junior High. That is to say, there is little chance that many books of poetry will top the *New York Times'* Bestseller list. But we should remember that poetry has many forms, and rhyming is not necessary in most of them. Most poetry centers more on some pattern in the syllables of expression than on rhyming the ending syllables, which would just be one way to create a pattern. The patterns of English poets are hard enough for most of us to grasp, but in reading the Bible we need to understand the patterns of Hebrew poetry. (As one example, Psalm 119 is an acrostic built on the letters of the Hebrew alphabet.)

The book of Psalms contains the fullest expression of Hebrew poetry, but it does occur elsewhere. The book of Job uses poetry, but so does the book of Exodus where Moses led the Israelites in a song of praise to the Lord after crossing the Red Sea. While there are many specialized categories in Hebrew poetry, the Bible student need only remember some basic forms in order to exegete a passage. The content of Hebrew poetry sets the patterns. A writer might express a thought and then provide further clarification of his meaning (Psa. 1:2), he might make a statement and build on it with various figures (Psa. 1:3), he might express an idea and then present the same thought in another way (Psa. 1:5), or he might state a fact and then present its contrast (Psa. 1:6). All of these should be pretty obvious categories.

Poetry is *the* medium of literature through which to express feeling. In writing poetry the feelings of the author take center stage. As a result, figurative language dominates poetry. That is not to say that poetry does not contain factual information. There are many Psalms referring to the history of Israel. But the focus of the Psalms is not on the *facts* of the events but rather on what feelings these facts should evoke. Therefore, it is improper to treat statements in the Psalms as if they were written in the epistles. Figures and expressiveness dominate the writing; therefore, the Bible student **must** consider them as part of the context. Psalm 51:5 provides a good example. David wrote, "Behold, I was brought forth in iniquity, And in sin my mother conceived me." David was certainly not talking about total depravity in this passage, but neither was he speaking of the sinfulness in the world. He was speaking in hyperbole about how he *felt* about his sinfulness. He felt like sin dominated him and that he could not remember life before sin. In verse four he stated that he had only sinned against the Lord, but he had also sinned against Bathsheba and certainly Uriah. David clearly did not believe that hyssop would literally purge him (Psa. 51:7). Figures dominate this passage *because it is poetry*. David was trying to get across the anguish of what it is to have sin in your life and how reliant we must be on God's salvation and forgiveness. Most of all, the poetry of the Bible should teach us the general lesson that it is impossible to fully express the tragedy of sin or the magnificence of God in purely literal terms.

FIGURATIVE LANGUAGE

The Bible is filled with figurative language. It would be hard to write such a voluminous work and avoid it. Figurative language is an integral part of communication. We fill our conversations and writings with similes and metaphors on a regular basis. Why some would expect God to avoid figurative language when communicating with mankind is beyond me. Over time, more than one expression from the Bible has worked its way, sometimes with slight alteration, into our ordinary speech. After all, it was Moses who first wrote by inspiration in regard to God's relationship with Israel that "He kept him as the apple of His eye" (Deut. 32:10).

Figurative language is both expressive and instructive. It helps to identify a new thought with something we already understand, using logical association. When David wrote, "Hide me under the shadow of Your wings" (Psa. 17:8), he aptly described the nature and extent of God's protection. Surely no one believes that God literally has wings. It is a figure denoting God's care. On the other hand, some have followed Philo and Origen in treating the entire Bible as an allegory. (This has regained some popularity with some modern theologians.) However, since Paul specifies that he is employing an allegory in Galatians 4:21-31, how would one understand his words allegorically? Simply put, the Bible employs figurative language in the same way that we normally do. It uses the regular modes of expression and when extending beyond these identifies the literary device. Jesus spoke many things in parables (Matt. 13:34), using stories of varying lengths to illustrate a particular trait He wished those listening to apply in their own lives. Jesus also used both similes and metaphors. Luke writes, "Then the seventy returned with joy, saying, 'Lord, even the demons are subject to us in Your name.' And He said to them, 'I saw Satan fall like lightning from heaven'" (Luke 10:17–18). (Please note that what fell from heaven was the lightning—not Satan.) Jesus used a simile to describe the figurative countenance of Satan as a result of their work. Jesus also used metaphors. He said, "I am the bread of life" (John 6:35). He did not mean that He had been transformed into hot cross buns. It was a figure. Similarly, when instituting the Lord's Supper, when Jesus said "this is My body," He meant it figuratively, and so should we understand it.

There are many more types of figures that are found in the Bible, but these should suffice to demonstrate that as Bible students we should recognize figurative language when we see it instead of trying to force some absurd doctrine into the text. There are, of course, some who will continue to see everything as figurative, and there will be some who view absolutely everything as literal. But the Bible uses both and should be interpreted accordingly.

PROVERBS

The book of Proverbs is a very unique contribution to the Bible. While the first nine chapters and then the final chapter develop themes over several verses in a series of proverbs (or with a proverb plus elaboration), the remainder of the book is filled with wise sayings that are generally one or two verses in length and that have little relation to the proverbs that went before or after. On occasion a few proverbs on a similar theme fall together, but the individual proverbs stand alone as well. Therefore, understanding these proverbs does not depend upon the immediate context so much as upon principles specific to proverbs. Proverbs itself is a book of accumulated wisdom, a book of very practical advice for handling real life situations. It emphasizes the themes of wisdom, listening to both God and parents, the importance of a good work ethic, the proper handling of money, marital fidelity, and character in government to name just a few. But no matter what the subject, these proverbs clearly declare the proper principles for success in life.

The form of many proverbs is similar to poetry, most often appearing as couplets. These couplets may employ parallelism (Prov. 10:18), they may build on one another (Prov. 10:22), or they may use comparison and contrast (Prov. 10:1). Proverbs also use figurative language to make the point more striking (Prov. 5:15-20). Whereas in other types of literature we must look to the whole in order to determine and understand the point, with a proverb we need not look any further because the proverb *is* the point. This does not imply, however, that the meaning of every proverb is obvious; the student must consider the historical setting sometimes in order to appreciate the wise man's thought (Prov. 14:4; 27:15).

It is interesting to note that the proverbs sometimes appear elsewhere in the book either verbatim or altered only slightly (Prov. 14:12; 16:25). Some of these offer a slightly different way to illustrate the point, while the reason for exact replication remains unclear other than the possibility of desiring emphasis or applying the same point in a different setting. The principles of proverbs imply the necessity of wisdom in understanding when a proverb applies and when it does not. In one notable example the casual reader might think that the writer blatantly contradicts himself: "Do not answer a fool according to his folly, Lest you also be like him," and "Answer a fool according to his folly, Lest he be wise in his own eyes" (Prov 26:4-5). The principle is that each is appropriate depending upon the situation; determining which requires wisdom.

Proverbs are *general* principles, which means there are some exceptions (Prov. 15:1). Unfortunately, many people seem eager to look for the exception instead of looking to apply the principle (Prov. 22:6). Proverbs deliver a wealth of wisdom in just a few words. The wise man will heed them.

PROPHECY

In the biblical context, a prophet is one chosen by God to give voice to His message. Therefore, prophecy is more than just prediction. It includes proclamations and pronouncements. Though we often think of "the prophets" as men who predicted events, we should also remember that much of their writing centered on proclamations of God's will, calls for repentance, and warning of God's coming judgment. In this their role was very close to that of a preacher's. What is difficult in studying their writings is determining when they are "preaching" and when they are "predicting." To determine this today's Bible student must recognize changes in tone and look for those times when the prophet's references do not make sense in the context of his own day or when the wording itself implies something supernatural (Psa. 110:1).

The danger is to treat every scripture as a direct prophecy. While few prophecies specify a particular time period — some prophecy goes so far as to cite a name (Isa. 44:28) — the prophets usually set forth a series of characteristics and circumstances that indicated a different time. Prophecies of the Messiah centered on His lineage, place of birth, and activity in order to identify Him to the people. These prophecies are *known* not only by their use of the term "Anointed One" but also by recognizing the relationship of the prophecy to the coming kingdom. This, along with noting when the prophet is calling for something beyond nature, helps the student to distinguish between a prophet's references to events in his own time, those in the near future, and those in the distant future.

To study biblical predictions is to study their fulfillment. Many today make the mistake of studying prophecy in order to find information pertaining to current events. They are so obsessed with the *idea* of prophecy that they subvert biblical interpretation to speculations about modern day fulfillment of prophecies that have already been fulfilled. This is truly unfortunate. These students will remain lost in a maze of self-created mystery, looking for a sign that the prophet never promised. The beauty of studying the prophets is to see God's message spoken with clarity to people in one age while also providing hope for all ages, a message of promise to Israel, fulfilled when God became flesh (John 1:14), and enjoyed by all who understand its ultimate blessings in Christianity.

EPISTLES

One of the things of note about studying the New Testament is the interest and focus of most studies. In younger Bible classes, teachers shed light on various episodes in the life of Christ for their charges. The book of Acts often receives much attention due to its discussions regarding conversion and the early church, and rightly so. The book of Revelation often draws substantial attention mainly due to how wildly people speculate about its meaning. In some places this is the full extent of New Testament study. Oh, people often have their pet verses from the epistles and refer to them to substantiate some teaching, but students often neglect the epistles for textual analysis. This is truly amazing, for the New Testament epistles provide the most relevant instruction pertaining to Christian life that is available. That is why they are there!

Letter writing is not much in vogue today. Greeting cards with professionally written sentiments and email with its casual approach to both form and grammar have replaced the extensive correspondence once common among all literate people. (Consider George Washington's Farewell Address, John Adams' correspondence both with his wife, Abigail, and with Thomas Jefferson, as well as the numerous letters written by soldiers during various wars.) One might wonder why God chose this format to deliver such instruction, but the answer, I believe, is fairly simple. An epistle allows the greatest variety in form and thought, making the epistle the perfect medium through which to present the finer points of Christianity. The New Testament epistles range from doctrinal discourse (Romans, Hebrews) to addressing particular doctrinal and practical problems (1 and 2 Corinthians), from concern at doctrinal instability (Galatians, Jude) to a sermon transcript on practical Christian living (James), from a form letter intended for many congregations (Ephesians) to a support letter to old friends (Philippians), from a letter to persons yet unknown (Colossians) to letters to individuals who were close personal friends (1 and 2 Timothy, Titus, Philemon, 2 and 3 John), and from encouragement and instruction for young Christians (1 and 2 Thessalonians) to calls for spiritual maturity (1 Peter, 1 John). An epistle allows the experiences of both the writer and recipient to come through clearly, so that we might more easily identify with the problem and more readily see and accept the solution. An epistle is formal enough to imply significance but personal enough to convey emotion. These epistles have been called "love letters," but that is often (and usually intentionally) misleading. They were not written to move people to tears but to move people to action and to change. Epistles can contain logical arguments and moving illustrations. They are as flexible as conversation. The gospel accounts are about the life of Christ. Acts is about the life of the church. The epistles are about the life of a Christian.

APOCALYPTIC LITERATURE

Apocalyptic literature has a long history but continues to perplex most Bible students today—and not without reason. The books of Daniel, Ezekiel, Zechariah, and Revelation in particular are certainly not straightforward presentations of a message. However, the prevailing view of interpretation in regard to these books has been defined more by unbridled speculation than any serious consideration of the characteristics of this type of literature. Regardless, the genre of apocalyptic literature developed for specific reasons, employed specific symbols, and fit into specific historical situations.

While brief apocalyptic visions had appeared in literature before, it was only with the advent of the Babylonian captivity that this style gained prominence. Apocalyptic literature employs various types of symbols designating concepts, qualities, leaders, and governments, as well as references to the Messiah and His kingdom, the church. The nature of these symbols grew out of nature, Israel's own history and literature, and from symbols borrowed from Babylon. Therefore, we cannot arbitrarily assign meaning to these symbols; we must interpret the symbols in line with how the original recipients would have understood them, and this is possible only by a thorough consideration of the historical context of the writing. (This is especially true of the numerical symbols employed by biblical writers.) Daniel, the prototypical apocalypse, helps immensely because Daniel explains various aspects of his earlier visions, giving us a firmer basis upon which to understand the nature of the literature. Some have argued that the purpose of the symbolism is to hide the meaning from an oppressor. However, this is unlikely just from a perusal of Daniel, since Daniel reveals the meaning of Nebuchadnezzar's dream to Nebuchadnezzar himself, a dream whose content prefigures the vision of chapter seven in particular, as well as the expansion that follows through the end of the book. These principles should be applied when studying the book of Revelation as well.

The theme of apocalyptic literature is: Be faithful in times of trial, because there is always hope when you do not compromise. The will of God will prevail. The symbolism helps to keep the principles and theme prominent so that, while the historical situation is essential to understanding the text, the historical situation itself becomes a type that can be applied when similar conditions arise. When a Bible student fails to recognize the symbolic nature of these writings, he is likely to begin down a path that leads to total confusion and addictive speculation. Therefore, it is essential to understand that these works were intended for people in particular circumstances and should be interpreted in light of *their* situation—not our own.

SERMONS

The word "sermon" typically brings to mind a homily delivered from the pulpit on Sunday. However, while it is true that all sermons should come from the Bible, it is also true that the Bible records several sermons for our benefit. Therefore, when we read these, we should consider them as a unit unto themselves, even while maintaining the overall picture from the writing in which they are found. It is entirely proper to consider the Sermon on the Mount (Matt. 5-7) as a whole while also studying it within the overall framework of Matthew's work. So we should consider it homiletically as well as textually. For this purpose, the people present when the sermon was delivered are the original audience rather than the recipients of the book in general.

Since these sermons were delivered orally first, the structure is more significant because a speaker must organize and present his lesson in such a way as to create a more lasting impression. As a result, sermons rely on familiar concepts, structure, and illustration more than an epistle, even though the content might be very similar. Jesus linked different points about the Old Law together by the rhetorical device "You have heard...But I say." In this way He provided common ground on which to remember the points while also emphasizing the main point—that the Pharisees' interpretation of the Law was inaccurate and that Jesus could explain it correctly. He showed that the Pharisees' focus was wrong, emphasizing the "show" of obedience without the heart of obedience. He then illustrated their hypocrisy. All this supported His thesis in regard to the inadequacy of their brand of righteousness (Matt. 5:17-20). Jesus addressed common real life situations that would bring to mind the sermon when encountering the situation. He used lively illustrations that always centered on His point. And this is just one example of a recorded sermon.

Luke records Peter's sermon on Pentecost (Acts 2), Stephen's sermon to the Jewish leaders (Acts 7), and Paul's sermon in Athens (Acts 17). In each instance the subject was different, the audience was different, the speaker was different, and some aspects of style were different, but the sermon served the same function. **Each sermon was a pointed address calling on those present to recognize their responsibility to the Lord.** We should also consider some of the speeches of Moses, Joshua, and the prophets as possible sermons. It is even possible to view the entire book of James as a sermon transcript. Today an audience with good listening skills has given way to a passive audience trained by television. This has made the presentation of sermons a little harder on the preacher. Perhaps, then, there are not only doctrinal but also practical lessons we can learn by studying the sermons of the Bible.

CONCLUSION

The nature of the literature *does* make a difference in how you interpret it. Certain types of literature lend themselves more toward figurative language than others. Certain literature types emphasize events while others emphasize doctrinal concepts. Each type has a particular purpose and role within the canon of Scripture. But in order to appreciate that purpose and role, we must keep it in mind while we are studying.

One book can contain more than one type of literature. The book of Daniel is historical for most of the first part of the writing but apocalyptic in the latter half. The book of Leviticus opens by giving instruction regarding the offering of various sacrifices but also includes historical events and codified law. Second Peter is an epistle that mentions some proverbs. Jude is very likely an epistle that responds to false teaching built upon Jewish apocalyptic literature of the intertestamental period. Therefore, while the epistle itself is not apocalyptic in nature, understanding the language and background of apocalyptic literature is essential in order to comprehend the message of the letter. So the Bible student needs an understanding of every type of literature, not just a general idea of a book's "classification." Literary context represents the framework of the writing. Therefore, by identifying the structure a Bible student can more readily understand the author's approach and point. This helps in developing an outline that is consistent with the author's, which assists the student in grasping the development of the theme in the various sections of the writing. Most of all, a Bible student must always remember that the purpose of studying biblical literature is not ultimately to appreciate its literary structure or the mastery displayed by the author. The purpose, as many of the authors noted themselves, is to learn something from God and to apply it in life. "And truly Jesus did many other signs in the presence of His disciples, which are not written in this book; but these are written that you may believe that Jesus is the Christ, the Son of God, and that believing you may have life in His name" (John 20:30–31).

A Bible student should identity the literary context of the material under discussion in light of:

- History
- Biography
- Poetry
- Figurative Language
- Proverbs

- Prophecy
- Epistles
- Apocalyptic Literature
- Sermons

Recommended Reading

Grant, Michael. *The Ancient Historians*. New York: Barnes and Noble, Inc., 1970.
Grant, Michael. *Greek and Roman Historians: Information and Misinformation*. London and New York: Routledge, 1995.

Questions for Discussion

1. Take some time to review other works of ancient literature, then compare them with works in the Bible of a similar genre in regard to quality.
2. How does one determine the genre of literature he is reading?
3. What is the starkest contrast between types of literature?
4. What genres might students easily confuse? How might this affect their interpretation?
5. In your opinion, what type offers the most challenges to a Bible student?

Assignment

Give three biblical examples of each type of literature discussed and how this affects its interpretation.

CHAPTER 10

Historical Context

INTRODUCTION

Bible study frustrates many people because they assume they should be able to pick up a Bible, read from it, and interpret it as if it were written today. But while the Bible's message most certainly applies today, it was not written yesterday. Writers of the various books of the Bible wrote in the language of the day, within the framework of that time, and for certain people living in a particular area—all of which differ from our own situation. This means that the people who originally received scripture understood by course of circumstance many things that we do not. As a result, there was no need for the writer to include *this* information when penning his work, but there *is* a need for Bible students today to study this information in conjunction with the text.

If we are to interpret the Bible correctly, we must understand it as its original recipients understood it. Therefore, we must understand what the original recipients understood. But this requires a study of matters not specifically addressed in the Bible. The Bible refers to various nations, various leaders, and various titles that no longer exist. The events recounted on its pages occurred on the other side of the planet where few of us have visited. Furthermore, words can have historical connotations that translation does not reveal. Therefore, even reading Scripture in the original languages does not resolve all of the differences between then and now.

Reading about the ten plagues sent against Egypt due to Pharaoh's unwillingness to allow the Israelites to go into the wilderness to worship are impressive enough just from a casual reading, but knowledge of Egyptian religion sheds additional light on the message of the plagues. Likewise, the inspired health regulations recorded by Moses stand out in ancient history, but this fact might elude a Bible student unfamiliar with some of the regular medical practices of the day, particularly in Egypt. In the New Testament one can read the account of the trial of Jesus and see the injustice, perhaps even wondering how Pilate could have made his decision, until learning more about the relationship of a Roman procurator with the emperor and Pilate's own history with the Jews.

Due to the nature of gradual revelation, the people we read about in the Bible did not understand all that we can today because they did not have access to all of the information we do today. The written record we now enjoy is a part of the process in which some of the people who are named in the Bible took part but did not live to enjoy the completed process. People sometimes quickly judge Abraham for his taking a concubine without considering how much spiritual information to which Abraham had access. In the same manner, people often become very critical of the apostles as they read Matthew, Mark, Luke, and John, forgetting that they did not have the benefit of these works, later works, or extensive doctrinal treatises on the nature of the Messiah's mission.

Historical context is probably the most difficult aspect of context to implement regularly. The text itself includes most elements of context in some way; however, historical context requires the Bible student to consider historical information outside the pages of God's Word in order to shed light on persons, places, and practices named in Scripture without explanation. Who was Tiglath-Pileser? What was a "high place"? Is there any way to verify the accuracy of certain biblical prophecies whose fulfillment is not mentioned in the Bible or to provide external evidence for those the Bible does mention? What did scribes and lawyers do? Where did the Jews get the idea for synagogues? And, finally, why do most people ignore these questions?

The events recorded in the Bible did not occur in an historical vacuum. In fact, understanding the Bible requires some familiarity with a *majority* of ancient civilizations because of their interaction with biblical figures. It does not require a degree in ancient history to understand the Bible. But the more historical knowledge of this kind a person has the easier it will be to see not only the obvious moral lessons of the Bible but also the backdrop against which these events and pronouncements occurred. This helps us realize, more than ever, that the Bible is not a series of short stories. It is a record of real events, real people, and real places, and it is about the very real God who started history, works in history, recorded history, and will end history.

GEOGRAPHICAL CONTEXT

Most Bible students have consulted one of the maps located at the back of their Bibles. However, for most this also represents the entire attention ever given to the geography or topography of places named in the Bible. And while it is nice to see a visible representation of Paul's journeys, there is far more to geography than just locating a name on a map.

In some instances, perhaps, the location alone might prove significant and helpful. When the LORD commanded Jonah to go to Nineveh, Jonah responded by boarding a ship bound for Tarshish (Jonah 1:1-3). While the reader probably understands the basic point — that Jonah was trying to avoid going to Nineveh — an appreciation for the geography provides a vivid portrayal of Jonah's actions. Nineveh was many miles to the northeast of Israel, lying on the upper Tigris River. Tarshish, on the other hand, was a Phoenician colony located in what is now southern Spain. So while God called for Jonah to go far to the east, Jonah tried to go as far west as possible.

In certain instances knowing the topography of the region is essential in order to understand the text properly. In Matthew 20:17 it says that Jesus and His apostles were going *up* to Jerusalem, but prior to this they had been in the area of Judea beyond the Jordan (Matt. 19:1), which is northeast of Jerusalem. In today's jargon, which tends to be map oriented, it might seem odd to think of going "up" somewhere while traveling toward the south. However, for those familiar with the terrain, and especially in a time and place where the most common form of travel was walking, the designation "up to Jerusalem" made perfect sense when one considered that Jerusalem was built in the mountains rising up above the Jordan valley and the Dead Sea. "Up" describes their movement in terms of elevation, not map direction.

In many other instances, becoming familiar with the location helps the student understand its significance. Mount Carmel provided the backdrop of the Mediterranean as well as a view of Ahab's palace in the distance. As the site of Baal worship that had previously been used as a place to worship Jehovah, it was the perfect place for the contest Elijah proposed (1 Kngs. 18:19-40). The likely backdrop around Caesarea Philippi provided an excellent object lesson for the difference between a small rock (Peter) and a large shelf of rock (Peter's confession) (Matt. 16:13-18). Knowledge of geography often helps the student understand various prophecies, since the prophets often mentioned certain place names to stand for the whole country.

Geography, therefore, is about more than maps. It pulls together the location, description, topography, and history of a particular place in order to provide additional insight into the scene described on the pages of Holy Writ. It may take a while to learn about every place mentioned, but it is time well spent.

POLITICAL CONTEXT

For those unfamiliar with ancient history it might seem odd to discuss the political context of the Roman Empire or any of the other nations mentioned by the writers of Scripture. Since most remain uninitiated into the inner machinations of non-democratic politics, the political dynamics at work—and recorded by the inspired writers—often get overlooked by the modern reader. To be sure, not every political citation conveys dramatic information, but even general references provide evidence of familiarity with the situation of the day.

A cursory reading of 1 and 2 Kings and 1 and 2 Chronicles demonstrates the importance of considering the political landscape not only of Israel and Judah but also of their neighbors—allies and enemies—since these factors contributed to their decisions and to their fate. When Daniel refers to Belshazzar giving him the title of "third ruler in the kingdom," he implies a particular political situation in which Belshazzar would be serving as co-regent with the power to inaugurate a third ruler. Critics dismissed this for years, but Daniel proved to have a better understanding of

Babylonian politics than some historians. While not taking away from Isaiah's prophecy regarding Cyrus (Isa. 45:1ff), it is helpful to know the political context that led the king to the decision to end the captivity. And these are just a few samples from Israel's history.

The New Testament demonstrates just as much interest in political matters. While the New Testament's references to various emperors might be viewed simply as a dating method, it is significant that the writers did not just refer to the emperor or a year but included additional information. Therefore, when Luke mentions the call for registering individuals that led Joseph and Mary to go to Bethlehem, he included the Emperor's decree, the time frame based upon a famous area authority (specifying his first tour of duty in the province of Syria rather than his role in the A.D. 6 registration, though this later date is subject to debate as well), and the requirements of that registration (Luke 2:1-3). Luke's description of the political landscape in the region at the time John the Immerser began his ministry is amazingly precise (Luke 3:1-2), recording the names of all office-holders notable in Judea. In the book of Acts, Luke mentions a famine during Claudius' reign (Acts 11:28). Appreciating Paul's appeal to Caesar (Acts 25:11; 28:19) requires knowledge of Roman citizenship and the climate of the time under Nero, which changed dramatically during his reign (Phil. 4:22).

A Bible student might be perplexed by Pontius Pilate's behavior during the trial of Jesus unless he acquaints himself with the political problems of the Procurator and his relationship with the Jews, including how they might be able to cost him his job. It would also be wise to study Jewish politics from the early second century B.C. through the end of the first century A.D. in order to understand the politicization of Judaism, which explains much about what these leaders feared they might lose because of Jesus' arrival on the scene, as well as the problems they created for the early church.

Political context encompasses far more than a timeline. It includes the internal and external conflicts at every level of government and the climate of the time (e.g. *Pax Romana*). Therefore, it is an essential component for serious Bible study.

RELIGIOUS CONTEXT

The events of September 11, 2001, drew attention to the relevance of religious context in order to understand why people do what they do. Those unfamiliar with Islam still struggle in their attempts to explain such horrific actions. But in order to appreciate the religious context of these events one must not only read the Koran but also various interpretations of the Koran. Religious context refers to the reality of the situation without reference to the accuracy of the views people hold. The religious context of the Bible refers to where people and society were spiritually prior to instruction and helps us understand why the inspired instruction took a particular approach.

Bible students often take religious context for granted because much of the Bible revolves around Judaism. Therefore, people believe that most of their practices either can be explained by references to the Mosaical Law or are self-explanatory. However, some accuse the author of Hebrews of misunderstanding the Law's designation for the location of the items of the tabernacle (Heb. 9:1-7) without considering that he, besides being inspired, knew very well the *practical* side of the instructions and location (Lev. 16:11-13) instead of viewing it as some model where the utensils never move. We take the existence of the Pharisees and Sadducees for granted in the New Testament, but many seem uninterested in trying to establish their origin (Matt. 22:15-16, 23) so long as they have a basic understanding of some of their beliefs (Acts 4:1-2). However, one cannot *fully* appreciate Jesus' reply to the Sadducees question about the resurrection without knowing that they only accepted the Pentateuch as authoritative (Matt. 22:29-32). Also, one might believe that the New Testament writers were "hung up" on discussing the Mosaical Law and circumcision unless he knows that these, along with the temple (Acts 21:27-31), were *the* doctrines of emphasis in their day.

A student might read Paul's apology at Areopagus in Acts 17 without considering the significance of this location for such philosophical discussions. Few people trace the treatment of Samaritans in the New Testament to their appearance in Nehemiah. And at which mountain did the Samaritans worship and why (John 4:20)? Why did Christianity's change of status in the eyes of Rome from a sect of Judaism to a mystery cult affect their treatment? In a general way, an understanding of the Roman psyche helps immensely to explain Mark's choice of material in the account of the gospel bearing his name. Therefore, religious context is significant. It sheds light on many of the questions people have that many teachers gloss over.

CULTURAL CONTEXT

Those who travel, and even those who read, understand the significant differences between cultures that exist in this world. American culture tends to revolve around business, but religion, tradition, and government dominate other areas of the world. Paris fashion is definitely NOT Tehran fashion. Courtship and marriage ceremonies differ throughout the world. And the face of George Washington does not grace the currency in every country. Even our own military is a distinct culture, employing a different method of keeping time (22:00, 5 bells) as well as having distinct rituals. Why then would we ever expect simply to open up the Bible, a book written over a span of over 1500 years in various places and completed more than 1900 years ago, and understand all of its cultural references?

To complicate matters further, the Bible does not present just one culture; its events take place in several different cultures. Therefore, one should learn not only about Hebrew culture (which changed through the years) but also about Egyptian culture, Babylonian culture, and Roman culture to name a few. In today's world Abraham's request for his servant to place his hand under Abraham's thigh would raise a few eyebrows (Gen. 24:1-9), but it was an understood way of accepting a request as binding (Gen. 47:29). Likewise, an uninformed Bible student might suspect that Naomi's advice to Ruth, and the subsequent encounter between Ruth and Boaz, contained some illicit connotation (Ruth 3:1-15) instead of recognizing this practical way of seeking an audience with an important man to discuss a private matter with a virtuous woman (Ruth 3:11). Paul's keeping of Jewish culture is still a matter of debate (Acts 21:23-24).

It also helps for the Bible student to understand the significance of smaller matters that sometimes lie hidden behind translation. The text is often specific about the coins used, which often referred to specific practices as well as specific amounts. When the Pharisees sent a group of Herodians—a sect known for their loyalty to Rome—to Jesus to ask about paying the amount required by law of all who were on the census records, the wording specified the practice as well as the amount—a *denarius*, a Roman coin that was approximately worth a day's wage for a laborer. However, on a different occasion, when those who collected the temple tax came, the text mentions both the Greek *didrachma* (Matt. 17:24), or two drachmas worth, and a *stater* (Matt. 17:27), a single coin which was the same as the Jewish shekel, the amount of the temple tax for two people. One must also watch for the differences in Jewish time keeping, sundown to sundown, and Roman time keeping, midnight to midnight. Knowledge of military watches also helps in discovering the particular time of events. An understanding of culture—Jewish, Roman, and Greek—also helps in interpreting the differences in the approaches of the synoptic writers. Cultural context is not a peripheral matter for the Bible student; it is integral.

An appreciation for and understanding of cultural context can also keep the Bible student from making improper assumptions or evaluations, as well as shedding light on puzzling passages. It is essential to remember that the Roman Empire was *not* a single culture but rather a combination of various conquered cultures answering to a single government. So when Paul mentions a particular cultural practice in one city or area, this does not mean that it existed throughout the Empire (1 Cor. 11:2-16). Therefore, preparation for a textual study must include a consideration of the setting. While one might read the book of Daniel and understand much of the earlier portions of the book without extensive knowledge of Babylonian culture, such knowledge can provide additional information pertinent to the text. Through this study we can conclude that Daniel and his friends were made eunuchs. We can also better understand the temptations that existed for them in Babylon itself and the extent of the idolatry. We can also learn why Darius could not change his own ruling.

The letters to the seven churches recorded in the second and third chapters of the book of Revelation well illustrate the variation of spiritual situations created by various settings. The city of Smyrna had a larger Jewish population (Rev. 2:9). Pergamos was both home to a large statue to Zeus as well as home city to the worship of Asklepios, symbolized by a serpent. Is it any wonder then that Jesus described it as "where Satan dwells" (Rev. 2:13)? Thyatira was the home of two temples, one to the Lydian sun god (see Rev. 2:18) and one to a feminine god (see Rev. 2:20ff). Sardis' location was excellent for self-protection, yet people had snuck in on more than one occasion (see Rev. 3:3). One might not fully appreciate the words of Revelation 3:12 to the church at Philadelphia without some understanding of the practices of the Imperial Cult. And one might miss the full message of the Savior's letter to Laodicea if unaware of that city's renown as a market for wool and eye salve (see Rev. 3:17).

Without an understanding of cultural context, Bible students might assume too much and draw wrong or incomplete conclusions. Some have condemned beggars without recognizing begging as the welfare of the first century. Likewise, an understanding of period clothing might help in explaining the point of a particular scripture (Matt. 5:40; Luke 6:29; John 21:7). So it is not only helpful but often essential for the Bible student to know he must consider how the culture impacted a particular writing. Otherwise, he might superimpose his own culture over the text and so do harm to its meaning.

SITUATIONAL CONTEXT

For many years now some people have questioned the relevancy of the Bible. They point out that it was completed more than 1900 years ago and had an audience in situations that do not exist today. In order to combat such skepticism, preachers have emphasized, and rightfully so, that the Bible is indeed relevant and that it still applies today, despite the chronological distance lying between its completion and the present day. However, some have concluded that relevancy and application mean that a student should look at the Bible as if it were written today. This is not so. While some of the statements of action and principle are still valid, some of the statements made are directed specifically to the situation of that day. Since we do not have the *exact* same situation, the passage cannot apply in *exactly* the same way. This does not diminish its relevance or the necessity of making appropriate application. To the contrary, such an approach draws attention to the principles that are relevant in every situation and how they should be applied to the current situation following the example of the past. However, this is quite impossible if the student is unaware of that situation.

One of the most pertinent portions of a spiritual situation is whatever false concept has intruded upon the people being addressed by the writer. The Bible often addresses these false teachings directly; however, that is not to say that the Bible *names* them. Following the meeting in Jerusalem about what God said concerning the Gentiles, part of the letter sent out to the brotherhood said, "Therefore I judge that we should not trouble those from among the Gentiles who are turning to God, but that we write to them to abstain from things polluted by idols, from sexual immorality, from things strangled, and from blood" (Acts 15:19–20). It might seem strange to see "sexual immorality" included in that particular list (or "blood", for that matter) unless one is familiar with the nature of idolatrous practices at that time. The problem of Jewish teachers trying to incorporate Christianity into Judaism and its practices (or vice versa) was at the heart of many of Paul's encounters. But if a person does not understand or fully appreciate the Jewish teachings of the day, he might miss the full impact of Paul's discussions about the abolition of the Old Law (Eph. 2:14-16; Col. 2:14). The book of Jude even provides an example of why it is helpful to have some knowledge of the extra-biblical literature of the day. Besides quoting from the Pseudepigrapha, many of Jude's word choices have an apocalyptic background that is a recurring theme in that collection of works, indicating the nature and origin of the problems he was addressing.

Besides idolatry and Judaism, Christianity also encountered problems due to the influence of various philosophies popular at that time. Paul wrote his epistle to the Colossians in order to combat the twin influences of Judaizing teaching and early Gnostic philosophy (which were probably related), a problem that John later addressed in his epistles in a way that indicates its development and increasing influence toward the end of the first century. Unfortunately, the casual student will miss some of the subtle inspired instruction because he remains unfamiliar with the implications, and even the terminology, of Gnosticism.

John's reference to Jesus as "the Word" is instructive in regard to His role but it is specific in countering Gnostic teaching. The doctrinal significance of the discussions about creation found in both John, 1 John, and Colossians remains today; however, a person with knowledge of the Gnostic belief in "emanations" of God as an explanation of creation can understand and appreciate the reason for the extent of the discussion and the precision of the language the Holy Spirit employed. Only someone familiar with the Gnostic teachings of both docetism and asceticism can put references to Jesus' coming *in flesh* in their full context (John 1:14; Col. 2:8-9).

One particular discussion during a Bible class indicates both the approach many people take to Bible study and why it is insufficient. A man frustrated with the detail of my exegesis once turned to Colossians 1:9, read it, and commented, "Now that verse just means what it says!" The verse in question reads, "For this reason we also, since the day we heard it, do not cease to pray for you, and to ask that you may be filled with the knowledge of His will in all wisdom and spiritual understanding" (Col. 1:9). However, unknown to this man, the terms "knowledge," "wisdom," and "understanding" all occur frequently in Gnostic literature, emphasizing the "special" knowledge of the self-proclaimed spiritual elite. Paul emphasizes in the following verse that it is knowledge from God that matters rather than the self-generated philosophies of a group of arrogant men—a direct assault on that particular error. But it just means what it says, which is true... if you really know what it says.

Some situations, such as those exposed in the Corinthian congregation, are "embedded in the text," but others require a degree of investigation. The words generally contain clues which, if studied, lead to a study of the situational context, which leads to a better understanding of the text.

CHRONOLOGICAL CONTEXT

When studying the Bible it is essential to keep in mind the time period under consideration and to realize that certain situations were temporary rather than perpetual. Our God never intended certain situations to continue indefinitely but rather instituted or allowed them within a particular time frame as it fulfilled His purposes. The Jews had difficulty accepting this concept when it applied to the fulfillment and abolition of the Old Law (Matt. 5:17; Eph. 2:14-16) even though God told them of this eventuality (Heb. 8:6-13; Jer. 31:31-34). Some people today have the same problem in their approach to Bible study when they appeal to the Old Covenant as their authority for certain aspects of worship today (e.g. Psa. 150) or to the thief on the cross as an example of salvation (Luke 23:39-43). You see, *when* these things were said *does* matter. We must discern what applies *today* in the present time period — which covenant and which situations — and what does not.

It is important for the Bible student to remember when reading the Bible that these things were written during a time period when God was communicating information and confirmation of His Word by means of the miraculous provision of the Holy Spirit (Mark 16:17-20). Therefore, references to miraculous gifts cannot apply directly today since God ceased providing these gifts when the inspiration of His written Word was completed (1 Cor. 13:8-10). It would be improper to attempt a direct application of Romans 1:11 because Paul is no longer living (2 Tim. 4:6-8) and able to impart miraculous gifts (Acts 8:14-19). Some people are obsessed with the idea of demon-possession, failing to realize that God allowed this phenomenon during the first century so long as He also provided the means miraculously to handle it (Matt. 8:16). A similar but more subtle example is how people often wish to apply many references to the Holy Spirit today in a direct manner without first establishing the historical context and time period that illustrates how the original recipients would have understand such references. They would have understood references to the Spirit as their source of spiritual information (Rom. 8:1-4, etc.).

Abiding by this interpretive principle might also keep people from straying into the land of absurd speculation that so often dominates explanations of the book of Revelation. Students fail to place it in its historical context and mistakenly attempt to understand it as if it were written today. But the Bible was not written today. It was written over a period of 1500+ years. Therefore, we need to know *when* it was written, what was going on when it was written, and what spiritual situation existed when it was written.

CONCLUSION

Historical context is a concept that remains lost on most Bible students. They prefer to place the Bible in the context of their own experiences rather than in the time and circumstances of the original writers and recipients. This is both sad and dangerous. It reveals a lack of diligence and a lack of concern for interpretive accuracy. After all, the consequences of failing to consider historical context can be severe. Without historical context our Bible study lacks depth and perspective. At the heart of this is the assumption that we understand more than we actually do (1 Cor. 10:12).

Critics might suggest that historical interpretation places the emphasis on man-authored documents instead of on the divinely-authored book. However, this would be untrue and unfair. The question is not whether or not historical considerations *supersede* the Bible; they do not. But historical information does *supplement* the Bible and enhances our understanding of the Bible in the process. Historical context is not just about knowing ancient history; it is about knowing how that history illuminates what the Bible says. If the Bible had been written in our own time, in our own country, in our own language, and in our own culture, then we would be able to understand it upon that basis. However, since the Bible was *not* written in our own time, *not* written in our own country, *not* written in our own language, and *not* written in our culture, then we must *learn* those things in order to understand what the original recipients understood. This is not a matter of judging "original intent." It is a matter of determining "original meaning" from the "original words" in their "original context" (1 Cor. 2:12-13; 2 Tim. 3:16-17; 2 Pet. 1:19-21).

Historical context is crucial for accurate interpretation. To understand a document of the 15th century B.C., one must first place it in a 15th century B.C. context. To understand a first century document, one must first place it within a first century context. This often requires knowledge and study beyond the pages of the Bible, but, once done, it makes the message come alive. It helps us see the people mentioned as real people, the places cited as real places, and the events that occurred as real events. Thus, historical context contributes a heightened sense of reality to Bible study. This is important because when we think about the children of Israel and the apostles as real people in real situations facing real problems, we become less critical of their shortcomings, we identify with them more, and we are more likely to apply God's message to the very real situations we encounter in life (Jas. 1:22).

Historical context includes:

- **Geographical context**
- **Political context**
- **Religious context**
- **Cultural context**
- **Situational context**
- **Chronological context**

Recommended Reading

Ferguson, Everett. *Backgrounds of Early Christianity, Third Edition.* Grand Rapids, MI: William B. Eerdmans Publishing Company, 2003.

Gower, Ralph. *The New Manners and Customs of Bible Times.* Chicago, IL: Moody Press, 1987.

Jackson, Wayne. *Background Bible Study.* Montgomery, AL: Apologetics Press, Inc., 1986.

McGarvey, J.W. *Lands of the Bible.* Cincinnati, OH: The Standard Publishing Company.

Oppenheim, A. Leo. *Ancient Mesopotamia: Portrait of a Dead Civilization.* Revised Edition completed by Erica Reiner. Chicago and London: The University of Chicago Press, 1977.

Saggs, H.W.F. *Civilization Before Greece and Rome.* New Haven and London: Yale University Press, 1989.

Sherwin-White, A.N. *Roman Society and Roman Law in the New Testament.* New York: Oxford University Press, 1963, Special edition for Sandpiper Books Ltd. 2000.

Whiston, William, compiler and translator. *The Works of Josephus: New Updated Edition.* Peabody, MA: Hendrickson Publishers, Inc., 1987.

Questions for Discussion

1. Does geography help explain Naaman's mindset in 2 Kings 5?
2. How would looking at the events surrounding Christ's trial from a political point of view help in understanding what happened?
3. How might having a knowledge of ancient religious beliefs regarding astronomy help in understanding the significance of certain events surrounding both the birth and death of Jesus?
4. How does a student determine if a practice is based on culture?
5. How might remembering that the Bible was written during the time of miraculous inspiration affect one's interpretation of various passages?

Assignment

Identify the situational context of the book of Colossians.

CHAPTER 11

Immediate Context

INTRODUCTION

*g*eneral, literary, and historical context provide the basic framework for understanding those elements that affect the student's comprehension of what a person wrote. Immediate context addresses the specifics of what the writer actually said. Knowing that a book is part of the New Covenant, is an epistle, and was written just prior to the Neronian persecution provides the background for what was said—which does affect interpretation—but immediate context refers to the smaller elements that pertain to writing in grammar, syntax, structure, and style that make reading comprehension possible. Immediate context therefore refers to how words, phrases, sentences, and paragraphs relate to one another, how the facts and references presented provide information, and how to determine the significance of each.

Studying immediate context essentially means gleaning every last detail available from a text, examining the material from every possible angle, eliminating what is impossible, recognizing patterns and minute distinctions, and establishing common relationships so that all of the information takes shape in such a way that every conclusion reached remains consistent with every *other* conclusion. If a student is to understand the overall meaning, he must recognize themes under discussion, but if a person is to recognize themes, he must identify the author's structure. Identifying written structure requires the recognition of parallel thoughts versus supportive points. Making this distinction means that a student must realize when material is related closely and when it falls under the general structure of the book. But a student must understand the meaning of words (or how to determine such) and a basic comprehension of diagramming sentences. (Of course, diagramming the sentence structure in the original language would be ideal.) Words carry meaning, contrary to Nida's insistence on a sentential theory of meaning. Sentences only have meaning because of the words employed and the relationship between the words in the sentence. Understanding the meaning of words and grammar are essential in order to understand context.

Too often a person reads through a text based upon a previous understanding and then forces unnatural meanings on words and unnatural relationships on phrases in order to justify his position—definitions and relationships that this person would never try to defend universally. This leads to an important point: Consistency is essential in examining context. Context is what comes *with the text*—not what we bring to it.

SURROUNDING MATERIAL

The most obvious aspect of immediate context still remains hard for many to apply. Although dividing the text into chapters and verses has proven extremely helpful in locating passages, unfortunate divisions sometimes wreak havoc on both the context and the Bible student. (In some cases, the punctuation provided by translators presents problems as well since there is no inspired punctuation.) But even beyond the obvious problems, this also can cause a student to consider a verse independently of those verses around it—even if he has just read them! It is therefore essential for the Bible student always to remain aware of the relationship between what was previously said and the verse being studied. In the same way, it is important for a student to avoid making decisions about the meaning of a text too early because the material that follows may provide additional information pertinent to that previous section.

Some have misinterpreted Paul's meaning of 2 Corinthians 1:22 as referring to the personal indwelling of the Holy Spirit. The New King James Version reads, "who also has sealed us and given us the Spirit in our hearts as a guarantee" (2 Cor. 1:22). While a first glance might seem to support this interpretation (especially given the translation), the proper translation and context do not. This difference, however, is not merely a question of the impact of the words "sealed" or "guarantee." The student should recognize that this verse is only part of a sentence and that this phrase should be interpreted within that context. Therefore, he should consider what information 2 Corinthians 1:21 might offer. It reads: "Now He who establishes us with you in Christ and has anointed us is God" (2 Cor. 1:21). Notice Paul's use of pronouns. The pronoun "He" refers to God, "you" refers to the Corinthians, and "us" refers to Paul and those like him—most likely the apostles since he refers to a divine anointing, or to Silas and Timothy. Now if "us" refers to Paul and the apostles in verse twenty-one, and verse twenty-two is a continuation of what he was saying in verse twenty-one, then the "us" and "our" referred to in verse twenty-two must also be references to Paul and the apostles. Moreover, verses eighteen through twenty emphasize the trustworthiness of the message Paul had preached to them. So verses twenty-one and twenty-two were explaining *why* the Corinthians needed to accept the message Paul preached (as opposed to that preached by the Judaizing teachers), which was one of Paul's primary purposes in writing the entire book. The literal translation of the phrase then makes perfect sense: "who also marked us with a seal and gave the earnest of the Spirit in our hearts," the earnest thus emphasizing the guarantee provided by the Holy Spirit that the message was from God.

In 2 Corinthians 2:3-4 Paul mentioned his first letter, which provides an important reference point for what follows. When he mentions someone who had caused grief in verse five, due to the prior verses the most likely interpretation is that he referred to someone he also mentioned in 1 Corinthians. But the *following* verses make this much clearer, referring to a punishment already inflicted along with the present need to forgive him, comfort him, and reaffirm their love for him. Then in verse nine Paul refers again to 1 Corinthians, noting their obedience to his words. Therefore, identifying the person in verse five required knowledge of the first letter and appreciation for the material surrounding that verse.

The author placed his material in a particular order with related information joined together to make a coherent whole. Attempting to interpret any small part of that whole without respect for what the author said in the related material will inevitably produce inaccurate conclusions, leading us to attribute meanings to the author that he himself would find offensive.

CIRCUMSTANTIAL REFERENCES

While the references within a passage referring to various events and occurrences rarely have doctrinal implications in regard to that passage, they do shed additional light on the text simply by making the application more vivid and adding to the student's recognition that these events actually occurred and that God expects the principles cited to be applied. It is important to consider whether an address occurred following a defeat, during a siege, in the midst of captivity, or after a great victory. When the prophet Azariah addressed King Asa in 2 Chronicles 15, he told Asa that he would enjoy the Lord's blessings as long as he remained faithful to him. He was reminded of the nation's unfaithfulness and the consequences. However, this was not after a defeat but after a victory.

Some of the notes added at the beginning of the Psalms are extremely helpful in this regard. At the beginning of Psalm 34 it says, "*A Psalm* of David, when he pretended madness before Abimelech, who drove him away, and he departed." However, the reader must realize (through a quick search of the name "Abimelech") that this is a common name (or title) for Philistine kings. But Old Testament history indicates that the note refers to Achish, king of Gath (1 Sam. 21:10-15). By reading this passage one understands that David faked insanity in order to save his life. This adds perspective to the interpretation of Psalm 34 regarding the many ways God delivers.

While it may seem a small thing to note when Paul wrote while being held by the Romans, this adds to the strength of his writing when he mentions his "bonds in Christ" (Phil. 1:13). Also in the book of Philippians, it may take reading through the book on more than one occasion to realize that the reference to the "fellowship in the gospel" (Phil. 1:5) addressed the relationship shared by Paul and the Philippians due to the congregation's ongoing financial help. Likewise, a consideration of Acts 18:1-20:3 helps immensely in discovering that the source of Paul's anxiety and fear prior to writing 2 Corinthians (2 Cor. 1:8-11) was the uproar in Ephesus created by Demetrius the silversmith.

These circumstantial references may seem of little value at first glance, but they sometimes unearth textual treasures. They fill in gaps of understanding and help to bring the entire picture of the text into focus. In some cases these "small matters" bring up points otherwise overlooked. Learning to consider and appreciate such references will help the student remember that nothing God says should ever be treated as meaningless.

THEME

Within a passage of scripture it is often helpful to identify the theme of the passage in order to assist interpretation. By taking note of recurring words or ideas the student can detect patterns of thought that will indicate the overall concept connecting verses so that, should a verse or phrase that falls within that section prove to be difficult, knowledge of the theme would provide help by limiting the possible explanations of the wording. Themes often encompass entire chapters. In the case of 1 Corinthians 15, the obvious theme of the resurrection helps to identify the meaning of the celestial bodies and terrestrial bodies in verse forty, though some have created doctrines from this verse that far exceed the context of the resurrection, thus illustrating the value of identifying the theme.

In Romans 7 the theme is the Christian's relationship to the Law of Moses. Most people accept this in the earliest verses (Rom. 7:1-4) but many argue that Paul was referring to the "ceremonial law" but not to the "moral law." However, the context will not allow this. While still addressing the Law, Paul wrote, "What shall we say then? Is the law sin? Certainly not! On the contrary, I would not have known sin except through the law. For I would not have known covetousness unless the law had said, 'You shall not covet'" (Rom. 7:7). Since Paul quoted from the Ten Commandments to cite an instance from the abolished Law (Eph. 2:14-16; Col. 2:14), his earlier references referred to the moral law as well as the ceremonial law. The theme was that the Christian was not amenable to *any* of the Law of Moses but to the New Covenant, which became the theme of the following chapter. While Jesus' exhortation in the Sermon on the Mount regarding laying up treasures in heaven rather than on earth (Matt. 6:19-21) does have a "wealth" application (Matt. 6:24), the theme throughout chapter six in the sermon's second section emphasizes that a person should not seek recognition among men but should seek salvation from God. Recognition is a small reward, but kingdom citizenship is far greater.

The theme of a text is sometimes obvious and sometimes elusive. However, without considering this ongoing relationship of ideas, a student may assign a meaning to a smaller portion of the text without realizing the principles underlying it. But it is just as possible to assign a theme to an entire text too broadly and include material that does not belong. In Matthew 24 many people overlook the fact that the disciples asked two different questions (Matt. 24:3) and that Jesus gave two distinct answers—the first referring to the destruction of Jerusalem (Matt. 24:2) which would be preceded by signs, and the second referring to Judgment Day which would come without warning. (Note the change in thought between verses thirty-four and thirty-six.) So failing to distinguish thematic material properly can lead to exegetical fallacies. A theme is a general reference point, but if the internal material does not fit, a student needs to change his opinion of what constitutes the theme.

ECCLESIASTICAL TERMINOLOGY

Someone unfamiliar with the language of the Bible might easily become "lost in the language." After all, there is a great deal of terminology that one might call "theological" or "ecclesiastical" included that may seem unrelated to real life—at least to the beginning Bible student. There are two reasons for this. First, spiritual matters do require spiritual terminology to some extent. Few "secular" words can communicate the full meaning of "atonement" or "righteousness." Second, some of the wording in our translations has developed traditionally within a religious or biblical context. In these cases, the use of "ecclesiastical terminology" often proves detrimental to the Bible student because he may attach a traditional meaning to the word that influences interpretation.

Many think of the "church" as an edifice, but the New Testament always uses it to refer to the Christian people. You do not greet a building (Acts 18:22)! Since the word *ekklesia* literally means "called out *people*," referring to the unity produced by responding to God's message, it may refer to the entire church of Christ throughout the world (Matt. 16:18; Col. 1:18), to a particular congregation (Acts 11:22; 1 Cor. 7:17), or to the assembly of a congregation (1 Cor. 11:18; 3 John 10). Some have already made efforts to substitute "good news" for "gospel," which would be quite literal since *euangelion* means "good message." Since "gospel" has come to mean specifically the message of the New Testament, the underlying meaning is sometimes lost in the process of studying. Students **know** it means "good news" and that it refers to God's message, but they often lose this emphasis due to familiarity with the wording (Eph. 1:13). Students' assumptions about "grace" produce similar problems. "Favor" would work equally well as a translation and might help the Bible student approach the text without preconceived ideas as to its meaning. The word itself can refer to the condition of favor (Eph. 2:8), the manifestation of favor (Tit. 2:11), or to our response to God's favor—thanks (Col. 3:16).

The key for the Bible student is to make himself aware of these types of words and their original meanings in order to interpret according to actual meaning rather than through the goggles of ecclesiastical oversight. If your interpretation is correct, then correcting the wording will not matter. But if your prior interpretation no longer fits, then it is time to reconsider what you believe in keeping with the new information learned (Acts 17:11).

TITLES

Titles or designations provided by the inspired writers often supply additional information pertinent to the text, imply a certain quality of character, or establish the extent of the role. A study of the names referring solely to Christ has been the subject of more than one book, and these rarely consider the full implications of the inspired appellations. Few people seem to recognize the Holy Spirit's use of the name "Christ" as designating Him as the Messiah, the Lord's Anointed, and even fewer have considered the timing of some of these occurrences as they pertain to a discussion of Judaism. This is but one example among many.

Throughout the writings of the prophets God's spokesmen refer to various countries by naming a prominent area or city rather than citing the "official" name. They often call Israel Ephraim. In Ezekiel, a piece of apocalyptic literature, the prophet refers to the "seed" or "sons of Zadok" (Eze. 40:46; 43:19; 44:15; 48:11). Unless one consults the history of Israel, he will likely miss this symbolic reference to the priest who remained faithful to David (1 Kings. 1:6-7). Ezekiel used these titles to refer to the character of faithfulness required of those who would serve the Lord.

The descriptions given to congregational leaders have also proven confusing to some. Luke records that Paul and Barnabas appointed "elders" in every congregation (Acts 14:23). The Jews had long used such terminology to refer to the older men in a community who had the experience and knowledge to lead people, though theirs was more of a civic concept (Acts 4:5). But elders of the congregational community bore the burden of spiritual leadership since the church is a spiritual community (Acts 20:17). These men—always in the plural in the New Testament—were also called bishops (1 Tim. 3:1), better translated "overseer," as those responsible for keeping a watch over the flock's spiritual condition, and pastors (Eph. 4:11), a term that means "shepherd." That these refer to the same congregational level of leadership is buttressed by the interchangeability of these titles and their related verbs (Acts 20:28; 1 Pet. 5:2-4; 1 Tim. 5:17). So while the titles themselves are fairly generic, referring to either a characteristic or function, the specific qualifications required by Paul (1 Tim. 3:1-7; Tit. 1:5-9), which were the basis of appointment and the means by which the Holy Spirit voiced His approval (Acts 20:28), imply a particular spiritual work described by those titles. The only time a preacher used one of these titles regarding himself was when it was used to describe an additional responsibility—not his work as a preacher (1 Pet. 5:1-4).

Transliterated words cause many problems in interpretation,

including references that have become titles or classifications. Unfortunately, the English transliteration sometimes takes on a life of its own to the point that people forget the meaning of the underlying word. "Presbyter" is a transliteration of *presbuteros*, which means "elder," but "presbyter" tends to convey more than the meaning of the original word due to its denominational connotation. The word *apostolos* means "one sent or commissioned" or "ambassador" and therefore can refer to more than the apostles of Christ (Acts 14:14; 2 Cor. 11:13). It simply depends upon who sent them. The term *prophetes* has become simply "prophet." Today most people assume that "prophet" refers to someone who predicts, not recognizing the root idea of "one who voices forth" serving as God's spokesman. The word *angelos* refers to a "messenger," as does its Hebrew equivalent *mal'ak*, which could be either a heavenly being or a man (2 Cor. 11:14). But transliterating it as "angel" forces a meaning on it that is not inherent in the word and that often steers the student in the wrong direction.

"Deacon" is a transliteration of the word *diakonos*, which means servant, emphasizing the readiness to fulfill another's wishes with the additional idea of responsibility. (The verb form is translated as serving or waiting tables in Acts 6:2, an apt description of someone who is ready to "take orders." This definition itself implies that "deacon" is not a position of leadership in the sense of making decisions.) So the word *diakonos* could refer either to a particular position of responsibility as a congregational servant who fulfilled the qualifications described in 1 Timothy 3:8-13 or *generically* to one who served in a more limited capacity—to a preacher whose service was in proclaiming the gospel (Col. 1:23) or to a woman like Phoebe who worked in the Lord's service in a capacity that pleased God (Rom. 16:1) but that was not a congregational position of deacon since she could not meet the inspired qualifications. Every Christian can serve in some way, but not every Christian can serve in the position of "deacon." "Minister" is a little incomplete in describing a preacher; he should be called a "minister of the gospel" because this specifies the nature of his service. "Evangelist" means "gospel preacher" or "one who spreads the good news."

The titles found in the New Testament clearly are function-oriented, though some continue to confuse both the functions and the titular descriptions. It would be quite impractical to list all the relevant names and titles found in Holy Writ. Hopefully the Bible student has gained awareness of the significance of these names and titles and will not pass over them without notice in the future. Students should consider biblical titles with the implied function or characteristic in mind, noticing how this enhances an understanding of the text under consideration and sometimes helps to draw out the specific meaning.

PEOPLE AND PLACES

Since most students of the Bible become familiar with the names of people and places found within the pages of Scripture, they do not feel compelled to investigate them further when they occur within a particular passage. The origin of the names themselves might prove of some interest. Timothy's name is Greek, showing his father's influence, while the meaning of the name itself, "honoring God," says something about his mother's. Titus is a Roman name. John Mark's names indicated both his Jewish birth (John) and possibly his Roman citizenship (Mark).

At the close of the epistle to the Colossians Paul mentions a great number of people by name. If the Bible student is to glean more than very generic lessons from this portion of Scripture, he must consider the small amount of information available about each person and use it. In this same book Paul mentions the cities of Laodicea and Hierapolis (Col. 4:13). By combining the description of Epaphras, his work, his relationship with Colossae, his relationship with the congregations in Laodicea and Hierapolis, and the locations of these cities, the Bible student can establish that Epaphras was from Colossae and served as a traveling preacher in the small area that included these three cities, probably having been taught by Paul when he was in Ephesus. Therefore, identifying people and places assists in providing information about practices in the early church (as verse sixteen implies the regular congregational exchange of apostolic epistles).

The various gates into the city of Jerusalem had names describing their position or purpose (Neh. 3). It may not mean as much to other people, but in my opinion those who worked on the refuse gate deserve special recognition (Neh. 3:14)! It can be quite easy to skip over genealogies and passages with repetitive phrases, but God saw fit to include these names and places for a reason. There is a divine reason why Tamar, Ruth, and "her *who had been the wife of* Uriah" received attention in Matthew's account of the genealogy of Jesus. In each instance there was something significant about how they came to give birth to an ancestor of the Messiah. God's purpose will be served! Why was the lame man laid daily at the gate called Beautiful? There is a reason. Why did Paul go to Areopagus in Athens? There is a reason. But Bible students must be interested enough to pursue the answers. Taking the time to notice the location and purpose of a place included and considering the individual role of a particular person mentioned may seem like small matters, but they can provide marvelous insights into the writer's world and purpose in writing.

WORD CHOICES

Most people use thousands of words everyday, but it is doubtful that they ever spend ten minutes deciding on the exact right words for a situation. Presidential speechwriters, on the other hand, have the responsibility of choosing the best turn of phrase that fits the Commandeer in Chief's thoughts and modes of expression. People react to these words; therefore, they must select them carefully. But when the Holy Spirit chooses words (1 Cor. 2:10-13), His choices carry the purpose of God. Therefore, Bible students who thoughtlessly pass over the words of inspiration and casually explain each word with a synonym have somewhat missed the point. The particular words chosen at particular times can carry great meaning, and the Bible student who knows to look for these subtleties will gain great insight into the verbal precision of the Scriptures.

In the same way that there is a reason for the change of name from Saul of Tarsus to Paul, so also Paul's own choice of descriptions at various times serve a purpose. A brief perusal of the opening of his epistles demonstrates how carefully Paul chose words. When he emphasizes his apostleship, he brings attention to the authority of the message He presents. When he chooses the word "servant," it carries with it a sense of humility, downplaying his own importance. To

Philemon he described himself as simply a "prisoner." The purpose for these choices might change depending upon the audience, but they remain significant. While the Galatians required a reminder of Paul's apostleship and authority, Timothy and Titus knew this. Therefore, a reminder of Paul's apostleship emphasized that they should rely on the authority of the message from Christ rather than their position. To the Thessalonians apparently Paul's name itself communicated all that he required.

The various designations of the gospel message itself deserve greater scrutiny. The word "gospel" means "a good message," drawing attention to its purpose in saving mankind (Rom. 1:16). "Word" generally draws attention to the origin of the message, emphasizing divine expression, and to its divinely determined content (2 Tim. 4:2). Doctrine tends to express the communication of spiritual information with the response of the people in mind (2 Tim. 4:3). Truth indicates that the message is the communication of God's ethical system (John 17:17). While discovering the particular meaning of a word requires a word study and synonym comparison, once accomplished it provides the Bible student with a wealth of additional information to consider. Different words communicate different things; therefore, word choices matter.

IDIOMS

Every language and culture uses words and various expressions in ways that would seem odd and even funny when translated or presented in a culture unfamiliar with the expression. Imagine for a moment the confusion that the phrase "kicked the bucket" might produce among people without an understanding of the intended meaning — which does not rely at all, in this case, on the meaning of the actual words. "Have you lost your mind?" might provoke looks of incredulity. While the Bible student rarely faces instances this blatant, some expressions might prove troublesome without some assistance.

Translators often eliminate this problem for the Bible student by exchanging the original idiom for one that the reader would more likely understand. There is certainly a time and a place for this practice, but translators can also go overboard. Ahab, king of Israel, once told Benhadad, the king of Syria, "Let not the one who puts on his armor boast like the one who takes it off" (1 Kings 20:11). Surely Bible students can understand this idiom. There is no need to insert, "Don't count your chickens before they hatch!" On the other hand, the first century phrase *en de te mia ton sabbaton*, translated "Now on the first *day* of the week" in Acts 20:7, communicates the correct idea, whereas a literal rendering, "But on the one of the Sabbaths," might confuse the reader. "The Sabbaths" referred to the period of days from Sabbath to Sabbath; therefore, it referred to the week. Unfortunately, translating this literally might lead some to the false conclusion that Luke was referring to Saturday. In 2 John 12, the apostle says, "Having many things to write to you, I did not wish to do so with paper and ink; but I hope to come to you and speak face to face, that our joy may be full" (2 John 12). The original idiom in this verse is "mouth to mouth." However, I think you will agree that this idiom would imply something far different to today's English audience.

In the New Testament "fruit of the vine" refers specifically to the product of the grape; therefore, it would be unacceptable to use watermelon juice just because a person thinks the words might allow it. The idiom does not. Others have taken the Hebrew idiom "three days and three nights" (1 Sam. 30:12) and attempted to adjust the chronology of Jesus' death, burial, and resurrection according to His reference to Jonah (Jon. 1:17; Matt. 12:40), believing that it requires exactly seventy-two hours. They miss the idiom. Idioms are a product of language and culture. They occur sparsely within the text, but they must be considered as part of the text—according to the nature of the idiom.

LISTS

Within the framework of many books of the Bible, the writers set forth lists of various kinds. Jesus Himself presented a list of sins in Mark 7:21-23. Paul employed lists of one kind or another in several of his epistles. He often catalogued various types of sins, depending upon the particular problem He was addressing (Rom. 1:29-31; 1 Cor. 6:9-10; Gal. 5:19-21; Col. 3:5, 8; 1 Tim. 1:9-10), but he also created positive lists of individual characteristics (Gal. 5:22-24) and collective characteristics (Eph. 4:4-6), lists of descriptive characteristics (Eph. 6:13-17) and lists describing a particular action (1 Tim. 2:1). The writer of Hebrews describes Jesus in a series of characteristics on more than one occasion (Heb. 1:2-3; 7:26-27) as well as God's Word in a series of descriptions (Heb. 4:12). He also famously makes a list detailing the faith of various Old Testament characters (Heb. 11:1-40). James adds a list about the wisdom necessary to teach (Jas. 3:17). Peter describes Christians using Old Testament terminology (1 Pet. 2:9-10) while later listing characteristics helpful in getting along with one another (1 Pet. 3:8-9) and in his second epistle a listing of characteristics essential for spiritual maturity (2 Pet. 1:5-7). These do not even exhaust the New Testament examples. If one were to consider the many series of exhortations included in various places (beginning with the Beatitudes), that group might be larger still.

Identifying the fact that the Holy Spirit has inspired writers to cite lists of various sorts is not earth shattering. But Bible students need to consider how to analyze the information contained in such lists. These lists provide a great deal of information. Most of the time writers use words that might be considered synonyms, but their inclusion in a list implies important distinctions worth investigating. What is the difference between wickedness and maliciousness or covetousness and envy? Paul's use of these words in Romans 1:29 demands that such differences exist. In Paul's list of the works of the flesh in Galatians 5:19-21, Paul arranges the sins in such a way as to create categories, beginning with sexual sins, and the distinctions between these sins have important implications (Matt. 19:9). In this same passage he places outbursts of wrath, selfish ambition, envy, and revelries in the same overall class with murders and idolatry. This certainly should cause some people to pause for thought.

So when Bible students come across one of these lists they need to examine the list, looking for similarities in words, differences in words, and categories by which to organize the words. Where the list occurs also should be a consideration. Why provide an extensive list at this particular point? Is there a special reason for emphasizing the specifics a list makes possible? Lists help the author fill in details of the general point he is making. Lists provide information for the Bible student on many levels – if he is looking for it.

CONJUNCTIONS

Conjunctions are one of the most important keys to determining various elements of immediate context. The old turn of phrase, "Whenever you see a 'therefore' you need to check to see what it's 'there for'," states a truth that applies beyond just that one particular conjunction. By their very nature conjunctions explain the relationship between words and phrases. Since Paul said, "I beseech you **therefore**, brethren, by the mercies of God, that you present your bodies a living sacrifice, holy, acceptable to God, which is your reasonable service" (Rom. 12:1, emp. mine, KWR), the Bible student needs to know *why* "therefore" is in the text and to what it refers. Paul maintains that adequate reasons exist of God's tender mercies that they should respond favorably to Paul's plea. To ignore the "therefore" is to ignore the motivation cited. In each case a student must determine whether the conjunction refers to the previous verse, the previous paragraph, the previous chapter, or the entirety of the book that preceded it.

Notice Paul's use of conjunctions in the short sub-section of 2 Corinthians: "Therefore, when I was planning this, did I do it lightly? Or the things I plan, do I plan according to the flesh, that with me there should be Yes, Yes, and No, No? But as God is faithful, our word to you was not Yes and No. For the Son of God, Jesus Christ, who was preached among you by us—by me, Silvanus, and Timothy—was not Yes and No, but in Him was Yes. For all the promises of God in Him are Yes, and in Him Amen, to the glory of God through us" (2 Cor. 1:17–20). In verse seventeen Paul used "therefore" to refer to the discussion in the previous verses regarding why he changed his mind about the timing of his arrival in Corinth. In verses nineteen and twenty he began with "For" in support of his assertion of verse eighteen. However, it is the conjunction that begins verse eighteen that offers the most insight into the immediate context. Translators tend to treat the phrase "But *as* God *is* faithful" as simply a bolstering of Paul's own point. However, since the "*as*" is an addition to the text, it might well read, "But God *is* faithful." Either way the "But" offers a mild contrast with what preceded it—in this case, Paul's own decision making. What then is the point? Paul was confronting a situation in Corinth where Judaizing teachers were attempting to use his change of plans as a tool not only against him personally but against the gospel he preached. Therefore, he emphasized in this context that however much his own decisions seemed to vary to them, there was no question about the veracity and immutability of the gospel message he preached.

Conjunctions appear regularly in the biblical text, but they are not just convenient placeholders within paragraphs. They are essential to the construction and meaning of that text; therefore, the student should consider their meaning, their placement, and their implications based upon when and where they occur. Conjunctions help a student remember that passages do not occur in isolation; they are part of a larger unit. Coming to understand those relationships is what context is all about.

TONE

Tone is at once both a consideration and a reflection of the context. Unfortunately, writing does not easily communicate the tone of the author, but this is not to say that it is impossible to detect. Paul himself mentions the tone or tenor of his writing when in his epistle to the Galatians he wrote, "I would like to be present with you now **and to change my tone**; for I have doubts about you" (Gal. 4:20). However, writers rarely provide such an obvious statement in regard to their tone or to the tenor of someone's statement they record. It is therefore up to the Bible student to recognize such matters by way of analyzing the vocabulary employed, the force of the message under consideration, and the reaction, if recorded, of those present.

Hollywood seems intent on portraying Jesus as if He were the greatest whispering orator of all time. They carefully select passages for the actor to recite. Such portrayals of Jesus speaking the Sermon on the Mount ever so softly to His audience is to press the imagination to its limits. Even allowing for such a tone while citing the beatitudes (which is doubtful), does anyone really believe Jesus whispered, "For I say to you, that unless your righteousness exceeds the righteousness of the scribes and Pharisees, you will by no means enter the kingdom of heaven" (Matt. 5:20)? Why do people not perceive that such strong statements could have been presented forcefully? The answer says more about their own expectations for preachers today than anything else. Paul avoided the flowery oratory of his day when preaching (1 Cor. 2:1-5) so much so that his enemies attempted to use this fact against him (2 Cor. 10:10). The whole of this passage demonstrates the point of tone. "For even if I should boast somewhat more about our authority, which the Lord gave us for edification and not for your destruction, I shall not be ashamed — lest I seem to terrify you by letters" (2 Cor. 10:8-9). When Paul says, "lest I seem to terrify you by letters," he is using sarcasm in reference to the accusation rather than stating it as fact. The prophet Micaiah also used sarcasm when he mimicked the response of Ahab's prophets for hire (1 Kings 22:12, 15). Ahab recognized his sarcasm immediately and demanded a more respectful answer (1 Kings 22:16), though he did not like the truth (1 Kings 22:17).

Surely anyone who has read Matthew 23 can acknowledge the harsh overtones that Jesus used in condemning the scribes and Pharisees. Certainly the expressive tenderness of the Psalmist comes through in Psalm 23! The Bible student should acknowledge these differences that result from the words and recognize them as an integral part of the overall context of the message.

COMPARISON AND CONTRAST

The human mind creates associations and distinguishes differences as an inherent component of thought. A person's eyes are "the color of the ocean." We make lists of pros and cons. We weigh the talents of any given basketball guard against Michael Jordan. People are either for us or against us. Comparison and contrast allows us to measure the extent of likeness and distinguish the level of discord. Comparison should help us realize men of all ethnic backgrounds have much in common, though history demonstrates a concentration on the contrasts presented by ethnicity. But comparison and contrast assist the student greatly in Bible study, aiding him in the discovery of unstated information that the comparison and contrast implies.

The Bible offers a myriad of comparisons and contrasts. The book of Hebrews compares and contrasts Jesus with Moses, the priesthood of Jesus with the priesthood of Aaron, and the sacrifice of Christ with the sacrifice of bulls and goats. Paul often contrasts the Old Covenant with the New (Rom. 7-8; Gal. 3-4; 2 Cor. 3). The whole of Jesus' life implies comparison and contrast (Matt. 16:13-16). The gospel invites men to compare their lives to God's standard (John 12:48; 17:17) and to contrast their behavior with Jesus Christ's (1 Pet. 2:22-23). Paul compares both the behavior and opportunities of Jews and Gentiles in the opening chapters of Romans (Rom. 1:18-3:31) and the divergent receptions he received as a preacher in his second epistle to the Corinthians (2 Cor. 6:8-10). However, while most recognize these more straightforward comparisons and contrasts, many doctrinal gems lie just below the surface waiting for a student willing to discover them.

In the thirteenth chapter of 1 Corinthians, Paul presents a contrast that some overlook. After describing how love behaves, Paul returns to his discussion regarding spiritual gifts. "Love never fails. But whether there are prophecies, they will fail; whether there are tongues, they will cease; whether there is knowledge, it will vanish away. For we know in part and we prophesy in part. But when that which is perfect has come, then that which is in part will be done away" (1 Cor. 13:8–10). The short series in verse eight, by comparison, establishes the subject matter as the spiritual gifts discussed in chapter twelve. Paul then refers to knowledge and prophecies in verse nine as being "in part" or "partial." In verse ten Paul guarantees that these miraculous activities, which are only "in part," will cease "when that which is perfect has come." The phrase "that which is perfect" could be translated more precisely as "the complete thing." So Paul pointed to the cessation of miracles at the time when that which completely fulfilled their purpose would come on the scene. Miracles, Paul says, were insufficient as a means of declaring God's will that would be replaced when God's will was available in a complete form. Thus, since the purpose of miracles was to communicate and confirm the gospel, once the gospel reached a form where it could be presented as a whole unit, miracles would cease. "The complete thing" therefore to which Paul referred was the completed New Testament. Since the Holy Spirit completed the New Testament at the end of the first century, after which it was shortly compiled into a single unit, miracles ceased at that time as well. Through comparison and contrast, while also using historical context and word meanings, the Bible student can discern the meaning of the phrase "that which is perfect." Miracles were an inferior means of communicating God's will; the Bible is superior.

The book of Hebrews opens with two comparison and contrast sections, using angels as the point of contrast in each. In the first the writer contrasts angels with Jesus to demonstrate that Jesus is not an angel but deity (Heb. 1:5-14). He emphasizes that the Messiah had a special relationship with God and a particular, developed character that the angels did not enjoy (Heb. 1:5), that the Messiah is worthy of worship (Heb. 1:6) while angels fulfill subsidiary roles in fulfilling God's will (Heb. 1:7), and that the Messiah sits on an eternal throne (Heb. 1:8-12) as a result of His victory (Heb. 1:13) while angels serve Him for man's benefit (Heb. 1:14).

In Hebrews 1 the writer presents both sides of the contrast, but when comparison occurs statements pertaining to one side imply the opposite for the other. If a person describes two people named Bob and Fred who look very different, and tells you that Bob is tall, then you rightly conclude that Fred is short. It is possible in some cases for Bob and Fred both to be tall, but when the discussion itself differentiates according to physical appearance, knowing the nature of the contrast and the trait of one person automatically distinguishes it from and identifies the trait of the other. In Hebrews 2 the author contrasts angels with Jesus to demonstrate that Jesus did not become an angel but became a man (Heb. 2:5-18). In this case, after supplying information to demonstrate the humanity of Christ, he did not always provide the opposing trait of angels, but the contrast implies them, though people rarely study Hebrews 2 with this in mind.

In these two chapters, if Jesus and angels had the same characteristics, there would be no contrast. If there is no contrast, there is no difference. If there is no difference, there is no argument. If there is no argument, there is no point in writing it.

ASKING THE RIGHT QUESTIONS

The Nobel laureate Mahfouz Naguib once said, "You can tell whether a man is clever by his answers. You can tell whether a man is wise by his questions."[1] No one who studies the Bible understands everything—and certainly not on the first reading—which *should* mean that people have questions. Many materials purporting to assist people in their studies ask questions that address only the surface issues of a text rather than the real meaning. On the day of Pentecost Peter quoted Joel's affirmation, "And it shall come to pass That whoever calls on the name of the Lord Shall be saved" (Acts 2:21). If a person poses the question, "According to Acts 2:21, what must one do to be saved?" the expected answer would be "He must call on the name of the Lord." However, such inquiries require a minimum level of thought and necessitate nothing more than reading the verse and filling in the blanks. And this question often is one of the more difficult queries posed! Did this question lead the student to any greater understanding of the verse than he could have obtained by reading it? No. So why ask it? All it accomplishes is making the student feel good about his current knowledge (or reading ability) without helping him to grow in his understanding. As John Maxwell, the leadership guru, has said, "Wrong questions shut down the process of creative thinking. They direct thinkers down the same *old* path, or they chide them into believing that thinking isn't necessary at all."[2]

Questions that benefit a Bible student explore meaning and application without taking anything for granted. Joel's inspired words are not self-explanatory. A student must identify his reference to "the Lord." Is this speaking of God the Father or God the Son? Why does the phrase "in the name of" appear at all? What action does "call upon" imply? Considering some doctrinal views in the religious world, one might also ask: "Who is *not* included in 'whoever'?" These questions challenge the Bible student to look within the context for the answers.

Follow-up questions are also essential to draw out the deeper meaning of a text. Asking, "Does the Holy Spirit dwell within a Christian?" only introduces the subject. "How?" addresses what is really at issue. If a student only asks the first question, he learns very little. Asking the second calls on the Bible student to study a great

1 Quoted by Gwen Yount Carden. *Listen Up! The smartest things you'll ever hear from the famous and not-so-famous.* Boca Raton, FL: American Media Mini Mags, Inc., 2003, p. 75.
2 John C. Maxwell. *Thinking for a Change.* United States of America: Warner Books, 2003, p. 111.

deal if he is to answer it correctly. After a student answers the obvious questions he should ask himself "How?" to address the application and "Why?" to force himself to give adequate contextual reasoning that justifies the original answer. Some people feel threatened and pressured when asked "How?" and "Why?" because they often reveal ignorance. But ignorance will become a *perpetual* problem for those unwilling to ask and answer hard questions.

Basic questions ask people to look at a verse; good questions ask them to consider the context. Basic questions address facts; good questions address meaning. Basic questions require basic answers; good questions require good answers. Bible study should begin with basic questions; it just should not end there.

SIGNIFICANCE

In 1 Corinthians 2:12-13 the apostle Paul describes the miraculous process of inspiration, affirming the Holy Spirit's role in assuring that every word written fit exactly what God wanted—the doctrine we call verbal plenary inspiration. Since God is infinite, and since God has a purpose, then all God does He does with purpose. Regarding inspiration, this itself implies the necessity of God's careful involvement in inspiration down to the presence or absence of articles or the choice of a particular preposition. Every word of inspiration holds a special significance for the simple reason that God inspired every word.

Some find it fashionable to skip over vast amounts of scripture (or just the most difficult portions) without comment. While surveys have their place in Bible study, they also leave much unexplained. Many accept this and move on, but to a person who dedicates himself to understanding God's will, leaving what may be treasures of wisdom unearthed is an unthinkable option. Granted, not every passage of scripture carries equal doctrinal impact. The genealogy recorded in Genesis 5 does not have the same appeal as the accounts of creation, the fall, Cain and Abel, or the worldwide flood. Yet the information recorded in Genesis 5 offers insights and background necessary to appreciate the whole picture. This chapter tells us the length of a normal lifespan prior to the flood. It notes that Adam and Eve had daughters as well as sons. It tells us of the marvelous character and life of Enoch. Then it introduces Noah and his family who figure prominently in the next section of scripture. These are bridges in the inspired record, but Bible students would do well to enjoy the scenery while crossing them.

The differences in recording the same events, which some consider contradictions, actually provide insight into the writing. Mark's choice of material demonstrates how well he knew his Roman audience. The various accounts of Paul's conversion provide different perspectives and serve different purposes, each offering a few individual tidbits on its own. Regardless of the material, Bible students should ask themselves questions that search for significance: Why did God include this in the text? How does this verse or passage support the author's case? Why did He use a particular reference? Why *this*? Why *now*? In Romans Paul waited until after addressing Gentile sin to detail the Jews' own problems. Then he gave a series of Old Testament quotations, all but one of which referred to the Jews specifically as a sinful people. By explaining God's relationship with both Jews and Gentiles, their amenability, and their access to revelation, Paul presented a powerful case for justification through Jesus Christ.

There is significance in the words, the phrasings, the argumentation, the choice of material, and the figures chosen by the Holy Spirit. The Bible student's responsibility is to search for that significance. You must guard against forcing a particular significance on a passage that it does not teach, but if you fail to look you may miss the whole point of the writing.

IMMEDIATE AND REMOTE CONTEXT

Preaching trends have vacillated between an emphasis on remote context in topical sermons and an emphasis on immediate context in textual and expository sermons. The remote context mainly consists of what we have called "general context" and provides a framework of doctrinal understanding, while the immediate context examines the intricacies of paragraphs and verses. Each has its place, but each has also been abused. The only way to understand and use remote context correctly is first to understand the immediate context of those passages that provide the principles and framework of a study.

Also, some people have twisted exposition of immediate context into an opportunity to make a passage say whatever they wish it to say without regard for what the Bible says elsewhere. Good Bible study does not take an either/or approach to context. The immediate context and the remote context work in harmony, and the Bible student should consider both in his studies.

Jesus often referred His hearers to scripture as He taught them and corrected their understanding. New Testament authors also frequently quoted passages of scripture from the Old Testament in order to support their arguments. The purpose in each instance was to demonstrate how the other statements made within the conversation, sermon, or epistle remained consistent with what God said. The writer of Hebrews referred to the great heroes of faith in Hebrews 11 to demonstrate that his theme of salvation through a faith that obeys what God says was consistent with God's actions throughout time. Likewise, his earlier discussion in chapters three and four showed that God punished those who did not listen to Him—a lesson the writer did not want his readers to learn the hard way.

When the writers referred to an Old Testament passage, they expected their readers to consider the context of that passage. When Paul quoted Psalms 116:10 in 2 Corinthians 4:13, "I believed, and therefore I spoke," he did not use it simply because the words sounded good or fit what he wanted to say. Rather, the context of Psalm 116 reveals that the Psalmist felt great distress yet trusted the Lord to deliver him. This is exactly Paul's point in 2 Corinthians. When Matthew quoted Jeremiah in Matthew 2:18, he understood and expected his readers to understand that the passage referred to Judah's pain at the hands of a foreign leader and applied this principle to the situation Judah felt at the decree of Herod to kill all male children under two years old.

Jesus used remote context when he quoted Deuteronomy 6:16 to explain the devil's misinterpretation of Psalm 91:11-12. The verses Satan quoted were true, but he had applied them beyond the framework of remote context. Bible students should consider the immediate context of any passage they use as a "prooftext," and they should consider the remote context of the Bible to guard against inserting opinion into immediate context. Complete contextual consistency is the hallmark of good students of the Bible.

CONCLUSION

Most people consider immediate context the simplest part of Bible study. After all, it means what it says! But immediate context requires the Bible student to consider every aspect of the text before him. He must determine the relationship between a particular paragraph and the surrounding paragraphs. He must learn what this related material indicates about the text under consideration along with any important information that the text might offer in regard to the surrounding material. Immediate context pushes the Bible student to identify the impact of every word upon the meaning of the text. It provides small tidbits of information that may prove to be valuable nuggets if mined further.

Thorough analysis of the immediate context by means of comparison and contrast brings the Bible's implications to the forefront for consideration and study instead of leaving essential teaching obscured by hazy thought. By asking probing questions about the words, the phrases, the relationships between various words, and the significance of a text, the Bible student begins to peel back layers of divine thought that existed all along (Acts 8:30-35; 17:11). When the student places this newly gleaned information alongside similar findings and continues his work, the beauty of the Lord's message will never grow boring and will always refresh the soul.

Sadly, personal comfort levels often keep us from exploring immediate context to its fullest extent. Most people remain satisfied understanding most of the words and the basic point of a passage. However, without deeper investigation these will likely *miss* the real point of a given passage at various times. This approach is spiritually barren because a person will rarely if ever learn something new but will continue to review the same thing over and over again, convinced each time that his interpretation is correct because it agrees with what he thought the previous time. But an interpretation that does not address the *whole* passage and that provides only a minimal amount of reasoned explanation is not an interpretation at all; it is an opinion. It is the in-depth analysis of the immediate context that establishes the meaning God intended. And if we fall short of that, why are we studying the Bible?

Immediate context includes:

- Surrounding material
- Circumstantial references
- Theme
- Ecclesiastical terminology
- Titles
- People and places
- Word choices
- Idioms
- Lists
- Conjunctions
- Tone
- Comparison and contrast
- Asking the right questions
- Significance
- Relationship to remote context

Recommended Reading

Large, James. *Titles & Symbols of Christ*. Hodder & Stoughton, 1888; reprint, AMG Publishers, World Reference, 1994.
Stone, Nathan. *Names of God*. Chicago, IL: Moody Press, 1944.

Questions for Discussion

1. Considering various elements of immediate context, how might a person's view of inspiration affect his interpretation?
2. What ecclesiastical term has caused the greatest misunderstanding?
3. What titles have an historical basis?
4. How do you know when something is an idiom?
5. What question should always be on the Bible student's mind?

Assignment

Choose a passage of Scripture, and then examine every aspect of its immediate context, recording your conclusions on a separate piece of paper.

CHAPTER 12

Biblical Principles

INTRODUCTION

The Bible was not written yesterday, nor was it addressed with a United States zip code. So while it applies to all men today, the means and manner of application might differ *if* the application cited in the New Testament is tied to the culture, time period, or location. The situation today does not coincide *exactly* with the situation of the apostles, but exact correspondence in culture and situation is unnecessary in order to apply the lessons of the gospel because the gospel announces principles that pertain to every age and every culture in addition to its pattern for the church and particular do's and don'ts. The difficulty lies in discerning when a precept is a principle and when it is a specific part of God's pattern. At times this is a daunting task. It is no new problem, but it has taken on new manifestations and greater prominence today due to current efforts to justify the abandonment of God's pattern and the adoption of doctrinal changes based upon modern culture.

So what makes a biblical principle a principle? After all, it is one thing to call something a principle and quite another to prove that it is a principle. A principle, as the word suggests, is a foundational precept. It is a fundamental truth that underlies other concepts and supports them. Principles do not change, though their applications might. God has not always required *all* the same actions in worship. Under both Patriarchal Law and Mosaical Law animal sacrifices were accepted actions of worship. Under the New Covenant animal sacrifices are no longer accepted but remembering the sacrificial death of our Lord in communion is now divinely legislated (1 Cor. 11:23-29; Acts 20:7). Underlying worship in all of these covenants is the principle that only divinely sanctioned worship is acceptable worship

(Gen. 4; Lev. 10:1-2; John 4:24). In Jesus' discussion of worship with the Samaritan woman He referred to spirit and truth as essential elements of worship—correct attitude and correct action. This principle implies a limit on correct actions for our worship, which means that you must look for worshipful actions in the New Testament that prove acceptable to God rather than worshiping in whatever way suits your disposition.

Some people wish to accept some generic biblical principles while rejecting any specific instruction. Some accept biblical principles but reject any application of those principles. Others see only specifics, attempting to avoid the responsibility of determining and applying any biblical principles. But you cannot live a generic Christian life. You cannot obey if you do not know what to obey. You cannot "walk in Christ" (Col. 2:6-7) by moving to Nazareth. To have the mind of Christ (Phil. 2:5-8), you must learn to think like Christ, which is why you must learn to think in terms of biblical principles.

DETERMINE THE CONCEPTUAL DEPTH

Although the New Testament contains many principles and non-specific precepts, it also includes examples of how those principles and precepts apply. Sometimes the application precedes the principle; sometimes it follows the principle. The Bible student must therefore determine the difference between an action that illustrates one application of the broader binding principle and an action that is itself specifically bound.

While Jesus instructed His disciples, Luke records, "And behold, a certain lawyer stood up and tested Him, saying, 'Teacher, what shall I do to inherit eternal life?' He said to him, 'What is written in the law? What is your reading of it?' So he answered and said, '"You shall love the Lord your God with all your heart, with all your soul, with all your strength, and with all your mind," and "your neighbor as yourself."' And He said to him, 'You have answered rightly; do this and you will live.' But he, wanting to justify himself, said to Jesus, 'And who is my neighbor?'" (Luke 10:25–29). The lawyer, when prompted by Jesus, recognized the two major principles underlying the whole law, as

Jesus stated elsewhere (Matt. 22:37-40). Therefore, Jesus replied to his query by telling him to apply those principles and he would inherit eternal life: "do this and you will live." The lawyer, however, wished to avoid applying these principles universally by making them part of his character, desiring instead to apply them depending upon the circumstances and his own prejudices. Jesus responded by telling the story of the Good Samaritan (Luke 10:30-35). He then asked the man, "So which of these three do you think was neighbor to him who fell among the thieves?" (Luke 10:36). Thus, Jesus' purpose in relating the story was to force the man to recognize that "neighbor" referred to all fellow men. The lawyer's answer, "He who showed mercy on him," was a synopsis of the Samaritan's actions. "Then Jesus said to him, 'Go and do likewise'" (Luke 10:37). But was Jesus telling the lawyer to go look for an injured man on the road to Jericho? No. When Jesus said, "Go and do likewise," he was referring to the principles cited — not the specific application within the story, though that would apply should the situation arise. The application serves the principle — not the other way around.

The conceptual depth of this account goes far deeper than assisting helpless victims of crimes. The broader statements of love are the point; the story assists us in understanding that true love produces action consistent with that love and that true love should extend to all mankind without partiality. Therefore, accepting and applying principles requires us to integrate them as part of our character, which will then produce corresponding behavior. The lawyer accepted the principles of love intellectually, but his prejudices and selfishness kept him from integrating those principles into his character, which caused him to limit their application. In any text a student should find the broadest concept stated or implied that fits the context. This becomes the basis for application when the exact circumstances do not exist today.

DETERMINE THE BACKGROUND OF SUPPORT

Some of the recent controversies in the church hinge on whether a person should adapt his understanding of the scriptures to "keep up" with modern culture. It did not take long for feminist culture to affect enough women in the church to produce a movement calling for women deacons, women elders, women preachers, and women taking other leading roles in worship. They argue that those passages that traditionally have kept them from fulfilling these leading roles reflected the culture of the Roman Empire and Jewish society but that God did not intend to bind them on a culture that recognized the equality of women. The key to interpreting these passages is to determine the nature of the background support used and evaluate whether or not it uses culture as the determining factor in calling for the prescribed action, as well as whether or not we are comparing apples with apples. In 1 Corinthians 14:34-35 Paul told the Corinthians, "Let your women keep silent in the churches, for they are not permitted to speak; but they are to be submissive, as the law also says. And if they want to learn something, let them ask their own husbands at home; for it is shameful for women to speak in church" (1 Cor. 14:34–35). In this specific instance Paul directly addresses the role of women in assemblies (churches). Paul's use of the phrase "as the law also says" demonstrates that he was establishing consistency with "precedent" rather than reflecting current culture. Therefore, culture was not the basis for this limitation of the woman's role in worship. A quick perusal of the immediate context also demonstrates that the cited limitation of those who could lead in worship was one in a series of divinely authored regulations given in this chapter. In 1 Timothy 2:11-12 Paul makes a more generic pronouncement in regard to spiritual leadership, extending beyond congregational worship: "Let a woman learn in silence with all submission. And I do not permit a woman to teach or to have authority over a man, but to be in silence" (1 Tim. 2:11–12). However, his two supporting reasons are significant: (1) man was created before woman, and (2) woman was deceived. These are not cultural issues; they are historical facts that have no relationship to culture. Therefore, Paul — and the Holy Spirit who inspired Him — intended this statement to apply in every culture.

The question as to whether a doctrine or practice is based on culture or the social circumstances of the day is legitimate. But the answer to such issues should be based on an understanding of the historical background of the time and a close examination of the argumentation used by the writer—not on *modern* culture, as is so often practiced today. Jesus did not base His view of marriage and divorce on culture—or even on the Old Law—but on God's design for marriage in the beginning (Matt. 19:1-9). So before calling something a cultural matter, consider the argument.

DETERMINE THE ORIGIN OF THE BEHAVIOR

Some people mistakenly identify every behavior recorded in the New Testament without respect for the origin of that behavior, either in an attempt to impose the incidentals of biblical culture on Christians today or to attempt to transfer some portion of God's pattern for the church to the level of cultural relativity. But such distinctions exist within the framework of the Bible, and it is essential for people to recognize those distinctions in order to understand the Bible. Some wish to bind the washing of feet (John 13) while others claim that the New Testament's designation that men, and men only, serve in the roles of elder, deacon, and preacher is actually a cultural matter. Therefore, it is incumbent upon the Bible student to establish not only *what* command was given but also *why* it was given. Students must distinguish between what is incidental (being in an upper room) and what is required (partaking of the Lord's Supper). Furthermore, one must discern between the principle and the cultural application of that principle. To do this one must first become familiar with that culture and then evaluate the practice based upon the biblical author's argumentation and context.

An important question to consider is: Did the practice in question exist prior to a divine command? Is the practice accepted as is, regulated and changed somewhat, or instituted? The acceptance of a practice would mean that it existed previously and was morally acceptable but would not require the exact manner as the only acceptable method. The regulation of a practice assumes its existence but then provides additional instruction on what is necessary for that condition to be acceptable to God. The institution of a practice occurs when some new action has been introduced. These three designations are critical if one is to understand biblical and cultural distinctions.

The Bible assumes the existence of fasting as a practice undertaken to dedicate a person's time and attention to important spiritual matters. The practice itself is accepted, as Jesus demonstrates (Matt. 4:2). When He mentions fasting in the Sermon on the Mount, He further regulates it—if one should choose to practice it—by addressing the attitude that some had adopted (Matt. 6:16-18). But nothing about fasting was ever instituted. Therefore, it would be acceptable if done for the right reasons, but it is not required. In the eighteenth century some in America attempted to justify slavery through appeals to the Bible. But God did not institute slavery, nor did He accept it morally. He did regulate the existing practice in Judaism to curb its abuses (Lev. 25) and then demonstrated through Paul's letter to Philemon that the principles of Christian love would lead to its abolition (Phm. 10-21). Therefore, while the Bible did not condemn the institution of slavery specifically, it does not accept it as righteous behavior.

Two of the common objections made in regard to specific commands of the New Testament stem from failing to distinguish between the acceptance, regulation, and institution of practices. Since the Bible was written within the framework of particular cultures, it should surprise no one that cultural practices of those times and places should receive mention by the biblical writers. However, that the Bible mentions and accepted some cultural practices of the day does not mean that God expected or allowed the culture to dictate how Christians should conduct themselves.

The posture of hands raised heavenward was a posture of prayer for centuries prior to Paul's writing to Timothy (1 Kings 8:22-54). When Paul told Timothy, "I desire therefore that the men pray everywhere, lifting up holy hands, without wrath and doubting" (1 Tim. 2:8), the context centered on proper spiritual leadership and what God expected of man in order to accept his prayer. Since the lifting up of hands as one accepted posture already existed, what stood out was Paul's point. Paul simply referred to the common cultural practice of those who led public prayer in order to emphasize that the character and attitude of the person leading mattered (as well as the gender). Likewise, a kiss was the normal greeting during the first century, and still is in some places today. Therefore, when Paul said, "Greet one another with a holy kiss," (Rom. 16:16; 2 Cor. 13:12) he was not instituting and requiring a practice but regulating an existing practice. The form of greeting existed as part of the culture prior to the command. What Paul did require was that the greeting be "holy." Christians should recognize when greeting other Christians that they share a distinct relationship and bond.

If applied in the same manner, it would not be wrong to practice any of the aforementioned items, but it would be wrong to require what were the cultural practices in the past of others today. We could lift our hands as a posture for prayer so long as it is not treated as the backdoor to Pentecostalism. We could wash one another's feet. If a sincere Christian is unable to distinguish between these cultural matters and biblical commands, it would be better for him to practice a morally acceptable activity from another culture that God does not require than for him to disobey biblical commands. But few who mention the difficulties of understanding these matters desire to adopt the culture of first century Christians; to the contrary, they want the Church to adopt the culture of today's society. Lest we forget, Paul told the Romans: "And do not be conformed to this world, but be transformed by the renewing of your mind, that you may prove what is that good and acceptable and perfect will of God" (Rom. 12:2).

DETERMINE BIBLICAL CONSISTENCY

Before a student is at liberty to call some idea a biblical principle, he must establish that the concept is consistent with everything else taught in the Bible. Some charlatans have taken the precepts of Christian giving (1 Cor. 16:1-2; 2 Cor. 9:6-7), combined them with promises of God's care (Matt. 6:25-34), and created the damnable doctrine of "tithing your way to prosperity." This fails the test of consistency for various reasons. It encourages covetousness. It falsely interprets God's promised care for the necessities of life in terms of monetary wealth. It elevates the amount or percentage of the gift to a higher level than the heart of the giver. It ties God's blessings to worldliness. Furthermore, it implies that financial prosperity is an expression of God's favor while poverty indicates God's displeasure, a false concept since at least the days of Job.

Those who quote some passages about faith in order to promote the doctrine of "faith only," which they regard as a New Testament principle of salvation, must disregard *other* passages about faith in the process. Jesus does indeed say, "Do not be afraid; only believe, and she will be made well" (Luke 8:50). This verse conveniently provides the two important words "believe" and "only" together. However, the situation and promise did not pertain to salvation but to the healing of a young girl; additionally, Jesus' actions were done to build belief rather than as a result of belief. So the doctrine of "faith only" in regard to salvation could not come from this passage contextually, regardless of the wording. Likewise, Paul's statement in Romans 5:1, "Therefore, having been justified by faith, we have peace with God through our Lord Jesus Christ" (Rom. 5:1), does not teach salvation by faith only. "Only" is nowhere in the text, and to interpret as if this is the final word on justification without looking elsewhere in the Bible is dishonest. But neither is a so-called principle of "faith only" consistent with other statements in the Bible. James said, "You see then that a man is justified by works, and not by faith only" (Jas. 2:24).

Following a sermon from Nehemiah 3, one man argued that the Lord did not expect "non-homogenous groups" in the church to work together. How he expected to reconcile his belief with specific declarations regarding Christian unity (Eph. 2:14-16; 4:1-3; Gal. 3:26-29), Christian charity (Rom. 12:10; John 13:34-35), forbearance (Col. 3:13), the mind of Christ (Phil. 2:5-8), and Paul's example (1 Cor. 9:22), escapes me. A biblical principle will never be in conflict with any other passage of scripture or known truth. Far too often people take their pet ideas, call them principles, and then go looking for at least one place in the Bible that might support what they want. Not so with biblical principles. Biblical principles require biblical consistency.

DETERMINE THE AUTHOR'S REASONING

Determining the proper manner and extent to which we are to apply a principle derived from scripture depends upon the author's own stated reasoning. How did he limit the application? How far did he extend it and why? Asking "Why?" is essential in order to distinguish between the particular cases cited and the reasoning that applies to other coordinate situations.

In 1 Corinthians Paul addressed many problems, among which was the instance of sexual immorality that required congregational discipline (1 Cor. 5). Though many overlook the connection, Paul continues to address this problem in the sixth chapter of that book. His overall structure addressing the sexual immorality includes: how to handle it (congregationally) (1 Cor. 5), how *not* to handle it (Do not go to court) (1 Cor. 6:1-8), the moral knowledge they should have applied to the situation (1 Cor. 6:9-11), and a refutation of attempts to justify sexual immorality (1 Cor. 6:12-20). Within this last section Paul not only condemns sexual immorality but also provides a principled explanation as to what makes it wrong. Therefore, once a student determines how each "part" of the context fits into this principle, the principle can and should be applied to other matters that fall beneath the parameters of that principle.

A Bible student should therefore begin by examining a text in search of the reasons given by the author as to why he makes the inspired moral judgments in his conclusion. Consider Paul's reasoning in 1 Corinthians 6:12-20: "All things are lawful for me, but all things are not helpful. All things are lawful for me, but I will not be brought under the power of any. Foods for the stomach and the stomach for foods, but God will destroy both it and them. Now the body is not for sexual immorality but for the Lord, and the Lord for the body. And God both raised up the Lord and will also raise us up by His power. Do you not know that your bodies are members of Christ? Shall I then take the members of Christ and make them members of a harlot? Certainly not! Or do you not know that he who is joined to a harlot is one body with her? For 'the two,' He says, 'shall become one flesh.' But he who is joined to the Lord is one spirit with Him. Flee sexual immorality. Every sin that a man does is outside the body, but he who commits sexual immorality sins against his own body. Or do you not know that your body is the temple of the Holy Spirit who is in you, whom you have from God, and you are not your own? For you were bought at a price; therefore glorify God in your body and in your spirit, which are God's" (1 Cor. 6:12–20). Paul begins with one principle addressing ethics, argues further based upon the principle of fulfilling God's purpose, arguing that this should be considered from an eternal viewpoint, draws specific conclusions based on principles drawn from remote context, calls for corrective action, reminds them of consequences, both physical and spiritual, and closes with yet another principle. Thus, Paul argued against sexual immorality through appeals to ethics, God's purpose for man, scriptural implications, consequences, and the ownership of the body.

In 1 Corinthians 6:12 Paul cited his reasoning to explain why sexual immorality is wrong, beginning by addressing the ethical fallacy of moral equivalency that some apparently used to justify the behavior in question. Paul responds by emphasizing that just because something is possible does not make it the right thing to do. All activities, good and bad, are an available choice to man, but that does not mean that all activities are morally equivalent (1 Cor. 6:12). Having established this principle, Paul applied it to sexual immorality. The fact that God created the human sex drive does not imply that He set no limits in regard to its expression. Sexual immorality is not morally equivalent to eating, as apparently some were arguing. There are important moral distinctions between the two. God created food to provide for man's sustenance while he lives upon the earth. Therefore, eating food fulfills the purpose for which God made it. Furthermore, the relationship between food and the body is temporary. But God did not create man or his body for the purpose of giving himself over to his lusts, as in committing sexual immorality, but for the purpose of doing the Lord's will (1 Cor. 6:13). (Notice the change from the name "Christ" to "Lord.") Furthermore, Paul argues, the purpose of the Lord's coming was not just to provide for the redemption of the soul but also for the resurrection of the body (1 Cor. 6:14). Therefore, our bodies do not really belong to us but to the One who gave His own body for us. So what we do with our bodies is a moral matter, and what we do with our bodies affects our relationship with Christ. What we choose to do with our bodies demonstrates the one to whom we have truly given ourselves and to whom we belong. We can either give Christ control of what we do with our bodies or we can give that control over to someone else (1 Cor. 6:15). Paul then points his readers to the scriptures to demonstrate the implications of a sexual relationship. No one can successfully deny that sexual immorality is incompatible with the Christian life because from the very beginning God intended the sexual relationship to be shared only in the union of marriage between a husband and wife (Heb. 13:4). Therefore, giving your body to someone outside marriage unites you with sin (1 Cor. 6:16). Moreover, someone who has become a Christian entered a spiritual union with Christ and thereby promises to remain true to the conditions of that union, with the implication drawn from his prior argument (1 Cor. 6:14-15) that this spiritual union takes priority over a physical union (1 Cor. 6:17).

Based on the reasons Paul cited in 1 Corinthians 6:12-17 Paul makes the necessary application: Every Christian should avoid sexual immorality for the plague of sin that it is. But Paul does not stop at this point, choosing instead to offer additional reasons why a Christian is morally obligated to abstain from such behavior. Sexual immorality, he emphasizes, does not just violate God's law; it involves the body itself in the sin, a body that is supposed to be at Christ's disposal, and the body itself bears some of the consequences of that sin because the body itself has become the instrument of sin (1 Cor. 6:18). When you commit a sin such as this, you are taking the same structure which is supposed to represent a place compatible with God's holiness and treating it as a brothel. While Christians were to make their bodies the instrument through which God's will, revealed by the Holy Spirit (originally by miraculous means and now through the Word of God), was accomplished, committing sexual immorality turns the body into the instrument of sin and becomes abhorrent to God because it offends His holiness. No one has the right to use his body in this way, because we do not own our bodies (1 Cor. 6:19). God secured ownership of our bodies when Christ died on the cross for us. Therefore, whatever we do in life – including with our bodies – must reflect God's will, God's character, God's greatness, and God's ownership (1 Cor. 6:20)

Based on Paul's reasoning, we can extract the general principle: What you do with your body affects your relationship with God. The purpose of man is to glorify God by reflecting God's character (Eph. 4:24). This is accomplished by means of a life lived in a human body; therefore, anything that uses that body improperly, harms that body, or limits that body's ability to fulfill its purpose is detrimental to man's purpose and sinful. So while the specific application of this passage addresses the sin of fornication, Paul's argumentation provides some reasons—such as the divine ownership of the body—that pertain to other issues. Illegal drugs, alcohol, and the improper use of legal drugs all harm the body and therefore violate this principle, as would specifically failing to care for the body properly. We should thus care for our bodies and protect them in light of how they can be used to fulfill God's will.

DETERMINE SIGNIFICANCE

Bible students sometimes attempt to minimize the effect of a principle by limiting all discussion to the specific application used by the inspired writer. The partial purpose underlying this technique, in the spirit of the community church movement, is to eliminate barriers to fellowship by redefining what constitutes a barrier. Thus, they treat the modern applications of principles pertaining to Christian doctrine and conduct as matters of opinion, binding, in theory, only those specific applications cited by the biblical text.

The most notable example of this practice comes from John's second epistle, where he writes, "Whoever transgresses and does not abide in the doctrine of Christ does not have God. He who abides in the doctrine of Christ has both the Father and the Son" (2 John 9). Proponents of a limited application argue that the context indicates that John's reference excluded only those who accepted the Gnostic doctrine which denied the incarnation of Christ (2 John 7). Since John identified Gnosticism as the problem in verse seven, they argue, then his reference to "the doctrine of Christ" in verse nine must mean "the doctrine *about* Christ." Opponents of this view interpret "the doctrine of Christ" to mean "the doctrine *belonging to* Christ," encompassing the whole of the New Covenant. Therefore, the first view accepts the limitation of fellowship only in regard to the denial of the incarnation while the latter treats this statement as a principle pertaining to the whole of Christian doctrine.

The significance and extent of application indicated by John is determined, however, not simply by an argument over the meaning of the phrase "the doctrine of Christ" but on the basis of the breadth of the apostle's statements in context. If John's first reference to "the doctrine of Christ" is limited to the denial of the incarnation, then what follows should be equally limited. Since "does not have God" refers to a severing of fellowship, then "has both the Father and the Son" refers to the existence of fellowship. Does John teach here that the only doctrine necessary to enjoy fellowship with God is belief in the incarnation? What about Christ's deity or resurrection? Do they not matter? Where does such an argument end? The *significance* of this passage is not limited to one doctrine but to all Christian doctrine.

Even if a person takes verse nine of Second John as a reference to Gnosticism, based upon verse seven, the principle must apply beyond this particular doctrine, as verses five and six demonstrate. John first emphasized the importance of loving one another, recalling the commandment given by Jesus on the night of His betrayal (John 13:34-35). His purpose is two-fold: to confirm that love and its accompanying behavior (1 Cor. 13:4-7) are commendable and to emphasize that love is defined by the commandments of God. One of these commandments is to remain true to Christian doctrine and practice as it was originally revealed, a principle already mentioned by John in verse four, "I rejoiced greatly that I have found some of your children walking in truth, as we received commandment from the Father" (2 John 4). "Walking in truth" refers to all of God's revelation to man and includes the commitment to God's truth—in doctrine and in life—that is the basis for our fellowship (2 John 1-2). When John warned against the false teaching of Gnosticism and those who promoted it, he was explaining why it was unacceptable to extend hospitality to them (2 John 10-11), even though hospitality is an act of love, which is commanded (Rom. 12:13). Having departed from the truth, false teachers have abandoned the basis for the completely open and accommodating relationship of fellow Christians. Since they have no fellowship with God (2 John 9b), a faithful Christian should not assist them in their error or give them the idea that their ideas are acceptable, including the extension of hospitality to them (since this enabled them to travel and spread their false message).

John referred to the general principle of walking in truth to demonstrate the principle these false teachers had violated by their Gnostic teaching. The consequence of failing to walk in truth, whether by acting contrary to truth or teaching contrary to truth, is the breakdown of fellowship with God—another principle (Amos 3:3)—which then had to apply to the Gnostics. But John's identification of Gnosticism and the denial of Christ's incarnation as "anti-truth behavior," which causes God to withdraw His fellowship, does NOT exclude other false doctrines from fitting this category as well. John's exhortation not to assist these false teachers was founded in another principle yet, which Paul stated elsewhere: "And have no fellowship with the unfruitful works of darkness, but rather expose them" (Eph. 5:11). Assisting false teachers involves Christians in their work. Supporting false doctrine places a Christian in opposition to truth, which in turn breaks his own fellowship with God. So while loving one another is a Christian principle, it does not override the principles of walking in truth and light in order to maintain fellowship with God (1 John 1:5-7). To the contrary, since Christian love involves obedience and adherence to truth (John 14:5; 1 John 5:3), offering assistance and support to those upholding error is not loving at all. One Christian principle does not override others. They must work in harmony with one another or they do not work at all.

DETERMINE THE MODERN EQUIVALENT

After recounting the Israelites' spiritual difficulties following their departure from Egypt, Paul told the Corinthians, "Now all these things happened to them as examples, and they were written for our admonition, upon whom the ends of the ages have come" (1 Cor. 10:11). The situations of the Corinthians and the Israelites were not identical, nor were their problems. They *were* similar. It was this similarity that made the Israelites an appropriate example for the Corinthians, and it is the use of such examples that demonstrates the proper application of principles.

By their very nature, principles require the Bible student to assess the ancient application, derive the lesson, and then make modern day application. To accomplish this, one must first understand the relationship between the principle and the original application, then, using logical association, he can establish what is equivalent to those circumstances today. However, he must remember not only how the situation is similar but also how it differs if he is to avoid drawing unwarranted conclusions. The New Testament speaks of both bondservants and masters (Col. 3:22-4:1; Eph. 6:5-9), but the thirteenth amendment finally abolished slavery in America. However, taking that difference into account, these passages are not irrelevant because they still offer valuable instruction pertaining to behavior in *any* work environment. Employees have many options available to them (quitting for one) that bondservants did not enjoy, but they are the modern equivalent for people in the workplace who are under another's authority. This approach—recognizing the differences but applying the lesson insofar as the situation correlates to the modern equivalent—is the foundation for the application of principles, as the account in Leviticus 10:1-7 of Nadab and Abihu's sin and the consequences that followed demonstrates.

Following the giving of detailed instruction regarding the proper manner for offering sacrifices, Moses writes, "Then Nadab and Abihu, the sons of Aaron, each took his censer and put fire in it, put incense on it, and offered profane fire before the Lord, which He had not commanded them" (Lev. 10:1). "Profane" indicates that God did not recognize their sacrifice as acceptable; the last phrase, "which He had not commanded them," explains why. God does not accept that which He does not request—the principle of silence and the necessity of establishing divine authority (Col. 3:17; Heb. 7:14). God's response to their sin was swift and decisive: "So fire went out from the Lord and devoured them, and they died before the Lord" (Lev. 10:2). God will judge those who do not abide by His authority (Rom. 2:6; John 12:48). The fact that today God reserves the punishment for sin until Judgment Day does not diminish the certainty of the principle (Heb. 9:27).

Building upon verses one and two in Leviticus 10, the LORD adds an additional thought: "Moses said to Aaron, 'This is what the Lord spoke, saying: "By those who come near Me I must be regarded as holy; And before all the people I must be glorified."' So Aaron held his peace" (Lev. 10:3). This further explanation of Nadab and Abihu's sin implies the principles of worship: (1) God is to be the center of worship (Matt. 4:10; Rom. 1:25), (2) the worshipper must maintain the right attitude in worship (Heb. 12:28-29), and as verses one and two demonstrate, (3) the action of worship must have divine approval (John 4:24). It is not enough to offer worship; it must be directed toward God, keeping Him as the focus, by someone with a reverent attitude using actions that God Himself has accepted as pleasing worship. The modern movement toward "entertainment" violates the first principle as clearly as mechanical instruments of music used in worship violate the last.

Moses then moves beyond the judgment against Nadab and Abihu to the lessons implied for the benefit of those who lived. "Then Moses called Mishael and Elzaphan, the sons of Uzziel the uncle of Aaron, and said to them, 'Come near, carry your brethren from before the sanctuary out of the camp.' So they went near and carried them by their tunics out of the camp, as Moses had said" (Lev. 10:4-5). The separation required implies the principle of holiness. They were to be "set apart" from what is common or evil (Ex. 19:22), placing anything that might defile them "out of the camp" because it did not correspond to the character required by God. This separateness provides the foundation for many of the moral pronouncements of holiness found in the New Testament (2 Cor. 7:1; 1 Pet. 1:16), along with the church discipline commanded in order to maintain the purity of the Lord's church (1 Cor. 5:6-7; Eph. 5:27). Jude alludes to this very passage when calling upon Christians to exercise wisdom as well as caution when attempting to convince others of their lost condition: "but others save with fear, pulling them out of the fire, hating even the garment defiled by the flesh" (Jude 1:23). Christians must avoid all compromise or accommodation of sin in the same way that the clothing of Nadab and Abihu was considered unclean as a result of their sin.

In the last two verses in this section, the LORD sets forth what some might consider a harsh declaration: "And Moses said to Aaron, and to Eleazar and Ithamar, his sons, 'Do not uncover your heads nor tear your clothes, lest you die, and wrath come upon all the people. But let your brethren, the whole house of Israel, bewail the burning which the Lord has kindled. You shall not go out from the door of the tabernacle of meeting, lest you die, for the anointing oil of the LORD is upon you.' And they did according to the word of Moses" (Lev. 10:6–7). The key to this passage is the phrase "for the anointing oil of the LORD is upon you." It demonstrates the principle of righteous priorities. Aaron, Eleazar, and Ithamar had spiritual responsibilities that deserved priority regardless of what happened. Doing God's will must take priority over *everything* else (Col. 3:1-2). The priestly responsibilities took priority even though Aaron had lost two of his sons. Jesus said that following Him takes priority over all family obligations and relationships (Luke 14:26). There is never a time when God excuses man for failure to comply with His will. God and God's will must always take priority (Matt. 6:33).

The last sentence of this section is significant: "And they did according to the word of Moses." Obedience is a principle. God required it of Adam and Eve, He required it of Aaron, and He requires it of us. God always has required it. Yet many today cover their eyes to this reality when it comes to salvation. For "though He was a Son, yet He learned obedience by the things which He suffered. And having been perfected, He became the author of eternal salvation to all who obey Him" (Heb. 5:8–9). Jesus was obedient unto death (Phil. 2:5-8), but some do not seem to believe that God requires obedience in baptism as a prerequisite to putting on Christ (Gal. 3:26-27). Yet we should never limit this principle to one particular command. Obedience must extend to the whole of God's will — not just one or two pet commands. There is no excuse for disobedience (2 Th. 1:7-9). There is no command too hard to obey (1 John 5:3). There is no middle ground in obedience (Rom. 6:16-18). As Israel discovered that day, it *is* a matter of life and death. A Bible student must make sure that the application he employs truly fulfills the principle and sufficiently addresses the whole text. Hebrews 11 surely emphasizes the principle of faith, but even a cursory examination of this text shows that this emphasis is not to the exclusion of obedience. One principle does not cancel out another principle. When a conclusion and application put principles in conflict with one another, a student should not abandon one of the principles but should instead abandon the false conclusion that he has drawn and its application.

DETERMINE THE APOSTLES' HANDLING OF PRINCIPLES

The apostle Paul provides an excellent example of the proper handling of a principle and how to apply it in his first epistle to the Corinthians. The Corinthians apparently had listened to people who wished to discredit Paul's work. Among the implied charges against him was the argument that what he said had little value, which, these alleged, explained why he did not ask for financial compensation. In reply, Paul explained that he had every right to expect financial compensation for his efforts instead of supporting himself (1 Cor. 9:6), pointing out that this was consistent with every other type of work with which they were familiar (1 Cor. 9:7). He concluded by showing that the gospel he had preached was of far greater value to them than any amount they could ever offer financially (1 Cor. 9:11). Having said this, he was free to explain that the reason why he had not asked for financial support was so that any such *request* would not become a hindrance to people's faith (1 Cor. 9:12). Within this context Paul referred to a principle from the Old Law to buttress his argument in favor of the financial support of preachers.

After reasoning with the Corinthians based upon their own experience and common sense, Paul appealed to the Old Law, which would have carried added weight since the Corinthians seemed attached to it, as 2 Corinthians implies. "Do I say these things as a mere man? Or does not the law say the same also? For it is written in the law of Moses, 'You shall not muzzle an ox while it treads out the grain.' Is it oxen God is concerned about? Or does He say it altogether for our sakes? For our sakes, no doubt, this is written, that he who plows should plow in hope, and he who threshes in hope should be partaker of his hope" (1 Cor. 9:8–10). Paul's argument concerned the propriety of paying a preacher, but those who have difficulty applying principles must find his appeal to Deuteronomy 25:4 very confusing. How could a command not to muzzle an ox that is treading grain apply to preachers? Paul's explanation of the principle is significant. While this command did help oxen, certainly the people understood that God valued people over oxen (though this may be news to some animal rights activists) and that this was said in order to establish a principle for people (especially since oxen cannot read). Why should they not muzzle an ox that is treading grain? The ox is working for their benefit; therefore, he should at the very least be allowed to benefit somewhat from his efforts. Reasoning *a fortiori*, extracting a general principle from a given statement to apply to another similar or stronger example, Paul explains that the same should be true for a preacher. He is working to benefit others; therefore, he should be rewarded for his efforts. Not only should he receive something, he should *expect* to receive something, and those who receive the benefit of his work are expected to provide something for his benefit. Paul appealed to the Scriptures, derived a broader principle from what was directly stated by applying logic and other biblical knowledge, and then applied that principle to the situation regarding preachers, establishing the God-approved pattern regarding the application of biblical principles.

A CASE STUDY IN PRINCIPLE: 1 CORINTHIANS 11:2-16

Perhaps the most difficult passage pertaining to the relationship between principle, culture, and application is 1 Corinthians 11:2-16. In this discussion the Bible student must determine whether Paul's references to the covering of the head are specific divine legislation or are only the application of a divine principle within the culture of Corinth. The words Paul chose, the correlation with remote context, and the examination of Paul's argumentation are important in discerning when he refers to the principle and its origin versus when he refers to the application and its origin.

Paul first acknowledges the Corinthians' correct attitude in general of accepting apostolic instruction (v. 2) before introducing the matter in which they had failed to apply the lessons received — maintaining respect for the roles God has given to men and women (v. 3). Therefore, having established that man is the head of woman in God's spiritual hierarchy of roles, Paul applies this to the problem in Corinth: Who should and who should not wear a covering while praying and prophesying (vs. 4-6)? Paul does not introduce this particular practice and distinction between men and women; he assumes its existence in Corinth. The Bible student should note carefully the reason Paul gives for determining why a man should not wear a covering and why a woman should: the wrong practice would "dishonor" the head. But what brought the dishonor? Paul does not say; he takes it for granted that the Corinthians would understand. How could he do this? In Corinth having the head veiled indicated respect for the head of the house. This meaning and distinction was especially strong in Corinth, which had a large population of *hetairas*, a group of women who wore no veil as a declaration of their independence from men and the mores of society. For a man to cover his head was an indication that he was not in his proper role, and for a woman to uncover her head was a statement that she was in submission to no man and therefore not in her God-given role. So a Christian man who covered his head was an embarrassment to Christ because he failed to take his God-given role. A Christian woman who uncovered her head embarrassed her husband and the congregational leaders — men — because this signified she did not recognize their leadership.

In verse six Paul states the seriousness of the situation by suggesting that a woman who uncovers her head is in a similar moral situation as that of a woman whose head has been shaved. Thus, Paul uses yet another cultural reference to explain the effect of their ignoring their culture. A shaved head was a punishment for a woman who committed adultery — an embarrassment to her husband indeed. So Paul was demonstrating that a woman's uncovered head in Corinthian culture signified her lack of respect for the leadership of men just as much as a shaved head indicated adultery. If she then showed a lack of respect for male leadership, she was failing to respect God's plan and was identifying herself with an element of Corinthian society that was disreputable, bringing shame on herself, on her husband, and on the church.

After specifically addressing the differing roles God has given men and women, Paul demonstrated how this applied in Corinthian culture. But some argue that if the covering of the head was a cultural matter then the subordinate role of women must also be cultural. However, this is to try to treat the principle and the cultural application as if they were one and the same. Paul stated the principle in verse three, not tying it to culture but to apostolic instruction (v. 2). In verses four through six, on the other hand, his language changes from declaring God's will to the existing cultural norms in Corinth that helped determine the manner of application.

Some people try to use this passage in order to argue for a broader role for women. Paul's inclusion of "prophesying" in verses four and five is important because it indicates the taking of a leading role in the communication of the gospel. Paul does imply here that women could take an active role spiritually, but he limited this role in two ways. First, within the context of the book (1 Cor. 14:34-35) Paul said that women should not speak in any leading way in the worship assembly, specifically mentioning praying, preaching, and leading singing in the context. Second, in the immediate context of *this* passage, Paul said that men were given the leadership role spiritually before women. Therefore, Paul's statement does not condone women leading in the worship assembly but rather emphasizes that they are to keep to their God-given role whether in the assembly or out since he does not mention the assembly until verse seventeen. In fact, this discussion emphasizes the behavior of Christian women in society as 1 Timothy 2:9-15 discusses the behavior of Christian women in the church and 1 Corinthians 14:34-35 discusses the behavior of women in the assembly.

When Paul then explains why it would be inappropriate for a man to cover his head, he contrasts the lowliness implied by such behavior in Corinth with the divine expectations underlying creation for man to reflect God's spiritual image (Gen. 1:26-27; Eph. 4:24) and point to His greatness, because God made man first and for Himself but made woman second and for man (Gen. 2). Therefore, a man covering his head to worship in Corinth would undermine the purpose for which God made him. This does not mean that God values women less or that she has no role. She has the important responsibility of bearing children, which should remind every man that he owes his existence to the care and effort of his mother and that men and women are dependent upon one another fulfilling their roles (v. 11-12).

To this point Paul's discussion has noted that God gave different roles to men and women (v. 3), that these differences affect the roles of men and women in spiritual matters, especially worship (vs. 4-5), that

Christians should take the outward symbols of these roles seriously (vs. 4-5), and that the underlying basis for these roles was determined from creation (vs. 7-11). Therefore, culture can determine the specific application of the principle (vs. 4-5), but it does not override the principle (v. 3).

Within Paul's elaboration on the priority men have in spiritual roles and the respect women should give for God's choice in giving man this position, Paul says, "For this reason the woman ought to have a symbol of authority on her head, because of the angels" (1 Cor. 11:10). Women ought to retain the symbol that she is under another's authority "because of the angels." While God has stated specifically the limitations on the role of women in the home, in worship, and in the church, the outward symbol of respect for authority depends upon the culture. While the speculation about the final phrase in verse ten seems endless, this phrase, as with any difficult passage, should be interpreted with a great degree of dependence on the immediate context. Since "angels" means simply "messengers," the context determines whether heavenly or human messengers are intended. The entire context centers on the woman's relationship to men; therefore, human messengers should be the first choice until good evidence demands otherwise, suggesting that those who brought God's message to the congregation—preachers, teachers, elders—were in mind (cf. Hag. 1:13; Mal. 2:7) and that a woman should do nothing that would give people the impression she did not respect them in their role.

One of the most difficult aspects of this particular passage is that Paul argues both the principle and the cultural application in the same passage. Therefore, it is important to note once again his choice of words in verses thirteen through fifteen. In verse thirteen he argued that the Corinthians should not have required a specific statement in regard to the covering of the head because they should have been able to make the proper application of the divine principle to their particular situation: "Judge among yourselves." He had stated the principle regarding the role of women to them previously. The only question was whether or not a woman in Corinth who uncovered her head was abiding by that principle. The New Covenant is filled with principles, requiring the Christian to digest the principle thoroughly and make the application within his culture in a way that is "proper" —

consistent with the principle. Several years ago in the United States, if a woman wore pants, it was generally interpreted in society that she was attempting to take over the role of a man. (You sure can tell who wears the pants in that family!) Therefore, it would have been wrong for a Christian woman to wear pants as long as society interpreted the wearing of pants as a statement of disdain for the authority of men. Why do some women not change their last names when they marry? Does this not indicate that they are unwilling to submit to the authority of their husband? The Corinthian application of this principle helps us understand how to apply it in our own culture.

Paul's argument in 1 Corinthians 11 includes yet another important example in illustration of the principle. Paul wrote: "Does not even nature itself teach you that if a man has long hair, it is a dishonor to him? But if a woman has long hair, it is a glory to her; for her hair is given to her for a covering" (1 Cor. 11:14–15). The important word here is "nature." Do these verses condemn long hair on men and short hair on women? If so, how do we determine the exact line between short and long hair? And would such an interpretation not imply that men should not shave since this would be interfering with what nature teaches? These problems suggest that the common use of "nature" today is likely not intended by Paul. It is therefore not a question about how well a person's hair grows naturally but rather what is appropriate in respect to his gender and role.

The definition of the Greek word *phusis* is broad enough to include what nature produced physically as well as what comes naturally as a result of habitual practice based on maintaining existing distinctions. Since Paul has just appealed to the Corinthians' own sense of judgment in regard to what is appropriate and since the connection between verses thirteen and fourteen implies opposite answers but similar standards, then Paul's reference to "nature" in verse fourteen must indicate yet another social situation in Corinth which the principle of verse three would affect. As a woman who failed to cover her head and a man who covered his head were both inappropriate due to what this implied about their respective roles, so too any change in appearance that would identify a person with the opposite sex is inappropriate because it attempts to blur the distinctions between man and woman that God intended to be obvious physically and respected spiritually.

Notice the connection between the application regarding the veil in verses 4-7 and the application regarding physical appearance in verses 13-15 that Paul implies by using the terms "shame" and "glory." "Shame" implies humiliation in the sense of being in a position lower than is appropriate; "glory" indicates "reflected splendor." It is shameful for a man to fail to take the role of leadership that God has assigned him, but it is to a woman's credit when she submits because this is the role God has assigned her. Moreover, a man's appearance should reflect that he has taken on the responsibilities assigned to him by God, and a woman's appearance should reflect that she has placed herself in submission. Some belittle such distinctions of appearance and propriety, arguing that the mindsets of leadership and submission matter rather than the symbols. However, according to Paul, both the inward attitude and the outward manifestation are important.

Paul closes this discussion with a critical phrase, the interpretation of which is key in determining the distinction intended regarding principle and application. He writes, "But if anyone seems to be contentious, we have no such custom, nor do the churches of God" (1 Cor. 11:16). The central issue depends upon how one identifies the "custom" in this verse, but this identification is best accomplished by examining the context of the verse.

If Paul's reference to custom refers to being contentious, then this deserves note as by far the mildest rebuke Paul ever recorded. The Greek word *sunetheia* refers to an established practice in society that rests on tradition. Paul never refers to church practices as if they carry authority *because* the church practices it. The force of the "If... then..." idea inherent in this sentence is important. The application of the second clause depends upon the existence of the first. Paul first presents the likely existence of someone who would object to the applications presented, then he offers the answer to that possible objection. The most likely problem, one that dogged Paul where the Corinthians were concerned, was the accusation that he was being inconsistent. The "then" portion of the sentence is intended to explain why that is not the case. The latter two phrases show a distinction between "we" and "the churches of God." Paul included himself in some category other than the church where this custom was not practiced. While Paul sometimes used "we" to refer to the apostles as a group, the context of this passage indicates a different designation. The Roman approach to governing allowed for the conquered societies to maintain their distinct cultures as long as they did not interfere with or threaten the Roman government. Therefore, distinct cultures developed in different areas and among different people. Since Paul included himself in a category besides the church that distinguished him culturally from the Corinthians, then "we" must refer to Jews. This also explains the inclusion of "neither the churches of God." The applications Paul made for the benefit of the Corinthians earlier in the chapter were based in Gentile culture, and more specifically Corinthian culture. These customs were not part of Jewish society or the church as a whole. Therefore, some might see requiring the Corinthians to make these applications as inconsistent unless they realized the biblical principle stated in verse three and the unstated principle implied by Paul that Christians should abide by the customs of society when they are more restrictive than God's precepts so as not to offend or give the wrong impression of Christianity to those in society.

Many commentators mistakenly align this passage with the discussion of worship and the assembly that follows. However, careful consideration of the preceding section reveals a section addressing the proper conduct of Christians in Gentile society. Herein Paul cited the principle for which he based his applications regarding the conduct of women in 1 Corinthians 11:2-16 as well as the various cultures under consideration: "Give no offense, either to the Jews or to the Greeks or to the church of God" (1 Cor. 10:32).

CONCLUSION

Biblical principles are those truths that remain constant throughout the entire revelation of God. Therefore, understanding biblical principles is essential for an overall understanding of the Bible, which in turn is necessary for understanding any given portion of the Bible. As a result, the Bible student must accept as principles only those ideas that the Bible presents consistently.

Without exception, *God always requires man to have divine authority for what he does* (Matt. 21:23-27). So when man fails to follow this principle, *God holds individuals accountable for their own decisions and their own sins*, while recognizing that sin often has consequences beyond the individual, such as the spread of sin and the existence of death (Rom. 5:12). The LORD warned Adam and Eve from the beginning that *sin will be punished* (Rom. 6:23). As a result, if man is to be saved, *there must be atonement for sin* (1 John 2:2). But while God extended His love to man fully in the person of Jesus Christ (John 3:16), *the Lord still requires faith and obedience for justification* (Rom. 5:1; Jas. 2:24; Heb. 5:8-9; 11:6). Furthermore, *one must stay true to God by staying true to God's instruction* (Amos 3:3; Col. 2:6-7), knowing that *God will bless those who are seeking Him* (Matt. 6:33; Heb. 11:16; John 14:1-3).

Principles are the essence of God's commands. Sometimes they remain unstated, but they always underlie the specifics. Saul was told to destroy the Amalekites and all their possessions. When he saved the king and the best of the animals, Samuel condemned him for the failure to obey (1 Sam. 15:22). We have no command to destroy the Amalekites or anyone else, but what God has instructed us to do we must obey. Specific commands change, but principles remain true regardless of time. God has always required faith (Heb. 11:6); He has not always required baptism. However, He *has* always required obedience; therefore, since baptism for the remission of sins is commanded in the New Covenant (Acts 2:38), failure to obey violates a biblical principle.

Biblical principles represent the essential responses man must make as a result of God's character. If you do not understand and submit to the various applications of biblical principles, you do not understand and are not submitting to God Himself (1 Pet. 1:16). The whole of God's Word is written to explain to man how to draw near to God (Jas. 4:8) through repentance (Acts 17:30) and the adoption of God's character (1 John 3:9; 2 Pet. 1:4). Biblical principles are the building blocks upon which Christian character and a relationship with God are erected. If you reject any given principle, your spiritual edifice will be deficient, built not upon the foundation of Christ but on a personal wall of self-deceit. Without the guiding pillar of biblical principles, a Bible student will wander in the wilderness of sin.

To determine and apply biblical principles you must:

- Determine the conceptual depth
- Determine the background of support
- Determine the origin of the behavior
- Determine biblical consistency
- Determine the author's reasoning
- Determine its significance
- Determine the modern equivalent
- Determine the apostles' handling of principles

Questions for Discussion

1. What is the conceptual depth of Luke 9:23?
2. What background of support is important regarding the Lord's Supper?
3. Distinguish between principles, cultural matters, and incidentals in Genesis 24.
4. Given 1 Timothy 2:4, 2 Peter 3:9, and 1 John 2:2, what CANNOT be a biblical principle?
5. What is the modern equivalent of washing feet?

Assignment

Determine, cite, and apply the principles contained in the first chapter of 1 Corinthians.

CHAPTER 13

Tools

---------- ❖ ----------

INTRODUCTION

ost people understand the necessity of obtaining the best tools with which to work in order to make the most out of their efforts. A good mechanic can accomplish far more with the right tools than he could with only a screwdriver. The same principle holds true in Bible study. While the proper approach discussed previously remains essential, appropriate tools help the Bible student maximize his effort. Tools for Bible study expedite the learning process. However, this does not mean that the fastest way is the best way. It seems the first thing most people do when they are preparing a lesson or trying to find the meaning of a passage is to run to the bookshelf to find a commentary. This is mistake because it is essentially a shortcut. It bypasses the actual process of Bible study. At the least the commentary will color a student's thinking and approach to the passage. At the worst it will become a crutch whereby he comes to trust the commentator absolutely. This is NOT Bible study.

A Bible student must know (1) what tools he needs, (2) how to use those tools effectively, (3) when to use those tools, (4) which tools to use when, and (5) why to use those tools. Studying the Bible requires a Bible (obviously), a few books that provide important and relevant information shedding additional light on the text, something to record questions for investigation and conclusions reached so far, the right environment, and a student willing to do what it takes to apply all of these things correctly. But these tools are useless unless a person knows how to use them. Therefore, a Bible student needs to take the time not only to obtain the proper tools but also to practice using them. While this does require an investment of time in the beginning, in the long run the time saved will more than make up for it. As mentioned above, having the right tools and knowing how to use them is not enough. It is important to know WHEN to use them. Many people spend far too much time at the very beginning of their study in every book they own EXCEPT the Bible. This leads to many "wild goose chases," and hurts the Bible student's focus. A proper understanding of the tools is necessary in order to evaluate when a particular work will be most helpful. A student can waste a great deal of time looking in a Bible dictionary or encyclopedia for information on a word where a word study book would be far better, and vice versa. Finally, a Bible student needs to know why he is using his tools. Are they serving a useful purpose, providing busy work, or just taking up space?

The right tools make studying the Bible a very enjoyable process, and today's Bible student has access to a great variety of helps at a reasonable price. Of course that also means that there are many works available that may not actually benefit a student much. Therefore, a student should remain very selective about what he includes in his library. More is not necessarily better. It is far better to spend money on what will truly help in studying than to throw a few dollars around here and there on books that do not contribute anything of value to your understanding or to the studying process.

TOOL #1 – A GOOD BIBLE

It stands to reason that in order to study the Bible one must have and use a Bible; however, it is also important to have a *good* Bible. Unfortunately, many people do not spend enough time or energy when preparing to purchase a Bible. Most buy one as close as possible to the last one they had as a matter of "verbal comfort." Others prefer whatever is the newest, sleekest, most modern sounding Bible currently on the market. Rather than critique every aspect of various Bibles, it is more profitable to come to a greater understanding of what makes a good Bible.

In Bible study a student should use only a translation that highly respects *verbal* inspiration and translates the words (rather than the "meaning") of the original language. Translations that attempt to translate meaning often eliminate other possible interpretations and at times obscure the real meaning, even unintentionally. Also, word studies, which are difficult to begin with, are easier the closer the translation is to the original text. The King James Version, New King James Version, American Standard Version, New American Standard Bible, and English Standard Version fit this description best, though each has problems in certain places. One might also include the Revised Standard Version among these, but the New Revised Standard Version's word choices and modernism exclude it from serious consideration in this category. While other versions are probably easier to *read*, those cited above are most definitely better for study. The choice from among these depends upon your preference of Greek text, your comfort with older language forms, and readability, though ease of memorization might also figure in.

Besides choosing a Bible translation one must also choose the "style" of Bible. There are many "Study Bibles" available, which include cross-references, chain references, and supplemental materials. Many of the cross-references provided are linked to a word in one scripture rather than to the context itself and are therefore more confusing than anything. The chain references are worse. The exception to this is the citation of those instances where scripture itself is quoted (or is later quoted). Much of the supplemental material, such as basic introductions for books, timelines, and maps, is helpful; however, those study Bibles that include explanatory notes cause more trouble than they are worth. It is essential for the Bible student to understand the distinction between what God says in the text and what men have said in the margins or in the notes. For this reason I recommend a wide-margin Bible where a student can write down his own cross-references and notes. This encourages actual Bible study instead of taking some short cuts that often lead to nowhere. Finally, one might consider a large print or even giant print Bible. This certainly allows a person to read more easily as the Bible sets about a desk, which gives the student more time to contemplate the meaning.

A student's choice of Bible will have an effect upon his study. The wrong choice of Bible can lead him to wrong conclusions and thereby inhibit rather than help his study. When choosing a Bible, a student has the responsibility to keep in mind that his ultimate purpose is to come to a correct understanding of God's will. You might use other translations for comparison and study helps for reference, but for Bible study a person needs a *good* Bible.

TOOL #2 — A GOOD PLACE TO WORK

While a good working environment might not immediately come to mind when considering tools for Bible study, it certainly affects your ability to concentrate and meditate. Since these are essential in order to understand something as important and sometimes difficult as the message of God's Word, a Bible student should treat his surroundings as a significant component of the study itself. The best environment may differ depending upon the person and may even vary for an individual depending upon the nature of his study. The student should find a place that works well for him. Since every person is different, describing the perfect working environment probably remains out of reach; however, hopefully these suggestions will provide some guidance.

A student needs to find a place free from distractions. This does not necessarily mean that it must be noise free. In fact, too much silence can be just as distracting as a lot of noise. Some people like to have music playing while studying; others cannot listen to music or the radio without becoming absorbed in it. The key is to avoid interruptions. An office may provide a nice quiet atmosphere, but it also includes a telephone—which means telemarketers! So a student either should find someone else to answer the phone or simply turn the ringer off. How a person defines a distraction also comes into play. A more extroverted person may work better around people, while a more introverted person probably will work well in solitude. Therefore, an individual must know himself well enough to make these determinations. What can a person ignore and what takes attention away from Bible study?

A student should locate a place that has good lighting, especially natural lighting. Since studying the Bible requires quite a bit of reading, both of the Bible and of other materials, good lighting is a necessity. Better lighting is easier on the eyes and therefore keeps a person from tiring quickly. Lighting also has a remarkable effect upon attitude and outlook. Since studying the Bible can be frustrating at times, one should use as many things as possible to keep the correct frame of mind. A student should make sure that he has plenty of room to "spread things out." Bible study requires books and notes, possibly a computer, and any other number of odds and ends. It is often necessary to go back and forth between helps, so a good-sized desk or table is a must—even in the digital age. A student also should look for a comfortable setting. While the government's ergonomic standards sometimes appear laughable, a person needs to be comfortable while studying. He should take posture into consideration as well.

The individual student must discover the place which best allows him to concentrate and study. He should also find the time of day in which he can think clearly. Studying when tired produces poor results. Studying must occupy a high enough priority so that it receives full attention and full mental acuity. Some people set aside a small room in their home; others use the office setting at work during the lunch hour. Do whatever works. But, most of all, do it!

TOOL #3 — A GOOD DICTIONARY

Since understanding the Bible depends upon understanding the words contained in the Bible, it follows that a Bible student needs a good dictionary in order to check the meaning of words that he does not understand. It amazes me sometimes how people can go through several years of reading the Bible and yet never check the meaning of some of the words. The context often provides hints to a practiced reader, but this means that the reader only has a general understanding of the context and has gained nothing from that word itself. Therefore, Bible students need to get in the practice of keeping a dictionary at hand as they read to look up those words they do not understand fully.

In 1 John 2:2 the apostle wrote, "And He Himself is the propitiation for our sins, and not for ours only but also for the whole world." Now "propitiation" is not a word people use every day, nor does it appear in the newspaper or in much literature. It is therefore unlikely that a student will know its meaning at first glance. The context demonstrates that "propitiation" refers in some way to Jesus Christ in relation to sin. From general experience most people, in essentially a subconscious manner, simply begin substituting terms or phrases that work, according to what it is already known. This provides a good basis to conclude that "propitiation" means "sacrifice." However, respect for verbal inspiration demands that a student consider the reasons why John chose "propitiation" instead of "sacrifice." A dictionary can clarify the meaning and give hints as to the specific idea John had in mind that caused him to use that particular word. The definition of "propitiation" points to two other words: atonement and appeasement. Thus, "propitiation" emphasizes that there must be satisfaction for sin, that it must be punished in some way. But only a person of complete, righteous character (v. 1) offering Himself willingly could meet this need.

Many dictionaries are available, and any dictionary is better than nothing. But the better quality dictionaries are more likely to have the words included a student will need explained. There is no need to purchase a fifty-pound edition, but neither should a person get the smallest one possible. The Merriam Webster Collegiate Dictionary has proven itself useful and practical over time, though certainly other dictionaries will work just as well. There is one danger, however, in using English dictionaries. Their definitions may well reflect the accepted meaning of the English words but be contrary to the meaning of the underlying Greek or Hebrew words (baptism, for example). So proceed cautiously, but do use a dictionary. It is not a perfect tool, but it is a good place to start.

TOOL #4 – A GOOD BIBLE DICTIONARY OR ENCYCLOPEDIA

Once you have secured a good collegiate dictionary, you might wonder a bit about the reason for suggesting the purchase of yet another dictionary. But even a casual perusal of scripture will indicate that many terms found in the Bible do not appear in a standard dictionary. Webster's offers the basic definitions for most terminology, but this does not always help a Bible student. Throughout scripture the names of places, events, and people occur with which no reader today is likely to be very familiar, yet no ordinary dictionary will include these terms. Therefore, it is a good idea to include a good Bible dictionary or encyclopedia in a Bible student's library.

Since the events recorded in the Bible happened so long ago, much of the recorded information lies far removed from the situations of today. A good Bible dictionary or encyclopedia can help to bridge this gap by providing access to information regarding these places, people, and events that will assist a student in understanding the meaning of a passage. An explanation about the history of Pentecost helps explain the large crowd from various parts of the world gathered in Jerusalem on that day. An entry on Sennacharib would provide useful background on this Assyrian king, and a quick overview of the life of Jeremiah would prove effective in understanding the prophet's work and writings. Most Bible dictionaries also include short introductions to the books of the Bible as well.

While no Bible dictionary or encyclopedia is perfect—after all, they are works of men—there are several worth checking into. *Smith's Bible Dictionary* is an old standard, and various editions are available. *Unger's Bible Dictionary* and the *New Bible Dictionary* are pretty good one volume works. The *International Standard Bible Encyclopedia* is available in two editions, the older edited by James Orr and the recent edition edited by Geoffrey Bromiley. Each of these has strengths and weaknesses, both doctrinally and practically, but overall they would make fine additions to a growing library. Before making a purchase, a student should reflect upon how often he might use such a work and how in-depth he wishes to pursue background information. More is not always better if you prefer easy access or if space is limited. A Bible dictionary or encyclopedia is essentially a topical compilation of relevant facts from the Bible on a particular topic, a resource for the historical background of those items appearing in the Bible, and a tool to begin research on some doctrinal concept from the Bible. It is definitely something a student should obtain and use.

TOOL #5 – A GOOD BIBLE ATLAS

Geography is making a comeback in American universities, with some schools beginning to offer a major specifically in this field. It seems that they recognize once more the value of understanding the effects a setting has on a culture and even on events within that culture. This certainly proves true in regard to a study of the Bible because for most people the recorded events occurred in places far away as well as in a different era. Therefore, people have difficulty remembering the place names and do not appreciate the significance their position or topography might have.

A good Bible atlas can help alleviate this problem by providing maps of the areas under consideration during a particular time period as well as some facts about the conditions in that area. The topography of Judea becomes significant in order to explain why people in Galilee would go "up" to Jerusalem. The people did not think "north and south" as we tend to today; they thought topographically. Jerusalem was in the hill country of Judea; therefore, a person would notice the climb necessary to get to the city. An atlas also provides secular information about trade routes that helps explain travel patterns or significant natural conditions that might clarify why Megiddo became known for large and important battles. A knowledge of the location and conditions in that location helps to build mental pictures of the events that occurred there. Locating Mount Carmel as a high promontory overlooking the Mediterranean Sea helps to appreciate the scene when Elijah challenged the prophets of Baal, where he had the people slay the prophets at the foot of the mountain along the Kishon River, where he had his servant look to the sea, and how far he had to run to Jezreel. It also helps to see Beersheba on a map to see how far Elijah went to try to escape the wrath of Jezebel. One can understand why Jeroboam set up golden calves at Dan and Bethel after looking at a map.

Baker's Bible Atlas has a recently updated edition that has greatly improved the maps in addition to the helpful information in the text. There are also several atlases available with quality maps. Unfortunately, many use dates that follow modernists' interpretations of scripture and give modernistic explanations of some biblical events, such as the crossing of the Red Sea. In cases such as these a student must learn to ignore the arrows and explanation and use the clues found in the Bible text instead. J.W. McGarvey's *Lands of the Bible* provides detailed descriptions of these lands for those who truly want to experience the region. A student should also consider the Bible Land Passages video series available through World Video Bible School as an introduction to the impact of Bible Geography on Bible study. At the very least a Bible student should learn to refer to the maps in a good atlas to help appreciate the setting and circumstances underlying the events recorded in the Bible. The distances, the topography, and the "lay of the land" all give additional color to events that we know — in words — very well.

TOOL #6 — BASIC WORD STUDY BOOKS

Words are the foundational elements of communication — despite some of the current trends in Bible translation. Therefore, the meaning of words matters greatly and affects the meaning of the text in which those words are found. So it is essential to know the original meaning of the words God used in order to discover the original meaning of what God wrote (1 Cor. 2:12-13). However, there are a couple of problems that seem immediately evident. English dictionaries are designed only to give the *current* definition of words as used in society — not definitions automatically coinciding with the meaning of the New Testament writers. Secondly, since the Old Testament was written in Hebrew and Aramaic and the New Testament in Greek, the natural differences between these languages and English limit the helpfulness of English dictionaries, and Bible dictionaries do not address every word used. That is why a diligent student of the Bible should include in his library some basic word study books in order to give him access to the meaning of the words found in the original languages.

There are some works available to the English-only reader that will contribute tremendously to a better understanding of the original wording of the text. *Wilson's Old Testament Word Studies* contains entries based upon the words found in the King James Version and provides short definitions of the various Hebrew and Aramaic words with a fairly simple system to help the reader identify where the different words are found in the text. The student can then compare and contrast the different Hebrew and Aramaic words that were translated by one English word and find the more exact meaning. *Vine's Expository Dictionary of New Testament Words* also provides access for the English reader for the Greek words of the New Testament and gives more extensive definitions of the various words, though it does not specify where all of these are located. *Mounce's Complete Expository Dictionary of Old and New Testament Words* offers a modern update to Vine's, though this edition is not actually complete if you understand that to mean exhaustive.

There are other works available to the English reader via Strong's numbering system, requiring only a *Strong's Concordance* (see below) to indicate the correct number and dictionaries and lexicons, such as *Thayer's*, that are coded to *Strong's*. However, a couple of words of caution are in order. First, these are all works of men, so there is some doctrinal bias, and they do contain mistakes. A wise student learns these possible "predispositions" before trusting a work too much. Second, these present their conclusions but not their reasoning. Thus, a good student, even if he only knows English, should learn how to perform basic word studies on his own—a skill to be addressed later.

TOOL #7—A GOOD CONCORDANCE

Most people have used a concordance of one kind or another at some point in their lives. Many Bibles contain smaller concordances as part of the reference materials included with the Bible. Some have learned the value of a concordance in locating a particular passage they wanted to find. Others have used a concordance to find verses that use the same word, perhaps while undertaking a basic Bible study. Concordances have great value for the Bible student—if that student learns how to use them correctly. A concordance is simply an index of the various words used in the Bible. Most are older and based upon the King James Version; therefore, a student should use this as a general reference as well if it is not his study Bible. The best English concordances are probably *Strong's Exhaustive Concordance of the Bible* and *Young's Analytical Concordance to the Bible*, both available through Hendrickson Publishers. Both of these concordances provide complete lists of words found in the Bible along with part of the phrase in which they are found, a system to distinguish between different words in the original that are translated by the same English word, and short definitions of the original Hebrew, Aramaic, or Greek words.

Different concordances use different systems. Strong employed a numbering system, for which he has become well known, which placed all of the instances of an English word together in biblical order and then placed a number to the side designating the particular Hebrew, Aramaic, or Greek word. Upon locating the English Word a student can simply find the verse under consideration and thus locate the corresponding number. Then, using this number, he can turn to the back of *Strong's* to the dictionary portion where the author described the meaning of the word in the original language. This also means that a student could have some access to other verses where this particular word was used. Young, on the other hand, while also listing verses according to a word's occurrence in the King James Version, separated these into sections within the text so that all occurrences of the same word in the original language are found together, along with a short definition of that word. Both of these become simple to use after a little bit of practice.

Concordances are the best place to go when searching for a particular verse. All a student must know is one major word. ("The" or "a" will not work!) By observing the differences in the original wording an English reader can see that there might be some problems cross-referencing Matthew 15:9 with John 4:24 since the words translated "worship" differ. Concordances are a good point to begin a topical study because they provide many verses to consider on a topic if that topic is a biblical word. Even if it is not, a student can use related words in order to begin his research. However, as with any work of man, concordances are not perfect. Sometimes Strong's numbers have been printed incorrectly, though a corrected version is now available. Also, some of the definitions might be incorrect as a result of doctrinal bias. But a good concordance is a very useful tool for a Bible student to include in his library. A student should find one he likes and then get to work.

TOOL #8 — GOOD COMMENTARIES

Although an untrained Bible student can make a huge mistake by consulting commentaries too quickly, this does not imply that commentaries do not have a place in Bible study. The key is in knowing what that place is. A good commentary provides important background information to the book under consideration as well as helpful insights into the meaning and application of passages of scripture. Every commentator has his own strengths and weaknesses, so a student must consider first what he hopes to gain from a commentary.

It is a good idea to keep certain commentaries in order to "keep you from going off the deep end." Good commentaries can serve as a helpful check against the imagination, but a student needs to find works that are grounded doctrinally for them to help. For years the standard commentary sets fulfilling this purpose have been the *Gospel Advocate* series and *Barnes' Notes*. Neither of these offers a great deal of depth, which means that some of the tougher questions of exegesis go unanswered, but they do cover the basics quite well, which was their original purpose. The *Truth For Today Commentary* series is seeking to provide this role as the must-have commentary set for the next century and is worthy of your consideration. Some of the "classic" commentary sets written by individuals can help immensely. Adam Clarke filled his commentary with historical references and notes regarding the customs of the times. Matthew Henry, while weaker in exegesis, has a way with words that can help a student find "just the right way" to explain a passage. Matthew Poole, though lesser known, has some excellent insights. G. Campbell Morgan's works excel in exposition. Although not technically commentaries, A.T. Robertson's *Word Pictures of the New Testament* and *The Expositor's Greek Testament* along with *Vincent's Word Studies* give the reader an idea of the impact the original language has upon the New Testament. These all contain doctrinal bias, however, mixed in with their excellent philological studies, making discernment an important trait for the student using them, and some of their views are highly objectionable, beyond even basic doctrinal differences. Generally speaking, the best commentary for each book of the Bible should be purchased individually because they are not all found in the same set of commentaries; some, in fact, are not in a set at all. It requires a great deal of research just to decide which commentary on Revelation to purchase since there are several approaches that change the whole direction of interpretation. (I recommend Homer Hailey's commentary or Ray Summers's *Worthy is the Lamb*.)

As a friend remarked, "No one is completely satisfied with someone else's commentary." But neither should a student expect to be. A good commentary is like having an excellent Bible student for a friend. Consult it, consider its explanations, and make note of its applications. But never, ever depend upon it totally. The purpose of commentaries should be to keep the Bible student on track, to provide access to helpful information that the commentator has researched to take that load off the beginning Bible student, and to offer exegesis with adequate explanation and reasoning provided to help especially with difficult passages. However, every Bible student should remember this: The role of a commentary is to supplement personal Bible study — not replace it.

TOOL #9 — PAPER AND PENCIL

It astonishes me at the number of people who open up their Bibles to "study" but do not take notes. This typically means that the person is only reading — not studying. Taking notes improves retention of the information and makes conclusions and reasoning available for future consideration and evaluation. Therefore, taking notes means that a student does not have to start at "square one" every time he looks at a passage or topic. Conclusions and reasons that look good at first glance often appear much weaker the second time through. Putting thoughts on paper is an excellent way to force yourself to examine a passage or an issue more thoroughly.

A Bible student should establish a notepad especially for his Bible study. It should be large enough to put a few related thoughts on the same page but small enough to carry around without being bulky. Either a spiral bound notebook or a planner will work well. The spiral notebook ensures that all of the notes stay together but would require dividers or different notebooks for different subjects. A planner allows the student to take notes on different topics or passages in successive pages and then arrange them at a later date. Another consideration might be the student's handwriting. Planner pages usually have smaller ruled lines, while there is a wider array of choices available in spiral notebooks. A student should choose the size that allows for legible writing with the least wasted space.

The problem in suggesting that Bible students should take notes lies in the reality that most people do not know *how* to take notes. Taking notes truly is a learned art that requires practice in order to discover what works best for any given individual. Since people learn in different ways, taking notes should reflect the student's individual learning style. A good place to begin is by paraphrasing the passage he is studying or summarizing his understanding of a given subject. A student can then write down questions that remain unanswered. This provides a springboard for further study or a basis for later discussion with someone else. Outlining a passage or topic helps to guide the student in organizing thoughts in a way that he can more easily remember. Making lists or points is also very helpful. Anything learned from other books should also be paraphrased. This is an effective way to ensure that a student actually comprehends the material before using it. (Do not forget to note the book and page number for future reference.)

A student should generally use more than one style of taking notes in order to gain the most from a passage or topical study. Every approach offers a different way of looking at a passage or topic, and examining these from every side and angle possible is part of what makes a good Bible student. Ultimately a student might wish to put all of his notes into a readable form for later use. There are few ways better than "organized" writing (such as an article or research paper) to help train a student to reevaluate his work and spot weaknesses in his reasoning. Notes, then, are an important step in the process of Bible study. They help students build their knowledge, their abilities, and their spiritual lives.

TOOL #10 – GOOD BIBLE SOFTWARE

The computer age, while having its drawbacks, has created many possibilities for the Bible student. Research that previously would have taken hours can be completed in minutes and even seconds with the help of a good computer program. In fact, a student could find all of the tools already mentioned within various Bible software packages in some form. Therefore, it is conceivable for a student to do all of his work on a computer. But the first matter to consider before purchasing Bible software is for the student to determine what he needs the program to do. There is no need to buy an expensive program if a more inexpensive program will work. Some Bible shareware is available, and the Internet also provides access to many works. So the cost of Bible software ranges from free to thousands of dollars. Generally speaking, you get what you pay for, with perhaps a few exceptions. Rather than reviewing every product on the market, I will use my own choices as examples, and this has changed immensely over the last few years. I previously ran three programs while studying: a word processor to serve as a collecting place for all of the information gained from study; the *Master Christian Library* as a source for commentaries and other helps; and *Bibleworks for Windows* as my major Bible research software. However, my entire workflow has changed since I transitioned to *Accordance Bible Software.*

Accordance and *Logos* are leaders in the field of Bible software today. Both of them have versions for both Mac and Windows environments, both offer a great religious library, both have outstanding note taking capability, and both provide ready access to information in the original languages. However, more than this, they both make it possible to search throughout the user's digital library in seconds, thus allowing the student to find information in an instant that previously could have taken hours. Both *Accordance* and *Logos* include every translation you would ever wish to have, Bible dictionaries, Bible encyclopedia, lexicons for Greek and Hebrew words, word study helps for both Old and New Testaments, an editor in which to take notes in multiple files and attach to either chapters or to verses, extensive search capabilities in any version, searchable texts in the original languages with a "mouse pass over" function that requires no knowledge of those languages, and more. Everything is at your fingertips and can be transferred into your word processor with ease—sometimes directly. *Accordance* offers an interactive map, adjustable timeline, and photo library as well. Both programs also have mobile apps, allowing the user to hold a complete religious library in the palm of his hand. However, this may be too much program for some, and it does come with a price, though this too has improved with time. Nevertheless, especially for those interested in in-depth research in the original languages, the cost is well worth it for the time saved. I prefer *Accordance* primarily because of the "under the hood" performance quality its programmers have integrated into its design, particularly with the Mac. *Logos* offers a broader library, especially in works in public domain. Therefore, your choice depends upon how you study, which works you typically use or wish to use, and the general aesthetics and design of the program.

Bible software offers many advantages to a Bible student, but there are some other matters to consider. First, even the greatest software in the world is useless if a person is not willing to learn how to use it, so there is a learning curve for Bible software. Second, reading is more difficult on a computer screen, and there is something special about having a book in hand to write notes in and highlight passages, though the advent of the iPad has made great inroads in leveling the experience. Third, studying with a computer can provide a temptation to do everything too quickly, which is a true disadvantage so far as Bible study is concerned. However, if properly used, Bible software can become a powerful part of a student's library at a price that is much less than what the books purchased separately would cost.

When I began studying the Bible, I had no Bible program for my computer. I also had no computer. I relied on the book version of all those items listed above as well as others in my personal library. However, today I do the vast majority of my work on the computer, using *Accordance* to perform almost all of the tasks I previously accomplished with books piled across my desk. In the end, the greatest drawbacks of Bible software are that the company must make a book or reference work available and that, for many of us, you simply cannot replace the feel of holding a book in your hand as you read and study. Other than these, and the aforementioned temptation to do everything too quickly, the advantages all lie with computer software.

TOOL #11 — TIME

People today do everything in a hurry. While baseball, a leisurely sport, formerly enjoyed popularity as America's pastime, more and more people today prefer sports such as football, basketball, and hockey, where time is an essential element so that a player's abilities are tested most when he must "beat the buzzer" or conduct a great "two-minute comeback." Employees today generally get paid according to time worked. "Time is money." In all of this hurrying, the value of meditating, of slow and deliberate reflection, often gets bypassed. This cultural phenomenon, unfortunately, has affected how people look at the Bible.

A person cannot read the Bible like the morning newspaper and get any real benefit. Neither should anyone accept the notion that reading a passage of scripture as an evening ritual passes for Bible study. Bible study takes *time*. Many of the works about studying the Bible have attempted to cash in on popular opinion by suggesting how *easy* Bible study is and how *quickly* one can learn the Bible. Many modern translations err because of this same mindset that attempts to make understanding the Bible as easy as possible for people — providing either what the Bible student should study to learn himself or misleading the student due to an oversimplification of the text. So while many have attempted to shorten the time necessary to study the Bible, such actions do not always work for the student's benefit. In fact they contribute to the problem because students never learn the skills necessary to study and learn on their own — always requiring the direction (or inviting the misdirection) of another.

True Bible study will always take time because time is necessary in order to meditate upon a passage and think through a doctrine. People often accept the most obvious possibility because they have not taken the time to see its flaws or even to consider that there might be another option. A Bible student must learn to set aside specific portions of his day in order to delve into the Word of God. This might be a daily or a weekly practice, but the key is to set aside enough time so that the student is able to look at every possible perspective that pertains to a topic or a passage of scripture. The best way to begin would be to schedule personal Bible study at a regular time daily, setting aside at least an hour, unless this is impossible. In this time a person should pray, read, meditate upon the reading, and then note questions, conclusions, or items for further study. It might even be wise to schedule these for specific periods within that hour.

A wise student of the Bible will learn to use his time spent driving and waiting in line for the purpose of reviewing, mulling over, or refining thoughts from previous study. Sadly, people today do not put enough stock in spiritual thought as a whole (Rom. 8:5), which is why real, earthy Bible study has been replaced by feel-good emotionalism that does not stem from God's Word. Paul called upon us to reflect on matters that have spiritual and moral value (Phil. 4:8). But you can think on these things only by first knowing what they are, and that requires spending time studying God's Word.

TOOL #12—AN ACTIVE, ALERT MIND

The tools discussed to this point have referred to external factors required in order to facilitate a good study of the Bible; however, all of the tools previously cited would be to no avail if the student does not enter the study with an active, alert mind. This demands attention because individuals so often complete all of their other tasks prior to opening their Bibles, bringing a tired and lethargic mind to one of the most important portions of the day. Even if Bible study becomes part of the nightly routine, a person may learn very little because his mind continues to drift into other matters. This does not imply that one cannot study in the evening but only that he must do so early enough to ensure that the text or topic receives full attention.

An active mind probes every facet of the subject at hand, asking questions and searching through the text as a detective searching for clues at a crime scene. When a person's mind is tired, he tends to accept his prior understanding far too easily, which provides no benefit and no growth. (However, neither does this mean that a different conclusion is the standard by which to measure Bible study.) The more alert a mind is going into the study, the more perspectives it will be able to perceive and the greater depth it will be able to explore. The shallow perusal that generally passes for Bible study in most places only soothes the person's conscience; it rarely satisfies the needs of the soul.

Bible study requires individuals to keep many facts, references, and questions in mind at the same time. Good Bible study requires students to analyze all of these factors, considering possible variables (word meanings, situations, grammar, and syntax), and then to synthesize them for evaluation. Imagine for a moment the effort required just to determine the proper chronology of the life of Christ. And this does not pertain to any doctrine, *per se*. An active and alert mind requires energy, a fact that might shock some people. It does take energy to think—quite a bit, in fact! But it is energy well spent.

In order to ensure a more active and alert mind for Bible study, a student should first clear his mind of other concerns. Prayer is a wonderful way to accomplish this (Phil. 4:6). However, there is nothing that helps keep a mind active and alert better than a high degree of interest in the subject. A lack of interest is what usually curtails most Bible study. As a student's interest in God's will grows, so also will he attune his mind to the spiritual. Interest without effort accomplishes nothing; but intense interest coupled with diligent effort prepares the mind for the discovery of great things, and that is what Bible study is all about.

CONCLUSION

One of the most amazing things to observe among some "handymen" is the mistaken belief that having all of the best tools will automatically ensure quality workmanship. Nothing could be farther from the truth. I could have the best tools available and would still probably have trouble constructing a three-legged stool or a basic table. Others I know, working with very basic tools, can build beautiful furniture. Tools are only part of the process; they are not a substitute for practice and skill. The same principle applies to the tools of Bible study.

However, having the *right* tools is important. Many preachers (of which I am one) have invested great amounts of money in books only to discover that there is a "core" group that receive use far more than the others. Preachers often purchase books in order to prepare for various studies that most people will never need. Therefore, it is wise to be realistic about the likelihood of using a book before purchasing it. Some books make good reference material, even though a student rarely needs them. Some books are excellent reading that, once read, may never be picked up again, yet they may have contributed greatly to the student's understanding. The most important factor is to know *why* to buy a book in the first place. Since space is limited it has not been in the realm of this study to examine every book available but only to recommend where to begin. Some of the choices that a student makes will depend upon his strengths and weaknesses, as well as current level of spiritual maturity. It is essential, though, to gather an assortment that covers every aspect of Bible study before emphasizing one in particular, which might create an imbalanced study.

The greatest obstacle presented by some of these tools remains the possibility that a student will begin to trust the tools absolutely instead of using them to access additional information through which to gain a greater understanding and trust in God's Word (Psa. 119:105). Some people treat tools as an end unto themselves. Others find no use whatsoever for them. But a Christian who wants to investigate the meaning of God's Word in more than a superficial way will put great thought into the purchase of just the right tools for his library, learn how to use them, and then put them to use immediately. Tools are not skills though. They can only do so much. Therefore, Bible students need to know what the tools can do, what they cannot do, and how to tell the difference.

A Bible student needs to utilize these in his Bible study:

- **A good Bible**
- **A good place to work**
- **A good dictionary**
- **A good Bible dictionary or encyclopedia**
- **A good Bible atlas**
- **Basic word study books**
- **A good concordance**
- **Good commentaries**
- **Good Bible software**
- **Paper and pencil**
- **Time**
- **An active, alert mind**

Recommended Reading

Jackson, Wayne. "Tools for Bible Study." Chapter in *A Study Guide to Greater Bible Knowledge*. Montgomery, AL: Apologetics Press, Inc., 1986.

Woods, Guy N. "An Annotated List of Useful Books." Chapter in *How to Study the New Testament Effectively*. Nashville, TN: Gospel Advocate Co., 1992.

Questions for Discussion

1. In your opinion what tool discussed is overlooked the most? Why?
2. Since everyone's interests and abilities differ somewhat, how should one begin to make selections for his personal library?
3. How does a person determine if a work is "good"?
4. How do you determine what environment best suits you?
5. How do you make time for study?

Assignment

Consulting as many tools as possible and profitable, learn what you can about Acts 2:7-13.

CHAPTER 14

Textual Studies

INTRODUCTION

Despite the extensive theoretical treatment of Bible study covered previously and the numerous examples provided, in order to address a particular passage a student must have some practical method at his disposal or he might end up staring at his Bible for some time, still overwhelmed by the challenge. Truthfully, most who study the Bible have experienced that exact feeling at some point—frustrated by a difficult passage to the point of losing all hope of discerning the correct interpretation. However, a combination of diligence, skill, and experience will help these moments occur less frequently. Even then, it might require several forays into the same material over a long period of time to comprehend the fullness of the penman's thoughts.

Studying the text *should be* what Bible study is all about. Unfortunately, this sometimes becomes lost in the shuffle. People often become interested in a particular text only because of the subject it addresses, because of a question that has arisen, or because of a subject under study instead of studying it from a desire to understand the text itself. When this happens, textual study often is reduced to a cursory examination without depth, context, application, or introspection. People end up looking to the text for answers to questions they bring to the text instead of letting the text itself lead. As a result, the Bible student may substantiate a truth from the text, but only at the expense of missing many other lessons and perhaps missing the real point. Most people look to 1 Corinthians 6 to address questions about Christians going to court against one another, but they seldom connect this with the previous section regarding the dispute between the father and son (1 Cor. 5:1), even though fornication remains the focal point for Paul until the close of chapter six.

A textual study should attempt to examine a given text thoroughly, addressing every part and every aspect of the material. While the student should never lose sight of the broad themes and general lessons, a good textual study should cover the "jots and tittles" as well. The differences in wording between 1 John 1:8 and 1 John 1:10 may seem insignificant on the surface, but until you can provide an adequate contextual explanation, you really cannot claim to understand the text—even though you may understand the basic point and every word John writes.

Textual study is the heart of Bible study. Once a student learns the process and method by which to approach the Bible, the wealth of spiritual knowledge unearthed will create a passion for God's Word that will not easily be quenched. Short cuts may produce an easier path to understanding (and sometimes misunderstanding), but diligence that grows from a passion for truth will build the character and enrich the soul, making the right skills well worth the effort necessary to develop them.

READ THE BOOK

A student's first instinct generally leads him to turn immediately to the passage of interest and begin attempting exegesis. While he may comprehend the words and even understand the author's basic point, inevitably he will miss many of the finer elements embedded in the text simply because he is approaching it from an isolated viewpoint. The Bible student should not attack a passage out of nowhere. He should approach it gradually and contextually, and the best method by which to accomplish this is reading the text *with purpose*.

Whether the student's purpose in studying a given passage is topical or purely textual, he should read through the entire book of which the passage is a part before he attempts exegesis. This first reading helps to familiarize the student with the language, structure, tone, theme, and basic content of the book. But the student must look for these while reading. A cursory reading might be profitable in gaining overall impressions, but at some point a student must read the book for the express purpose of gleaning background information pertinent to contextual study.

Assume for the moment that you are studying from the book of Philippians. By reading through the entire book first, you learn immediately that it is an epistle (literary context) written to the church at Philippi, which was mentioned in the book of Acts (general context). You can see that the author is the apostle Paul and that he was in prison at the time but expected to be released soon. Furthermore, references to the praetorium and Caesar's household indicate that this most likely was written from Rome, all of which help establish the time of writing (historical context). Paul's use of the word "fellowship" in chapter four in direct reference to the Philippians' giving assists in interpreting his meaning in the opening section of chapter one (book context). Therefore, this original reading of the entire book provides many of the clues necessary to begin research into the context — which should always precede exegesis.

Unfortunately, for many Bible students this first reading of the book is also the last. In the course of a study through a book, the student should re-read the entire book prior to the study of each section of scripture. This is important because it reinforces the lessons learned from the study of previous sections, helps the student see any foreshadowing the author is employing in preparation for upcoming sections, and assists in developing an understanding of the current section under consideration based upon its role in the book, keeping the student focused on the text for both exegesis and application so that it does not become just a pretext for a favorite topic. Reading through a book keeps the text in the right perspective — the perspective of the author rather than the perspective of the student.

OUTLINE THE BOOK

After reading through a book of the Bible to discover general information and generate adequate familiarity, the student should slowly develop an outline of the book. While this may seem a daunting task at the outset, hopefully a few short suggestions will suffice to demonstrate the basic approach along with the accompanying benefits. Outlining itself seeks to place a summary of the material visually on a page in such a way as to show relationships in the development of the author's thought and the relative importance of the supporting material. In outlining a book of the Bible, the student's goal is to discover the outline employed by the author.

The first step in outlining is to assign a tentative title to the book based upon your reading. *Tentative* is the operative word; the title should be subject to modification as the outline develops. At this stage the title can be as generic as necessary, but it should capture as closely as possible the thrust of the entire book. In attempting to give a title to 2nd Corinthians, I once began with the preliminary title of "Lessons You Should Learn," because of the original difficulty I had in establishing Paul's unifying theme. Eventually, however, after more thorough study, I settled on "Spiritual Discernment" as a way of describing the problem behind the Corinthians' situation. But most books of the Bible are much easier to title and outline.

After deciding on a title for the book, the student should attempt to entitle each chapter according to its content. Sometimes the chapter divisions are unfortunate, but they provide a good place to begin, especially in longer books. This also provides an opportunity to observe patterns. Most agree that the book of Hebrews was a call for Jewish Christians not to return to Judaism. Chapters in the book of Hebrews almost title themselves. Chapter One: Jesus is God, not an Angel. Chapter Two: Jesus is a Man, not an Angel. Chapter Three: Jesus is a Better Messenger than Moses. Chapter Four: Israel was Punished because of their Unfaithfulness to the Law. Chapter Five: Jesus is a Better High Priest than Aaron or his Sons. Chapter Six: Be Diligent in Treating Jesus as High Priest. Chapter Seven: The Priesthood had to Change for Jesus to be High Priest. Chapter Eight: A Change in Priesthood Required a Change in Law. Chapter Nine: Jesus offered a Better Sacrifice than Bulls and Goats. Chapter Ten: Remain True to what Jesus Died for. Chapter Eleven: The Roll Call of Faith. Chapter Twelve: Be Faithful to the End. Chapter Thirteen: Remain True to Christianity.

In order for the chapter summaries to come together into an actual outline, the student must further determine the relationship of the related chapters, what defines them, as well as evaluating whether the distribution of material does not coincide with the chapter divisions. In Hebrews the first two chapters discuss the nature of the Messiah, chapters three and four discuss Christ as a Lawgiver, chapters five and six cover Christ as High Priest, chapters seven and eight pertain to the role of the Old Covenant, chapters nine and ten revolve around Christ as a sacrifice. Chapters eleven through thirteen develop the thesis from faith to faithfulness to complete commitment to Christianity. This summation allows the student to observe a definite relationship between the discussion of Christ as Lawgiver (chs. 3-4), Christ as High Priest (chs. 5-6), Christ as Surety of a Better Covenant (chs. 7-8), and Christ as sacrifice (chs. 9-10). When comparing the notes on these chapters, the student can further note a pattern of one chapter building faith in Christ as being better followed by a chapter exhorting faithfulness to Him in that role. The first two chapters do not address Christ in a role but His deity and humanity — each of which are important to the four roles discussed, making these two chapters an excellent introduction. Furthermore, considering the pattern of faith and faithfulness applied to each role, the longer treatment of both faith and faithfulness in chapters eleven and twelve as a fitting summation and chapter thirteen directly applying these to the whole of Christianity makes designating these final three chapters as a conclusion quite easy. When these relationships are placed in the traditional outline form, they look like this:

An Outline of the Book of Hebrews

I. Introduction Heb. 1-2
    A. Thesis Heb. 1:1-4
    B. The Messiah is God Heb. 1:5-2:4
    C. The Messiah is Man Heb. 2:5-18

II. Body Heb. 3-10
    A. The Messiah is the Better Lawgiver Heb. 3-4
        1. Have faith in the Messiah as God's Lawgiver Heb. 3:1-19
        2. Be faithful to the Messiah as God's Lawgiver Heb. 4:1-16
    B. The Messiah is the Better High Priest Heb. 5-6
        1. Have faith in the Messiah as the High Priest God recognizes Heb. 5:1-14

    2. Be faithful to the Messiah as the High Priest God recognizes Heb. 6:1-20
  C. The Messiah is the Surety of a Better Covenant 7-8
    1. Have faith in the Messiah's Covenant. Heb. 7:1-28
    2. Be Faithful to the Messiah's Covenant. Heb. 8:1-13
  D. The Messiah is the Better Sacrifice Heb. 9-10
    1. Have faith in the Messiah as your sacrifice Heb. 9:1-10:22
    2. Be faithful to the Messiah as your sacrifice Heb. 10:23-39

III. Conclusion Heb. 11-13
  A. God has always required faith of His people. Heb. 11:1-40
  B. God has always required faithfulness of His people. Heb. 12:1-29
  C. God now requires that faith and faithfulness in Christianity. Heb. 13:1-25

The division of the sub-points in the outline of the book of Hebrews (II.D.1-2) illustrates the need for flexibility in outlining and following the content rather than the artificial divisions of chapters — even though this proved immensely helpful as the starting point. Unfortunately, not all of the books of the Bible outline quite this easily. Most books do not have an obvious introduction and conclusion or, if they do, are much briefer, making it more difficult to classify them as a true introduction. Some would place the written prayers at the opening of Paul's epistles as a kind of introduction, though these often lead directly into the first point. Also, the literary type sometimes alters whether the outline should follow events or form rather than doctrinal points.

Returning now to the book of Philippians, consider the possible titles and the emphasis of each chapter. Since much of the material seems unrelated on first reading, a general title might not even help, making the evaluation of each chapter take on even greater importance. Following the introductory prayer, references to the gospel dominate the first chapter, which means that "the gospel" should be included in some way in the chapter's title. The second chapter is dominated by the description of the mind of Christ (Phil. 2:5-11), but the outline should designate how this pertains to the individual

Christian—having a spiritual attitude. The third chapter begins with a warning against false teachers—an important clue—then proceeds to call on the Philippians to march ever forward in Christianity. The final chapter of Philippians contains a series of exhortations which might ordinarily be considered part of a conclusion except that he presents new material. The dominant thought of these exhortations seems to center on controlling one's thoughts. In these four chapters Paul thus emphasized an important source of information, an important attitude, the necessity of determination, and the existence of a particular mindset. But for what purpose? In this case the author has employed a developmental approach in his outline, each point building on the previous point. The gospel is the beginning point which should produce a spiritual attitude in those who study it. These, when applied with determination, will produce faithfulness, but the Christian should strive for more than just external submission to Christ but a thoughtful internalization of these principles. Paul has thus provided his plan for spiritual maturity which (1) begins with the gospel, (2) requires a spiritual attitude, (3) produces faithfulness, and (4) is manifested by a spiritual mindset. This plan, which forms the body of the epistle, lies between the introduction and conclusion which both include Paul's thanks for their generosity, which acts as a unifying element for the whole book.

As the book of Philippians illustrates, identifying the major points in chapters does not complete the work of outlining a book. Understanding Paul's theme of "Spiritual Maturity" and the four major elements necessary to achieve it are only the beginning. The development of these points is important to demonstrate not only *what* Paul desired for the Philippians but also *how* he intended for them to achieve it. Therefore, after the student has established a basic outline he should identify the substructure of each point—roughly identified by chapter—by noting the author's more subtle changes in thought—changes which generally, though not necessarily, correlate to paragraph divisions.

While most modern versions either typeset their translation in paragraph form or provide some method to suggest paragraph divisions, the Bible student should never rely on them. After all, these translations often disagree about the proper place to create a new paragraph. Their suggestions are sometimes helpful, but ideally the student should ignore them and use them only to see if they happen to agree with his own conclusions. Authors often employ major conjunctions to signal just such a change. Though it is somewhat hidden in translation, Paul used the phrase "Now concerning" to introduce several larger sections in 1 Corinthians. "Therefore" should cause a student to look carefully whether the author is concluding the point just made or perhaps beginning a new one building on the previous section. But this should never become a hard and fast rule. Once again, the content should drive the choices made.

Begin the process by notating on a piece of paper the divisions already established, including the chapters and verses covered by each. Leave plenty of room to add sub-points as they come to view. Then, while reading through the book (yes, again), write down those verses where the author seems to change the nature of his discourse, however slightly. This now provides an avenue for analysis upon which to develop the outline. Mentally "roping off" each of these sections, identify what this paragraph says specifically in relationship to the heading given to the overall section and write that down as a tentative title for the paragraph containing those verses. The title should capture the whole idea of the paragraph while including a reference to the basic thought of the larger section. Continue this process throughout the book. The paper should now contain a title or heading for every paragraph in the book, leaving no verse untouched. This paper should now provide a quick review of the entire book's content. Going section by section, identify what point a given section makes in regard to the overall heading that distinguishes it from the others in its section. A title that combines the section heading with these differences becomes a sub-point.

The title of the second chapter of Philippians, once the title of the book and the title of the chapter are combined, becomes "Spiritual Maturity Requires a Spiritual Attitude." But development of this section depends upon identifying the paragraphs and how Paul describes this attitude and its importance. The chapter begins with a call for unity but quickly turns to the attitude necessary to achieve it (Phil. 2:3-4). Although verse five contains yet another exhortation to the people, the content shifts to center directly on the example of Christ, suggesting a change in paragraph. Paul concludes his discussion of Christ in verse eleven, returning to the Philippians' responsibilities, as "Wherefore, my beloved" makes obvious. Paul's expectations of the Philippians continue through verse eighteen, though his own feelings become intermixed. In verse nineteen Paul recommends the character of Timothy and does the same for Epaphroditus beginning in verse twenty-five.

All this suggests at least five paragraphs, each mentioning a spiritual attitude in some way but with a different emphasis both in person and in manifestation. Regarding persons, the first paragraph (2:1-4) pertains to the congregation, the second to Christ (2:5-11), the third to individual Christians (2:12-18), the fourth to Timothy (2:19-24), and the fifth to Epaphroditus (2:25-30). However, such a division rarely helps the Bible student in understanding the practical lessons implied by the author. Therefore, the student should next consider what manifested trait stands out in each section: congregational unity (2:1-4), obedience (2:12-18), service (2:19-24), and sacrifice (2:25-30). The section about Christ is more difficult to entitle until one realizes that the whole chapter revolves around it and that this paragraph (2:5-11) refers to each of the points found in the other sections. Therefore, Paul argued that: (1) a spiritual attitude leads to congregational unity, (2) a spiritual attitude is characterized by the life of Christ, (3) a spiritual attitude leads to greater obedience, (4) a spiritual attitude leads to service in the kingdom, and (5) a spiritual attitude leads to the willingness to make sacrifices for the cause of Christ.

These sections equally support the heading of "Spiritual Maturity Requires a Spiritual Attitude" and indicate that such an attitude will be manifested in ways similar to how they were in Christ, in unity of thinking, in obedience to God, in service, and in sacrifice. Thus, Paul's teaching regarding spiritual attitude stresses individual recognition of the status of man before God which is then applied in his relationship in the church (seeking unity), in his relationship with God (obedience), in his relationship to the work (service), and in his relationship to life itself (sacrifice). Moreover, the specific attitude that makes all of these possible might further be identified as "humility." So by developing the outline of the book the student must make distinctions and analyze relationships between paragraphs, which in turn contribute to a better understanding of the book, the chapter, and each individual section. This approach helps the student understand the focus of each paragraph and how it fits into the whole book and keeps the context always "front and center."

READ THE PARAGRAPH

After defining the parameters of his study by consulting his outline, the student can give his attention to a particular passage of immediate interest. To this point a student has read over every section of scripture in the book several times and, by outlining the book, developed a basic understanding of each paragraph. This, however, only enables the process of in-depth textual study. At this point the student should concentrate on just a few verses. In order to do so, he must once again read the paragraph—this time with a different purpose.

Prior readings sought to establish general comprehension of the material, which allowed the student to pass over confusing verses and avoid difficult questions. However, paragraph study demands attention to detail; therefore, reading should now give attention to the author's vocabulary and grammar. In order to accomplish this, the student must read and re-read the material, considering the author's emphasis by examining the inspired words. Since previous study has set the context for the paragraph, the student should now isolate the paragraph and concentrate on the manner in which the author has communicated his point. Reading the paragraph at this point helps to focus the student on the material. In fact, the key to breakthroughs in understanding often lies in the student's willingness to read and re-read the paragraph patiently, each time considering a different viewpoint or grammatical emphasis.

A simple way to begin analyzing a paragraph is to read the passage with different emphases on parts of speech. In the first reading highlight the verbs (and/or participles). Since many verbs communicate action, attention to them often helps the student understand the author's development of the material. Also, noticing the author's use of active and passive voice and transitive and intransitive verbs may help establish patterns or draw attention to distinctions in taking direct responsibility, accepting circumstances, and developing matters of character or quality. On the next reading take note of the nouns employed, emphasizing first those directly associated with verbs. Then continue on with pronouns (noticing differences in first, second, and third person), adjectives, and prepositional phrases until every word in the paragraph has received attention. Read the passage with the author's viewpoint in mind. Then read it again from the recipient's point of view. If anyone is mentioned, considering that person's point of view might prove helpful. This grammatical approach also points out repeated words and related words, which deserve special attention. Throughout this process reading the paragraph out loud each time can provide additional assistance, bringing more than one of the five senses on board to help.

Consider how reading with varying emphases helps draw out Paul's points in Philippians 2:5-8. First, read this passage emphasizing the verbs, particularly those describing the action of the main subject—Christ. "Let this mind be in you which was also in Christ Jesus, who, being in the form of God, **did** not **consider** it robbery to be equal with God, but **made** Himself of no reputation, **taking** the form of a bondservant, *and* coming in the likeness of men. And being found in appearance as a man, He **humbled** Himself and became obedient to *the point of* death, even the death of the cross." The succession of these verbs show that humility is the thoughtful determination and willingness to act in regard to what is needed by others instead of based upon one's perception of personal status. Noting the other verbs in the passage also makes a point. Even though "**being** in the form of God," He chose "**coming** in the likeness of men" and being "**found** in appearance as a man." These are statements of condition that also show the progression from His existence in heaven as deity, worthy of worship and equal with the Father, to the incarnation in which He submitted to the Father to the perception that He was then subject to the struggles of life as any other man. Thus His humility led Him to accept a situation below what He deserved. Also, "**became** obedient" highlights that humility precedes and leads to obedience.

Emphasizing different aspects of the text helps to highlight areas that might otherwise go unnoticed. Repeated words often pass under the reader's radar unless the nature of his reading draws this repetition out. Emphasizing nouns, especially by reading out loud, one must notice the repetition of "God," first referring to deity as a description of characteristics and then as a name. "Form" appears twice, supplying verbal evidence of the direct contrast Paul uses to emphasize the extent of Christ's humility—from Master to servant. At the close of verse eight, the repetition of "death" with the addition "of the cross" shows that Jesus' humility and obedience did not simply last until the end of His life but that it required Him to give His life. The differences between "men" and "man" and "likeness" and "appearance" show the importance of recognizing nuances of vocabulary.

Many people read the Bible daily, but few read it with focus. Most reading is just about the words; focused reading is about the content. These few suggestions hopefully will provide a method to transform reading from a daily ritual to an active and beneficial part of Bible study. While this emphasis on parts of speech should not be carried too far (especially since sometimes this does not reflect the grammar of the original language), it does help a student learn to begin considering the importance of grammar and the small, but important, distinctions of the author's vocabulary.

DEFINE THE TERMS

Reading the paragraph thoroughly should make the student aware of the importance of the author's word choices. But this is only the beginning. Good textual study must include an investigation into the exact meaning of the terms chosen and the implications of that choice. One of the most difficult skills a student must learn is how to evaluate the relative importance of the various words. A word may appear pretty straightforward yet contain great depth of meaning. This is complicated by the fact that the English translations sometimes have difficulty translating the full meaning of the word in the original language. (For the English-only student, comparing translations of a text can be helpful in identifying important or difficult words—if those translations translate the words themselves rather than the "thought" or "meaning.") Therefore, a student must remain curious enough about these word choices to discover the meaning of the original word as well.

The text of Philippians 2:5-8 provides several examples of just how important defining the terms and investigating word meanings can be to interpretation and contextual understanding. When Paul described Christ as "**being** in the form of God," he chose a word, *huparcho*, which refers to the state of circumstances rather than referring to identity, which a derivative of *eimi* would tend to indicate. Therefore, by his choice of verb alone Paul showed that Christ could change His circumstances while retaining His identity (John 1:1, 14). The word "form" is interesting as well, especially when one considers that deity has no external form. This same word, *morphe*, appears later to dramatize the change in form Christ underwent — "taking the **form** of a bondservant." Only when one understands the Greek idea of *morphe* as a model (similar to our use *model* citizen) can he appreciate the point that Christ manifested the ideal character regardless of the change in His circumstances and in a way that reflected those circumstances. The word translated as "robbery" in the New King James Version and "a thing to be grasped" in the American Standard Version poses many difficulties. This word draws attention to the strength or force by which one holds onto something. These translations offer a strong defense of the deity of Christ. But while this passage does teach the deity of Christ, its emphasis is on His humility. Jesus did not consider His existence in heaven as deity as an existence that He had to hold onto. Rather than clinging to His existence as it had always been, the Savior willingly exchanged it for the lowly form of humanity.

Few people contemplate the full implications of Paul's statement regarding Christ that He "made Himself of no reputation" (Phil. 2:7). Does it mean that He came without presenting credentials or a resume? Does it mean that He came anonymously? Does it mean that Jesus did not rely on His previous "history" in heaven when He was upon the earth? All of these things are undoubtedly true; however, none of these interpretations accurately or fully reflect Paul's point. The American Standard Version translates this phrase very literally: He "emptied himself." Thus, defining this phrase more specifically opens up interpretative possibilities that remain hidden in some translations. However, knowing the literal meaning of this phrase alone does not explain its implications. That remains the responsibility of the Bible student. He must then ask: Of what did the Lord empty Himself? What did He give up? To some, contemplating such a question seems anathema. But using Christ as the ultimate example of humility, Paul drew attention to the extent of the sacrifice Jesus made when He took on human form. The incarnation, by its very nature, would limit Him. To be human is to have a limited presence, limited power, and limited knowledge. To be human is to have the moral freedom to choose between good and evil. Therefore, when "the Word became flesh," He emptied Himself of omnipresence, omnipotence, and omniscience. The very act of combining Christ's spirit with flesh meant that He became temptable and that His character no longer would be defined by the nature of His eternal existence but by His moral choices. He emptied Himself of all those divine attributes but retained divine identity. By emptying Himself of these traits, He placed Himself in the position where only through humble obedience could He manifest the character of deity that He previously held by right of existence. What a sacrifice! What humility! What a lesson! And all of this—for us!

These few examples from Philippians 2:5-8 should illustrate not only the importance but the necessity of defining the terms used by the biblical writers. While not every word will offer the level of insight as those cited above, and while not every context will share the doctrinal impact of this particular passage, the Bible student should always define the terms found in a passage. Defining terms often keeps a student from assuming he understands the material simply because he recognizes the words. It also guards the Bible student against drawing points from English words in a way that does not reflect the meaning of the original term. When all of the words and their meanings are fully understood, defining terms can take what seemed to be a self-explanatory verse and lift the understanding to new heights.

TAKE NOTES

Without consulting the information provided regarding Philippians 2:5-8, write down what you have learned to date. If you have trouble doing this, you are not alone. Most of us have difficulty retaining information for any length of time. We believe we understand it when we read it, so we do not invest additional time working to remember it. However, if you had taken notes on this material, you could easily review previous lessons and recall points of interest. Now, if this is true when reading another person's conclusions, it should be obvious that taking notes in such a way as to substantiate your own conclusions is even more important.

Textual note taking should center on the various aspects of context and address those matters that are not obvious. Copying the text (or almost) does not constitute taking notes. Copying a quote from a commentary at this point is premature. Taking notes from the text should focus on personal reasoning based upon an evaluation of the context. Taking notes might begin with a series of definitions from a lexicon or word study book on important words from the text. However, rather than simply copying the definition, a student should also add what significance that definition holds for the interpretation of the passage being studied. All notes should include a personal touch and connection to the passage. Otherwise, the notes will lack coherence and show little continuity. Garnering the definitions of "robbery" and "made Himself of no reputation" will help very little unless there is a simultaneous search for relevance and significance. What are the theological implications of Jesus' decision not to "cling to" equality with God the Father? A question such as this, stimulated by a definition, is a powerful note all by itself because it provokes additional study and demonstrates the significance of the passage under consideration. In fact, creating a list of difficult questions about a passage is an effective note taking technique in its own right when followed with contextual argumentation in seeking to find the answers.

A Bible student should always be prepared to state his conclusion about the meaning of a passage once studied. A good Bible student will be prepared to provide the argumentation that led to his conclusions. Taking notes forces the student to put his thoughts on paper where flaws and inconsistencies are more easily detectable. Taking notes also makes conclusions and argumentation from a previous study readily available should questions arise about the validity of those conclusions. Finally, taking notes provides the means to advance in spiritual understanding each time a passage is studied.

When a student takes notes, he can later reevaluate his thinking and conclusions, correct or refine them, and move on toward greater depth.

ASK QUESTIONS ABOUT THE TEXT

A few years ago I heard a man deliver a "talk" from the pulpit in which he quoted from a periodical a series of questions. He offered no biblical answers to the questions posed. He just asked the questions. Such a use of questions undermines faith. The purpose of asking questions is not to create distrust or just to draw attention to problems. Asking questions should assist in isolating particular areas for study in the process of producing a solution. The purpose of asking questions about the text, then, is to draw attention to areas that require study and to what one must discover in order to understand the text.

Asking questions is a bit of an art. After all, how do you know what you do not know? In order to ask questions, the Bible student must combine honesty, curiosity, and perseverance, seeking to uncover every last morsel available in a given text. Additionally, one should never stop with "Who?" and "What?" Ask yourself "How?" and "Why?" constantly. When Paul said, "Let this mind be in you which was also in Christ Jesus" (Phil. 2:5), the student must inquire what mind was in Christ Jesus. Furthermore, how does one acquire such a mindset? And why is it so important? If the student never becomes curious about Paul's use of "form" or the meaning of "robbery" in Philippians 2:6-7, he will never investigate the original meaning of these words or their historical context. Without asking why Christ humbled himself, according to the text, the student will never recognize that just being a man, which is so obviously a status lower than God and an existence that depends upon God, is a cause and the basis of humility. Most never think much about *why* Christ was obedient unto death, yet this is important for a Christian to know if he is to emulate Christ's mindset.

While there is no set number of questions that will necessarily cover a text, the student should ask at least ten questions regarding every paragraph that are specific to that text. In studying Philippians 2:5-8, a student should ask at the minimum. (1) How do we take on the mind of Christ? (2) What connotations surround the word "form" practically and historically? (3) Consult various translations of verse 6. What is the meaning and why? (4) Was Christ equal with God or did He just not aspire to it? (5) Consult various translations of verse 7. What did Jesus give up when He came? (6) What contrast is created by "form of a bondservant"? What is the form of a bondservant? (7) What is the difference between "likeness of men" and "appearance as a man"? (8) What was the basis of Christ's humility? (9) How did Christ express His humility? (10) Why did Paul add "even the death of the cross"? The right questions will be difficult, but once answered contextually they will contribute to spiritual growth.

OUTLINE THE PARAGRAPH

In the same way that outlining the book assists the student in evaluating the relationships between sections, outlining the paragraph forces the student to develop a more detailed understanding of the general point. Outlining a paragraph requires a person to reconstruct the author's reasoning on the basis of the text itself. By restricting themselves to the immediate text, students force themselves to get only the information provided by the text. When outside information finds its way into the outline, the text itself is compromised and its particular focus often lost. When a student simply outlines the paragraph at hand, the material speaks to the student instead of the other way around.

A student should follow the same basic approach to outline a paragraph as learned in outlining a book, though the less material available makes outlining more difficult because the student must learn to recognize more subtle distinctions made by the author. By drawing on the lessons learned from the reading, the student should be able to identify the focus of Paul's discussion in Philippians 2:5-8 as well as the supporting points. "Let this mind be in you which was also in Christ Jesus, who, being in the form of God, did not consider it robbery to be equal with God, but made Himself of no reputation, taking the form of a bondservant, and coming in the likeness of men. And being found in appearance as a man, He humbled Himself and became obedient to the point of death, even the death of the cross" (Phil. 2:5-8). Using Christ as the ultimate example of a mindset that pleased

God, Paul showed that such a mindset makes personal sacrifices (Phil. 2:6-7a), serves others (Phil. 2:7), remains humble (Phil. 2:7-8a), and obeys God (Phil. 2:8). Now all that remains is to develop the outline by identifying the exact examples Paul uses to support each of these basic points. Attention to every word is absolutely necessary in order to keep the examples text-driven instead of only a pretext to bring in other examples. Christ sacrificed His existence as untemptable God, His equality with the Father, and His divine attributes, as well as the grandeur of heaven. These points all come straight from the text or its direct implications. Christ's taking on the form of a servant shows that being human places one in a position where service to God should be understood as natural. The weakness of the human condition places man in a state of reliance on God. Christ's service for others was directly related to His recognition of the human responsibility to serve God. Likewise, humility should be the simple matter of recognizing man's status when compared to God. Jesus, though previously being in the form of God and being divine in identity, understood that the human condition is a lowly condition characterized by need for God, a need that should motivate and regulate man's behavior. Finally, Christ's obedience was a process exhibited throughout life (based on a study of the Greek word translated "became"), was more important than life ("to the point of" death), and necessary for the well-being of others ("even the death of the cross"). When the student's outlines maintain structural integrity through an even treatment of material and parallelism, he can develop his understanding of the text one layer at a time, building a better understanding based upon previous work but also opening up new possibilities to refine that previous effort.

In my outline of 2 Corinthians, the theme is identified as "Spiritual Discernment," which includes a lengthy section entitled "Spiritual Discernment of the Preacher and Preaching" (2 Cor. 2:12-7:16) as Paul explains his actions and attitude to the Christians at Corinth who had listened to the Judaizers' criticisms of Paul. Within this section Paul explains to the Corinthians why they need preaching (2 Cor. 5:12-7:1), arguing in one longer paragraph that they need preaching because they need the gospel message (2 Cor. 6:1-13).

By outlining the book the student sets the book context for 2 Corinthians 6:1-13 where Paul centers on people's need for the gospel as the driving force in the life of a preacher. But how does he manifest this? According to Paul, when a preacher is convinced that people need the gospel he will behave in a particular way. He will plead with them to obey the message: "We then, as workers together with Him also plead with you not to receive the grace of God in vain. For He says: 'In an acceptable time I have heard you, And in the day of salvation I have helped you.' Behold, now is the accepted time; behold, now is the day of salvation" (2 Cor. 6:1-2). He will be a living example of the message, modeling character, sacrifice, and faith: "We give no offense in anything, that our ministry may not be blamed. But in all things we commend ourselves as ministers of God: in much patience, in tribulations, in needs, in distresses, in stripes, in imprisonments, in tumults, in labors, in sleeplessness, in fastings; by purity, by knowledge, by longsuffering, by kindness, by the Holy Spirit, by sincere love, by the word of truth, by the power of God, by the armor of righteousness on the right hand and on the left" (2 Cor. 6:3-7). The preacher must learn to face criticism and not let praise go to his head: "by honor and dishonor, by evil report and good report; as deceivers, and yet true; as unknown, and yet well known; as dying, and behold we live; as chastened, and yet not killed; as sorrowful, yet always rejoicing; as poor, yet making many rich; as having nothing, and yet possessing all things" (2 Cor. 6:8-10). Most of all, he should seek the well being of others: "O Corinthians! We have spoken openly to you, our heart is wide open. You are not restricted by us, but you are restricted by your own affections. Now in return for the same (I speak as to children), you also be open" (2 Cor. 6:11-13). So the paragraph divisions — reworded as instructions for a preacher's life (since Paul lived this way) — would be (1) plead with people to obey the gospel, (2) be an example to the people in character, sacrifice, and faith, (3) face criticism and do not let praise go to your head, and (4) seek the well being of others. By wording the outline in this way, the student will learn to incorporate application into his study — which is the point of Bible study.

In order to make these contextual divisions within the paragraph found in 2 Corinthians 6:1-13, it was necessary to observe the distinction in Paul's plea, supported by an appeal to the Old Covenant, and his explanation of his own behavior (in which comparison and contrast indicated three separate points). Then, within this long list provided by Paul, one had to notice the change from the series of positive characteristics to the listing of opposite ways in which Paul was received. The final section stands out syntactically since it does not present a list, but only when it is considered within the general framework is one likely to notice Paul's emphasis on his own desires for the Corinthians being so primary, which is the real point. Therefore, by noting subtle changes in the author's mode of expression within a paragraph or by paying heed to grammatical parallelism, the student can discover and reproduce the outline of the author, which is the ultimate goal of the Bible student.

Outlining paragraphs is a great challenge to the Bible student, but also an exciting process as one's understanding of the passage begins to take shape and then contributes to a better overall comprehension of the will of God. Outlining is essentially diagramming thought. As diagramming sentences helps to visually represent the grammatical relationship between words, outlining a passage helps to demonstrate visually the contextual relationship between thoughts. The challenge is to examine the text with the highest respect for the inspired wording and then reproduce the content, altering the form from poetry or prose to an outline in such a way as to maintain the same emphasis as the writer, always keeping the material in its position of relative importance within the framework suggested by the author.

First and foremost, outlining is a visual expression of textual analysis. It highlights the main points and then details the supporting material. Most introductions and commentaries suggest outlines such as these. However, they often supply so little of the argumentation of the author that one can barely capture any flow of thought. Such an outline offers very little, practically speaking. If the wording of the outline does not explain the unifying elements of the material, then the process will provide only limited assistance. So while outlining begins with extensive analysis of the material, good outlining also requires textual synthesis. Some tend to confuse textual synthesis with *eisegesis* — the introduction of personal opinion into the text. But textual synthesis is simply the rewording of the information to reflect the cohesiveness of the author's material, especially as the student directs the outline toward modern day application. When an outline reflects only the analysis, it is exegetical. When an outline contains both analysis and synthesis, it is expository.

KEEP IT IN CONTEXT

Context is one of those things that people often take for granted. After all, few students would admit to perverting the context intentionally in their exegesis of scripture. Therefore, it is important to maintain some guidelines to encourage regular reference to the principles and subjects of context that determine meaning. A common tendency in textual studies is to begin drawing conclusions and making applications before the context as a whole has come into focus. The first few words or phrases sometimes seem familiar to the student so that his association of the passage with other ideas or passages may end up coloring the way he interprets the passage at hand. In order to prevent this the Bible student must discipline himself to refrain from drawing a conclusion until the entire context has received attention. The methods by which he can do this vary, but the purpose of any of them is to force patience and thoroughness in regard to the wording of the text under consideration.

Considering context means, among other things, that you must know where the author is coming from and where he is going, what he has already said and what he is about to say, in order to understand correctly and appreciate what the author is saying. Many quote or refer to verses regularly to support their positions even though the verses they use do not even refer to the same subject. Untold numbers have supported their absence from a true worship assembly with the words "For where two or three are gathered together in My name, I am there in the midst of them" (Matt. 18:20). However, this verse refers not to a worship assembly but to the actions of witnesses who verify that a person is at fault and subject to discipline based upon divine authority, as the previous verses demonstrate (Matt. 18:15-19). In 2 Corinthians 9:15 Paul said, "Thanks be to God for His indescribable gift." A very easy assumption would be to identify this "gift" as Jesus Christ. However, the context does not bear out this interpretation. One must return to 2 Corinthians 8:9 to find that idea mentioned, and then it occurs only as a minor point in a broader discussion. Contextually, this verse is the final statement Paul makes in his discussion of giving, which covered chapters eight and nine. Also, in the verses immediately preceding this one, Paul has emphasized how much good can come from giving to God. Therefore, the "indescribable gift" of 2 Corinthians 9:15 is actually the opportunity God has given us to give. As Jesus said, "It is more blessed to give than to receive" (Acts 20:35). In Matthew 18:20 the phrase "gathered together" immediately causes people to think of an assembly. In 2 Corinthians 9:15 the reference to a wonderful gift from God automatically leads us to think of Jesus Christ (John 3:16). In both instances people have allowed general context to overshadow immediate context to the detriment of the inspired text and their own understanding of scripture.

An inherent part of context, though one of the most difficult aspects to master, is the ability to put yourself in the position of both the author and the recipients in their own time and environment as you study. Obviously, the more you know about each will help. The purpose of identifying the author and recipients in the first place is to assist in understanding their relationship and situation, thereby providing insight into the point of view expressed in the text. It is very easy, and quite common, for Bible students to attempt a direct interpretation of a text, as if it were written to them personally the day before. But this ignores the historical aspects of the document and presupposes an exact replica of the social and spiritual context under which conditions the words were originally penned. Paul's description of his activities in the first chapter of 2 Corinthians would be meaningless to us today. Only by considering the Corinthians' point of view by immersing yourself in the events described in scripture can one accurately determine their reasons for doubting Paul. Many Christians have stated their bewilderment at the disciples' inability to understand Christ's mission, but these criticisms are based on our own access to the entire New Testament — something the twelve apostles did not have. Many commentators have attempted to identify Paul's thorn in the flesh (2 Cor. 12:7-10); however, they generally assume that this was some physical ailment or condition, pointing to the word "flesh." But Paul usually used "flesh" to emphasize the weakness of man in facing trials. Also, the context of the entire book of 2 Corinthians, and especially the last four chapters, centers on his self-defense as a gospel preacher and a condemnation of the Judaizing teachers who had infiltrated the church at Corinth. From Paul's point of view, the problem that plagued him more than anything was this team of false teachers who followed him everywhere he went trying to undermine his work. Therefore, the Judaizing teachers are a far more likely candidate for the "thorn in the flesh" than Paul's eyes or any other health problem.

Keeping the text in its context requires the student to constantly tie each portion of the text back into the major theme of the section and the message of the book. If an interpretation of a particular verse or phrase does not flow as part of the overall section, then it is likely that the interpretation is wrong and should be reconsidered. Remember: context is about consistency. Sometimes interpreters, for various and sundry reasons, insert inconsistency into the text because it is necessary in order for them to maintain a particular doctrinal position or because they focused too narrowly on a verse without reference to the context. So, as a general rule of contextual interpretation, if your current interpretation of a phrase or passage does not fit well with the rest of the material, it is time to reevaluate your interpretation.

PICTURE THE PASSAGE

It is significant that the Lord determined that the written word best communicated His message to mankind. He did not choose pictures, nor did He choose an ongoing oral tradition. God desired a permanent, available means of communication which presented an appeal that stimulated the intellect rather than just the senses. However, the growing visual culture has made reading itself less desirable for many. And while people may not be illiterate, they often see only the words on the page rather than the vivid depiction of actions, events, and images.

The Bible is filled with riveting accounts of history and brilliant character development which create the backdrop for its discussion of morality and doctrine. But students today get lost in unfamiliar territory when reading through the Bible because they treat Abraham, Moses, Paul, and even our Lord, as names rather than as real people living real lives. Our understanding of what they lived through will remain incomplete until we visualize it. We need to picture the flood and place ourselves on the ark with Noah. We need to see the actual work of a shepherd in our mind's eye when we read of Moses or David tending sheep or writing from that vantage point (Psa. 23). We need to see the cultural temptations of Daniel in Babylon and feel the loneliness of Paul when surrounded with false religion in Athens (Acts 17). We need to recognize the real world politics involved in the Jewish opposition to Christ and the decision of Pontius Pilate. Our God may not have provided pictures to accompany His inspired words, but His words created vivid descriptions that should generate in our minds a lasting impression.

Thinking in word pictures is foreign to an English reader for the most part. To most of us, words are words and pictures are pictures, and never the twain shall meet. But in oriental thinking, words are pictures. Therefore, in Hebrew, Aramaic, and Greek (the original languages of the Bible) even non-historical passages contain inherent visual images due to the word choices employed by the writer. When Paul said that Jesus "did not consider it robbery to be equal with God" (Phil. 2:6) the wording suggests a picture of a person clutching an object as tightly as possible so that it will not escape his grip. The image created by the word is itself powerful. Even the English word "appearance" in Philippians 2:8 suggests the outer trimmings of life as opposed to the essence of one's existence. But we must give our attention to these word pictures in order to learn from them.

Few of us today write in picturesque phrases with the glowing imagery of an eloquent poet. Few of us even read the works of literature that contain them. But we all must revive our awareness of the beauty, force, and strong images behind the words of the biblical text. When we begin to see the pictures involved in the words it gives the text a wonderful sense of reality and proximity that enhances our understanding of God's Word.

PARAPHRASE THE PASSAGE

After thoroughly investigating a passage, one of the best ways to retain the lessons learned is to paraphrase the passage, incorporating as much of the explanation and application gained from the study as possible, while maintaining as much of the flow of thought contained in the original as one can. This is best accomplished by paraphrasing one phrase at a time and by turning the long and complicated sentences of the text into shorter and simpler sentences in the paraphrase.

In the case of Philippians 2:5-8 the text reads, "Let this mind be in you which was also in Christ Jesus, who, being in the form of God, did not consider it robbery to be equal with God, but made Himself of no reputation, taking the form of a bondservant, and coming in the likeness of men. And being found in appearance as a man, He humbled Himself and became obedient to the point of death, even the death of the cross." By rewriting this passage in more modern syntax and adding in important lessons to emphasize, the paraphrase becomes something like this: "Everyone should learn to think the same way that Christ thought. Though He was deity in every way and with every characteristic, He did not consider His equality with God, the Father, something He had to maintain. Instead He divested Himself of these characteristics when he took on all of the characteristics of humanity—including free moral agency—though His identity and essence of deity did not change. Then, finding Himself in human form, and living a human life, he humbled Himself before God, becoming completely obedient even though it included dying a horrible death on a cross for our sins."

The purposes of paraphrasing a passage at the completion of the study are many. First, paraphrasing is the simplest way to record one's observations of a text. It can include as much or as little reasoning as the student feels is necessary and does not take a tremendous amount of time. Second, paraphrasing a passage forces the student to consider the meaning of every portion of the text. While a person may overlook or ignore a difficult phrase even while teaching the text, he cannot do so when paraphrasing it. Therefore, paraphrasing is a useful check to ensure that every aspect of the text receives attention. Third, paraphrasing forces the student to think through the passage. True learning occurs only when a student can put the information into his own words. Paraphrasing therefore encourages greater comprehension.

Paraphrase should never be confused with translation (though some translators themselves get confused on this point). Paraphrase is intentionally and inherently interpretive. Paraphrasing the text attempts to record conclusions about the text in an easily accessible way so that reviewing lessons learned from a previous study may lead the student to deeper insights the next time through the text, after which one can correct the paraphrase accordingly.

MAKE APPROPRIATE AND PERSONAL APPLICATION

A person does not fully understand a text until he can apply its principles correctly to the current situation. It is therefore necessary first to note the differences in the situation discussed in the text and our own and then to identify the "common denominator" between the two based upon historical context. This serves as the basis for application. The Bible student must then parallel the application made by the author with an application that fits the present situation that is consistent with the text.

In the case of Philippians 2:5-8, Paul's discussion regarding the mind of Christ is historical and theological. It is so foundational and based in principle that no allowances are required for differences between the historical situation of the Philippians and our own. Since the basic command calls for a new way of thinking, the student must pay close attention to the lessons that follow in order to identify the type of thinking required. As covered previously, Paul emphasizes that thinking like Christ requires a spiritual attitude, one that is humble, that sacrifices, that serves, and that obeys. However, we must be willing to test these general lessons in real situations where maintaining a spiritual attitude becomes difficult. Jesus' humility is demonstrated by the extent to which He showed it when His very being surpassed all else in existence. His willingness to sacrifice begins not on the cross but when He chose to leave the perfection of heaven for the confines of the earth. His service is performed on the basis of His humanity—not His social status. Finally, His obedience was complete throughout life, even when it cost Him His life in the cruelest manner possible, and which He willingly accepted because of His love for others. Having the mind of Christ therefore indicates far more than an emotional identification with the Savior; it indicates a purposeful and meaningful way to think and to live with quiet determination based upon God's will.

Humility is not the most difficult when we recognize someone else's superiority in a given area. Nor is humility a degrading of oneself. Rather, *humility is the attitude that takes the best course of action for others without regard for self* (Jas. 4:10). We become humble when our love for others motivates us entirely rather than a concern for how others perceive us. Some people like to think that their financial contributions are tremendous sacrifices. Yet Jesus gave up the tranquility of heaven to experience the enmity of sinful man (Luke 9:23). If we gave up everything we have and everything we are, we have given up nothing compared to Jesus Christ. Jesus recognized that humanity itself is a position of need, making service man's natural duty before God and his fellow man (Mark 10:45). We should serve others because we come to understand our purpose as men rather than because we seek recognition or advancement. Jesus was tempted (Heb. 4:15), but Jesus always obeyed, recognizing that God's will *always* supersedes man's (Matt. 26:39). It is only when we can lay down our will completely at the Master's feet that we can begin to appreciate the extent of obedience Christ gave His entire life.

Application occurs when the reality of the text becomes the reality of your life. Making appropriate and personal application requires a student to assume the perspective of God rather than the perspective of man and so open himself up to criticism and correction. Such an action is never easy, but it is the only way the inspired text will reach and touch its intended object—your will and your soul.

CONCLUSION

While the method of studying the text we have discussed has definite steps, and though you may have felt comfortable reading through this process, applying this in a regular way to every portion of scripture is more difficult than any description of method can communicate. Each text has its own difficulties, which is why the student must proceed carefully through every aspect of contextual reasoning, even when some of the answers seem obvious. A failure to consider all of the suggested steps might very well leave a student with confidence in a very wrong conclusion. Some of this is very tedious work at first, but the effort exerted in learning the process will become easier with time.

During most textual studies the student will come face to face with various problems. He may stare at a passage for hours, read it over and over again, or get a headache trying to ascertain its meaning. This should never become discouraging; it should be expected. After all, a Bible student's understanding and application of a text has far greater ramifications than missing a question on Jeopardy. This is why it is important to look at the text from several points of view, and also why there are times when it is best to set it aside for a while to keep momentary frustration from becoming a permanent mental block.

There are also many things that can distract a person from the text. Most people certainly have plenty going on in life that makes it impossible to sit down for hours at a time to study the Bible. Even when they do there are often many other things floating around in their minds that inhibit concentration. Attention to prayer and a good study environment can help these external distractions immensely. Internal distractions, on the other hand, are far more difficult to address. Sometimes a student, in his zest for deeper study, can begin seeing things that simply are not taught in the text. Exegesis (bringing out the meaning) can become eisegesis (inserting meaning) in a hurry without a strong background in general context and self-discipline. A student can become so focused on the meaning of one word that it begins to affect every aspect of how he interprets the passage. This is one problem that paraphrasing helps immensely.

Studying the text of the Bible should always receive the greatest attention and time from the Bible student because the text is what God revealed and how God chose to reveal His will. Textual studies therefore keep the student in closer contact with the Word and its context. However, with this in mind, I offer one last word of caution: Bible students studying a given text sometimes become so caught up in the individual paragraph that they lose sight of the general context and begin to draw far-reaching conclusions and build doctrines based upon limited study. The in-depth method suggested here is similar to helping a botany student understand the complexity and intricacy of an oak tree. But his knowledge will cease to be helpful if he forgets the purpose and beauty of the forest.

To do a textual study and to understand a text you must:

- **Read the entire book**
- **Outline the book**
- **Read the paragraph**
- **Define the terms**
- **Take notes**
- **Ask questions about the text**
- **Outline the paragraph**
- **Keep it in context**
- **Picture the passage**
- **Paraphrase the passage**
- **Make appropriate and personal application**
- **Know how the text fits into the bigger picture**

Questions for Discussion

1. What might make the first couple of times you read a book all the way through a little easier?
2. What kind of notes help you the most?
3. What best helps you to outline a book and paragraph?
4. What part of the suggested method is easiest for you? Hardest? Most helpful?
5. What distractions hurt you the most in your Bible study? Why?

Assignment

Do a textual study of the paragraph of which James 4:14 is a part.

CHAPTER 15

Topical Studies

❖

INTRODUCTION

*T*hough textual studies should become the mainstay of the Bible student, rarely does a single passage cover every aspect of a given subject. Therefore, it is necessary to study the Bible topically as well as textually. However, one must understand the nature of each type of study. In a textual study one should continually refer to general context, which is, in a sense, a consideration of what the Bible says on the subject beyond the specific text under study. In a topical study the student must constantly check the immediate context of verses he is citing to ensure that he is using the text properly in garnering information on the topic. Therefore, whether one prefers textual or topical studies, both skills are necessary to do either one well.

Beginning Bible students sometimes err in topical studies by immediately consulting a concordance, topical dictionary, or cross-reference chain. While these may seem to ease and speed the process, they often short circuit the learning process and create problems along the way. Each of these can prove to be a useful tool, but they can also create false impressions because the connections they represent are based on single words or someone else's interpretation rather than the student's own reading of the context of each passage. The most egregious example must be references to "S/spirit." Any time a student comes across this word in the text he must make his own evaluation of how the author uses it. The Greek word *pneuma* can refer to the Holy Spirit (1 Cor. 2:10), man's spirit (1 Cor. 2:11), an attitude (1 Cor. 4:21), or wind (John 3:8). Only the context can determine this, and sometimes the context itself is difficult (Rom. 8:26-27; Heb. 1:7). Yet some people ignore these difficulties while performing topical studies because they never really consider for themselves the context of their references. Instead they accept without question the evaluation of someone else or proceed without any evaluation whatsoever. This practice leads to dangerous assumptions rather than meaningful interpretation. These assumptions then become part of the student's understanding of the text, when the student has not studied the text itself at all.

Despite these dangers, topical studies serve an important function. They compile all the biblical evidence on a given subject to perform a thorough examination of every aspect covered by inspiration. By doing this properly a student cannot simply choose a passage he believes favors his point of view; he must address all passages, including those that might pose great difficulty for his point of view. After all, the point of a study is not to defend one's personal point of view but to discover truth (Prov. 23:23; John 17:17). Some matters addressed in the Bible require topical study because no one passage provides a clear picture on its own. One might even argue that portions of the book of Proverbs lend themselves better to topical study than to textual study. Therefore, becoming a good Bible student requires learning both skills well.

CHOOSE A TOPIC

Someone who has never attempted a topical study of any kind might think that choosing a topic would be pretty simple. It is not. For a person unfamiliar with Bible study the choice of topic might prove to be one of the most difficult aspects of the study itself. If you do not know enough about the Bible in the first place, how can you know where to begin?

Some create studies according to theme. They select an idea that appeals to them and search for several examples throughout the text. Following this approach one might find "All the Lies Told By People in the Bible." While the material might come from the Bible, and while it might prove interesting in some respects, this approach does not teach you much about what God expects of you in your own behavior. Thematic studies can be interesting, but they often force connections that help the Bible student very little. This approach may have its place in reviewing what a student already knows, but it offers very little in helping a student learn.

Though the novice Bible student may know little about the process of Bible study, he should determine immediate areas of need and interest by simple exposure to others who have more knowledge. Listening to a sermon, participating in a Bible Class, or reading a book can provoke many questions for the ready learner. That learner must be prepared, however, to investigate the topic in order to determine the correct answers.

Therefore, when considering appropriate topics for study the Bible student should:

(1) Choose biblically. A student should choose a topic that originates from the Bible rather than what someone else says about the Bible. Novices often attempt to study something like "the rapture," without realizing that it is not even found in the Bible. To be a Bible student one should study smaller aspects of important Bible doctrines such as Jesus Christ, redemption, and the church rather than obscure suggestions from others. There will be time for these later.

(2) Choose systematically. The Bible student should enter his study with a purpose and a plan. He should know what he wants to learn from a given study and why he wants to know it, even if it is just introductory information. No one can study everything at once; therefore, developing a proposed track of study from the beginning is important. A person studying the church might inquire into its worship, organization, activity, and membership. Categories always help the learning process.

(3) Choose by textual interest. A student may have developed an interest in a topic as a result of a textual study, realizing that the text did not cover the subject in its entirety. The text of Matthew 12 might provoke the question: Why did Jesus perform many miracles but not perform one in this situation? A topical study of miracles could explain this.

(4) Choose with priority. A beginning Bible student often feels inclined to leap immediately into topics of extreme controversy, failing to realize that these subjects often require attention to great subtleties that even the advanced Bible student overlooks if he does not exercise great care. Rather than jumping into controversy, the novice Bible student should build his skill level first, addressing those areas that he might not find the most attractive but that remain essential. Every student should begin with a study of salvation. Such a study actually requires even greater effort in attitude, respect for authority, and context than most topics because it is filled with emotion. Therefore, it is perfect for developing skills in studying a topic because there is a wealth of information available that the student must consider as he works through the biblical view, which often contrasts with what he was taught previously. Most of all, there is nothing more important for any soul than personal salvation. Your eternal destiny depends on understanding this correctly, which is why it should receive the highest priority in your study. Following this the student might consider studying various areas of disagreement between religious people in order to determine the biblical view on these matters. As a general rule, the closer to salvation a topic stands, the higher priority it should receive in your study.

(5) **Choose with personal interest**. While individual preferences and interest should not guide a person's student as a whole, a Bible student's interest in various topics certainly assists in motivating a person to study. Therefore, interest should remain a consideration when choosing a topic for study. It may be that an upcoming Bible class will address a particular issue and you wish to prepare for it. Perhaps you feel that your prayer life needs some work and believe that combining a topic in Bible study with this need will help. (It certainly should.) Certain events in life might provoke interest in particular subjects such as what happens after death, why do bad things happen to good people, or the relationship a Christian should have with government. These are all legitimate topics for Bible study, and I would always encourage people to turn these personal interests into a Bible study so that they grow accustomed to turning to the Bible for the answers to life's questions.

The suggestions offered here by no means comprise a complete list. Part of studying a biblical topic is the process of learning to see the need for further study either as you read through the Bible or observe situations in life. If someone accuses you of gossip, it might be a good time to study the Bible's definition and view of gossip and the proper use of the tongue. If the preacher says something with which you disagree, consider examining the topic yourself in order to determine the truth on the matter so that you can correct either yourself or the preacher using the Bible as the standard. At first you may have difficulty thinking of a topic; eventually you will have problems deciding which topic to study first.

NARROW THE TOPIC

Once a student has decided upon a topic he often jumps in headlong without thinking the subject through. This can lead to a never-ending study in frustration as the beginning student becomes overwhelmed with the amount of information available on his topic. Therefore, it is imperative for him to narrow his topic adequately in order to ensure that the study does not get out of hand.

Narrowing a topic requires the student to consider exactly what he wishes to learn about the subject. A desire to study prayer is admirable, but one should contemplate how many different aspects of prayer exist. Do you wish to study prayer in relation to worship, the proper content of prayer, the character of those who pray, whose prayers God hears, or accepted postures of prayer? Each of these is a study all its own because of the wealth of information provided in scripture. However, the novice will not know this because he is by definition new to this information. Therefore, it may become necessary to begin a general study on a subject of interest but remain willing to narrow it as the amount of information available becomes mountainous. This is important because of how many beginning students have allowed Bible study to intimidate them specifically because the whole thing seems overwhelming. Shorter, specific studies in the beginning help the beginner learn the process without allowing him to get bogged down by an ocean of scripture references.

It is possible to narrow a topic to the point that a true topical study becomes impossible. There certainly is value in understanding the basic construction of Noah's Ark; however, the information provided is limited. You can learn what wood was required, the dimensions of the ark itself, that it had three levels, that it had a door, and that it had a window. Careful study might even help you understand that this was a rectangular barge rather than a ship, as so many of the pictures depict it. It might even be worth considering the nature of the window as an opening around the top of the entire ark. But the specifics of how many compartments or stalls were included is not available. Furthermore, all of this information comes from one text. It is straightforward information. Most of the arguments that surround Noah's ark involve either the veracity of the account (and inspiration) or doctrinal principles derived from the example. Therefore, Noah's ark has its limits as a topical study even though understanding it is important.

After making your choice of subject, state your purpose in studying the topic with great precision. The better you understand for yourself what you wish to gain from the study the better you will remain focused on that topic. It will also assist you in combing through the Bible as you sort out what texts are specific to your topic and which are only related. This process will ultimately save you time and help build a background for future studies.

LOCATE PERTINENT PASSAGES OF SCRIPTURE

After a student determines what topic he wishes to pursue, he must locate all passages of scripture that address the subject. The order and process of this step are what distinguish a true topical study from a thematic study. Rather than immediately deciding various points and lessons, the student should wait and let the Bible speak.

A student should begin his search for scriptures that pertain to his topic by considering what words are generally associated with this subject. If a person decides to study "miracles," he should also consider various ways in which references to miracles might occur in scripture. (Of course, he must first have narrowed his topic. He must decide if he wishes to study the nature of miracles, the miracles of Jesus, miracles in the Old Testament, miracles performed by the apostles, the means by which miracles were performed, or the purpose of performing miracles.) Thinking of key words requires time, thought, and a general familiarity with the language of the Bible. The student must consider various synonyms for his subject as well as retaining a list of generic words for passages that emphasize principle. A list regarding miracles should include not only "miracle" but also "sign" and "power." Depending on the nature of the study, it might be necessary to include passages that refer to healing as well.

After forming this beginning list the Bible student should turn to a concordance or use a Bible program to find when the selected words are used in the Bible. However, that they are used in various places in the inspired text does not guarantee that they apply to your topic in every instance. This is where chain reference and topical Bibles often cause many problems for the beginning student. Therefore, everyone should learn an important rule: Do not rely totally on your concordance. Words can be used in different ways and in different contexts; it is important to read the entire verse and surrounding verses of those references found in the concordance to verify that it does indeed apply to your topic. "Sign" might refer to something miraculous or it might not. The student must decide.

On a piece of paper or on a spreadsheet, place the words used as the basis for the study at the top of a column, then record the verses found beneath the word in its column. There will likely be some repetition in this process since many passages will use more than one word on the same subject. After completing this initial process you may eliminate repeated references from the page. While reading through these passages other words previously not considered should come to view. In fact the student should actively search for these. When they are discovered simply add them to the list and include them in the process.

There will always be a few passages that are central to a topical study (e.g. Romans 13 on civil government), but do not neglect the others. While not every passage will prove equally helpful, if it addresses the topic it should have a role in the study and in shaping the student's understanding.

DEFINE, REFINE, AND DISCOVER

After establishing a list of words that pertain to the subject, the student must define those words, refine his understanding of any nuances pertaining to those words, and discover how this affects the verses under consideration. Most people have developed the tendency to allow the context to help them with the meaning of individual words. Most of us were taught this in grade school. However, in studying the Bible this can lead one astray because it assumes a correct understanding of the context prior to examining the words that make up the context.

A Bible student must understand the meaning of the words he reads in order to understand the meaning of the verse. Therefore, he should write or type out the verses that refer to his topic and then create a list below each verse of the words in that verse that require additional attention. If a student cannot cite a definition of a word that distinguishes it from other biblical words, it belongs on this list. What is the difference between anger and wrath? What distinguishes patience from longsuffering? To answer these types of questions the student should consult an original language lexicon or two and write the word's definition adjacent to it on the page, leaving plenty of room for longer explanations if needed.

It will not take long before a diligent Bible student realizes that defining biblical words is more difficult than one might first imagine. One word in Greek or Hebrew might be translated a number of different ways, and translators might have relied on one English word to translate more than one Greek or Hebrew word. Therefore, the student must refine his definitions to account for these problems. It may even prove necessary to do another word search based upon the words of the original language. A student might believe he understands "love" until he realizes the number of Greek words translated by this one English word. Each Greek word must be distinguished from the others in how the student understands it and thus defines it.

The purpose of this process is true intellectual and spiritual discovery. By analyzing the meaning of words contained in a passage, the student has more information at his disposal in order to determine how these words interact in the context. As Paul begins to conclude his epistle to the Romans, he describes himself as "a minister of Jesus Christ to the Gentiles, ministering the gospel of God, that the offering of the Gentiles might be acceptable, sanctified by the Holy Spirit" (Rom. 15:16). The word "minister" signifies public service, similar to what the Levites did around the temple. The word "ministering" alludes to the work of the priest in the temple. The word "offering" implies the image of the sacrificial work of the priesthood. Thus, in a book dedicated to the unity of Jew and Gentile in the church through adherence to the gospel and turning away from the Old Law, Paul drove his point home by saying that the role he had in Christianity had taken over the roles of the Levites and priests as God's approved servant. Defining and refining the words of Scripture leads to wonderful discoveries from God's Word.

ROUGH IT OUT

Once the student has gathered the information from the scriptures pertaining to his topic, he should attempt to organize this information in order to make the material more easily understood. Good organization helps to reduce both the clutter on a page and the clutter in the mind. While there may be many general ways to organize thoughts, the best, and most easily adaptable, is outlining. However, instead of outlining material already existing in a cohesive unit, as in the study of a text, now the goal is to take information with a more limited relationship and create ties that seem natural and seamless.

After collecting information from the various scriptures found, the student can begin to ask questions about that material to clarify meaning and consider how all of the verses relate to one another. Depending on the topic, many verses may have very similar thoughts or offer limited insight. A word search on all forms of "heal" produces many references that only allude to healing as an historical incident without providing any specific information to explain the account. However, even in these cases one could note who did the healing, what was healed, and consider the context to determine why it happened. Proceeding in this fashion and categorizing the references accordingly, one soon realizes that accounts of healing are dominated by Jesus, that the diseases healed had external symptoms and were beyond medical or natural capabilities, that the healing was complete and immediate, and that the healing was usually done both due to compassion and in order to produce or build faith. These general conclusions, gleaned from an overview of the passages discovered, already distinguish the miracles recorded in the Bible from what people call miracles today.

Since the people who could work miracles was limited, one might then look again at the references in order to determine what made it possible for them to do so as opposed to others. This creates another category under the general heading of "Miracles." A third consideration might be to wonder why miracles, as defined by the Bible, no longer occur. It would not take long to realize that the number of references gathered, especially after adding in additional word searches referring to specific types of miracles, requires a series of studies on miracles rather than a single outline.

After determining which area to study, the student should create a rough outline using the groups already formed under that heading, then he should further analyze and classify them, grouping related passages together. These groupings and sub-groupings form the basis for the outline. By recording the basic lesson or lessons learned from each, the student can note similarities and then look for progression of thought. After studying the passages in their context, the student can sketch out a rough outline of his conclusions, which he can then check for logic and consistency.

SAMPLE OUTLINE: THE CESSATION OF MIRACLES

Introduction
1. We live in a world that espouses many different religious beliefs.
   a. Calvinism
   b. Catholicism
   c. Mormonism
   d. Islam
   e. New Age Mysticism
2. One of the most popular of these "new" religions is the charismatic movement.
   a. It does not have denominational boundaries.
   b. It teaches that we have continuing revelation and miraculous gifts
3. This view is false because it denies what the Bible has already said.

4. There are four reasons given in scripture why there are no miraculous gifts today and no continuing revelation.

Body

I. No One Today Receives Holy Spirit Baptism
  A. There is only one baptism valid today. Eph. 4:4
  B. There are only two choices.
    1. Holy Spirit Baptism
    2. Water Baptism
  C. Consider how each was received:
    1. Holy Spirit baptism was promised. John 16:13; Acts 1:5
      a. Only Jesus could give it because He promised it. Acts 1:5
      b. This was fulfilled.
        (1) Pentecost Acts 2:4
        (2) House of Cornelius Acts 10:44
    2. Water baptism is commanded. Acts 8:36-39; Matt. 28:19
      a. It was to be carried out by men. Mark 16:15-16
      b. It was still necessary for salvation after Holy Spirit baptism. Acts 10:47-48
  D. Therefore, water baptism is the only baptism today, and no one can receive miraculous gifts or revelation through Holy Spirit baptism.

II. No One Today Has Received the Laying on of the Apostles' Hands
  A. This includes all of the gifts listed in 1 Corinthians 12:8-10.
  B. These gifts were obtained solely by the laying on of the apostles' hands. Acts 8:14-17
  C. All of the apostles are dead.
  D. No one now living was living when the apostles were alive.
  E. Therefore, no one today could have received miraculous gifts by the laying on of the apostles' hands.

III. The Time of Miraculous Gifts Has Ended 1 Corinthians 13:8-10
  A. If "that which is perfect" has already come, then miraculous gifts have ceased.

1. It is compared with knowledge and prophecy, which represent all of the spiritual gifts considered in context.
2. These gifts were to reveal the word of God, but were only capable of revealing it "in part."
3. We have the completed word of God, or "that which is perfect."

B. Therefore, miraculous gifts and continuing revelation do not occur today.

IV. We Do Not Need Further Revelation

A. We are warned not to believe it even if it comes from an angel of heaven. Gal. 1:6-9
B. We have the faith which was "once delivered to the saints." Jude 3
C. We already have all things that pertain to life and godliness. 2 Pet. 1:3

Conclusion

1. There are some who insist that God's provision of miraculous gifts never ceased, failing to appreciate the stated purpose of these gifts as well as statements indicating their limited existence (1 Cor. 13:8-10).
2. This has nothing to do with "limiting God" and everything to do with accepting God's will.
3. During the first century, God provided miraculous gifts through the Holy Spirit, first to Jesus (Matt. 3:15-17), then to the apostles (Acts 1:5; 2:4ff) through the baptism of the Holy Spirit, and finally, through the laying on of the apostles' hands, to other Christians (Acts 8:14-19).
4. That they performed miracles — *actions that could not occur naturally* — is clear. But sometimes people lose sight of their *purpose*.
5. The purpose of these gifts was always to provide evidence that the message preached by God's spokesmen was indeed from God (Mark 16:17-20; Heb. 2:3-4).

FINAL WARNINGS

Topical studies actually open the door to a variety of pitfalls if one is not very, very careful. A topical study does not have some of the natural advantages that a textual study enjoys. A textual study has natural limits imposed by the text itself, while some topical studies could go on endlessly. A textual study has a more obvious focus, while a topical study requires thorough inductive research in order to determine a focus. A textual study almost screams "CONTEXT, CONTEXT, CONTEXT," while a topical study can wander about almost imperceptibly. In a textual study the student can more easily check to see if he has addressed the entirety of the passage, while such a test is almost impossible in a topical study. Therefore, with these difficulties in view, the Bible student should heed some warnings while undertaking a topical study.

Stay on topic. One of the easiest traps to fall into, and one of the most difficult to escape, is the temptation to let each passage or subtopic under consideration take on a life of its own to the point that the original focus on the topic recedes far into the background so that it ceases to be the focus. This is affectionately known as "chasing rabbits." It would not take great effort for a study of the miracles of Christ to morph into a study of Christ's casting out demons. From there it is a small step toward a full-fledged study of demonology, which offers its own series of rabbits to chase. A good Bible student may be tempted through curiosity to pursue these other interests, but he must have the discipline to write them down as subjects for the future and then return to the topic at hand.

Be thorough. A student might find it tempting to limit the words or texts he considers in order to keep his study within reasonable limits. However, this approach might suppress important material and so skew the conclusion. The topic should be limited, but the investigation of the topic must be complete. A person is not going to get a full picture of forgiveness if he does not include verses using a form of "remission." He should also consider as many passages referring to sin as possible. It is a difficult problem: How do you know when you have all the evidence if you do not know the full extent of the evidence? This is where consulting some sources proves valuable.

Keep all verses in context. It is so easy to put a verse down in the topic column based on a perusal of a concordance. However, that does not guarantee that the verse belongs there. It is the Bible student's responsibility to check the reference and its context to ensure that it truly is "on topic." This is why textual study should precede topical study. You must be able to evaluate the context of several different verses in a topical study. In the study of the cessation of miracles, contextual interpretation of 1 Corinthians 13:8-13 is essential, and that is just one example.

Topical studies are difficult to do well because they require the student to be mindful of so many different principles while also applying contextual rules to the texts that pertain to the topic. Topical studies require discipline as a student. The student must focus on his topic, thoroughly search out and digest the information available, and then handle the located texts, which might be several, with respect to the context of each passage. A good topical study can lead to a better grasp of a topic and provide insight into various scriptures. But they are not easy. You have been warned!

SUMMATION

The summation of a topical study fills a very similar role to the paraphrase in a textual study. It pulls together all the pertinent information gathered in the process of the study after extensive analysis and attempts to synthesize that material into a cohesive unit, including significant doctrinal points and practical application, written in paragraph form in order to communicate those conclusions formed as a result of the study.

The length of the summation will depend on the extent of the study. A brief study requires only a paragraph for summation, while the summation of a more extensive study would compare to a brief essay. Therefore, the form the student uses in summation should remain adaptable, depending upon the nature of the study itself. For a brief summation a strong topic sentence is sufficient introduction. However, a longer summation should follow the style and structure of an essay, including a "funneled" introduction with a precise thesis statement.

Regardless of its length, the summation should begin by

stating the topic studied and expressing the overall conclusion from the study. A topic sentence regarding the postures of prayer might be: "God provides very specific guidelines for many aspects of prayer; however, the posture a person takes while praying is not among them." A summation of the study on the question of modern-day miracles might read: "According to the information provided in the New Testament, no one living today can perform a miracle as the Bible uses that term."

A summation should follow the logical progression of the outline created during the study. "The New Testament records only two means by which Christians were able to perform miracles: baptism of the Holy Spirit (Acts 1:8; 2:4; 10:44-45; 11:15-16) and the laying on of an apostle's hands (Acts 8:14-19). Since there was only one baptism in the church by the time Paul wrote Ephesians (Eph. 4:5) and since baptism in water was commanded for all men (Matt. 28:18-20) while the baptism of the Holy Spirit was promised (John 14:26; 15:26; 16:8-13), then Holy Spirit baptism does not occur today. Also, since the apostles have all died and since all men who had the apostles lay hands on them have died, then no one living today has received the laying on of the apostles' hands. Furthermore, the Bible itself argues that miracles would cease when the written revelation was completed (1 Cor. 13:8-10) since they existed specifically to provide and confirm that message (Mark 16:20; Heb. 2:1-4) which is to exist without alteration or addendum (Gal. 1:6-9)." As illustrated above, a student's summation of a topic should include scripture references to substantiate his conclusions and document for others his argumentation.

The concluding thoughts of a summation should explain the pertinence of the study and how this applies to one's understanding of the Bible and to life in general. In regard to miracles one concludes: "No one living today can credibly claim to be able to do true miracles as the result of Holy Spirit baptism or the laying on of the apostles' hands. Those who make these claims are in error and are teaching contrary to the word of God. While God still makes marvelous things possible through His providence, none of these occurrences is the equivalent of a biblical miracle. God does not miraculously speak to men today because that time has passed. The gospel is the power of God unto salvation (Rom. 1:16). It is up to all men to use it!"

CONCLUSION

Topical studies fulfill a vital role in Bible study, examining various portions of scripture that are related by subject in order to produce a comprehensive view of that topic and so build a greater understanding of the Bible's general context. The great themes of the Bible, including studies on sin, worship, and salvation, require topical study in order to understand the doctrine well. How could one possibly explain God thoroughly from one text? Topical studies bring doctrinally related texts together to form a cohesive unit through contextual analysis, comparison, and topical synthesis.

However much one might love studying the text of the Bible, there are simply some questions and themes that a textual study cannot address well. Therefore, topical study is an essential tool in order to become an effective Bible student. To determine God's interaction with Gentiles prior to the church the student must consult every passage possible that provides some insight pertaining to the overall theme. Indeed, it is often because people rely on one or two passages without more extensive investigation that they create doctrines foreign to the overall context of the Bible.

Since topical studies are not bound by a set number of verses in a particular place, and because they can adapt themselves to various themes on a number of questions, they offer a versatility that the textual study cannot match. A topical study could address the actions of worship, the attitude of worship, the definition of worship, the object of worship, the character of the worshipper, the worship leader, the question of order versus spontaneity, and the purpose of worship. While one must go to the scriptures in order to develop these topics, there is no one passage on any of them that covers the subject entirely.

Topical studies can be as simple or as complex as the student wishes. As a result, many lazy Bible students limit their efforts to a few word searches here and there built largely upon prior knowledge (or ignorance). However, the topical study can be very challenging when the student is willing to be thorough and inquisitive. Furthermore, it is often through a topical study that a student finds a text he wishes to study more extensively.

In some quarters topical studies receive little attention and even less appreciation. However, others spend their time almost exclusively in topical studies and, through lack of regular practice, lose the contextual skills that are required even in topical studies. Topical studies are necessary, they are versatile, and they are challenging. They will never have the personal flavor of an in-depth contextual investigation, but they provide the means to address grand themes in a way that a study of one paragraph could never provide. Therefore, a good Bible student will always keep topical studies in his repertoire, understanding their role in tying together the delicate textual strands provided in various passages to create a seamless garment of doctrine, tightly woven together intellectually to produce something valuable in its own right.

To do a topical study you must:

- **Choose a topic**
- **Narrow the topic**
- **Locate pertinent passages of scripture**
- **Define, refine, and discover**
- **Develop a rough outline**
- **Be very careful!**
- **Summarize the study**

Recommended Reading

Brownlow, Leroy. *Why I Am a Member of the Church of Christ*. Fort Worth, TX: Brownlow Publishing Company, Inc., 1973.

Elkins, Garland and Thomas B. Warren, editors. *The Church – The Beautiful Bride of Christ*. Jonesboro, AR: National Christian Press, Inc., 1980.

Fox, Marion. *A Study of the Biblical Flood*. Oklahoma City, OK: Five F Publishing Company, 2000.

Questions for Discussion

1. What makes choosing a topic so difficult for most Bible students?
2. Which is more difficult: a topic that is too narrow or a topic that is not narrow enough?
3. What is most important for the Bible student during the "discovery" phase of study?
4. Is outlining more difficult over a text or on a topic? Why?
5. Why should you bother writing a summary?

Assignment

Do a topical study to determine the proper conditions necessary to partake of the Lord's Supper in a manner pleasing to God.

CHAPTER 16

Textual Criticism

INTRODUCTION

The study of textual criticism does not receive much attention either from the average Christian or from many preachers. There are many possible explanations for this. First, some confuse textual criticism with historical criticism. Second, many people do not understand the actual purpose of textual criticism as a discipline. Third, textual criticism requires some knowledge of the original languages. Fourth, the admitted inconclusiveness associated with textual criticism can generate ambivalence rather than interest.

Historical criticism, often called "higher criticism," gained popularity in the nineteenth century in conjunction with German rationalism. It attempted to explain the origin of the Bible in naturalistic ways. In historical criticism proponents will argue that Moses did not write the Pentateuch but that these first five books were compiled over time and that a redactor created the current form during the Babylonian captivity (the Documentary Hypothesis). So questioning the authenticity of the books of the Bible is the opening premise of historical criticism. Textual criticism, on the other hand, accepts the authenticity of the Bible, so that determining the precise wording of the original author is the premise of the entire discipline.

Canonicity refers to the principles by which we determine which books belong in the canon of Scripture and which books do not. During the Reformation a great debate raged concerning what books actually belonged in the Bible. The Catholic Church accepted more books than the Reformers, a collection that we refer to as the Apocrypha. If we are to know God's will in its entirety, we must first determine *where* that will can be found and what books are spurious.

We must know whether or not we should revere and study the books of 1 Enoch and the Gospel of Thomas because this has a major bearing on what we should believe. Textual criticism reduces this principle from determining which books are inspired to which words in those books are inspired.

The reason why textual criticism exists as a discipline is that we have no original manuscripts of the books of the Bible. Rather, we must rely on copies of these books. Therefore, while the originals were perfect and without defect, being inspired by God, the copies we have were made after the cessation of miraculous gifts, which means that human error entered the arena of copying texts. As a result, while we have thousands of manuscripts documenting the text, these manuscripts differ from one another ever so slightly. Therefore, in a given text there may be two, three, or more different possibilities as to how the text should read. Textual criticism is the discipline by which we determine which words are inspired and which are not.

Since textual criticism centers on finding the original wording of the author, it naturally requires a person to have some familiarity (the more the better) with the original language of that author. It is hard to understand why some versions in 1 Corinthians 2:1 read "testimony" while others read "mystery" unless you realize how close these words are in Greek (*marturion, musterion*). One also might believe there is some conspiracy in certain texts to remove references to Christ's deity, as in 1 Timothy 3:16, where some versions read "God" while others read "who," until your studies reveal that the copyists used abbreviations for references to deity, the one for "God" looking almost identical to the word for "who" in handwritten Greek, especially in uncial (capital) lettering.

The problem of textual criticism lies in the disagreement regarding what principles should form the basis for determining the original text—the number of manuscripts, age of manuscripts, internal characteristics, external characteristics, order of discovery, geographic distribution, etc. The priority that scholars give to these and other factors has created a divergence in how to determine the original text and therefore a divergence in what different people believe the original text in some places actually is.

One difficulty with textual criticism is that it focuses attention on the disagreements in the manuscripts. So it is important to note that, setting aside minor differences such as word order and spelling, the manuscripts agree with one another 99% of the time, and no variations to our knowledge affect doctrine. But if we are truly concerned about precision and accuracy, textual criticism deserves our attention.

PROVIDENTIAL PRESERVATION

Textual criticism creates more than one problem for those concerned about the integrity of God's Word. To some any change whatsoever from the Greek text (and sometimes the English translation) with which they are familiar is tantamount to heresy. Therefore, they reject textual criticism itself. But there are some who argue for the accuracy of the *Textus Receptus*, the Greek text underlying the King James Version, based upon the doctrine of providential preservation.

In his first epistle Peter wrote, "Since you have purified your souls in obeying the truth through the Spirit in sincere love of the brethren, love one another fervently with a pure heart, having been born again, not of corruptible seed but incorruptible, through the word of God which lives and abides forever, because 'All flesh is as grass, And all the glory of man as the flower of the grass. The grass withers, And its flower falls away, But the word of the Lord endures forever.' Now this is the word which by the gospel was preached to you" (1 Pet 1:22–25; cf. Isa. 40:6-8). Without controversy the Bible itself teaches that God will providentially preserve His message for all time. However, there are great difficulties in attaching this doctrine to a particular Greek text.

While the Bible certainly teaches that God will preserve His special revelation to man, it does not in any way indicate how or where. Thus, considering the nature of providence (i.e. "perhaps" in Philemon 15), it is simply impossible for men to designate which text or which manuscripts God preserved providentially and which He did not. If we argue that God providentially preserved the Byzantine text for Erasmus to use in publishing the *Textus Receptus* (a designation that actually appeared in 1633 in the Elziver brothers' preface to their text), we must also admit that He providentially preserved Codex

Sinaiticus and Codex Vaticanus for Westcott and Hort to use. If we treat the Renaissance and Reformation as the only periods of God's textual providence, we must give some reason why. Why reject the textual tradition that existed prior to Erasmus? Why reject the textual discoveries following him? God has preserved much evidence for us in the various manuscripts, translations, and quotations available from antiquity, thereby fulfilling the promise He made in 1 Peter, but He has not designated which manuscripts He would have us use. This remains in the realm of judgment. Before anyone suggests otherwise, he must identify some Bible citation that would indicate a divine preference for particular manuscripts. God intentionally chose to allow the autographs (the originally penned documents) to elude our grasp, preferring in His wisdom to provide thousands of handwritten copies from over a thousand year period.

Another problem that one must consider in addressing providential preservation is the variety within the *Textus Receptus* tradition itself. The longer reading in 1 John 5:7, included in both the King James and New King James, did not appear in a Greek text until Erasmus' third edition. The King James Version itself was based upon Stephanus' work, which was a revision of Erasmus' work, and then ultimately Beza's work. In fact, the word "edification" (*oikodomian*) in 1 Timothy 1:4 that appears in both the King James Version and New King James Version did not enter the *Textus Receptus* tradition until Beza's work, and only then because it was the reading in a manuscript that Beza himself discovered. The previous editions of the Textus Receptus agree with other manuscripts that the reading should be "stewardship" (*oikonomian*). Thus, one could hardly call this the result of providential preservation. Scrivener's version of the late 19th century sought to correct some obvious problems in these earlier editions (that were not really the fault of the editors). So one cannot just announce a preference for the *Textus Receptus*; he should also explain which *Textus Receptus* he prefers and why.

It would be a tremendous error to treat the *Textus Receptus* as if it were originally compiled immediately after John wrote Revelation and then just rediscovered during the Renaissance with everything in between being erroneous and everything afterward being fraudulent. But it would also be a mistake to discard the textual base underlying it as if it were irrelevant. God preserved ALL of the more than five thousand manuscripts we now have at our disposal. The textual critic has a responsibility to use them or at least to provide a good, well-reasoned argument why he does not. God's providence has preserved His message, but this does not extend to a particular manuscript, text-type, or published edition. To argue such actually begs the question about the nature of God's providence and how it is known. It is a dangerous matter to confuse tradition with doctrine – in any situation. Therefore, tradition or longevity does not automatically constitute a manifestation of God's providence in regard to the identity of the original text any more than it does in regard to the identity of the New Testament Church.

RIGOROUS ECLECTICISM

With the 1881 publication of the *English Revised Version* of the New Testament and the printing of a bold textual theory the following year, B.F. Westcott and F.J.A. Hort set the world of textual criticism "on its ear." Although others had made suggestions on a similar basis before, these were the first to use the evidence of newly discovered manuscripts to formulate a Greek text of the New Testament without any reference to the *Textus Receptus*. Though originally instructed to revise the King James Version, these two men convinced the translation committee to follow their theory and text.

Westcott and Hort's theory sprang from the discovery earlier in that century of various manuscripts that were much older than the majority of manuscripts available. Since manuscripts were copied by hand and since copying by hand inevitably produces errors they reasoned that the older manuscripts would contain a more accurate representation of the original text. They further argued that the traditional text of the *Textus Receptus* had come into existence much later than the documents they used as the result of a recension of the text produced in order to create an official edition, possibly to keep people from questioning its legitimacy.

Westcott and Hort began not with the *Textus Receptus* but with these older manuscripts as their base text, particularly utilizing Codex Sinaiticus, discovered by Tischendorf, and Codex Vaticanus, which was the property of the Vatican. Due to their age these manuscripts, which were fairly complete, were shown great deference. Westcott and Hort even maintained that when these two manuscripts agreed one could be certain that he possessed the original text. Therefore, their text was the result of choosing which manuscripts to follow — rigorous eclecticism. These two men then labeled the resulting text-type as "Neutral," as opposed to the Byzantine text-type represented by the overwhelming majority of later manuscripts and the Western text-type that seemed to predominate in the western Mediterranean. (A text-type is essentially a "family" of manuscripts that tend to read the same way, though no two are exactly alike.) There also came to be some question about a Caesarean text-type that seemed to be a mix of Byzantine and "Neutral" readings. For this reason, Westcott and Hort's theory was originally termed the "Genealogical Method," because they attempted to reconstruct a "family tree" for each text-type in order to determine the original parent manuscript readings — an approach that automatically favored the oldest manuscripts.

While this is necessarily brief and perhaps an oversimplification of their theory, it does present its basic tenets. Thus Westcott and Hort based their text on the propositions (1) that the oldest manuscripts are more reliable, (2) that there had been an official recension of the text which created the Byzantine text-type, and (3) that their own text was neutral. The problem with their theory and text is that the evidence does not support their claims.

While there is no question that Codex Sinaiticus and Codex Vaticanus are ancient (4th century), this does not imply that the text they represent is older than that of later manuscripts. There is simply no way to tell how many times a text had been copied prior to the copy we now have. A thirteenth century manuscript could conceivably represent a text that had been copied fewer times than a fourth century manuscript. For rigorous eclecticism to work, one would have to know the date of the reading — not just the date of the manuscript. Secondly, their total rejection of later manuscripts centers on the proposition that these later documents were the result of an official edition which smoothed out the readings. However, there is absolutely no historical or archaeological evidence for this assumption. Thirdly, even those who appreciate Westcott and Hort's work have recognized that their text was not neutral. The text-type was later renamed *Alexandrian* because almost all of the manuscripts of this family come from a very small geographical area centered in upper Egypt, a place where the climate is very conducive to preserving such manuscripts. Instead of being a "neutral" text, their text was simply representative of the text of Egypt during the fourth century.

Westcott and Hort opened up the floodgates in textual criticism. Eventually, their theory caused the editors of the Revised Standard Version to eliminate Mark 16:9-20 from their translation—a move that created such a stir that following editions included it, but with a lengthy explanatory note. They created a rather heated dialogue that continues to this day. However, very few scholars today subscribe fully to rigorous eclecticism or the genealogical method, the closest probably being Philip Comfort.

REASONED ECLECTICISM

Though the rigorous eclecticism espoused by Westcott and Hort did not achieve the acceptance desired by its proponents, it did have a significant effect upon the world of textual criticism. While they did not convince people to accept their "neutral text," they did create enough doubt in the *Textus Receptus* for critical methods to become acceptable and even preferred. Textual critics realized the limitations of following particular manuscripts and began applying the reconstructive methods of textual criticism employed in other ancient writings where few copies are extant.

Instead of giving high priority to particular manuscripts, this method, called "Reasoned Eclecticism," utilizes "reasoned" principles by which to examine each reading and its variants. Most eclecticists agree to the following twelve principles, which I have paraphrased from Kurt and Barbara Aland (pp. 275-276), adding my own comments after each one.

1. **Only** *one* **reading can be original, and the original is one of the readings.** This ought to be obvious. God wrote only one reading. Also, it is foolishness to create a reading that is never found among the evidence.

2. **Only the reading that best satisfies both external and internal criteria can be original.** This is acceptable as stated, but only when the "external and internal criteria" are acceptable. They give this principle early, but define it by later principles.

3. **External considerations should precede internal evidence.** This is essentially saying that even if the grammar does not work critics should follow the earlier manuscripts.

4. **Internal evidence should never be the sole basis for a decision, especially when opposed by the external evidence.** Even if the internal evidence (as defined by principles below) should indicate a particular reading, it would be unacceptable to a reasoned eclecticist if that conclusion does not fit predetermined conclusions about the external evidence. (See below.)

5. **The Greek manuscript evidence is superior to the evidence of early translations and the church fathers.** While this makes sense, considering some of the limitations of translations and quotations, one other unstated reason why they include this as a principle is because of how much the translations and quotations support conclusions other than their own.

6. **Manuscripts should be weighed, not counted, and no individual manuscript should be followed to the exclusion of others.** This is an explicit declaration of independence from both the majority of manuscripts and rigorous eclecticism. In effect, they wish to discount totally the Byzantine family of manuscripts. How to "weigh" a manuscript, on the other hand, is based largely in the assumptions of rigorous eclecticism.

7. **Though theoretically possible, it is unwise to accept a reading that appears only once in the available manuscripts.** This principle is meant to distance reasoned eclecticism even further from rigorous eclecticism.

8. **The reading that best explains the other readings is most likely the original reading.** This is the core principle of reasoned eclecticism. The problem is that in many instances

there are two equally valid explanations. In such cases they generally fall back to the "external evidence."

9. **Variants should be considered within the context of a manuscript tradition.** By essentially taking all of the Byzantine manuscripts and treating them as one in the textual apparatus of their editions, the reasoned eclecticist is indicating the "weight" and his understanding of the "context" of manuscript traditions. This is a matter of likelihood within a text family — once again a return to rigorous eclecticism.

10. **The more difficult a reading is, the more likely it is the original reading.** Think about this one! The poorer the reading, the more likely God wrote it. This principle is intended to deny Byzantine readings outright since they are known to be "smooth" readings of higher quality grammar.

11. **The shorter reading is probably the original reading.** This shows a prejudice toward the Alexandrian text family — the Neutral text of Westcott and Hort — since its readings are typically, though not always, shorter.

12. **The best textual critic is not a theoretician but someone who has experience in collation of some early manuscript.** Since the Alands are in charge of most of the manuscript evidence, they also have great control over those who look at it. Essentially, they are saying, "We are only the ones qualified to be textual critics and to tell others who are qualified to speak about textual criticism." This is a very good example of the arrogance of academia.

MAJORITY TEXT THEORY

The Majority Text Theory is on the surface the simplest of theories; however, adherents of all the other approaches often mischaracterize it. Those who prefer a providential preservation approach generally refer to the testimony of an overwhelming majority in order to support their view that one should remain true to the *Textus Receptus*, yet they often greet any mention of abandoning minority readings in the *Textus Receptus* with great resistance. Those who follow either rigorous or reasoned eclecticism frown, and sometimes throw philosophical barbs, at the Majority Text Theory because it rejects many of the assumptions of their theories. Therefore, the Majority Text Theory is perhaps the greatest minority in the textual criticism debate.

Majority Text Theory emphasizes external evidence; however, instead of giving weight to certain, older manuscripts or text-types, Majority Text Theory turns instead to the vast number of manuscripts and insists that they *all* be included in the evidence. One of the dictates of eclecticism insists that manuscripts should be weighed, not counted; therefore, this demonstrates a very different approach. According to Majority Text Theory, manuscripts *should* be counted because in normal textual transmission the errors that occurred, regardless of the reason, would vary from manuscript to manuscript and statistically the majority would maintain the original reading. The major difference between eclecticism and majoritarianism is the extent and nature of the external evidence that receives greater reverence.

The Majority Text Theory also uses another aspect of external evidence: history. Majority Text adherents note that the recension (official edition) originally postulated by Westcott and Hort, though accepted by all eclecticists, does not have any historical support. Eclectic theories, then, rely on a history based on the silence of the evidence. That is a little more than shaky scholarship. The Majority Text Theory notes this lack of evidence and suggests that the reason there is silence about a recension is because one did not occur. Furthermore, they note that both the geographical distribution and amount of textual variance in the manuscript evidence fit the statistical model based on a normal transmission history.

This does not mean that there are no downsides to the Majority Text Theory. Since the vast majority of Greek manuscripts that are extant are later manuscripts, this means that the Majority Text Theory does not take into account in any way the age of a manuscript. Critics point out that there are no examples of a Byzantine text-type prior to their postulated recension date. However, the climate of the Byzantine Empire was not as conducive to the preservation of ancient manuscripts as the climate of Egypt. Also, Harry Sturz demonstrates in his work that while there may not be manuscript evidence of a text-type, all the readings are represented in the early papyri. Since the individual majority readings themselves (not the Byzantine text-type) have early support for their validity as an ancient reading, Majority adherents maintain that they should at the least not be ignored or treated with less respect than Alexandrian readings (as eclecticists tend to do). Essentially, rigorous eclectists emphasize the Alexandrian majority of the oldest witnesses to the exclusion of later evidence while Majority proponents want the whole of the evidence considered without respect for the age of the manuscripts. Reasoned eclecticists lean toward the older witnesses and ignore Byzantine readings, which are in the vast majority. So in reality the majority reading does not even get equal status for consideration because of the subjective rules of eclecticism that are designed to eliminate the majority readings.

The majority text edited by Hodges and Farstad does not take into account the evidence of the early versions or the quotations found in the church fathers. While these should not carry the weight that the Greek manuscripts do, they should be considered. Also, there are certain sections, such as at the first of John 8, where a majority reading would be difficult to create exactly, and then might make the grammar totally unacceptable. The book of Revelation presents a similar daunting task. However, the more recent edition of the Majority Text edited by Robinson and Pierpont address these deficiencies quite well, approaching the text with a less mechanical formula and including all types of evidence while showing deference to the Byzantine text.

The Majority Text is not perfect, and some might be surprised at what readings it does *not* support. It is, however, an important argument that deserves consideration. However, since the publication of the Robinson-Pierpont edition, the Majority Text has begun to receive more attention from scholars—a type of respect academia had previously chosen to withhold.

CONCLUSION

Textual Criticism has received much criticism of its own. Some believe incorrectly that the motives behind textual criticism are similar to the modernists in the historical criticism movement that has treated the Bible as simply the work of men. The efforts of the Jesus Seminar are just one example of their attitude toward scripture. But textual critics are generally motivated by a very high regard for inspiration and scripture. Their respect for inspiration is such that they yearn to determine exactly which words are inspired and which are not. The problem is that textual critics differ on the approach one should take to make these types of decisions.

Any discussion of textual criticism automatically emphasizes the differences and distinctions of each school of thought, and the process of textual criticism shines light on the variant readings that exist within the textual evidence. This can lead some to imagine that the message of the text is in doubt, which is why we must always keep these matters in perspective. Many of the differences between the texts resulting from the different theories amounts to variant spellings and the order of words. These do not affect the meaning of the text at all. The more noticeable differences involve additions/ omissions or the use of different words. While we would not wish to minimize what it would mean either to accept an uninspired word or reject an inspired word, there is no instance in which any of these alter any doctrine of the Bible. In Colossians 2:18 the inclusion of the word "not" does indeed affect interpretation in that passage, but the context clearly indicates the nature of the problem. Whether they were looking into things that they had not seen or Paul was simply referring to claims of visions these false teachers had made, there is no change in what the Christian is to do. Therefore, textual criticism does affect interpretation of particular passages, but the texts are so consistent that the teaching regarding spiritual responsibilities is not affected in any way. The same could be said of word choices. While there is certainly a difference between "the testimony of God" and "the mystery of God," no one doubts that both refer to the gospel. There is a different emphasis, obviously, but the basic interpretation remains unaffected. In fact, few critics disagree on the appropriate word here, despite the fact that a variant reading is available.

When Westcott and Hort decided to depart from their instructions and create a new Greek text in 1881 and when the Revised Standard Version, which did not include Mark 16:9-16, was published in 1946, textual criticism was indeed a controversial subject. However, the latter half of the twentieth century, with the growing strength of reasoned eclecticism, produced more of a moderating influence in the field. The publication of two different editions of a majority text have helped as well. Therefore, the two versions that differ the most textually are probably the King James Version and the American Standard Version. Most of the differences in today's versions are due to translational differences rather than textual differences. This should help ease our minds some when we realize that the detectable differences between Greek texts affects a very small percentage of readings and does not affect the meaning of the gospel whatsoever.

Unfortunately, many enter the debate on textual issues without even bothering to acquaint themselves with the history or theories that produce such questions. Therefore, KJV-only advocates accuse others of being irreverent for removing the name of God from the Bible in many places, without considering the textual problems at issue — or that this might include every instance of "God forbid" in the KJV, which is an idiom, translating a Greek phrase in which *theos*, the Greek word for "God," does not appear. This leads to an emotional debate rather than a scholarly one. On the other side, reasoned eclecticism has allowed some to pick up a Greek text believing that they can choose whatever variant they wish. This makes textual criticism subject to personal whims and doctrinal pre-dispositions.

What overall lessons should we learn? (1) The differences in the texts used today are not great enough to spend time worrying about them. (2) Before arguing about textual variants one should read extensively about textual criticism. (3) Before accusing a translator of bias one should consider the text he followed.

Theories of Textual Criticism:

- **Are various means seeking to determine which words God inspired**
- **Providential preservation**
- **Rigorous Eclecticism**
- **Reasoned Eclecticism**
- **Majoritarianism**
- **Do not create differences in doctrine**

Recommended Reading

Aland, Kurt and Barbara. *The Text of the New Testament*. Translated by Erroll F. Rhodes. Grand Rapids, MI: William B. Eerdmans, 1987.

Brotzman, Ellis R. *Old Testament Textual Criticism: A Practical Introduction*. Grand Rapids, MI: Baker Book House Company, 1994.

Comfort, Philip Wesley. *Early Manuscripts and Modern Translations of the New Testament*. Wheaton, Illinois: Tyndale House Publishers, Inc., 1990.

Comfort, Philip Wesley. *The Quest for the Original Text of the New Testament*. Grand Rapids, MI: Baker Book House, 1992.

Metzger, Bruce M. *The Text of the New Testament: Its Transmission, Corruption, and Restoration*, Third enlarged edition. New York, NY: Oxford University Press, 1992.

Pickering, Wilbur. *The Identity of the New Testament Text*, revised edition. Nashville, TN: Thomas Nelson Publishers, 1977.

Sturz, Harry A. *The Byzantine Text-Type and New Testament Textual Criticism*. Nashville, TN: Thomas Nelson Publishers, 1984.

Westcott, B.F. and F.J.A. Hort. *Introduction to the New Testament in the Original Greek*. Peabody Massachusetts: Hendrickson Publishers, 1988, reprint from New York, NY: Harper and Brothers, 1882.

Wurthwein, Ernst. *The Text of the Old Testament*. Translated by Erroll F. Rhodes. Grand Rapids, MI: William B. Eerdmans, 1979; reprint, 1992.

Questions for Discussion

1. What factors constitute external evidence for textual criticism?
2. What factors constitute internal evidence for textual criticism?
3. How might studying the geographical distribution of the manuscripts affect one's understanding of the textual evidence?
4. Since the transmission history of the Old Testament and New Testament differ greatly, how might this affect the textual criticism of each?

5. Which theory do you find most compelling? Why?

Assignment

Examine the textual evidence for Acts 8:37 using each of the four theories.

CHAPTER 17

Translation

INTRODUCTION

The translation question, that is, the controversy regarding which translation is the best and whether or not there are translations that should not be used, is a subject that seems to give rise to strong emotions, provoke polarization, revive traditionalism, and give credence to pseudo-scholarship (on both sides). It has come to the point that anyone carrying a KJV is thought to be a traditionalist and any person carrying an NIV is presumed to be a liberal. Neither of these attitudes is correct. I have known liberals who carried the King James as well as men very sound in doctrine who preach from the NIV. Therefore, to imply that the translation itself indicates doctrinal disposition is illogical.

The choice of translation itself is not—or at least **should not** be—a matter of fellowship but a matter of judgment. There is no direct statement, account of action, or implication that gives authority to a particular translation of the Bible. This is so because translation, at its best, is inexact. Therefore, discussions pertaining to translation necessarily involve matters of degree, which puts the whole matter into the realm of judgment. Jesus and the apostles used and quoted from the Septuagint, despite the fact that it was flawed at times, employed idiomatic translation in places, used a different textual base, and included non-canonical material (the apocrypha). Shall we condemn Jesus and the apostles for their using it? The absurdity of such an action should be obvious. Therefore, the translation question should be debated in the realm of judgment without any condemnation involved.

That is not to say that the translation question is irrelevant. In matters of judgment it still behooves us to choose that which is *expedient*, what is the best fitted for its intended purpose within the context of what is authorized. If there is biblical authority to build a building in which to worship, and there is, then the difference between building a $500,000 structure and a $5 million edifice is a matter of judgment. Choosing to build the $5 million building would certainly seem to be poor judgment and a poor use of the Lord's money in many cases (though less so as inflation rears its ugly head), but could we not also meet in a pole barn that would cost much less than $500,000? Judgment and expediency must play a role. The same is true in translation.

Many people do not understand that what separates the translations and what causes so many differences are the underlying differences in the Hebrew and Greek texts chosen and the differences in translational philosophies between the various versions. In the Greek alone, as considered previously, translators could choose from the *Textus Receptus*, the Westcott-Hort text, the United Bible Societies text, the Majority text, and the Byzantine textform. Translators also must determine how literally or freely they will translate. Various opinions have produced a continuum between literal/unreadable to easily readable/inaccurate. However, no mainstream translation of which I am aware set out purposefully to be inaccurate or unreliable; the translators simply defined these terms differently in keeping with their particular theory. The underlying theories often account for many of the discrepancies between versions, and we should begin our evaluation at this point.

Preachers, elders, and Bible class teachers are often called upon to give an evaluation of a translation or to recommend one. But relatively few possess even a hint of the skills required to do so, though most have proceeded to recommend some translation and warn against others. We have carried this so far that many "evaluations" are strictly the product of a personal opinion that was formed without the benefit of any real understanding of what is involved in translating and what should be involved in an evaluation of a translation. Therefore, should we not evaluate those who evaluate? Failure to do so is traditionalism, accepting the word of men without appropriate biblical evidence (Acts 17:11). Just for the record, comparison and contrast between versions is not the same as an objective evaluation.

I write this neither in defense of any of the suspect versions nor as an attack upon them. I simply hope to draw attention to the fact that this question is multifaceted and should be studied honestly without any pontificating. We move forward on the premise that knowledge is to be preferred to ignorance and truth to traditional thought or "progressive" musings.

TRANSLATION PHILOSOPHY

To those unfamiliar with the challenges of translation the mere mention of "translation philosophy" may appear absurd. Most people seem to view translation simply as the process of seeing a word in one language and then choosing the appropriate word in the other, and so forth, and so on. Unfortunately, translation is not as simple as that. If languages matched up in syntax, style, idioms, and vocabulary, then the translator's work would indeed be simple. But this is simply not the case. To the contrary, the original languages of the Bible do not match up evenly with English in **any** of the categories stated above. Therefore, the translator must determine the most appropriate way to bridge the gap between the two languages.

Over time a rainbow of ideas has developed concerning the most appropriate way to translate the Bible. As stated above, *an actual literal translation is impossible*. Do you recognize the following verse? "In but the one of the sabbaths, of gathering together of the disciples of the to break bread, Paul was dialoguing with them, ready to be out in the next day, prolonged and the word as far as midnight." Perhaps you recognized Acts 20:7 by various clues, but would it have made much sense if you had not been familiar with it? It certainly shows respect for the original language, but it does not communicate. Even an interlinear does not get this literal because the translators recognize the accompanying difficulties. Translating in this fashion I still had to make certain interpretive decisions necessary because of the various cases in Greek, even while trying to be literal. My word choices are interpretive to some degree, though I have tried to keep them as literal as possible. The foregoing exercise simply points out the impossibility of actual literal translating.

On the other end of the spectrum lies "free translation." This philosophy does not even attempt to match up words or phrases with the original language. The translators who translate "freely" put emphasis upon the receptor or target language (English in our case) and on style instead of upon the source language and its grammar and syntax. Therefore, they freely interpret the passage from the original language and then reword it in what they consider the most acceptable and most readable style in English. Translating the same verse as given above, they might write, "When the Christians met on Sunday to take the Lord's Supper, Paul preached an extra-long sermon for them that lasted past midnight because he was going to have to leave the next day." Technically speaking, I have communicated the meaning of the verse in modern language and in phrases we are accustomed to hearing. I have not violated the meaning of the text absolutely, but I have made some interpretive decisions regarding 1) emphasis by changing the order of words quite a bit, 2) the meaning of "to break bread," 3) phrasing at the end of the sentence, and 4) saying that the reason Paul preached so long was explicitly because he had to leave the next day. Therefore, the problem with free translation is that it allows the translator great freedom to insert his particular interpretation of a passage and eliminate other possibilities — though the translator may do this very innocently. Even if the translator chooses an interpretation that is correct, he may do so at the expense of other possibilities. Thus, *the translator has taken upon himself the responsibility of the Bible student, making the student subject to the interpretation of the translator.*

Now if we have admitted that neither literal nor free translation is reasonable, the first because it is unreadable and the second because of its highly interpretative nature, what does a translator do? Most translations recognize this problem and therefore fall in between literal and free. The varying degrees between are determined by their philosophy of translation in how to meet the problems of both literal and free translation. The focus of the debate then becomes: *What is the proper balance between literalness and freedom in translating the biblical text?* Translators must decide how much to emphasize the original languages and how much to stress the effect the writer intends upon the reader. They must determine how closely to follow the original syntax and how much this might interfere with the reader understanding the text. They must debate the advantages of translating a Greek word by several different English words according to the context versus adopting as uniform a use as possible, though this might restrict the word's meaning and usage. They must weigh the value in creating a readable style with the dangers of letting style override grammar.

The most influential factors in a translator's mind are his respect for the original text, which is his source, and his respect for his readership, whose understanding is his objective. Therefore, *translation philosophy is often determined by the translator's understanding of inspiration and by the degree of respect the translator has for those who will use his translation.* Surely you can now see how important it is to know the translation philosophy of a translation when choosing a Bible.

FUNCTIONAL EQUIVALENCE

The translation philosophy that grew very prominent in the twentieth century in translating the Bible is known variously as functional equivalence, dynamic equivalence, or idiomatic translation. Some translators used this philosophy years ago, but since the NIV came out, the use of functional equivalence as a philosophy has dominated the market, and it seems that with each subsequent translation the text becomes freer and freer—with all its accompanying difficulties. The functional equivalence philosophy attempts to identify idioms (figures of speech, colloquialisms, etc.) and then translate with an equivalent idiom rather than translate the words literally. Translators who follow this philosophy reword the text to create the same "impact" upon the reader as the original text would have for the original recipients. As a result, the "form" of the text has given way to the perceived "function" of the text.

Since these versions have gained a large following, it seems wise to point out some of the difficulties that naturally attach themselves to such a practice. Many simply assume that all translations are equal when the words "Holy Bible" are printed on the cover. Thus, when selecting a translation most people make choices according to how easy it is to understand. Therefore, while not condemning people for choosing a particular version, **it certainly behooves us to warn them of the dangers associated with a given translation.** However, the appropriate place to begin is with translation theory.

Functional equivalence defines accuracy by meaning rather than by grammar. It does no good to argue about the literal meaning of a Hebrew or Greek word when the translators did not intend to be literal. What we should discuss is the extent to which it is possible to translate meaning without injecting personal interpretation.

Functional equivalence follows Quine's Sentential Theory of Meaning. They propose that words have no meaning in and of themselves. *Bank,* for instance, could refer to a place where people keep money or the side of a river. They argue that only in a **sentence** does *bank* have any meaning. This is ridiculous. *Bank* has both meanings as a word. The sentence only provides the context to determine which one is appropriate.

Functional equivalence has low requirements for something to be considered an idiom. For something to be an idiom a given phrase must be used consistently in a given way. Even then the only reason to translate it by functional equivalence would be if it could not communicate this literally. However, many now make arguments for idiomatic use based upon "similar" uses or phrasings. This allows them to translate a phrase as an idiom when there is no instance of the phrase itself ever being used as an idiom.

Functional equivalence assumes Bible students do very little study. Translators who use this philosophy must admit that they are making the English text easier to understand than the message is in the original language. This is impossible without interpretation. The underlying assumption is that people are just reading the Bible and will not take the time to study it properly, so the translators must do some of their study for them. However true it may be that people do not study, that does not justify writing studied conclusions into the text.

Functional equivalence emphasizes the "impact on the reader." Any wording may "impact" various readers differently, making this point meaningless. This is another way of saying, "What that phrase *meant* to them was...."

Functional equivalence makes some assumptions about the original language. Most people who translate using functional equivalence argue that *Koine Greek,* the language of the New Testament, was written for common people, with the implication being that they had to have things simple, just like people today. The Bible was written on a high plain, using the language common to people throughout the Roman Empire—but not like some oversimplified primer. There is a touch of arrogance in their explaining what is difficult to people who could not grasp it otherwise.

Functional equivalence eliminates some possible interpretations just by its natural process. While it is not possible to always include every possibility available in the original language, functional equivalence often chooses one, with the reader never knowing that there were other possible interpretations.

All this is not to say that translations that follow this philosophy never translate literally. The NIV provides one of best literal translations of 2 Timothy 3:16 found in any translation. However, the method by which functional equivalence translators choose *when* to translate literally eludes me. **But what they really need to explain is the authority by which they inject so much of themselves into the text and then still call it** *God's* **Word.**

FORMAL EQUIVALENCE

The translation philosophy behind most translations before 1975 is known as "formal equivalence" or a "modified literal" approach. The "complete equivalence" advocated by the translators of the New King James Version is simply a modernized version of this same philosophy with a little more freedom allowed in translation. As its names indicate, this philosophy emphasizes the form of the text above the function and attempts to render the text word for word inasmuch as this is possible. The strengths of the formal equivalence philosophy lie in its respect for the grammar of the original languages rooted in a conviction of verbal plenary inspiration. Since that which is written (Scripture) is inspired (2 Tim. 3:16-17) down to the very words (1 Cor. 2:12-15), the specific words chosen by the Holy Spirit from the vocabulary available and the word forms chosen (noun, verb, adjective, etc.), as well as the way in which they are presented becomes important to the overall communication of the message. Formal equivalence recognizes that words carry meaning on their own apart from sentences. That is not to say that their use in the sentence is not important or that it has *no* effect but simply to point out that **words are the basic building blocks of language—not sentences. If this were not the case, lexicons could not exist!**

God, being infinite and having purpose, must be infinite in purpose, which means that every time He acts and every decision He makes is done with purpose. This necessarily includes the actions and choices made in inspiring His Word. To deny that the "particulars" matter when translating is to deny the force of verbal plenary inspiration. **If those "particulars" matter, it is important to include them in the translated text as much as possible.** *This* is the overall strength of the formal equivalence/modified-literal approach. However, formal equivalence is not perfect. It has problems and limitations in what it can provide to the reader simply because of the nature of translation. Sometimes those who realize the dangers involved in functional equivalence translating can overstate their case because they do not realize the imperfections of formal equivalence.

Complete word for word correlation is impossible. Because languages develop independently some languages have several words to describe the intricacies of a given concept while other languages use only one word. Greek has four words (*agape, philia, storge, eros*) to describe the different aspects of what the English language uses the word "love" to describe. Likewise, on occasion English has greater variety than Greek from which to choose. Therefore, sometimes it is necessary to write two or more words to stand for one word in the original language.

Words can be applied in different ways (and need to be translated as such) depending upon the context. It is quite impossible to translate a given word the same way every time. Even if the translator should always use the unaffected meaning of a word (more on this below), it does not necessarily follow that English readers will understand the connection that a Greek reader would have originally. This would also require using entire phrases at times to translate a word. The frequently occurring word *parakaleo* literally means "to call alongside" with the implied purpose of communicating something to another (with the intention of providing perspective). The Greeks relied on the context to indicate the nature of the communication and the perspective offered. In English this one word is translated as "comfort, exhort, beseech, beg, implore, encourage, etc.," depending upon the context. While you could translate this word as "to call alongside *for the purpose of* ___," doing so would likely distract the reader because such a phrasing is so foreign to ordinary syntax.

The differences in grammar between languages requires interpretation to some degree in some places—no matter how much the translator wishes to avoid it. The genitive and dative cases in Greek can be very flexible, even in their most basic employment. This is so true that A.T. Robertson, the well-known Greek grammarian, and his disciples argue that though there are only two forms known historically as genitive and dative there are actually five cases— genitive, ablative, dative, locative, and instrumental. This simply proves that **the** *form* **in the original does not supply all of the answers and therefore translating** *always* **requires** *some* **interpretation.**

All translations translate functionally to some degree. While the modified-literal approach prefers translating words rather than meaning, this does not mean that formal equivalence translations avoid it entirely. The King James Version is famous for its use of the phrase "God forbid," though neither word is literally found in the phrase *me genoito* (literally, "may it not become *so*"). I know of no translation that translates "*stoma pros stoma*" (2 John 12; 3 John 13) as "mouth to mouth," which is literal.

Formal equivalence is to be preferred because it attempts to translate the original words faithfully, while remaining quite readable. While functional equivalence translations are good for "Bible *reading*," formal equivalence translations are generally more accurate and better suited for Bible *study*.

NUANCES OF GREEK VERB TENSES

English verbs emphasize the concept of time to the reader. When we read in English we associate verb tense almost exclusively with time. However, the Greeks did not solely emphasize time in their use of verb tenses but also the *kind* or *aspect* of the action. Beginning Greek students often have trouble grasping the various Greek moods because they have very little to do with time while still employing tense. Some have oversimplified the *kind* of action by delineating the differences as "linear" action and "point" action, illustrating these differences visually with a line and a dot. However, this approach still emphasizes time (or duration) to the English reader, while the Greeks intended these tenses to represent various concepts related to the action presented by the verb, sometimes emphasizing the time and in other instances the aspect. Essentially, then, the variety of tenses available to an author writing in Greek allowed him to provide not only an account of the action but also perspective regarding that action. Herein lies the essence of the Greek verb and the accompanying riches to be mined by one willing to study the text accordingly.

Present. The present tense presents the action "in motion" as the focus of the verb. Therefore, should the verb in question concern existence or thought, while not literally employing motion, the aspect of the verb can carry the "process" of thought or the ongoing progress of existence. Yet we must also realize that the context can limit the extent of this process. "We know that whoever is born of God does not sin; but he who has been born of God keeps himself, and the wicked one does not touch him" (1 John 5:18). The apostle uses the present tense "does...sin" ("sinneth" in the KJV) to emphasize the persistence of sinfulness that the child of God avoids through repentance rather than referring to a life completely free of sin. Especially is this evident in that the verbs "keeps" and "does...touch" immediately following indicate the extent of the process intended. The child of God does not sin so long as he keeps on his guard; and so long as he keeps on his guard, Satan cannot touch him.

Imperfect. The imperfect tense continues to present the idea of progress or process but with certain limitations, the foremost of which is time. Thus, it presents an action in progress in the past, drawing attention to the process. Regarding Judas Iscariot it says, "he sought how he might conveniently betray Him" (Mark 14:11). "Sought" is imperfect; therefore, Mark wanted to convey that Judas' betrayal involved an ongoing process of seeking opportunity, implying persistence on the part of the one acting, while still emphasizing the beginning of the behavior.

Aorist. The aorist tense refers to events or processes in a manner that emphasizes the occurrence without reference to what went on to create the action, whether that was progress, process, or persistence. In the aorist the fact that it happened (or is happening, or should happen) is enough. This does **not** imply that the action does not involve process, nor does it mean that there are no consequences. The aorist simply does not refer to them. In his first epistle, John refers to the certainty of God's forgiveness of our sins when confessed and the surety of being cleansed, summarizing the whole process (1 John 1:8-10).

Future. The future tense presents an action in summary without regard for its duration. The certainty of its occurrence is the main thrust of the speaker or writer. Sometimes the future is even used as if it is an imperative (e.g. quotations from the Ten Commandments) (Matt. 22:37-40). The force is: You shall do such and such, or you will face the consequences. Thus, the future presents a summarized view of an action with certainty. (Be careful! Do not assume that "shall" or "will" always has a future verb behind it. Sometimes this comes from the subjunctive mood.)

Perfect. The perfect tense presents an action but brings attention to the consequences that the action had once completed. Paul affirmed, "I know whom I have believed and am persuaded that He is able to keep what I have committed to Him until that Day" (2 Tim 1:12b). There are three perfect verbs presented here, each one referring to the consequences of prior action. Paul's trust was based on what he had believed over time. The consequence? Continued belief and trust. Likewise, his being persuaded at that moment was rooted in prior persuasion. The third perfect in this sentence is not "have committed" but "I know." Paul's faith and persuasion were based on His experience with God's faithfulness.

Pluperfect. The pluperfect, rarely found, is like the perfect except that it limits the extent of the consequences in regard to the perspective of the speaker or author.

When these tenses are employed in the various moods, their meaning is modified accordingly. In the imperative mood, while it is difficult to denote a distinction in translation, the present tense means, "Take action," while the aorist tense means, "Get it done." The present imperative prohibition means, "Stop it!" But the aorist subjunctive prohibition means, "Don't even think about it!" These rarely come through in translation but are essential elements of the verbs in the original, though still somewhat debated. Greek verbs contain multitudinous treasures…if you know what you are looking for!

TRANSLATION PRINCIPLES

Translation principles are those fundamental ways that a translator looks at his work and what he uses to guide and guard his translation. While translation philosophy describes a general approach, translation principles form the framework of that philosophy and detail how it should be implemented. Through my observations of both the problems created by the difficulties of translation and the mistakes that translators have made, I offer the following principles as an approach to translation.

- **Arguments based on grammar or words are only valid when using the original language as the standard.** It is senseless to argue translations by comparing English versions.
- **The word's unaffected meaning should take precedence and then be applied in context as generally as possible.** Misunderstandings about the nature of worship usually stem from applying the word *latreia* in Romans 12:1 too narrowly.
- **The only pertinent meaning of a given word is the meaning it had when the author originally penned it.** What *psallo* meant some time before the first century has no bearing on what the New Testament writers meant when they wrote.
- **It is as important to note differences between words as it is to note similarities when seeking a word's particular meaning and nuance.** If the Holy Spirit chose different words in the original language, we must not act like they are the same just because they are translated by the same English word.
- **It is essential to consider the overall context of the Bible in order to choose the most appropriate rendering.** This would eliminate the problem of a possible contradiction

created by some translations in Matthew 5:17 and Ephesians 2:14-16 by translating two different Greek words by the same English word.

- **Prepositions should be handled with extreme care to make sure that the case and unaffected meaning of the preposition affect the translation more than context.** The preposition *eis* is always limiting because of its connection to the accusative case, and its basic meaning always has the "end" or "extent" in mind—even when used with "believe."

- **The translator should respect the original verb tenses, realizing that even slight modifications may interrupt a subtle point being made by the writer.** Many translations lose the nuances of the original by blurring the imperfect, aorist, and perfect tenses—and sometimes others.

- **Periphrastic constructions should retain both verbal and adjectival elements if at all possible so that as full a meaning as possible comes through.** While "will be bound" is simpler and shorter in Matthew 16:19 than "will be, having been bound," the second version communicates the existence of two verbs—a being verb and a participle—and communicates every aspect of each of them as fully as possible.

- **The translator should take care to denote words and phrases that are associated, as much as possible.** One of the most difficult things for a translator to do is communicate associations present in the original language that depend upon form but are not always obvious in English where forms are limited. However, as much as is possible, a translator should communicate these relationships.

- **All grammatical options should be explored instead of making assumptions concerning either grammatical tags or meaning.** It is inappropriate to make an argument based upon some titular designation assigned to a given phrase if other possibilities exist. Therefore, to insist that "gift <u>of</u> the Holy Spirit" in Acts 2:38 is epexegetical (genitive of apposition) is fallacious since the form could equally indicate ablative (<u>from</u> the Holy Spirit).

- The translator should leave as many of the options open as the original language *unless* this would create *grammatical* (not hermeneutical) difficulties. However tempting it may be, the translator's responsibility is to communicate the original text, not simplify it.
- The translator should generally avoid transliterating words if another word would accurately translate the original word's meaning. "Immersion" is a better translation than "baptism," and "messenger" is more accurate than "angel" — no matter what the context.
- Historical terms and titles *should* be transliterated in order to maintain historical integrity. While "denarius" and "ethnarch" may require some explanation, it also emphasizes the historicity and veracity of the Bible.
- The translator should avoid making interpretive decisions as much as possible and should provide a means for the readership to know when he has done so. While it is impossible to avoid interpretation completely in translation, this should be kept to a minimum. No one translating the Bible should dare to inject himself into God's Word. For this reason italics are a useful method of communicating most interpretive decisions (though it is important to let the reader know that this is the purpose of the italics instead of using them for emphasis).
- Idioms should be translated "idiomatically" only (a) when they can be firmly identified as idioms (b) when a literal rendering would <u>mislead</u> (c) and not just when it may be more difficult for the interpreter. Most idioms can be understood as written with a little bit of study; therefore, translating them idiomatically is unnecessary. But "mouth to mouth" means something entirely different to an English speaking audience; therefore, "face to face" is a better translation, though idiomatic (2 John 12; 3 John 14).
- The translator should avoid using "ecclesiastical terms" when adequate words exist to translate them generally. "Congregation" or "called out *people*" is more literal than "church" and eliminates some of the false assumptions some

people make. "Favor" is better than "grace." "Overseer" is better than "bishop."

- **The translator should employ the same word as much as possible for uniformity with the original text unless doing so should interfere with the meaning.** While *dikaios* does cover much territory, **translating** it as both "righteous" and "just" creates confusion, and the connection between "just" and "righteousness" is lost (Rom. 1:17).
- **When possible the translator should distinguish between words with similar meanings.** While requiring a great deal of ingenuity, distinguishing between the different Greek words for love or service is a great asset to the English reader. The Holy Spirit chose to employ different words because of the different nuances they have.
- **Readability and ease of comprehension should not be considered a test of accuracy—only a test of style—beyond ensuring that the translation employs proper grammar.** Oversimplifying the text often equates to oversimplifying biblical truth.
- **It is essential for the translator to maintain a high level of respect for the interpretive abilities of his readership.** This last principle is essential because it keeps the translator from assuming that he must explain *everything* to the reader.

While these principles are not really new and should not be considered as absolute rules, they provide a standard basis for interpreting the faithfulness a given translation displays toward the original text. They admittedly require great discipline and, on occasion, produce a translation that is not so smooth. However, they help immensely when considering anything with reference to the original text. Translating Hebrew requires an appreciation for imagery and the ability to translate the imagery as accurately as possible. Greek translation and Greek exegesis depend upon attention to detail in even the finer points of grammar and the subtle nuances brought out through more intensive word studies. Far too often translators allow "assumed context" to dictate translation more than grammar and unaffected word meanings. Unfortunately, preachers sometimes make the same mistake when referring to the original languages. Both practices are wrong.

TRANSLATION IN BIBLE STUDY: THE EARNEST OF THE SPIRIT

The phrase "Spirit...as a guarantee" appears twice in Paul's second epistle to the Corinthians, and a similar reference appears in the book of Ephesians. It often has been assumed that these passages refer to the indwelling of the Holy Spirit, but this is simply not the case. Rather than addressing the manner of the indwelling, I will limit this study to a contextual examination of the particular passages associated with "the earnest of the Spirit."

The word *arrabon*, which is translated "guarantee" in all three of these passages, is actually a transliteration from the Hebrew into the Greek. (See Genesis 38.) It refers to something given as a pledge in order to provide proof of sincerity and the willingness to complete the transaction. While all typically agree that *arrabon* has the idea of guaranteeing something, there is disagreement about what is being guaranteed and the nature of the pledge. The *de facto* interpretation of this phrase maintains that the Spirit Himself is the earnest. Many modern translations, including the New King James Version, translate this phrase, both in 2 Corinthians 1:22 and 5:5, as "the Spirit...as a guarantee," translating the phrase dynamically — and incorrectly — on the assumption that it is a genitive of apposition. (It could be translated quite literally as "the guarantee **from** the Holy Spirit.") But how can "the guarantee of the Spirit" serve as proof or a guarantee when, assuming for a moment that it is the Spirit Himself, we must accept that guarantee itself by faith? In all three passages the guarantee is mentioned as confirming that God is true to His word. But if we must rely on God's word for knowledge of the guarantee, where is the confirmation? Rather than leaving the question open, however, it is incumbent upon us to consider the context in search of an interpretation consistent with the wording.

As Paul began 2 Corinthians he had just emerged from the turmoil in Ephesus (2 Cor. 1:8; Acts 19) and the congregation at Corinth had begun to listen to some Judaizing teachers. Therefore, Paul wrote this letter to stem the tide of apostasy and to defend himself and, more particularly, the message he carried. Since Paul had not followed the exact travel plans he originally proposed to the Corinthians, these false teachers were using it as a means to defame Paul's character and — by extension — Paul's message. So Paul replied that even if his own character was inconsistent, God's character and message were not (2 Cor. 1:17-20). Paul then said, "Now He who establishes us with you in Christ and has anointed us is God, who also has sealed us and given us the Spirit in our hearts as a guarantee" (2 Cor. 1:21-22). The verbs are all tied together in this statement. God "establishes," and "has anointed," "sealed," and "given." Each of these verbs refers in some way to a designation of God's approval. "Establishes" specifically emphasizes God's approval as accepted by others, "anointed" indicates designation for a particular, God-appointed task, "sealed" refers to an outward sign demonstrating God's "stamp of approval," and having "given us the Spirit in our hearts as a guarantee" proves that God will follow through on what He has promised. But who was stablished, anointed, sealed, and was given the Spirit as a guarantee? Paul made a distinction in this passage between himself and those with him who preached the message (us) and the Corinthians who received God's message (you). (Note verse 19.) That this context has not changed is shown by verse 24: "Not that we have dominion over your faith, but are fellow workers for your joy; for by faith you stand." Therefore, the context of 2 Corinthians 1:21-22 demands that we recognize that the "the Spirit in our hearts as a guarantee" referred to by Paul was given to Paul and those with him for the benefit of and as proof for the Corinthians. Paul was arguing that the Corinthians had adequate reason to listen to the message he presented because God had backed up that message by providing proof in the form of miracles that it was indeed a message from God. Therefore, in 2 Corinthians 1:21-22 Paul was definitely not referring to the indwelling of the Holy Spirit but to the gospel and its miraculous confirmation provided by the Holy Spirit (Mark 16:20; Heb. 2:3-4).

Thus far we have established: (1) that any interpretation of "the Spirit…as a guarantee" should explain contextually and consistently what "proof" actually is being offered, (2) that the phrase translated "the Spirit...as a guarantee" in Greek does not grammatically make the Spirit the earnest but that it might equally mean that the Spirit is the source of the earnest, and (3) that the context of 2 Corinthians 1:21-22 indicated that "guarantee" referred to the provision of miraculous gifts to prove the divine origin of the gospel, with the emphasis being on the message presented. (A phrase not discussed was "in our hearts." Since *kardia*, "heart," refers to man's mind especially as affected by circumstances, it would require the person arguing for indwelling in this context to accept the Spirit's direct influence—as some are prone to do.) Let us then consider Paul's use of "the Spirit...as a guarantee" within its context in 2 Corinthians 5.

Although Paul left his self-defense briefly in 2 Corinthians 2 in order to call for the forgiveness, restoration, and acceptance of the man who repented, he soon returned to the matter at hand—whether the Corinthians should listen to him or to the Judaizers. Therefore, in chapter three he called upon the Corinthians to judge righteously and addressed the proper role of the Old Law and the superiority of the gospel. In chapter four he explained that suffering persecution or such like was not an argument against the gospel but rather demonstrated that God wanted people to accept the truth on its own merits rather than due to the earthly messenger. He then emphasized that he was able to endure such persecutions because of his trust in the hope of the gospel. Finally, Paul explained at the beginning of chapter five that part of that hope was to be unencumbered by the weaknesses and frailty of the human body—a subject he had addressed in his first epistle to them as well. Within this context he then wrote: "Now He who has prepared us for this very thing is God, who also has given us the Spirit as a guarantee" (2 Cor. 5:5), though once again the translation confuses the issue.

While it is certainly clear from 1 Corinthians 15 and elsewhere that all Christians will receive new bodies, that is not really the point that Paul is making in 2 Corinthians 5. Paul is in the midst of explaining his own behavior to the Corinthians. The Corinthians had been told that Paul's difficulties were proof that he was not God's messenger and therefore could not be trusted. Paul argued that it was the spiritual condition of the inner man that mattered—not his physical condition or treatment. Therefore, the physical condition of the body was not a proper indicator of God's acceptance. Moreover, Paul was trying to explain to the Corinthians why he would be willing to put his life on the line. The answer was simple: the preservation of the body was immaterial; the restoration and preservation of the soul is what matters. But how could he be so confident? God had given him some form of proof that there was life after death, that he would receive a new body, and that this condition would be far better than his present situation. His confidence was based in what God said because, he wrote, "we walk by faith, not by sight" (2 Cor. 5:7), and "faith comes by hearing, and hearing by the word of God" (Rom. 10:17). On what grounds had he accepted information about what would happen to him if he died? The message inspired by the Holy Spirit! And he could have confidence in this message because the Spirit had provided miraculous confirmation of its truthfulness (Heb. 2:3-4; 1 Cor. 12:1-12). This was the guarantee provided by the Holy Spirit.

The personal indwelling of the Holy Spirit could not offer any confirmation of the promises beyond this life because both would be on equal footing—known in exactly the same way. It would therefore be impossible for one to be guaranteed for the other. A guarantee must be detectable in some way that is detached from what is being promised, otherwise it would amount to arguing in a circle: Believe God's Word when it tells you about the life to come. Why should I believe it? Because the Holy Spirit dwells in you. How do I know the Holy Spirit dwells in me? Because God's Word tells us so. Does this alone establish that there is no personal indwelling of the Holy Spirit? No. That is not the scope of the study. However, it does establish that the personal indwelling view cannot be taught using this passage—at least not contextually.

The most familiar passage referring to the Spirit as a guarantee comes from the book of Ephesians. Emphasizing the divine origins of the church and God's plan for man's redemption, Paul notes the Father's role (Eph. 1:3-6), the Son's role (Eph. 1:7-12), and the Holy Spirit's role (Eph. 1:13-14). Of special interest is the underlying context of Paul's purpose in demonstrating that Christians, rather than Jews, are God's chosen people today. With this in mind, let us note Paul's final reference to the guarantee associated with the Spirit: "In Him you also trusted, after you heard the word of truth, the gospel of your salvation; in whom also, having believed, you were sealed with the Holy Spirit of promise, who is the guarantee of our inheritance until the redemption of the purchased possession, to the praise of His glory" (Eph. 1:13–14).

"In Him you also trusted" presents a contrast with those mentioned in verse twelve who had trusted first. Considering the overall context, Paul is likely distinguishing between the Jews and the Gentiles. The Gentiles of Ephesus had responded to the same saving message as the Jews, placing their hope in the Messiah after hearing God's message. "The word of truth" is not only a synonym for the gospel but also a way to emphasize its character. "Truth" is not just a contrast with a false religious message but also a contrast with an *incomplete* message. "For the law was given through Moses, but grace and truth came through Jesus Christ" (John 1:17). It is the message of the New Covenant which brings the good news of God's provision for man's salvation through Jesus Christ in the church.

The next phrase, "in whom also, having believed," presents an interesting problem. The phrase "in whom" is translated as a locative *en* followed by a masculine pronoun, paralleling the prior phrase. However, grammatically speaking, *en* could also be instrumental, translated as "by means of," and the pronoun could refer to "word," which is masculine in Greek, and therefore be translated "which." Thus, the phrase could read, "by means of which also, having believed," a very real possibility when used in conjunction with a passive verb. This is relevant when evaluating what follows.

When Paul told the Ephesians, "you were sealed with the Holy Spirit of promise," he could have meant by the preceding phrase that Jesus made this possible or that their belief made this possible, since both are indeed essential. But what was the purpose and meaning of the seal? A seal designates approval and ownership. It is by this means that these Gentile Christians could find assurance that they indeed belonged to God. But what was the nature of this sealing since Paul said it was done "with the Holy Spirit of promise"? Most, once again, believe this refers to a personal indwelling of the Holy Spirit, but does the context bear this out? "Spirit" occurs in the dative without any preposition attached, requiring the case and context to dictate the proper translation. When translators use "with" in this construction, they have interpreted the phrase instrumentally, which would mean that the Spirit was instrumental in the sealing. ("By" would also be a translation of the instrumental.) So this does not say that the Holy Spirit was the seal but that He provided the seal. It is significant that the Spirit is called "the Holy Spirit of promise." Saying "**the** promise" tends to indicate that he had a specific promise in mind, a promise that the Gentiles, in particular, should appreciate. As Peter preached on Pentecost, he quoted Joel's prophecy (Acts 2:16-21) that included the Gentiles ("all flesh") in the provision of God's complete revelation of His will (Acts 2:17-20) and the opportunity of salvation for all mankind (Acts 2:21) all in accordance with what He promised His apostles (John 14:26; 15:26; 16:8-13). Since "guarantee" appears within this context, it should be interpreted with regard for this context.

Remember, the context of Paul's reference to guarantee of the Spirit in Ephesians 1 indicates at least two things. First, the situation under discussion pertained to why the Gentiles who belonged to the church could have confidence that this made them part of God's chosen people. Second, the means by which they had obtained this standing was through their trust in what the Messiah had done for them and in the gospel as the complete and final revelation from God. "In Him you also trusted, after you heard the word of truth, the gospel of your salvation; in whom also, having believed, you were sealed with the Holy Spirit of promise" (Eph. 1:13).

While most identify "you were sealed with the Holy Spirit of promise" as a reference to a personal indwelling of the Holy Spirit, the wording and context would indicate otherwise. The purpose of Paul's reference was not to make these Gentile Christians feel special because they had some personal divine presence within them but to point them to the proof that God indeed accepted them—put His seal on them—as His people. This was accomplished by something provided by the Holy Spirit, and what He provided for them Paul had already mentioned more than once in the context—the word of God, the gospel, the divine message for mankind completed in its entirety, revealed in the first century by inspiration of the Holy Spirit (2 Pet. 1:19-21) and confirmed to be from God by miraculous power made possible by the Holy Spirit (Heb. 2:3-4; 1 Cor. 12:1-12). Since you can have confidence in God's Word and have confirmation that the gospel is God's Word, you can have confidence that God will keep His Word. The Gentiles could have confidence that they were Christians and part of God's chosen people when their lives matched what God's Word said. In other words, "whoever calls on the name of the LORD Shall be saved" (Acts 2:21). It does not matter who responds to the call of the gospel (Acts 2:38-39; 10:34-35). As long as they respond in accordance with God's revealed will (obedience), they can know that God has accepted them as His people, that He has added them to His church (Acts 2:47).

Paul then says, "who is the guarantee of our inheritance until the redemption of the purchased possession, to the praise of His glory" (Eph. 1:14). "Who" translates the masculine pronoun *hos*. While there is a textual variant on this word that reads *ho*, the neuter pronoun, the vast majority of manuscripts agree on *hos* and the older manuscripts are divided. (If *ho* is accepted, the antecedent could be "gospel" as easily as "Spirit.") If *hos* is the correct rendering, one would expect it to refer to a masculine noun. But "Spirit" is neuter in Greek. "Word," on the other hand, is masculine, making it the more likely antecedent than Spirit. This fits the rest of the context, implying that the completed word was the down payment God made to give us proof and confidence that we would receive an inheritance. The guarantee would perform this function "until the redemption of the purchased possession." God's complete and confirmed Word provides the evidence that assures us that He will also complete the transaction (redemption) by taking His people home to be with Him (John 14:1ff). Therefore, in verse fourteen Paul joins Jews and Gentiles together, describing them as equal recipients of "our inheritance." This inheritance we can anticipate together as God's people—the church, the people that God claims as His possession—whether Jew or Gentile. Paul then closes by repeating his phrase used solely of the Jews in verse twelve: unto the praise of His glory.

So how could these Gentile Christians be so sure that they were part of God's chosen people by belonging to His church? God gave them proof—the guarantee provided by the Spirit—when Christ sent the Holy Spirit to reveal all truth (John 16:13) by which the complete knowledge of what it means and what it takes to be God's people was made known to all mankind and for all mankind. When we do God's will, we can have confidence that God accepts us. This is the earnest of the Spirit.

The overall proof offered by the guarantee of the Spirit is threefold: (1) the divine origin of the message proved by miraculous gifts, (2) the message of the gospel itself, and (3) the confidence gained when our actions fulfill what the gospel requires. Since the miraculous confirmed the gospel, and since our obedience to the gospel confirms our status, then the heart of the earnest is the gospel itself.

CONCLUSION

Few people today appreciate the value of learning the original languages of the Bible. Learning Greek has fallen by the wayside for the most part, and the status of Hebrew is even worse. We lament the falling standards of the education system in America but then apply the same failed thinking to spiritual training. Why is it that fewer and fewer preachers have any knowledge of or — at the very least — appreciation for the original languages?

My own observation is that most of our schools have continued to lower their expectations in this regard. Learning any language does indeed take time, and having wrestled with curriculum myself, I understand the difficulties. But when language studies get placed on the back burner, it becomes obvious that the powers that be do not understand their importance. If providing a year's worth of study completely through a beginning grammar is just enough to make a student dangerous, then providing him with less is just plain ludicrous. This eventually leads him to quote the conclusions of others in regard to the original language without having any clue what he is talking about.

However, let us also realize that many students only realize the value of language studies after leaving school. Therefore, having not applied themselves fully during school and having neither time nor opportunity enough to extend their knowledge after school, they accept their ignorance of Greek. If this describes you, I hope to encourage you to rekindle your desire and retool your schedule to fit in time for language studies. If you live close enough to a school that offers *Koine* Greek or Biblical Hebrew, take it! If not, there are still ways to learn.

There is a plethora of beginning Greek grammars on the market today. Some of these are designed for private study. Ray Summers'

Essentials of Beginning Greek Grammar has enjoyed great popularity, though his explanations are often too concise without further explanation by a teacher. I recommend William Mounce's *Basics of Biblical Greek* to the beginning student because of its user friendly explanations and combination of inductive and deductive study, but his workbook exercises are drawn from the New Testament, which allows the student to rely, even subconsciously, on his memory of how a passage has been translated instead of pushing him to let the grammar lead the translation. Machen's grammar is still excellent, and his exercises come the closest to actual Greek syntax of all I have seen. Online courses and YouTube videos exist as well. Therefore, you can learn Greek if you really want to do so.

Unfortunately, the current trend among grammars is to abandon any exercises that require translating from English into Greek. While it is true that you will never be required to do this, translating into the language you are learning is the best way to teach a student how to think in that language. Otherwise, translation becomes a game of mix and match, and the meaning associated with the original is often lost on the beginner. Each grammar has its strengths and weaknesses, and there are other good grammars I have not named. However, the problem with studying a language on your own is that you have no one to correct your work and to detect particular problems you are having. Even videos are of little help in this regard. You really need a mentor of some kind who will help you along the way. This may require corresponding with someone, but it is better than not learning the language.

The best way to learn a new language is to study through a beginning grammar over a period of about a year in which you do some work at least five days a week. Then, follow this study up by going through a *different* beginning grammar with a different approach. Then you can move on to reading an intermediate grammar such as Dana and Mantey's *Manual Grammar of the Greek New Testament* or Daniel Wallace's *Beyond the Basics* or both. While studying these, begin translating passages before you preach or teach them, always checking yourself against a good translation.

These suggestions will not turn you into a scholar, but that is not our purpose. We do not need every preacher or Bible student to be a scholar (I hope!), but we do need to regain a serious perspective about our studies of the text. There are older, wiser, and more knowledgeable gospel preachers than I when it comes to Greek, and certainly Hebrew. However, most of these good men are many years my senior. Preachers and Bible students in younger generations need to be just as concerned and committed to language studies as those to whom we owe so much (1 Tim. 4:12-16; 2 Tim. 2:15; 4:2-5).

Translation:

- Is a matter of biblical expediency rather than religious authority
- May differ depending upon the philosophy of the translators
- That interprets meaning is called functional equivalence
- That interprets words is called formal equivalence
- Cannot always communicate the full impact of the original language
- Should follow strict principles in order to achieve verbal accuracy
- Can contribute greatly to a Bible student's understanding of the Bible

Recommended Reading

Deissmann, Adolf. *Light from the Ancient East.* Translated by Lionel R. M. Strachan. Reprint. Peabody, MA: Hendrickson Publishers, 1995.

Hightower, Terry, ed. *A Handbook on Bible Translation.* San Antonio, TX: Shenandoah Church of Christ, 1995.

Lewis, Jack P. *The English Bible from KJV to NIV,* 2nd edition. Grand Rapids, MI: Baker Book House Company, 1991.

Ryken, Leland. *The Word of God in English: Criteria for Excellence in Bible Translation.* Wheaton, IL: Crossway Books, 2002.

White, James R. *The King James Only Controversy: Can You Trust the Modern Translations?* Minneapolis, MN: Bethany House Publishers, 1995.

Woods, Guy N. *How to Read the Greek New Testament.* Nashville, TN: Gospel Advocate, Co, 1970, reprint, 1974.

Questions for Discussion

1. At what point does the inclusion of erroneous translation cause a Bible to be unreliable?
2. What did you learn about translation that you did not know prior to reading this chapter?
3. What should you know about the translators of a version of the Bible before purchasing it?
4. What value do you see in pursuing a study of the original languages of the Bible?
5. How might the translation you read affect your understanding of God's message?

Assignment

Selecting five different translations at random, determine the translation philosophy of each and provide examples from the text that demonstrate this philosophy.

CHAPTER 18

Word Studies

INTRODUCTION

Word studies receive only scant attention from most Bible students, partially because the suggestions made in order to determine word meanings amount to little more than a bibliography of Greek and Hebrew lexicons or word study books. As a result most Bible students believe that consulting these works *is* a word study. However, if these works disagree, how does one determine the meaning? Is it not possible that these works might be wrong or incomplete on occasion? It would be difficult to anticipate every possible nuance required in every study. Therefore, good Bible students should include learning the process underlying lexicography in order to evaluate the sources and conduct basic studies as a means of extending his own knowledge.

Lexical definitions. Any student attempting a word study should begin by becoming familiar with the definitions provided in Greek and Hebrew lexicons. Some of these lexicons are keyed to Strong's numbering system and therefore even a beginner who has no knowledge whatsoever of the original languages can still access them. Other lexicons require knowledge of at least the alphabet in order to locate the word in question. More advanced lexicons can contain quotations from various languages and can become a hindrance to study. The purpose of consulting these lexicons is not to form a final opinion but to provide a good place to begin a word study. A basic lexicon can provide immediate insight into the variety of ways a word can be translated and how difficult the study might become.

Independent research. Rather than simply accepting a few words offered by scholars, a good Bible student will learn how to evaluate these studies by discovering how the scholars decided upon the definitions given. This process is best served by either an original language concordance or a good Bible program, but the same process could be followed using a good English concordance that differentiates between the words of the original language rather than creating lists based solely on an English translation.

Scholarly opinion. Once a student has studied the use of the word in question by examining its usage in various contexts, he should also consult word study books to consider the studied opinion of various scholars. While it is natural to prefer a particular author or work, it is important to consult more than one opinion in order to maintain greater objectivity.

Word studies offer the student a glimpse into the linguistic associations of the author that often provide contextual hints through the nuanced meanings of the original language. Few Bible students will ever become lexicographers, but all Bible students should understand the nature of their work in order to explain not only what a word meant but also how it came to mean that.

DETERMINING TRANSLATIONAL POSSIBILITIES

For the Bible student who lacks much background in the original languages of the Bible, the best place to begin a word study is in a lexicon that can provide the basic information required to begin an analysis of a word. Different lexicons have different strengths and different weaknesses, which is why no Christian should rely on them — especially on just one — as the final say. Some limit themselves to biblical words, while others include words from other literature as well. Some lexicons offer a limited number of possibilities for translation while others list a different possible translation for (it sometimes seems) every occurrence of the word. Some lexicons have up to date scholarship while others did not have access to certain information when they were penned. Some lexicons offer information regarding the development of words while others only list possible translations. On occasion lexicons have included dubious translation suggestions that appeal to those of certain doctrinal dispositions. Therefore, when performing a word study, the student should bear in mind that a translation suggested by a lexicon is a beginning rather than the end of the study.

Depending upon which lexicon a student uses, the number of suggested meanings will vary. In the Bauer-Arnt-Gingrich-Danker *Greek-English Lexicon of the New Testament and Other Early Christian Literature* (BAGD) the possible translations for *logos* seem endless. Under the general heading of "speaking" the categories include a "word," an "expression," a "statement of definite content," "words uttered on various occasions," "the subject under discussion," and "written words and speeches." A second more specific subheading "of revelation of God" includes categories of "command" and "divine revelation through Christ." But the lexicon also notes that the same word refers to "computation, reckoning," "settlement (of an account)," "respect," "reason, motive," and two more that cannot even be put into noun form. The third major heading discusses *logos* as a divine name for Jesus. This type of over-analysis is overwhelming for most students, and though plenty of suggested translations appear, a person will know very little about the basic, underlying meaning of the word after reading the entire entry.

The best way to view this list of translational possibilities is to examine all of the words to see what they have in common and what ideas are suggested by those choices. All suggestions under the first major heading refer to a word or group of words in some way. All the possibilities in the second category suggest some aspect of the process of thought. The third major heading, which suggests "Word" as a name for Jesus, depends on the other two categories to explain its full implications. However, analysis of these translational possibilities demonstrates two key elements: words expressed in either spoken or written form and a thought process. This provides enough information to create a working hypothesis in regard to the essence of the word's meaning: *logos* might be defined as the word that best describes an expression of thought. This understanding is in accordance with every definition provided and also offers possible insight into why Jesus could be called "the *Logos* of God."

CONTRAST SYNONYMS

Few people today consider the precision capabilities of language. Rarely does a person consult a thesaurus in daily conversation in order to find the one word that communicates an exact image, yet writers often must consider the power of their word choices. It may be correct to say, "John walked into the classroom," but "John strutted into the classroom" communicates not only the action but also an attitude. English readers generally recognize these differences intuitively. However, the languages of the Bible used the same principle but often with different classes of words. So when a student compares and contrasts all of the Greek words in a particular class, the nuances of the various words begin to manifest themselves and he becomes more familiar with what the original audience understood when they heard or read the words.

One of the problems confronting the English-only Bible student is that he does not know what words in Hebrew or Greek have synonyms of interest. However, all he must do is consult a reference work such as *Wilson's Old Testament Word Studies* for Hebrew and Aramaic words and *Vine's Expository Dictionary of the New Testament* for Greek words to discover whether one English word translates more than one word of Hebrew or Greek. A peek inside a good concordance will reveal the same thing (distinguishing either by distinct numbers or separate lists). He should also consider English synonyms in order to determine whether they represent distinctions in Greek vocabulary or variety in the translator's use of vocabulary. By looking for the appearances of "word" in the New Testament one discovers that *logos* is joined by *rhema* as a Greek word translated in English as "word."

Furthermore, the Christian must determine which word is more specific and which is more generic. If both are specific or both generic, the student must decide the category of thought to which each belongs, when it was used, and why. The student makes these determinations by an examination of the various contexts and circumstances in which the synonyms appear. Consideration of the New Testament occurrences of both *logos* and *rhema* shows that *logos* places emphasis upon the reasoning underlying the expression while *rhema* emphasizes what actually has been expressed. However, by cross-referencing these lists of verses one quickly realizes that both words can refer to the same thing—each with a different emphasis. Jesus said, "He who rejects Me, and does not receive My words (*rhema*), has that which judges him—the word (*logos*) that I have spoken will judge him in the last day" (John 12:48). People reject what has been expressed and will be judged by the content and reasoning reflected in those expressions. The biblical text is filled with similar examples, illustrating why Christians should add the consideration of synonym contrasts to their Bible study repertoire.

DISCOVER THE ORIGIN OF THE WORD

The origin and development of a word can provoke insight into its application in the text and provide ready-made illustrations for the diligent Bible student. However, this information rarely appears in a general lexicon, though some lexicons do indicate the word cognate from which the word was derived. This allows a student to study the root word and then consider its origin as well. By combining the two studies and applying what is learned according to the appropriate part of speech along with a consideration of any prefixes or suffixes, a student can create a close approximation of the development of the word in order to explain not only *what* it means but also *why* that is what it means.

The Greek word *logos* is a noun derived from the verb *lego*, which means "to say"—a meaning one should expect since its verbal offspring means "expression of thought." However, an examination of the background of *lego*, available in some of the more extensive lexicons such as the *Theological Dictionary of the New Testament*, reveals that it originally had the idea of "picking or choosing." As the language developed, *lego* gradually narrowed its meaning to the choosing of words which were then mentally gathered together. Eventually the word became associated with the narration of those thoughts that had been selected; therefore, "to say" is an excellent translation.

For illustrative purposes one might also consider any words that the English language has adapted from the original. While Hebrew has had little impact on English, many Greek words eventually worked their way into the English dictionaries in one form or another.

The word *logos*, or more specifically its related adjective *logikos*, has given us the terms "logic" and "logical." This accords well with the hypothetical definition "expression of thought," indicating a more deliberative process which has been thought through to some extent. However, one should never take this too far. As we will discuss later, sometimes people can become overzealous and begin assigning the English definition to a Greek word. The point of this portion of a word study is that words *develop*; they can change. Words can evolve in their meaning. Therefore, it is important to know what the word meant when it was originally included in the document being studied (the Bible) and also understand when and how it came to enter the English language. Then one must also consider if the English word itself developed. However, despite these words of caution, considering the possible connections between the original language and English has value—not in determining meaning but possibly in illustrating that meaning once determined.

At this point in the study a student should have a working hypothesis of the word's meaning based upon his reading in the various lexicons. But this is not the end of a word study by any means. It has just become interesting!

DO AN INDEPENDENT WORD SEARCH AND STUDY

The weakness in most word studies is the reliance on secondary sources of information. Word study books and lexicons providing definitions of Hebrew and Greek words for the English reader are invaluable helps, yet some Bible students forget when consulting these works that they are not inspired. Most, if not all, of the editors and contributors involved in these projects enter them with a definite doctrinal disposition. Therefore, without any ill intent a very scholarly person could easily miss some information that might lead to a conclusion other than the one he believes personally. A quick comparison of different editions of the same lexicon might demonstrate changes that do not reflect new scholarship but rather a growing willingness to insert doctrinal opinion. This does not necessarily impugn the character of all those whose long hours made these books possible; it only demonstrates the need to check an author's reasons for providing the definitions he has given.

A student should begin this portion of the word study by finding every occurrence of the word under consideration as it appears in the Bible. A Greek-English concordance or a decent Bible program that either is keyed to the original words or has original language capability makes this task much easier than you might think. Then the student should take this list of occurrences and examine each text in its context in order to detect and label both different ways in which the word is used (with an emphasis on the functions of the word rather than the different translations of the word) and whatever unifying factors one might observe that remain true in every context. In this process a student should begin with the specific word of interest, but broadening the search to include all related words can help, especially when the number of occurrences is low, as with "propitiation." By analyzing each occurrence of the word carefully, a student should be able to check the hypothesized definition based upon the first portion of the study. The generic meaning-oriented definition must fit in every text or it must be reworked. This process usually helps the student understand the reasons behind the translation suggestions found in the lexicons, confirming their meaning while adding depth to one's understanding. On occasion independent study may unearth a possible interpretive "interpolation" in a lexicon. If you suspect this, inquire into the author's background and consider contacting the editor or another scholar for additional explanation (which must be from a lexicological, "word study" point of view rather than a theological point of view to be valid).

After practicing this method one might try adding word occurrences in the Septuagint and in historical writings of the same time period to verify the word's meaning in its cultural and literary context. This is, after all, what the lexicographers did in the first place.

DETERMINE UNAFFECTED MEANING

Nothing is more fundamental to biblical exegesis than understanding the words under consideration. For this reason, among many, it helps to keep a dictionary handy while studying. But since God did not inspire the Bible in English, the meanings of the words in the original language become significant. While very good English translations exist, it remains impossible to convey everything included in the original. Therefore, original language word studies can clarify the author's intent, though it might be obscured in translation, and bring out a relationship between words hidden in the English.

Most preachers therefore include at least one dictionary or lexicon in their libraries devoted to explaining the words of the original languages—Hebrew, Aramaic, and Greek. While there are many good works available along this line, preachers and teachers must understand their limitations. When a lexicon offers English words to consider as possible translations of a given word, these generally are *affected meanings*. They offer possible English equivalents based upon the various contexts in which that word is found. While most define the Greek word *logos* as "word," this is actually only one possible meaning, depending upon the context. *Account, message, speech, reason, saying*, and *expression* are all other viable alternatives that the lexicons provide. The fact that *word* may appear first in the series does not give it any greater weight. If a lexicon includes a word at all, its author or authors obviously considered it possible, and perhaps even preferable in some situations. In Matthew 5:32 the New King James translators used "reason" to translate *logos*. *Logos* refers to "a collection" and by first century times generally limited itself to the idea of a "mental collection," though Paul used the related word *logia* to refer to the collection taken on the first day of the week (1 Cor. 16:1-2). *Logos* therefore has an *unaffected* meaning that refers to "collected thought." For this reason content and logic are very much part of this word and its derivatives.

The question then becomes (though we are working somewhat backwards): What do all of these words have in common? How is it possible for all of these words to translate one Greek word? The lexicographers and translators have simply provided examples of how that word can be applied. What most people think are definitions are really applications of the *unaffected meaning* of the word within various contexts. But since contexts differ, not every application of a word's meaning fits well, or even correctly, into every instance where the word occurs. "Comfort" is one application of the word *parakaleo*. The related noun *paraklete* is translated "comforter" in John 14:26 in the King James Version and "Helper" in the New King James. However, when Peter said, "Be saved from this perverse generation" (Acts 2:40), he was not seeking to comfort the people (and only to help them in an indirect way), though *parakaleo* described these words. He wanted to *exhort* them. And, "exhorter" also might be a better translation in John 14:26 as well, considering the Holy Spirit's role in providing the gospel message! The *unaffected* meaning of *parakaleo* means simply "to call alongside" *in order to speak with and offer another perspective*. The nature of the conversation is known only by context. But it would be clumsy to translate *parakaleo* as "I call alongside *in order to speak with and offer another perspective*" every time it occurs. Therefore, the affected meanings—those meanings possible within the various known contexts in which the word occurs—are given as the translational possibilities.

The most obvious problem that has arisen due to this is the definition of *latreia* in Romans 12:1. Should it be translated "service" or "worship"? Lexicons do indeed provide "worship" as one affected meaning of *latreia*. Therefore, by including "worship" under *latreia* the lexicographer is saying that sometimes *latreia* refers to worship. However, this is quite different from saying that all actions included in the term *latreia* constitute worship. The question really should be: What is the unaffected meaning of *latreia*? What does it mean apart from any context? This is only revealed by considering its usage in *every* context—biblical (including the Septuagint) and historical—and then defining it in terms that incorporate its applications. Though it may be oversimplifying the matter, look for the universal common denominator of meaning. Since *latreia* always refers to that which has a religious character but is contrasted with worship (*proskuneo*) on several occasions, since it describes the work of non-priest Levites in the Old Testament doing activity that would be described, by themselves, as service but not worship, and since the overall context of the Bible argues in favor of worship as distinct and specific activity, then the unaffected meaning of *latreia* cannot be "worship."

The real problem is that translating *latreia* as worship blurs (if not erases) an important distinction between *latreuo* and *proskuneo* to which

Jesus Himself referred (Matt. 4:10). How then can we communicate the distinction between *proskuneo* and *latreuo*? Since *latreia* definitely refers to action done on behalf of another that is religious in nature and comes from the heart, the best translation for *latreia* is "religious service" or "devoted service." Service is activity done on behalf of another. It is very generic. While *latreia* does indeed carry a nuance emphasizing the depth of devotion given in service, it remains within the category of service rather than the category of worship. Worship is activity specifically directed toward God, **expressing** that devotion to God and demonstrating reverence for God. While worship is included as activity done on behalf of God, religious service is not primarily activity directed *toward* God, does not necessarily **express** *devotion* to or *adoration* for God, and does not of its own character demonstrate *reverence* for God. This does not mean that these attitudes are absent but that specific action rather than attitude is being emphasized. However, these distinctions only come out when you devote yourself to studying the *unaffected* meaning of words instead of just accepting the *affected* meanings as provided in a lexicon.

If nothing else, all this should serve as a caution against universally applying words found in lexicons. It is important to understand the process that went into forming the lexicon and making word choices, otherwise we might allow ourselves to either limit or extend a word's unaffected meaning and thereby do injury to the meaning of God's inspired Word.

DISTINCTIVE MEANING

Recent trends in Bible translating seem to have rejected a very fundamental principle underlying the entire discipline. Rather than performing word studies to determine the characteristic meaning unique to a particular word, the pendulum now seemingly swings toward ambiguity. Instead of recognizing the distinct unaffected meaning of words, doctrinal haziness demands that translation mask such distinctions, else controversy might erupt. As a result the clarity of the original now becomes lost in the vagueness of over-simplification. The ultimate result of this movement is to minimize the impact—in certain cases—of a word's distinctive meaning so that other possible translations are substituted that are easier to comprehend than the original but sometimes affecting the doctrinal impact of the passage in the process.

This practice in translation is unsuitable for the Bible because it fails to respect the language communicated by the divine Author. Since the Bible is inspired of God (2 Tim. 3:16-17) down to the very words recorded (1 Cor. 2:10-14), the failure to translate those words as faithfully and consistently as possible confuses rather than helps the reader because it confuses the text of the Author. God, being infinite, does everything with purpose. This includes the process of inspiration. When a translation or word study fails to appreciate the distinctions that God Himself made in giving His message, they have failed to communicate *His* message (2 Tim. 4:2-4), choosing instead to water it down with modern style.

While a student should observe the similarities between words and notice the categories of meaning and syntax to which words belong, he also should realize that different words exist for a reason. If two words communicate *exactly* the same thing, one is totally unnecessary. A brief study of language shows that this often explains why some words became obsolete. Various Greek words used in the New Testament communicate the general idea of one person speaking to another. However, the word choices may emphasize the content of what was communicated, the fact of communication, the sound of communication, or the exact quote that was communicated. Some who mock the practice of making these distinctions argue that nobody thinks with this precision in his speech or writing. However, they fail to realize that we do not need to do so because we make distinctions intuitively in our native language, as would the penmen of the Bible — with the added benefit of inspiration.

The arguments surrounding the Greek preposition *eis,* particularly as used by Peter in his sermon on Pentecost, has consistently served as a point of contention between those who teach the necessity of water baptism and those who deny it. When Peter said, "Repent, and let every one of you be baptized in the name of Jesus Christ for the remission of sins" (Acts 2:38), what did he mean by "for" (*eis*)? Does it mean "in order to," requiring water baptism or does it mean "because of," indicating that baptism is "the outward sign of an inward grace."

First, throughout all of the ancient secular literature written in Greek, there is no occasion in which the preposition *eis* occurs where the context indicates it means "because of." Therefore, those who would support this meaning must look to biblical literature. The Septuagint supplies no instance of a "because of" meaning; therefore, they are forced to find justification for a "because of" meaning in some passage in the New Testament.

They tend to skip over the most obvious passages of its 1773 uses. In Mark 1:4 and Luke 3:3 the writers record that John the Immerser went about preaching baptism of repentance "for the remission of sins." The phrasing matches Peter's words of Acts 2:38 exactly and simply cannot mean "because of," even according to ordinary denominational theology. Furthermore, as Jesus was instituting the Lord's Supper, He said, "For this is My blood of the new covenant, which is shed for many for the remission of sins" (Matt. 26:28). To teach or imply that Jesus died *because of* the remission of sins is both ludicrous and blasphemous. It makes a mockery of what He came to do in providing the means of salvation for mankind (Tit. 2:11; John 3:16). Therefore, those who insist on a "because of" meaning in Acts 2:38 cannot use any of the passages that are closest in syntax and wording.

However, before assuming that the matter is settled we should look at one more instance. Both Matthew and Luke record Jesus' words to the scribes and Pharisees who came seeking a sign of Jesus' authenticity as Messiah. In response to their query He used Jonah's three days and three nights in the belly of the great sea creature as an analogy to the sign of his coming death, burial, and resurrection. He then addressed the scribes and Pharisees themselves. "The men of Nineveh will rise up in the judgment with this generation and condemn it, because they repented at the preaching of Jonah; and indeed a greater than Jonah is here" (Matt. 12:41); cf. Luke 11:32). The word translated "at" in this verse is *eis*. If one were simply to choose from "because of" or "in order to" in this passage it might be easy to choose the former and become convinced that the preposition could indeed carry that meaning in Acts 2:38. However, this would amount to doing a word study backwards.

Rather than first assume that you have found an exception, you should consider the possibility that it is the exegesis that is incorrect—

not the word's definition. Jesus was not reminding the scribes and Pharisees that Jonah's preaching had produced repentance. His emphasis was not on the preaching but on the repentance itself. They needed to repent, and Jesus used the Ninevites as an example of true repentance. The purpose of *eis* as a preposition was to indicate *end* and *extent*. The *end* and *extent* of the preaching of Jonah was that the people of Nineveh did indeed repent and that their repentance matched up to what Jonah's preaching required.

When Peter told the Jews on Pentecost to "let every one of you be baptized in the name of Jesus Christ for the remission of sins," he was telling them what they needed to do in order to be saved from their sins; all of these things—repentance, baptism, remission of sins—still lay in the future for them (Acts 2:40-47). Peter's use of *eis* indicates two more things. First, the people needed to have "remission of sins" as their end in mind when they were baptized. Second, the people could be sure that their obedience did indeed extend so far as to procure the forgiveness they sought.

Some Greek grammarians' treatment of the meaning of *eis* provides a sad example of how predetermined theology can affect a person's scholarship. But on the positive side, this small word indicates the significance of word studies and why they should be part of our exegesis. Rather than allowing the precise meaning of the original word to become part of how they interpret the passages in which it occurs, some very learned men choose to interpret passages in a way that favors their previously determined position and then attempt to force a new meaning on a word that it never had when the inspired writer penned it. Such a practice implies that their interest in the Bible is something other than the discovery of truth.

CONSIDER AFFECTED MEANINGS

People unfamiliar with the process of translation often have difficulty appreciating the intricacies involved in simply choosing an English word by which to translate a Hebrew or Greek word. Since there is no direct correspondence between the vocabularies of any two languages a translator must make choices that are consistent with the unaffected meaning of the word but also that communicate in English.

This sometimes requires the use of several different words to translate one word in the original language. When the basic, unaffected meaning of the word cannot work in translation, the translator must make selections in English that are closest to reflecting the original meaning but which also fit the context. It is this combination of the word's unaffected meaning and its context that produces "affected meaning" — how the word is used in that particular instance.

The best example of this practice, and why it is sometimes necessary, is the Greek word *parakaleo* discussed above. This compound word literally means "to call" (*kaleo*) "alongside" (*para*). However, since its original meaning which emphasized a "summons" became overshadowed by the nature of the communication involved and because it occurs in so many different contexts, it would be impractical to translate it each time by its unaffected meaning of "to call alongside" or even by "to summon" (especially since another word, *phoneo*, more accurately fits the specific idea of a summons). Therefore, *parakaleo* has been translated by "called for" (Acts 28:20) (which is closest to the unaffected meaning), "comfort" (Matt. 5:4), "beseech" (Rom. 12:1), "pray" (Matt. 26:53), "plead" (Luke 15:28), "exhort" (Acts 2:40), "consolation" (2 Cor. 1:7), and "beg" (Matt. 18:32). Other translations add "intreat," "encourage," "petition," "urge," "invite," "appeal," and "ask" to their list of possibilities.

This is not to say that the unaffected meaning is irrelevant. It must always remain the guiding force in translation and in a word study. In each of the examples given regarding *parakaleo*, the underlying idea behind each word representing an affected meaning is some form of communication, but at the heart of each one is the proximity of those involved in the communication. Therefore, rather than referring simply to a sound or gesture to gain attention or to draw someone closer, *parakaleo* maintains a very personal element that the affected meanings attempt to communicate to the reader. Translating *parakaleo* as "I call alongside" or "I call to my side" has its advantages, but it also loses the personal touch of the original language and its intensity, which is why translators have opted for greater variety in its affected meanings.

It is essential for anyone doing a word study to understand the theory and purpose behind affected meaning. It is not the same as functional equivalence translating because the focus remains on the word rather than on the phrase, and the unaffected meaning should still be detectable. By recognizing the flow of thought from unaffected meaning to affected meanings, the Bible student will understand the differences in some of the translations, appreciate the nuances of the original words, and have greater insight into many passages of scripture.

CONSULTATION AND REFERENCE

Word studies should center, as much as possible, on an individual's independent study; however, a Bible student should neither discount the works of scholars nor ignore them. A Bible student should not allow the lexicons and word study books to become a crutch but neither should he ignore the value of the research they contain. As with all uninspired works, one must keep them in perspective and not base one's beliefs upon them absolutely, but they are valuable tools in the arsenal of the exegete and no one should ever dismiss them.

The proper role of these scholarly works in a word study is consultation and reference. A one-volume lexicon can provide direction and possibilities to consider while sorting through the evidence compiled through independent research. The larger lexicons often give a thorough explanation of a word's history that would require hours upon hours of investigation otherwise. Some writings illustrate the use of the word in its historical context. Works that offer comments on the text from the point of view of the original language can demonstrate how words and their affected meanings contribute to an understanding of a passage or how the grammar of the text affects its meaning. All of these deserve to find a permanent place in the Bible student's library.

If personal study had not revealed it, a quick check in a Greek to English lexicon would alert a student that the English words "righteous" and "just" translate the same Greek word, *dikaios*. Lexicons such as the works of Thayer, Danker-Bauer-Arndt-Gingrich, or Liddell and Scott would also indicate that it refers to some standard, while Moulton and Milligan's *Vocabulary of the Greek Testament* points out that fulfillment of these matters constitutes "duty" rather than outstanding personal achievement. The *Theological Dictionary of the New Testament* provides an extensive discussion of the word's legal connotations. The *Expositor's Greek Testament* shows how *dikaios* (righteous) is distinguished from *agathos* (good) in Romans 5:7 in that being righteous indicates a fulfillment of what you should have done anyway while good indicates higher character. The student should have arrived at similar conclusions through his own work, but these scholarly works provide a very helpful means to double-check that research and might offer insight beyond what a beginning student's first analysis indicated.

The average Bible student has little training in the original languages of the Bible, but this does not mean that he cannot learn the basic skills necessary to evaluate words and eventually come to understand scholarly works and elementary philology, lexicology, and lexicography. (Use that dictionary!) While the Bible student rarely aspires to these disciplines, he should learn their basic principles and purposes and thereby grow to appreciate them. Word studies are valuable to the Bible student, making those who study words essential.

SUMMARIZE THE STUDY

Once a Bible student has completed his research into the meaning of a word in its original language, he should summarize his findings. This is necessary in order to provide himself a written synopsis for later reference should he come across that word in a passage of scripture and not remember his previous conclusions.

A good summary includes all the elements of the word study in condensed form. It provides the various ways a word could be translated while contrasting its meaning with similar words. The student should briefly describe the word's history (etymology) followed by personal observations made in the process of the study. When a scholar's work has proved valuable, the summary should acknowledge that contribution. The word's unaffected, distinctive meaning should then be identified, along with the various affected meanings possible, with an explanation of how they were derived from the unaffected meaning of the word, using various biblical passages where the word occurs to illustrate these points.

A word study summary should also include adequate

reasoning to justify the conclusions reached. If a summary does not explain why a word means what it means, why it occurs where it occurs, or how it has significance that differs from others words, then it is completely unprofitable. A summary gains value when it succinctly and accurately characterizes the relevance of the original study. When it becomes merely an educational hobby, its validity has been somewhat compromised.

While the content of a word study summary should remain consistent for everyone, the style of the summary might vary depending upon the strengths and aims of the one conducting the study. A Bible student might summarize his word study by making a list of points for consideration, he might write a paragraph with minimal information, or he could pen an article or short paper discussing the full significance of the word. Each of these has strengths and weaknesses. The list separates each portion of the study into its own entity for individual evaluation and reference. A paragraph provides the essence of the study without excessive details. An article requires a writer's mechanics but generally makes the material more easily accessible to others.

After extensive reading, perusal of references, and examination of applications, the temptation to apply the information gathered to an immediate question without going to the trouble of summarizing the study might overwhelm the weary Christian. However, the diligence in preparing summaries when the material remains fresh will ultimately pay dividends should the need for an understanding of that word reappear at some point. While writing a summary does not guarantee that the student will retain the information in his memory, it will contribute to it, while also providing the best help any memory can have: written notes.

A BRIEF WORD STUDY:
HEAVENLY PLACES

The phrase "heavenly places" has created great consternation among commentators and preachers as they have struggled to identify the meaning of the phrase in each of its five New Testament occurrences (four in the KJV), all of which are found in Paul's epistle to the Ephesians (1:3; 1:20; 2:6; 3:10; 6:12). But while the English phrase "heavenly places" occurs only in these five instances, the Greek adjective (*epouranios*) underlying the translation is found another sixteen times, and its related adjective (*ouranios*) six times. Therefore, in order to gain a better understanding of the word's meaning, it is important to determine its usage each time it appears, contrast this with the related adjective and its usage, and then evaluate its meaning in the specific verses cited above by applying the information gained.

The difference between *ouranios* and *epouranios* is slight, grammatically speaking. They are both cognates of the noun *ouranos*, which means "heaven." The word *ouranios* simply turns this root idea into the adjective form, which we translate as "heavenly." In four of the six times it occurs, Matthew quotes Jesus using it to refer to His heavenly Father (Matt. 6:14, 26, 32; 15:13). Luke uses it twice—once to refer to the heavenly host (Luke 2:13) and once to refer to a heavenly vision (Acts 26:19).

However, translators have also rendered *epouranios* as "heavenly," despite the distinction made by the attachment of the preposition *epi* in composition. While writers often added a preposition to a word in order to strengthen its force, the preposition chosen retained its significance, because its significance is the reason why it was chosen! Matthew quotes Jesus using *epouranios* once (Matt. 18:35) where He emphasizes the distinction between an earthly lord and the heavenly Father. John quotes Jesus contrasting earthly subject matter with heavenly subject matter (John 3:12). Five times in 1 Corinthians 15 Paul used this word to emphasize the difference between our current bodies and the ones we will receive at the time of the resurrection (1 Cor. 15:40, 48, 49). The writer of Hebrews uses *epouranios* six different times, referring to our heavenly calling (3:1), the heavenly gift (6:4), heavenly *things* (8:5; 9:23), a heavenly *country* (11:16) and the heavenly Jerusalem (12:22). In the last two instances the idea of "place" is predominate, as is a contrast. In Hebrews 8:5 and 9:23 it contains no idea of "place" specifically but does present a contrast. However, in the first two instances (Heb. 3:1; 6:4), there is no direct contrast but only an emphasis on the fact that the calling and the gift came from God. Paul uses a similar emphasis as he closes his final epistle to remind us that the kingdom is heavenly in character (2 Tim. 4:18). It is spiritual in nature. But "heaven" as a place remains the root of the word. So what is the point?

The key to understanding *epouranios* lies in appreciating the significance of *epi*. The preposition *epi* is often translated very broadly; however, its most basic meaning is "upon," "over," or "*based* upon." If the physical position is emphasized, "upon" generally works well. If the verb is emphasized, then "over" suits it (as in *episkopos*, overseer). But if a concept is emphasized, then "*based* upon" seems to capture the meaning best.

In Philippians 2:10 Paul says, "that at the name of Jesus every knee should bow, of those in heaven, and of those on earth, and of those under the earth." This passage is difficult in its own right. As the italics indicate, "things" does not actually appear in the Greek, and the text could read "of **those** in heaven, etc.," following a masculine reading of the genitive case and allowing for possible ellipsis (*the knee* of those in heaven, etc.). If we consider the possibility that Paul is referring to the basis of a person's spiritual situation, then he is pointing out that those who base their lives on heavenly things will bow, but so will those who base their lives on earthly things, and so will those who are dead. If, on the other hand, these three categories refer to categories of the different Greek gods, the identification of whose knee will bow changes (without any admission of the actual existence of these gods) but the substance of the description remains the same.

The instances noted above help significantly in establishing a means by which to interpret Paul's use of *epouranios* in Ephesians, where it seems most difficult. In each verse it is translated heavenly "places." However, "places" is supplied by the translator(s) and limits the reader to a "physical location" interpretation, but this is not implied by the word itself. The translators were probably influenced by the preposition *en* that appeared in each of these instances. However, *en* can also be used instrumentally and be translated "by means of." Therefore, taking an instrumental view of *en* and understanding *epouranios* in a conceptual way, the translation becomes: "…by means of *concepts based* upon the heavens." This is how we have access to spiritual blessings (Eph. 1:3). This is how Christ rules (Eph. 1:20). This is how the church is unified (Eph. 2:7). This is how God's wisdom is expressed in the church (Eph. 3:10). And this is how the battle against Satan will be won (Eph. 6:12).

Paul was worried the Ephesians had forgotten that all they had spiritually did not originate with them. Therefore he wrote to emphasize that the power of Christianity is not in the men who submit to it but in the ideas and concepts given by God in the gospel (Rom. 1:16). "Heavenly *places*" are not places at all. It is a phrase indicating not only the superiority of spiritual concepts in life but also the divine origin of those ideas.

INCORPORATING WORD STUDIES INTO EXEGESIS

While word studies are interesting in their own right, the Bible student's purpose in examining the meaning of words in the original language should extend far beyond idle curiosity. Understanding a word's meaning often leads to previously unconsidered possibilities in the realm of exegesis. If a translation has not fully (or correctly) expressed a word's meaning, then studying that word might lead to looking at a text in which the word appears in a different way.

The book of Philippians is essentially a support letter. Paul wrote it in response to and in appreciation for the Philippians' sending of support to him while he remained in Rome under guard awaiting trial. This was the reason for his thanks and joy (Phil. 1:3-4) and the meaning behind his phrase "fellowship in the gospel" (Phil. 1:5). Paul had great confidence in the Philippians' financial support (Phil. 1:6-7) and had a wonderful relationship with them in general (Phil. 1:8). These points, taken from the immediate context, seem clear enough. However, while we have had no problem quoting and referring to the verses that follow—even preaching them with generic understanding and generic application—it seems that their contextual meaning has eluded us.

After Paul's short greeting, and immediately following his expression of thankfulness for their generosity, Paul writes, "And this I pray, that your love may abound still more and more in knowledge and all discernment, that you may approve the things that are excellent, that you may be sincere and without offense till the day of Christ, being filled with the fruits of righteousness which are by Jesus Christ, to the glory and praise of God" (Phil. 1:9–11). It is amazing how easy it is to give commentary on this passage without referring to the context! Its content appears so broadly stated that any application at hand might work, as the subtitle, "The Gospel Produces Righteousness," itself suggests. But this passage does have context, and that context should form the basis of its interpretation. What under discussion produces righteousness? Unless the student identifies this particular action, he really cannot claim an understanding of the passage. A careful reading of these verses should draw attention to words that characterize both motives and decision-making. These words deserve special attention within the study in order to determine what decision and whose motives Paul has in mind. Part of the difficulty in this instance is that the English text does not communicate the impact of the Greek. This is not due to any impropriety on the part of the translators but rather indicates the difficulty of both the passage and the variety possible in some key words. This makes the task of the Bible student more difficult but also emphasizes how important it can be to use original language sources in one's study.

By asking questions about this text it forces the student to consider possibilities he might otherwise overlook. What evidence of love did Paul have in mind? Why did Paul cite knowledge and discernment in regard to love? What knowledge and discernment did the Philippians lack? What is the difference between knowledge and discernment? Consider the Greek words for "approve" and "excellent" then explain. Did Paul question the Philippians' sincerity? How would the Philippians become a stumblingblock to others? What are the fruits of righteousness? And how are they "by Jesus Christ"? When are our actions "to the glory and praise of God"? How does all this relate to the context of the Philippians' gift to Paul? Having asked these questions, the Bible student now is under obligation to answer them to the best of his ability, first by taking notes and recording the answers to his questions, then by putting these answers together in a comprehensible format.

In verse nine Paul encourages the Philippians to continue to grow in love, but he qualifies it by emphasizing that it should be based on an ever-increasing knowledge (*epignosis*) and that they should be discerning in making their judgments (*aisthesis*). Therefore, while love is the correct motive for acting, we should employ wisdom in when and how we perform those activities. In verse ten the New King James Version says that we are to "approve the things that are excellent," but the significant words here have a broader meaning than this. The verb translated "approve" (*dokimazo*) means "to verify," testing the quality of something while expecting positive results. The participle translated by the phrase "the things that are excellent" (*diapheronta*) is from a compound word roughly corresponding to "carrying between two different options." The options are implied by "sincere" (*eilikrines*) and "without offense" (*aproskopos*), the considerations being the purity of our own motives and the possible harm our actions might cause others. Let us then consider the context with these definitions in mind.

Paul commended the Philippians for their love but cautioned them against letting their love keep them from gathering information and making informed decisions. He further called on them to consider not only the purity of their own motives but also the effects their actions might have upon others who are not necessarily as sincere, emphasizing his desire that they continue to produce the fruits of righteousness. But what was all of this about? The context is the key. While Paul was obviously thankful for the extent of the Philippians' generosity, he feared that their generosity might turn into gullibility. He did not doubt at all the purity of their motives in wanting to give to help spread the gospel, but he feared that they might give without discernment, simply "writing a check" each time someone asked for help. Therefore, he reminded them that their own motives were not the only consideration. They also needed to do what was best spiritually for that person, indicating that giving them money was not always the best thing to do. When they followed these principles the result would be "the fruits of righteousness."

Some people seeking financial support, which could include transients, missionaries, or those who promote benevolent causes, try to make elders and congregations feel guilty unless they contribute to *their* support. However, in Philippians 1:9-11 Paul taught the necessity of discernment along with the beauty of liberality. Where the Lord's money is concerned Christians need both.

This particular text contains many difficult words, but it is the exception. Most word studies will produce an added appreciation for the precision of the author's writing without leading to a revolutionary change in interpreting the passage. However, it is precisely due to these possibilities that a good Bible student will incorporate word studies into his regular examination of a text.

CONCLUSION

Some people who work in the original languages of the Bible have argued over the relative value of word studies and grammar. Some emphasize the benefits of precise grammar in conducting exegesis and resolving questions about the text while others argue that word studies provide deeper insight into the thought of the writer. The truth is: they complement one another beautifully. Both are important and both should receive attention because both are necessary to provide the complete picture. Grammar is the science of original language studies; word study is the art.

Word studies provide vivid illustrations. If a student contemplates the full force of James' call to "look into the perfect law of liberty" (Jas. 1:25), a study of the word *parakupto* would help immensely. Not only does its use in 1 Peter 1:12 show that the word implies heightened interest, but its use by both Luke (Luke 24:12) and John (20:5, 11) in reference to Peter's stooping down in order to look inside the sepulcher illustrates on a physical level the extra effort expected of the Bible student.

Word studies also can help to identify the historical use of a word, acting as a supplement to studies in historical context. While a general consideration of the historical context of 1 Corinthians might emphasize the Greek culture in which the Corinthians lived, it might require a few word studies in order to appreciate the number of words Paul employed that had direct reference to the religions and philosophies his epistle intended to expose. Paul's treatment of Gnosticism requires even deeper consideration in order to connect "persuasive words" (Col. 2:4) to the pithy analogies (*pithanalogia*) of the philosophical schools.

Word studies sometimes help in establishing an argument pertaining to doctrine or theology. A study of the Hebrew word *yom* shows that it rarely refers to an epoch or age and never does so when preceded by a numeral. Therefore, a word study indicates that it would be improper to accept an "age" interpretation of *yom* in Genesis 1, as the context itself bears out. Studying the text of Mark 12:30 a Christian might have difficulty distinguishing between the different ways in which Jesus calls for people to love. Examining the words in the original language helps to determine those differences and so sheds light on the meaning of the text.

Word studies have a value in Bible study that often goes overlooked. People sometimes argue that "it means what it says" while knowing little about the words by which God actually said it. The words of the Bible carry the meaning of the Bible (1 Cor. 2:12-13); therefore, while understanding grammar is necessary in order to understand the relationships of words to one another, this would be meaningless without a good understanding of the words themselves. A word study is neither a topical study nor a textual study; however, word studies can highlight nuances that prove beneficial to both.

To Conduct Word Studies the Bible student should:

- Determine the possible translations of the word
- Contrast the word with its synonyms
- Discover the origin of the word
- Do an independent study by examining each occurrence of the word
- Determine the word's unaffected meaning
- Decide upon the word's distinctive meaning
- Look for possible affected meanings of the word
- Consult scholarly works to check for possible errors in your work or additional insight
- Summarize the study
- Apply these conclusions where the word occurs in the text

Recommended Reading

Balz, Horst and Schneider, Gerhard. *Exegetical Dictionary of the New Testament*. Grand Rapids, MI: Eerdman's Publishing Company, 1990.

Bauer, Walter. *A Greek-English Lexicon of the New Testament and Other Early Christian Literature*. Translated and revised by William F. Arndt and F. Wilbur Gingrich. Second Edition revised by F. Wilbur Gingrich and Frederick W. Danker. Chicago: University of Chicago Press, 1979.

Jackson, Wayne. *Treasures from the Greek New Testament for the English Reader*. Stockton, CA: Courier Publications, 1996.

Kittel, Gerhard. *Theological Dictionary of the New Testament*. Volumes 1-10. Grand Rapids, MI Eerdman's Publishing Company, 1979.

Mounce, William D. *The Morphology of Biblical Greek*. Grand Rapids, MI: Zondervan Publishing House, 1994.

Rhodes, Kevin. "The Bible's Word: Righteousness." In *Looking Unto Jesus: The Author and Finisher of Our Faith*, edited by Tommy J. Hicks, "388-405. Lubbock, TX: Hicks Publications, 1999.

Thayer, Joseph Henry. *The New Thayer's Greek-English Lexicon of the New Testament*. Peabody, MA: Hendrickson Publishers, 1981.

Vine, W.E. *Vine's Expository Dictionary of New Testament Words*. Peabody, MA: Hendrickson Publishers.

Questions for Discussion

1. What portion of the word study appears to be the most difficult? Why?
2. What part of a word study causes you to value it the most?
3. How will you locate synonyms?
4. Explain the difference between unaffected meaning and affected meaning.
5. How do you determine when to undertake a word study?

Assignment

Complete a word study on the Greek adjective *hosios* (Strong's #3741).

CHAPTER 19

Mistakes Not to Make

INTRODUCTION

*A*s previously demonstrated, there are many considerations when studying the Bible, but the most precise answers ultimately stem from digging into the original language. A single word often shines light on a passage, since the Holy Spirit inspired every word with particular purpose. Therefore, the Bible student seeks to discover that divine purpose. However, original language studies present problems all their own. Modern translations have distanced themselves from literary exactitude, sometimes creating problems for the Bible student. Some teachers have misused the original languages to propagate error, whether ignorantly or knowingly. But especially in the New Testament, a detailed study of the text in its original language offers a treasure trove of information — if the student can avoid various mistakes along the way.

Careful translators do not choose words at random from a dictionary, nor do the lexicographers who provide such works. Scholars must study the way people used these words originally, tracing them from their first occurrences to the period under consideration — for the Greek New Testament, the first century A.D. By examining the use and history of these words, a student of Greek catalogues patterns of thought and contextual associations. Synonym comparisons further delineate the particular nuances of a given word. A translator or lexicographer then considers these nuances and chooses a word in his own language that best conveys the same meaning as the word in the original text. However, the differences in language make exact correspondence between words — and grammar — impossible. Unfortunately, the translator must often content himself with a word or phrase that comes closest to describing the idea prescribed by the original language. Since writers employ words in various ways and in various contexts, sometimes scholars translate one Greek word with many different English words, depending on the context. Likewise, English does not have a counterpart to some Greek words.

Therefore, original language studies, while beneficial, can lead to misunderstandings and misapplications, especially when pertaining to doctrinal matters. People often see what they want to see. But the purpose of Bible study – and original language studies – is not to promote our own understanding of scripture but to gain a *better* understanding.

ATTACHING AN ENGLISH DEFINITION TO A GREEK WORD

Some students have mistakenly taken an English word, provided as a definition in a concordance or lexicon, and attached a meaning it sometimes receives in English to the corresponding Greek word. This has proven especially true of transliterated words, English words derived from exchanging English letters for Greek letters. But no matter what word a translator may choose, a word's meaning only applies so far as the original Greek word allows.

The words "baptize" and "baptism" have prevailed in English translations in spite of their failure to communicate accurately the meaning of the Greek words *baptizo* and *baptisma*. In an English dictionary under "baptize" a person might find "sprinkle" and "pour" offered as acceptable alternatives to "immerse." But *baptizo* means "to dip, plunge, submerge, or immerse." No matter what the English word "baptize" has come to mean, the Greek words *baptizo* and *baptisma* always refer to immersion. Similarly, the word *angelos* is transliterated as "angel," though it can refer to any type of messenger, heavenly or human. Commentators often make doctrinal points about "angels" without bothering to establish whether the text refers to a heavenly messenger or a human messenger. They rely on the transliteration "angel" to make the argument—something it cannot do.

But transliterated words are not the only culprits. A word used in translation may have more meanings, a broader meaning, or a more limited meaning than the original Greek word. In these cases the expositor must understand the extension and limitation of the original word else he may reach a faulty conclusion. In Hebrews 10:25 the English word "forsaking" translates the Greek word *enkataleipo*. Some sources include "abandon" among its possible definitions. This may indicate a matter of preference, but the meaning of the word is governed by the meaning of *enkataleipo* — not by how someone defines either "forsake" or "abandon."

To some people "abandon" implies total abandonment — never to be heard from again. Following this interpretation of *enkataleipo* in Hebrews 10:25 one would be forsaking the assembling of the saints only when there was no intent of ever returning. Besides putting a subjective measurement into this verse (How do you measure either "intent" or "ever"?), this exegesis depends on an English definition (or supposition) regarding "abandon" rather than the definition and meaning of the Greek word *enkataleipo*. This word means "to leave in the lurch." It is a compound word joining *leipo* ("to leave"), *kata* ("down" or "behind"), and *en* ("in" or "among"). Once synthesized, these words indicate leaving someone or something in a down (bad) condition or leaving someone or something behind. In either situation the emphasis falls upon the **condition** — not how long it lasts.

In Matthew 27:46 the apostle records Jesus' Aramaic cry from the cross, "Eli, Eli, lama sabachthani?" which Matthew translated into Greek as, "My God, my God, why have you forsaken me?" "Forsaken" once again translates *enkataleipo*. Since God did not permanently abandon His Son but raised Him from the dead (Col. 2:12), the Holy Spirit's use of the word *enkataleipo* demonstrates that "forsake" refers to the condition of being left behind in a bad situation rather than to permanency or to the length of that situation.

In Hebrews 10:25 the writer explains the necessity of assembling together based on each Christian's responsibility to exhort others and provoke all to love and good works (Heb. 10:24). He argues that a person's absence in the assembly leaves others in a bad, even desperate, situation because he is failing to do his part as a Christian in building up and encouraging others. This presents evidence of a weakened faith and possible apostasy—not the apostasy itself. Therefore, one who willingly (Heb. 10:26) avoids the assembly is guilty of sin.

CHOOSING A SPECIFIC MEANING OVER A GENERIC MEANING

In their quest to aid the modern reader as much as possible, translators sometimes choose a specific affected meaning of a word when it is inappropriate to do so, demonstrating one particular problem of the functional equivalence theory of translation. However, even versions that translate word for word can contain poor word selection. Translators have an obligation to the English reader to avoid choosing one specific application of a word (affected meaning) rather than the generic idea behind the word (unaffected meaning) if it might affect the meaning of the text (and so potentially affect doctrine). The acknowledged difficulty of anticipating every possible misunderstanding that a choice might create only reinforces the seriousness of the issue.

In Romans 12:1 Paul uses the word *latreia*. This word refers to service rendered to another out of depth of devotion. In this *latreia* differs from the other major word groups referring to service such as *diakonia* (service rendered as an intermediary by carrying out the wishes or acting for the benefit of others), *douleia* (service rendered out of a binding obligation), *hupereteo* (service rendered in a subordinate role), *therapeuo* (service rendered voluntarily) and *leitourgia* (service rendered as a result of one's role). Louw and Nida improperly distinguish *latreia* and *leitourgia* by using "worship" as compared to "religious rites" instead of recognizing the distinction according to motive, "devotion" versus "role or duty." As a result, they fail to categorize *latreia* as service, choosing to place it in the category of worship, despite the problems this creates for translators, such as in Matthew 4:10 where Jesus uses both *proskuneo* (worship) and *latreuo*.

In certain instances even the King James Version translates forms of *latreuo* by "worship" (Heb. 10:2). The translators adapted the word to its context, but doing so was unnecessary and did not affect the meaning of the verse. However, many modern versions also render this word as "worship" in Romans 12:1. They have chosen to interpret *latreuo* in light of Paul's reference to sacrifice instead of interpreting Paul's reference to sacrifice in light of the meaning of *latreuo*. The latter interpretation agrees with biblical context which consistently indicates that worship is an action characterized by specific and intended direction toward God, as the Greek word *proskuneo* accurately represents. In Genesis 22:5 Moses wrote, "And Abraham said to his young men, 'Stay here with the donkey; the lad and I will go yonder and worship, and we will come back to you.'" The Christian teaches, studies, and lives righteously but in doing so is serving God out of devotion rather than worshiping Him, because these activities do not include the intention and direction God requires in other activities (John 4:24). Worship (*proskuneo*) is subordinate to *latreia* because our serving God out of devotion includes worshiping Him but is not equivalent to it.

In cases such as these the translators have taken a definition applied within one context (affected meaning) and extrapolated that definition to apply universally (or close to it). This practice is wrong and in this instance leads to the erroneous belief that everything in life is worship. Translators generally translate the word *dioko* as "persecute" (Phil. 3:6), but it would be inappropriate to translate the same word as "persecute" in Philippians 3:12 where "pursue" would be more accurate. The word means "pursue" with the context determining whether "persecute" is the best translation or not. If someone is pursuing a Christian in some way (so as to exert pressure or do harm because of that person's righteousness, Matthew 5:10), then "persecute" would be appropriate, *though not necessary*. But if a Christian pursues a heavenly goal, "persecute" would be incorrect. If a person insists on translating *latreia* as "worship" in Romans 12:1, he should also translate *dioko* as "persecute" in Philippians 3:12. Although people often cite context as an excuse to adapt definitions, those who do so have forgotten that even if one should choose a word such as "persecute" he could still substitute "pursue" and not change the meaning. One should always be able to substitute the broadest word possible that fits the meaning of the word in the original language without altering the meaning of the passage. If the meaning of the passage changes, prejudice has most likely overruled scholarship.

In Romans 12:13 Paul tells Christians they should be "given to hospitality." This literally reads: "pursuing friendship with (or, a love for) strangers." The New King James translators used "given to" to translate *dioko*. What would happen if someone took the affected meaning "given to" and used it to translate *dioko* in other passages? Was Paul "given to" the church prior to his conversion? Not at all. But he was "pursuing" it. The broadest definition fits in every context, but applying a specific meaning from one context to another instance of the word in a different context leads to erroneous translation and sometimes to doctrinal error.

THE ABUSE OF ETYMOLOGY

For many years now people who use mechanical instruments of music in their worship have pointed to the word *psallo*, emphasizing that it originally meant "to pluck or twang (as on a bow)" and then evolved to mean "to pluck or twang as on a stringed instrument." As far as the origin of the word is concerned, this is true, but the word did not stop its development at this point. Singing so often accompanied the plucking or twanging on a stringed instrument that singing developed into part of the definition. Eventually the word meant "to sing" independently of any instrument. Therefore, by the time the writers penned the New Testament *psallo* meant simply "to sing." If the author intended any instrument, he would supply it himself. In the two instances in the New Testament where the preposition *en* indicates the use of an instrument with *psallo* the inspired writers referred to *spirit* and *understanding* (1 Cor. 14:15) and *heart* (Eph. 5:19) as necessary instruments when Christians worship God in song. Besides these, no instrument is permitted.

The original meaning of the word *lego*, which is translated "to say" in the New Testament, was "to gather." It included the idea of picking out certain like things. *Lego* retained this concept in its derivative *eklego* which means "to choose, select, or pick out." The etymology of *lego* indicates that it meant to gather with the nuance of picking out or gathering similar concepts to be counted or gathered mentally. Then it developed to include the vocal enumeration of those things gathered mentally. Eventually the word referred to the narration of these thoughts. Therefore, it is translated "to say" in the New Testament. It means **the picking out of words to be laid alongside one another—first mentally, then orally**. For this reason *lego* emphasizes the content of speech more than other verbs referring to speech such as *laleo*. Without any doubt, when the Holy Spirit inspired the New Testament writers, *lego* meant "to say"—not "to gather." Regardless of the specific word, it does not matter so much **how** a word achieved its meaning, nor what it **previously** meant, nor what it might mean in the future, but only what the word **meant** at the time the writers penned it.

SAME ROOT BUT DIFFERENT MEANINGS

Some have maintained that since the word for bondage in 1 Corinthians 7:15, *douloo*, and the word translated bound in 1 Corinthians 7:27, *deo*, originally had the same root that they must also have the exact same meaning. Therefore, they conclude that *"bondage"* in verse fifteen addresses the marriage bond in the same way that *"bound"* does in verse twenty-seven. As a result, they believe they have discovered a reason other than fornication (Matt. 19:9) which would scripturally allow remarriage following a divorce. However, they have made an assumption similar to the one cited above: Although two words may have a common origin, this does not imply that they have a synonymous meaning.

The verb *douloo* developed as a derivative of the noun *doulos*, "slave" or "bondservant." The word *doulos* came from *deo*, which at that time meant the binding of a slave. Although *deo* originally meant the condition of being a slave, it evolved to mean any type of binding whatsoever. However, *douloo* did not experience this same verbal evolution. One can observe their shared origin in that they both refer to binding of some sort during the New Testament era, but the differences in these words determines the type of binding intended by the writer. The binding of verse fifteen is a binding of servitude or slavery (*douloo*), while the latter verses refer to a legal binding (*deo*). Other occurrences of *douloo* in the New Testament, as well as in secular writings, religious writings, and the Septuagint, show that the meaning of *douloo* is "to enslave" or "to bring into bondage" (Acts 7:6; Rom. 6:18; 1 Cor. 9:19; Gal. 4:3; Tit. 2:3; 2 Pet. 2:19). This is very different from the binding of a legal contract, which shows that Paul chose the two different words in 1 Corinthians 7 because in those two different verses he referred to two different types of binding.

THE IMPORTANCE OF CONTEXT

In the study of any language it is important to understand that language as well as the vocabulary. While some desire a translation where Greek words are translated by the same English words on every occasion (a noble but impossible task), others would prefer a translation where every instance of the word offers boundless choices of translation, depending upon what fits their fancy at a particular time. In both of these instances the people involved have forgotten one important fact: the original language has context too.

Sometimes it seems as if the guiding light in translation for many today after the text itself is "interpretational predisposition" rather than contextual considerations. When anyone builds an argument in a text based upon a particular word without considering its context, he has made a serious and dreadful mistake. This context must consist of the whole Bible, though, as well as the immediate context.

Translators who provide "abolish" as the translation for *kataluo* instead of a form of "destroy" unnecessarily introduce a contradiction into the New Testament between Matthew 5:17 and Ephesians 2:14-16. One must wonder why translators felt the need to deviate from the basic meaning of *kataluo*, to destroy utterly, and lighten the force of the word. In some instances one should consider whether this was transported into our English versions in order to protect the translators' own misunderstanding of covenant context. Whether intentional or not, to have a translation maintain that the Old Covenant was **not** to be abolished and that it **was** abolished certainly creates a problem for those who read it. It is certainly true that the context in English, both in Matthew 5:17 and in Ephesians 2:14-16, proves that the Old Law would be fulfilled by Christ when its purpose was completed and that it would then be abolished in favor of the New Covenant, as the writer of Hebrews also argues (Heb. 8:6-13). However, if translators consider the overall context of the Bible and the implications of their word choices they cannot translate *kataluo* as "abolish."

IMPROPER RENDERINGS OF PREPOSITIONS

An unabridged list of all the improper renderings of prepositions in the various translations could easily fill a book. This is true partly due to the difficulty that exists in fluidly translating each preposition in every instance in such a way as to maintain proper English syntax. But it is also true because many have used this perceived ambiguity as a license to translate prepositions according to personal preference of doctrinal meaning rather than by the conditions which should govern the translation of prepositions, including (1) the basic meaning of the word, (2) the case with which it is used, (3) and the context in which it is applied. A translator should apply these *in order* instead of allowing a personal interpretation to "sway" the context, the context to influence the case, and the case to overwhelm the meaning of the word.

The translation of Romans 1:17 has presented many difficulties to people due to those who have chosen to apply a very loose standard for idioms. As part of his thesis Paul wrote, "For in it the righteousness of God is revealed from faith to faith; as it is written, 'The just shall live by faith'" "In it," refers to the gospel (see verse sixteen). God's righteousness, then, is revealed in the pages of the gospel. But what follows is a mystery to many.

"From" is a translation of *ek*, a preposition meaning "out of" that is always used with the genitive case, carrying an ablative function of separation. It is used to indicate the "source" or "point of departure." The usages of "faith" being diverse, it is necessary to understand its use in Romans 1:17 in light of the context. The source or point of departure Paul already indicated is the gospel (Rom. 1:16), which is consistent with the use of "faith" in reference to the "body of belief" or "what is to be believed" (Jude 3).

The next preposition, "to," is a translation of *eis*, which is usually translated as "into" or "unto," is always used with the accusative case, and always points to and emphasizes the end as its focus, the end being understood in accordance with the context of the passage, which in this context is "faith." Therefore, Paul has "faith" as both the source and as the goal to be obtained. The first "faith" is a source, a beginning point, and the context already identified that source as the gospel message. The desired end, however, is also "faith." So the word of God is the source from which faith is produced as the goal to be obtained in the hearer. This short phrase in the thesis of Romans matches exactly Paul's later development on that same theme: "So then faith comes by hearing, and hearing by the word of God" (Rom. 10:17).

Unfortunately, many translators identify the *ek...eis* construction as an idiom with the force of "from first to last" whenever the same word follows both prepositions. First, there is simply no such thing as a "grammatical idiom," though some prepositions have applications beyond their literal meaning (*ana* used distributively, for example). Second, such a concept would require proof that the word (in this case, "faith") was used in the same sense in both instances. Therefore, translators have created an idiom mainly due to their failure to consider that "faith" has both an objective (the body of belief) and subjective (personal acceptance of that belief) application.

In the last phrase, a quotation from Habakkuk 2:4, the preposition translated "by" is once again *ek*. This emphasizes the source or point of departure for how a person lives: his faith. The meaning, then, is that our hope for spiritual deliverance ("shall live") depends upon our acceptance of God's message completely and our willingness to obey it in order to be righteous (just) in the sight of God (Jas. 2:24). A possible translation would be: "For *the* righteousness of God is being revealed in it out of faith unto faith, even as it has been written, 'Now the righteous *one* out of faith will live.'"

The literal translation of the preposition is not necessary; it is sometimes very awkward. But it should always be the first possibility so far as the translator is concerned. Sometimes it is necessary to be more liberal with the preposition in order to keep the English smooth, **but this should never go beyond the meaning of the word and the intent of the phrase and passage.**

THE USE AND ABUSE OF GREEK TENSES

Misunderstandings concerning the various Greek tenses are not far behind the faulty use of prepositions. The **present** tense indicates action limited only by the context. The **imperfect** tense indicates an action which is in the past but is being considered as a process instead of an event in that time period. The **aorist** tense signifies an action in the past which is thought of as a completed event or as a whole, even though it may have required a gradual process at the time. The **future** tense emphasizes the time of actions as beginning at some future date but does not express anything about the end of that action. The **perfect** tense points to an action or activity in the past which has brought about a condition which has present consequences. There are variations of some of these, but they are seldom used in the New Testament. The tense of a participle has similar meaning with the time restricted by the main verb.

In applying this we notice Acts 5:32: "And we are His witnesses to these things, and so also is the Holy Spirit whom God has given to those who obey Him" (Acts 5:32). Here the verb translated "has given" is aorist, showing that the giving of the Holy Spirit referred to in this passage referred to an event in the past without any ongoing consequences (in context). Therefore, it is improper to use this verse as proof of the giving of the Holy Spirit today in any way because even in Acts 5 it was considered a past event. If it were a situation that applied to Christians as a whole and for all time the verb should have been present tense. The context further shows that those under consideration were the apostles and that the reference made was to the baptism of the Holy Spirit on the day of Pentecost. There is a reason why Acts 5:32 does not read, "whom God "gives to those who obey him": Luke was referring to a past event rather than an ongoing promise and to the apostles rather than to all Christians.

THE PERIPHRASTIC USE OF PARTICIPLES

Another problem a casual reading of the English Bible cannot detect is the periphrastic construction in which a Greek participle may be used in conjunction with an intransitive verb, usually *eimi*, in such a way that translators treat it in English as if it were a single word. When translators fail to recognize the full significance of the words they translate or do not realize that in some cases there are doctrinal implications as a result, they will translate participles without giving careful consideration to the full extent of meaning involved. Since a participle is a verbal adjective, a word that has characteristics of both a verb and an adjective, translators should recognize and include, as much as it is possible, both aspects. Many grammarians have downplayed this important fact when classifying participles and have ignored the verbal aspects of the participle. As a result, when translators translate a participle as an adjective, all the verbal aspects of that word as a participle remain untranslated. Often the English form will appear as a regular verb, being a combination of the being verb and the participle. This is unfortunate because the vividness of the Greek language with its "descriptive motion" is lost, and the smoother rendering robs the Bible student of the full significance of these words.

In Colossians 3:1 Paul exhorts the Colossians to leave the things of the world behind and points them in the proper direction. The King James Version reads, "If ye then be risen with Christ, seek those things which are above, where Christ sitteth on the right hand of God." As Paul challenges these Christians he reminds them of their new beginning (Col. 2:12) and directs their attention to "those things which are above." The phrase which follows is a descriptive designation of what Paul means: "where Christ sitteth on the right hand of God." Most commentators and teachers would simply identify this as heaven and continue, but Paul is saying more than this. The word translated "sitteth" is a periphrastic construction combining the being verb *eimi*, "to be," with a participle from the word *kathemai*, to sit. When combined in their grammatical forms these two words produce "is" (*eimi*) "sitting" (*kathemai*) or "sitteth." This does not really change the meaning of the passage in a dramatic way, but it does take away from Paul's intent.

The apostle had just reminded the Colossians that in becoming Christians they had attached themselves to Christ. By being immersed in water, they had been buried with Christ (Col. 2:12). When they arose from the water, they were raised up with Christ (Col. 2:12; 3:1).

Paul is then showing Christians that they should not abandon their association with Christ after baptism. Paul's emphasis in describing "those things which are above" is not simply heaven, where Christ sits on the right hand of God. He is emphasizing Christ's presence there and exhorting Christians, those who have been buried and raised with Christ, to continue their association with Him by maintaining the proper direction in life. The descriptive participial phrase which follows, "sitting on the right hand of God," shows specifically Christ's authority and His victory, as well as where He is. "If you were raised up together with Christ, seek the things *which are* above, where Christ is, sitting at the right *hand* of God." The translators of the New King James Version recognized the problem in this verse and corrected it.

Although this past example has not confused people greatly and does not concern a controversial issue, it will serve well to illustrate the difference between combining forms into a construction with a loss of meaning and in translating with the intent to bring all aspects of the original words and their meanings to light. Perhaps observing another more telling instance of this problem will help demonstrate the harm that can come from overlooking the verbal aspect of these participles. In Matthew 16:18 Jesus declares that His being the Son of the Living God is the foundation upon which His church will be built. Then in verse nineteen He said, "And I will give you the keys of the kingdom of heaven, and whatever you bind on earth will be bound in heaven, and whatever you loose on earth will be loosed in heaven." Some have used this verse to teach that the church is the authority for doctrine and anything else and that God then accepts as authoritative whatever the church has set forth, beginning with Peter and the apostles. This view is not only contradictory to the nature of God and to explicit statements in the New Testament (Matt. 28:18) but is also based upon a poor rendering of a Greek periphrastic verb construction.

The phrases "will be bound" and "will be loosed" are both periphrastic constructions combining a being verb and a participle. In both of these instances, the being verb is the future indicative, third person singular, of *eimi*, "to be": *estai*, "it shall be." This verb then was followed by a perfect passive participle, either *dedumenon*, "after having been bound", or *lelumenon*, "after having been loosed." The perfect tense, remember, describes an action which took place in the past but has continuing consequences. **This force remains even in the participle**. Therefore, when Jesus used the perfect participle in this passage he was referring to a binding or loosing action which would have taken place prior to the apostles' teaching. Most translations lose this thought entirely because they treat the participles as adjectives, emphasizing the end (consequences) of the action without giving any attention to the tense of the verb part of the participle. However, although there were to be consequences from this action, they were not yet seen. The state of being was considered to be future (the significance of the being verb); therefore, since Christ had not died when He made the statement, that which was to be bound and loosed (the New Covenant) had not yet been given and was not yet in force (Heb. 9:15-16).

Jesus did not give Peter control over what would be taught, bound, and loosed following His death. To the contrary, He was letting Peter know that God would take care of those decisions and that in the future Peter would have the responsibility to announce these decisions to the world. "And I will give to you the keys of the kingdom of heaven; and whatever you should bind upon the earth will be, after having been bound in heaven, and whatever you should loose upon the earth will be, after having been loosed in heaven" (Matt. 16:19). What Peter spoke on the day of Pentecost and afterward was binding not because he spoke it but because God gave it to him to speak, as Christ also promised (2 Pet. 1:19-21; John 14:26; 16:13; Acts 2:4, 14).

THE IMPORTANCE OF CASES

In English we often have trouble knowing to which word an adjective or phrase refers. However, a careful consideration of the Greek construction would resolve many of these questions. Since in Greek an adjective or participle must agree in case, gender, and number with the word it modifies, noting these distinctions can correct some misunderstandings and erroneous teachings.

While discussing the Jews' equal need for salvation along with the Gentiles, Paul referred to the Gentiles when he said, "who show the work of the law written in their hearts, their conscience also bearing witness, and between themselves their thoughts accusing or else excusing them" (Rom. 2:15). The phrase which has caused some controversy is: "who show the work of the law written in their hearts." Some argue this phrase proves the existence of an inborn law within man, because it refers to the "law written in their hearts." These then argue that there is one law for Christians, the law of Christ, and another law for unbelievers, the law written on the heart. This has been twisted for various purposes, but the main reason for its existence is to try to eliminate the unbeliever's accountability to all of the law of Christ, particularly in the area of divorce and remarriage (Matt. 19:9).

Besides contradicting Scripture (John 12:48), this view of "the law written in the heart" is not even possible in Romans 2:15. In this passage "law" is a masculine noun in the genitive case, *nomou*, while "written" is a neuter adjective in the accusative case, *grapton*. Therefore, because they do not agree in case, gender, and number, "written" cannot modify "law." It does, however, modify "work," which is a neuter noun in the accusative case, *ergon*. This means that the **work** was written in their hearts—not the law. The phrase "of the law," *tou nomou*, describes the "work." The Gentiles were not directly amenable to the Law of Moses but certain pious "God-fearers" recognized in it communication from God and adopted many of its precepts, inasmuch as a Gentile could do this. They adopted the "activity" described in the law as their own personal standard of behavior ("written in the heart"). There is only one law in force today, and that is the law of Christ (Gal. 6:2) to which all men are accountable.

CONCLUSION

Certainly other problems exist as a result of a misuse of the original language of the New Testament, but it would be impossible to mention them all. However, when we choose a Bible, compare translations, recommend these works, and study for ourselves, let us keep these problems in mind so that we may approach the Scriptures honestly and with integrity, not being swayed by personal opinions but drawing conclusions from the Word of God itself.

When a Christian uses any of the scholarly works pertaining to the Bible that are available, it is important to keep these principles in mind. Though they have great value and deserve commendation for the work put into them, they are still the works of men and are subject to error. It is also wise to recognize the difference between lexicography and commentary, regardless of the book's title. Hopefully understanding the problems these men face and being aware of some mistakes men have made in the past will help you comprehend these things and assist you in your study of God's Word.

Bible students must not make the mistake of:

- Attaching an English definition to a translated word
- Choosing a specific meaning over a generic meaning
- Abusing the etymology of a word
- Failing to distinguish between words with the same root but with different meanings
- Forgetting that context exists in every language
- Rendering prepositions improperly
- Abusing or ignoring verb tenses
- Misunderstanding the impact of the periphrastic participle
- Ignoring the relationships designated by the cases of nouns

Recommended Reading

Chamberlain, William Douglas. *An Exegetical Grammar of the Greek New Testament*. Grand Rapids, MI: Baker Book House, 1941.
Dana, H.E. and Mantey, Julius R. *A Manual Grammar of the Greek New Testament*. Toronto: The Macmillan Company, 1955.
Mounce, William D. *Basics of Biblical Greek*. Grand Rapids, MI: Zondervan Publishing House, 1993.
Robertson, A.T. *A Grammar of the Greek New Testament in the Light of Historical Research*. Nashville, TN: Broadman Press, 1934.
Wallace, Daniel B. *Greek Grammar Beyond the Basics*. Grand Rapids, MI: Zondervan Publishing House, 1996.

Questions for Discussion

1. Which of these problems is the most common?
2. Which problem might you be most likely to fall prey to? Why?

3. Why would people who know the original languages of the Bible not correct some of these problems in translation?
4. What problem, once corrected, do you believe would have the greatest impact on an understanding of the Bible? Why?
5. How do you distinguish between language work and commentary in a book?

Assignment

Examine Ephesians 2:8-10 noting all possible options for translation that previous efforts might not have considered. Take note of how the information given above might help correct some misunderstandings in this text.

Can We Understand the Bible Alike?

❖

INTRODUCTION

*M*any people have experienced their greatest frustrations while attempting to study the Bible. With great sincerity of heart they opened the pages of Holy Writ only to become lost in the mass of details and overwhelmed by the cultural differences and historical references. They went to the Bible looking for answers but came away from the Bible with many more questions. They tried, they failed, and many of them gave up. Others approach the Bible with greater confidence. They read through a passage and think they understand it. But then they hear or read someone else's interpretation that argues it does not mean at all what they thought it meant. They then resign themselves to the studying sidelines, convinced that they can never learn how to discover the Bible's meaning for themselves. Or perhaps they decide to consult some commentaries in order to resolve the problem. Instead they quickly discover that the commentators also disagree with one another, and even offer an additional alternative interpretation not yet considered. It is no wonder that people ask the question, "Can we really understand the Bible?"

The Bible does pose some difficulties for the casual reader. Its penmen lived long ago. And it is not a novel; it is the revelation of God. But this is why the question "Can we really understand the Bible?" is so important! God inspired these Scriptures because He wants all of mankind to know some things. Does God require us to know the unknowable or attain the unattainable? Absolutely not. Jesus said, "And you shall know the truth, and the truth shall make you free" (John 8:32). However, when people see all the religious division in this world it should surprise no one that they ask "Can we understand the Bible alike?" It would not matter whether or not we understand a novel when we finish it. Its purpose is to entertain and sometimes to offer social commentary, but the consequences of misunderstanding it, if any, would be small to nonexistent. It does not even matter if we fail to comprehend a textbook on quantum physics if we are not going into that field. However, the Bible was not written to entertain us or to offer simple social commentary, and it is a textbook on a subject we all must understand—life. Therefore, the questions "Can we understand the Bible?" and "Can we understand the Bible alike?" pertain to the very existence of man and his purpose for being.

It is not okay to agree to disagree about what the Bible says. The stakes are too high. It is not all right for you to have your opinion and me to have mine. A wrong opinion about the life God expects us to live has devastating consequences. Such "tolerant" attitudes come not from a heart seeking God but from a tongue seeking an excuse to continue in sin. These are not interested in truth precisely because it condemns them. So let me assure you: **You** *can* understand the Bible, and **we** *can* understand the Bible alike.

OVERCOME MAN-MADE BARRIERS

Understanding God's will requires diligence and perseverance from the Bible student. Most of what it takes to understand the Bible is actually very simple, yet the very obvious existence of religious division implies that barriers to a common understanding of Scripture do indeed exist. However, God has not placed obstacles before people to prevent religious unity—man has. When the Allied soldiers stormed the beaches of Normandy, the tides were no real obstacle, nor were the cliffs. The obstacles that made the battle so deadly for many were man-made and man-placed; the machine-gun crossfire that stopped so many was aimed with the precision of a man. And so it is with understanding the Bible. The difficulties of knowing and doing God's will would be small indeed if there were not so many men on the opposing side creating obstacles and threatening the well-being of those who show interest in truth and unity God's way.

Men will question why anyone should think it necessary to understand the Bible on an individual basis. They believe you should share in their own lack of spiritual interest. Peter wrote of the angels' interest in what God was doing for man (1 Pet. 1:10-12), yet some men prefer to encourage ignorance rather than knowledge, to downplay its pertinence instead of cultivating spiritual interest. Peter wrote again, "as newborn babes, desire the pure milk of the word, that you may grow thereby" (1 Pet. 2:2). In order to achieve spiritual unity, we must share a relentless drive to know the truth (John 8:32; Prov. 23:23), and the wherewithal to go to the divine source (John 17:17).

Some men will give explanations designed to tempt you to accept their ideas before going to the Bible (Matt. 5:17). Some men will appeal to your pride (1 Cor. 10:12), arguing that you already understand everything you need to know (Matt. 19:16-22) in order to keep you from further investigation. Some men will flatter you and justify your sin in order to keep your allegiance and gain your trust instead of pointing you to God's Word (Rom. 10:17). Some men will discourage your preparation of heart to know, to do, and to teach God's will (Ezra 7:10) because it does not empower them. Some men attempt to influence our attitudes to place barriers in the way of our own learning.

Men may also throw up a barricade when it comes to understanding biblical authority. Instead of accepting the Bible's absolutes (John 10:35), they hedge. Instead of recognizing the Bible's stated precepts and accounts (Matt. 4:1-11; 12:1-8), they obfuscate and muddle. Instead of submitting to the clear implications of biblical instruction (Matt. 22:22-32), they argue that you cannot trust human reason (except for theirs, of course). Instead of accepting the limits placed on divinely approved action by biblical silence (Heb. 7:14), they rush ahead as if the Commander in Chief had called "Charge!"

Man-made barriers make Bible study more difficult; however, many of those creating these difficulties are themselves victims of Satan's powers of deception (2 Cor. 11:14-15). Therefore, not only must we overcome the obstacles they place in our way, we also, with meekness of spirit, should call for them to lay down the fiery darts of the wicked and exchange them for the panoply of God (Eph. 6:10-17).

UNDERSTAND GOD'S WORDS

Words are the building blocks and foundation of communication. When Paul wrote, "Now we have received, not the spirit of the world, but the Spirit who is from God, that we might know the things that have been freely given to us by God. These things we also speak, not in words which man's wisdom teaches but which the Holy Spirit teaches, comparing spiritual things with spiritual" (1 Cor. 2:12–13), he implied that the words of inspiration are the basis for understanding God's will. To understand anything written we must appreciate the meaning of words. Moreover, if we are to understand God's will, we must first pay close attention to *God's* words. As Jesus said, "It is written, 'Man shall not live by bread alone, but by every word that proceeds from the mouth of God'" (Matt. 4:4).

God is fully capable of communicating to man using words, and this is exactly how He has always communicated. From the very beginning God communicated to man using words: "And the Lord God commanded the man, saying, 'Of every tree of the garden you may freely eat; but of the tree of the knowledge of good and evil you shall not eat, for in the day that you eat of it you shall surely die'" (Gen. 2:16–17). The foundation of authority behind the Old Law was what Moses recorded when he wrote, "And God spoke all these words" (Ex. 20:1). In the first century, during the miraculous age, God still communicated using words. Jesus promised His apostles, "But when they arrest you and deliver you up, do not worry beforehand, or premeditate what you will speak. But whatever is given you in that hour, speak that; for it is not you who speak, but the Holy Spirit" (Mark 13:11). Jesus promised that God the Holy Spirit would communicate to man using words. While God no longer communicates His words miraculously *through* man, He still communicates His words *to* man. "All Scripture is given by inspiration of God, and is profitable for doctrine, for reproof, for correction, for instruction in righteousness, that the man of God may be complete, thoroughly equipped for every good work" (2 Tim. 3:16–17). The words God once communicated orally to man He now communicates to man in writing. Therefore, since God has always communicated His will using words, the only way to know and come to an understanding of His will is to know and understand the words He has written. If we respect God's words, we will not attempt to put words in God's mouth. A person cannot add "only" after "faith" in Romans 5:1 and still claim He respects God's words because such an action puts man's words on an equal plane with God's words.

To understand God's words a person must first respect what is inspired as God's Word—the collection of His words (John 12:48) by which He has communicated to man (John 17:8). God's words matter because they are at the heart not only of doctrine but also of salvation: "For this reason we also thank God without ceasing, because when you received the word of God which you heard from us, you welcomed it not as the word of men, but as it is in truth, the word of God, which also effectively works in you who believe" (1 Th. 2:13). If we reject the value of words, we reject the only means of truly understanding God's will, and so reject the message itself.

SEARCH FOR GOD'S MEANING

The way some people throw around opinions about the meaning of biblical passages you might think understanding the Bible is simple. Of course, at the same time, all of these people are throwing around very different opinions. In Luke's record of the early church he recorded this note of praise for the Bereans: "These were more fair-minded than those in Thessalonica, in that they received the word with all readiness, and searched the Scriptures daily to find out whether these things were so" (Acts 17:11). It is not enough to come up with *a* meaning from the text; we must search hard enough and long enough to make sure we have found *God's* meaning.

Anyone can offer an interpretation of Scripture. Satan even attempted to use a passage to get Jesus to sin (Matt. 4:5-7). Therefore, quoting the words of a verse is not always sufficient to establish the accuracy of the way you are using the passage. This also proves that reading the Bible, though important, is not enough (1 Tim. 4:13). Most of all, we should replace blind acceptance of someone else's assertions (Matt. 15:14) with diligent effort to determine the correct interpretation (2 Tim. 2:15).

Some try to undermine even the possibility of individuals conducting independent biblical research, arguing that men are not capable of understanding God's will. Ironically, most of these men attempt to argue in favor of their *own* understanding of God's will. But we are not only *capable* of understanding what God means in the Bible, we will be held responsible for doing so (Matt. 22:29-32). Therefore, we must give all diligence in order to complete this task (2 Pet. 1:10).

Searching for God's meaning in a text depends upon treating it *as* God's text. The Bible is not something a person should try to manipulate to one's advantage. Any attempt to manipulate the text alters the meaning and so alters the outcome, in which case it is no longer "good news" (Gal. 1:6-9). Many would-be interpreters play around with the inspired text like they are spinning a political candidate's dubious voting record. Searching for God's meaning requires us to respect the context—immediate, remote, biblical, literary, and historical—always adhering to logical consistency no matter what belief, doctrine, or practice we might have to give up personally.

People may use "smoke and mirrors" in order to create the impression that the Bible supports their position, but "the Scripture cannot be broken" (John 10:35). On Judgment Day nobody will receive an opportunity to convince God that an interpretation "has merit." God knows what He wrote, and God knows what He means. We also know what He wrote; therefore, we should focus all of our energy on making sure we know what *He* means, because that is the only interpretation that is going to matter. "Do not be deceived, God is not mocked; for whatever a man sows, that he will also reap" (Gal. 6:7).

ACCEPT GOD'S WILL

Sometimes people miss the most important points regarding the life of our Savior. They see in Him the spiritual strength they long for yet fail to understand the faith that gave it life. Jesus was victorious in life and in death not due to the strength of His own will but by the strength of His acceptance of the Father's. As He felt the full burden of God's scheme of redemption on the night of His betrayal, He prayed, "O My Father, if it is possible, let this cup pass from Me; nevertheless, not as I will, but as You will" (Matt. 26:39). This attitude described

Him not only at this critical moment but throughout His life upon the earth. Therefore, we must learn this very significant lesson: The most important step in understanding God's will is surrendering your own.

In Bible study one first must realize that the conflict that exists in religion is not due to God's giving competing versions of His will. "For God is not the author of confusion but of peace, as in all the churches of the saints" (1 Cor. 14:33). Conflict exists in the religious world because people have abandoned God's will in favor of their own (Matt. 15:8-9; 1 Cor. 1:10).

Accepting God's will is not merely a matter of accepting His will as true; it must include making it your own. "I have been crucified with Christ; it is no longer I who live, but Christ lives in me; and the life which I now live in the flesh I live by faith in the Son of God, who loved me and gave Himself for me" (Gal. 2:20). For this to become more than a noble pipe dream we must let God's word dwell in us richly (Col. 3:16) so that Christ dwells in our hearts by faith (Eph. 3:17; Rom. 10:17).

Whether we want to admit it or not, often our "understanding" of God's will becomes clouded by what we are willing to do and what we are unwilling to do. Which is more of a determining factor in the way you worship: whether it pleases you or whether it pleases God? "God is Spirit, and those who worship Him must worship in spirit and truth" (John 4:24). Does the strictness of what God says cause you to accept a message that does not have God's approval? That is certainly how some reacted (John 6:60; Gal. 1:6-9).

When Paul preached to Felix, Felix understood the sermon; he just did not want to accept it. "Now as he reasoned about righteousness, self-control, and the judgment to come, Felix was afraid and answered, 'Go away for now; when I have a convenient time I will call for you'" (Acts 24:25). God revealed the gospel (Rom. 1:16-17), you can understand and obey the gospel (Heb. 5:8-9), and you will be held accountable for your response to the gospel or lack thereof (2 Cor. 5:10). "I beseech you therefore, brethren, by the mercies of God, that you present your bodies a living sacrifice, holy, acceptable to God, which is your reasonable service. And do not be conformed to this world, but be transformed by the renewing of your mind, that you may prove what is that good and acceptable and perfect will of God" (Rom. 12:1-2).

CONCLUSION

There is so much confusion, so much division, so much controversy, and so much chaos in the religious world that it should surprise no one that people question whether or not it is even possible to understand the Bible alike. We have been conditioned to accept this situation as normal, and the world tells us to celebrate such diversity. But Jesus did not pray for diversity; He prayed for unity (John 17:21-23). Therefore, our Savior believed and taught that this unity is both desirable and possible because knowledge of the truth that brings unity is both desirable and possible (John 8:32; 17:17).

Truth must define us—define our doctrine, define our aspirations, define our faith, and define our actions. Sadly, many people are content with a faith that falls short of truth. But how can something be worth believing if it is not true? Do we really believe that accepting spiritual falsehood is in our best interest eternally? "Buy the truth, and do not sell it, Also wisdom and instruction and understanding" (Prov. 23:23).

Even the best method of Bible study cannot help a person who does not care about knowing the truth. You must love truth as a goal before you can discover truth as it has been revealed. "Oh, how I love Your law! It is my meditation all the day" (Psa. 119:97). Once you discover truth you must not only accept it for yourself but also stand and defend it (Phil. 1:17). The "nothing really matters" doctrine of postmodern theology is anti-Bible and anti-Christ. You cannot claim to cling to the Savior when you reject His message that saves (John 12:48; Jas. 1:21). But we need to realize that we must accept the whole rather than just a few parts we like. "You are near, O Lord, And all Your commandments are truth" (Psa. 119:151).

Religious discussions have all but disappeared for most people. Perhaps this is due to the argumentative approach some have taken in the past. The most natural response to an idea with which we disagree is to "throw up the shields" and "defend or die trying." However, should we be more concerned with winning a debate or with being right with our God? Desire truth—not victory. This must be the motto of a serious Bible student. The ultimate purpose of Bible study is not winning an argument but winning souls and winning heaven.

Can we understand the Bible? Absolutely! Can we understand the Bible alike? Yes, indeed! In fact, there is no other way to understand it! If we will reject our traditions and suppositions, if we will overcome our predispositions and upbringing, if we will accept only what God has said as He has said it, we can understand the Bible alike. Understanding the Bible is not easy, but there is no way to heaven without it. Understanding the Bible alike will require us to set aside our pride in order to pursue the truth, but this is a goal worth pursuing — not only for a moment, but also for a lifetime.

In order for people to understand the Bible alike they must:

- Realize divine truth is objective, knowable, and the only proper standard
- Overcome man-made barriers
- Understand God's Words
- Search for God's meaning
- Accept God's will
- Love truth, desire truth, stand by truth, and seek unity based on truth

Recommended Reading

Warren, Thomas B. *The Bible Only makes Christians Only and the Only Christians.* Jonesboro, AR: National Christian Press, 1986.
Whitten, Eddie, ed. *The Validity of the Restoration Principle.* Mesquite, TX: Biblical Bookshelf, 1989.

Questions for Discussion

1. Since truth is objective, is it possible for there to be more than one truth?
2. What barriers present the biggest problem for you personally?
3. Why do people accept differing interpretations when they cannot all be right?
4. Why do people equate their interpretation with God's even when logic does not allow it?

5. If people want true unity, why do we not accept a like understanding of scripture as the basis?

Assignment

Dedicate yourself to finding other people who are willing to study God's Word and accept God's will as the sole basis for their spiritual beliefs. Challenge one another's assumptions in order to break down the barriers of personal tradition that work against true spiritual unity.

CPSIA information can be obtained
at www.ICGtesting.com
Printed in the USA
FFOW02n1939110317
33226FF